CONTACT ZONES

CONTACT ZONES

Photography, Migration, and Cultural Encounters in the United States

Edited by
JUSTIN CARVILLE and SIGRID LIEN

Leuven University Press

Published with the support of
KU Leuven Fund for Fair Open Access
and
Terra Foundation for American Art

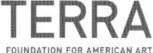

Published in 2021 by Leuven University Press / Presses Universitaires de Louvain / Universitaire Pers Leuven. Minderbroedersstraat 4, B-3000 Leuven (Belgium).

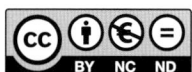
ISBN 978 94 6270 252 3 (Paperback)
ISBN 978 94 6166 357 3 (ePDF)
ISBN 978 94 6166 358 0 (ePUB)
https://doi.org/10.11116/9789461663573
D/2021/1869/17
NUR: 652

Layout: Crius Group
Cover design: Dogma
Cover illustration: Erich Salomon, *Blick durch die vergitterten Fenster des Internierungsgebäudes von Ellis Island auf die Wolkenkratzer von New York* [*View through the barred windows of the internment building of Ellis Island to the skyscrapers of New York*], ca. 1932, 17.9 × 24.2 cm, Erich Salomon archive Berlin, BG-ESA 462 [in, *Erich Salomon. "Mit Frack und Linse durch die Politik und Gesellschaft." Photographien 1928–1938*, eds. Janos Frecot et al. (Berlin: Berlinische Galerie, 2004), catalog from an exhibition at Berlinische Galerie, Berlin 2004, 245].

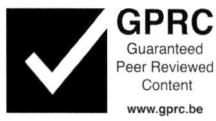

Table of Contents

EXHIBITING MIGRATIONS

DOCUMENTING MIGRATIONS

Acknowledgments

This collection of essays is drawn from a conference as part of a collaborative project Photography as Contact Zones: Migration and Cultural Encounters in America between the Institute of Art, Design & Technology, Dún Laoghaire (IADT), and the University of Bergen. The project and this publication are made possible through support from the Terra Foundation for American Art. The editors are eternally grateful to the Terra Foundation for American Art for its support of the project through its Academic Workshop and Symposium Grants. We would especially like to thank Julia Poppy and Sara Jakto for their guidance in completing the project.

At various points, numerous individuals helped with administrative and logistical support. At IADT, the editors would like to thank Alice Brennan, Linda Carroll, Pamela Gaynor, Thelma Gill, Karen Muldowney, Rachel Heffernan, Steven Nestor, Sarah Whelan, Paul Tynan, Rónán Ó Muirthile, David Smith, and Aoife Giles. Special thanks also go to Sean Daly who was our conference assistant, Leanne Sullivan for design and web-promotion, and David Monahan who helped with image files. At the University of Bergen, we would like to acknowledge the Bergen Maritime Museum and the Norwegian Freedom of Expression Foundation.

This book has been in the making longer than either the editors or the contributors had anticipated. Like much collaborative academic labor, it has been a global endeavor which has involved working across multiple time zones in Europe and the United States. It has also been completed in the midst of a global pandemic that has presented challenges—academic, the political, and the personal—for all those involved. The editors would like to thank all the contributors to this collection for their scholarship, patience, resilience, and friendship in what have been extremely challenging times. Finally, we would like to thank the Leuven University Press for their support in the completion of this book. A special thanks goes to Mirjam Truwant for her constant support and guidance, and for assisting with the application to KU Leuven Fund for Fair Open Access, which has facilitated the publication of the book in open-access format. And to the team of Leuven University Press for patiently navigating the final typesetting and design of this volume.

Introduction

Contact Zones

Photography, Migration, and the United States

Justin Carville and Sigrid Lien

Histories of migration to the United States are also a history of American photography. Yet, the relationship between these histories are rarely discussed in surveys of the history of photography in America. Neither are immigrants' uses and circulation of photographs discussed in the historiographies of the European immigration to the United States.[1] However, US migration history and the history of American photography can be conceptualized as what Swedish historian Gunlög Fur terms *concurrent histories*: two fields of inquiry that were mostly conducted in isolation but would "benefit from a concurrent analysis as a way of addressing the neglect of their interrelation."[2] Informed by comparative post- and decolonial thinking, Fur argues in favor of looking for moments of entanglements as a way of addressing such concurrences.[3] Inspired by such reflections, this book addresses the interrelationship between the histories of American photography and the histories of US migration by bringing together scholarship that explores the ways in which photography, migration, and the United States are entangled through cultural processes of temporal, geographical, aesthetic, and imaginative social contact.

Concurrent histories

How then may the concurrences between the histories of American photography and the histories of US migration be brought to the surface? This question requires a closer consideration of how each of these histories are typically narrated, and how they, as Fur puts it, "stand in an ambiguous and often conflicted relationships to other histories, in terms of time and space."[4]

One the one hand, there are surveys, such as Miles Orvell's history of photography in America, which representative of its genre is written with the purpose of uncovering "the 'Americanness' of American photography."[5] With the photographers' intentions as a point of departure, the survey presents a general overview of the works by canonized photographers within portraiture, landscape, documentary, and artistic photography. Early portraiture is discussed with an emphasis on great names within celebrity studio photography, such as Mathew Brady and Napoleon Sarony. Landscape photography, differentiated through notions of "aesthetic" versus "topographic," is construed as a line of development from, respectively, Carleton Watkins and Eadweard Muybridge, via Ansel Adams to Stieglitz, and from Timothy O'Sullivan to the New Topographics. Documentary is described as the general tendency stretching from the work of Jacob Riis, Lewis Hine, and the Farm Security Administration (FSA) photographers of the 1930s (including Walker Evans, Dorothea Lange, and Ben Shahn) to Steichen's *The Family of Man* and Frank's *The Americans*, followed by references to the works of Lee Friedlander and Diane Arbus. Finally, art photography is constructed as genealogy of merits starting with Alfred Stieglitz, Paul Strand, Man Ray, and Edward Weston to the work of Joel Peter Witkins, Cindy Sherman, Richard Prince, Barbara Kruger, and Nan Goldin.

Even though the survey aims to view the history of photography in America both "in terms of its own inner history and in relation to the larger cultural history of America,"[6] it is predominantly the "inner history" that is highlighted. This inner story accentuates individual, canonized photographers' intentions while striving to establish lines of development between their respective aesthetic practices. Consequently, what is left in the shadows is "the bigger picture." Not only does the overall question of the "Americanness" of American photography remain unanswered. More importantly, the relationship between photographic practices in America and the larger historical contexts in which they are embedded—particularly migration—is also an issue that is left in need of further exploration.

On the other hand, a closer inspection of histories of migration may similarly bring attention to blind spots. Anthony Moran, for example, identifies how such histories suppress certain kinds of truths—such as, for example, how "countries like the United States, Canada, New Zealand and Australia, despite important differences, are all structured by the fact that they are predominantly English-speaking settler cultures which have to a large extent supplanted indigenous peoples."[7] He demonstrates how evolving settler nationalism in settler colonies was justified through ideological discourses of "newness." This made it possible not only to proclaim the settler colonies as new societies, free of the burdening traditions and class distinctions of the "old world" that that the settler migrants left behind but also to regard indigenous peoples from whom they had wrestled their land as lacking histories and traditions of their own. Ultimately, this multiple "absence" of history entailed "that settlers could build their own utopias without hindrances."[8]

Accordingly, histories of emigration may often have a celebratory tone that emphasizes the hardship the settlers had to endure, including dangerous sea journeys, problems in adjusting to a new culture and language, the endurance and efforts required to clear land, and the setting up of homes and building of communities.[9] Such histories also tend to glorify processes of modernization; as Patrick Wolfe reminds us, settler-colonial discourse should by no means be regarded as pre- (or less than) modern. Indeed, he makes clear that "some of the core features of modernity were pioneered in the colonies."[10] As stated by Janne Lahti, the settler revolution

> involved, coincided, spurred, and was a consequence of industrial and transportation revolutions, massive population growth and outward migration from Europe, idealization of yeoman farming cultures, the rise of print culture and intense marketing (boosterism), mining rushes, the spread of market economy, and capital flows in extractive industries and agribusiness that crossed national borders and signified new forms of global integration.[11]

Photography was intrinsic to this multifaceted American modernity. It arrived in the mid nineteenth century, coinciding with the opening of the floodgates of migration in Europe and Asia. Addressing photography migration and settler colonialism in this wider context makes it not only possible to transgress nearsighted discussions of genres and photographic oeuvres but also to bring to light other more complex entanglements between the histories of photography and migration. Photography, as Carol Williams demonstrates with regard to British colonization of the Pacific Northwest, was instrumental in the construction of cultural and racial differences between settlers and Native Americans.[12] It was also, as Anna Pegler-Gordon's recent work on photography and immigration policy has shown, woven into America's new immigration laws of the late nineteenth and early twentieth centuries as a technique of racialized visual regulation of migrants arriving in America.[13] Moreover, photography was integral to the matrix of settler-colonial power as a tool for mapping vast and unfamiliar topographies. The photographers who mapped the American West from the mid nineteenth century for railroad companies or under the auspices of the US Geological Survey and Treasury Department—the Irish-born Timothy H. O'Sullivan, the German John K. Hillers, and the Norwegian Anders Beer Wilse, among others—were all immigrants, involved in this larger colonial apparatus.[14]

Last but not least, photography was of great importance to the newcomers in settler communities. They not only used photographs to represent and contemplate loss, dispersal, identity, and belonging but also as manifestations of their assimilation and adaptations to new environments, modern ways of living, and cultural differences.[15] Such photographic corpuses have the capacity to point to the blind spots of the settler-colonial history by stirring up fragments of the histories of those who were driven away, from, for example, the wide plains where many European settlers established their new existence.[16]

Photography has also been crucial in the processes of documenting the wider social, cultural, and political transformations of social landscapes in the wake of mass immigration and settler colonialism.[17] The Danish émigré Jacob Riis, regarded as a pioneer within the American documentary tradition, used photography to document the miserable conditions among impoverished immigrants in New York.[18] Likewise, the iconic photographs produced by the Farm Security Administration photographers during the 1930s and 1940s document rural poverty, internal displacement, and environmental damages predominantly caused by the broad development of settler migrants' monocultural agriculture.

A few decades later, the Swiss émigré Robert Frank published his famous *The Americans*. This photo book from 1958 presents an outsider's gaze on the anonymous segregated strata of American society, seemingly unified through banal national symbols.[19] At the time, Frank's *The Americans* was harshly received by critics for its iconoclasm of American exceptionalism through the relationships established between the symbols of idealized American values, and the harshness of everyday life in the book's sequencing of images.[20] However, the book and its legacy has come not only to define the subgenre of the American photographic road trip but also provided a model for photography's capacity to capture the national psyche by envisioning how American society saw itself and its place in the world.[21]

A closer inspection of American photographs from the nineteenth century to the present day would reveal a myriad of either explicit or implicit relationships with the histories of migration. The practices of early studio portraiture and landscape photography of the Western frontier; the origins of social documentary photography, pictorialism, early and late modernism, post–World War II photojournalism and photo reportage; and more contemporary conceptual and documentary work on race, ethnicity, and citizenship related to recent migration waves from Latin America, Africa, Asia, the Middle East, and the Caribbean, are all to a large extent shaped by migration histories and experiences in America.[22]

Alfred Stieglitz—whose canonical photograph, *The Steerage*, discussed in David Bate's contribution to this collection, of European remigrants on board the *SS Kaiser Wilhelm II* on his journey to Paris in 1907—brought to America the aesthetic philosophy and ideals of European pictorialism, in addition to introducing early modernist and European avant-garde works to American audiences through his 291 Gallery, and the 1913 exhibition of modernist art at the Armory Show.[23] The Italian-born photographer Tina Modotti, also a pivotal figure in early modernist photography, immigrated to San Francisco as a teenager in 1913.[24] László Moholy-Nagy, a central figure of the Weimar Bauhaus School, established a new Bauhaus

School in Chicago in 1937 as an émigré, reinforcing the European influence on American modernist photography throughout the mid twentieth century.[25]

Many of these examples already form part of the canon of the history of American photography. Fragments of this history have been the focus of scholarship that has, to varying degrees, illuminated or dampened the entanglement of photography with US migration history.[26] It is the aim of the essays collected in this book to explore specific examples of these concurrent histories.

Contact zones

The history of American photography and migration is not just a history of canonized photographers and their practices or a hagiography of émigré photographers. This book answers what we see as a need to address the questions of the broader work of photography in articulating and performing migration experiences. The work of photography in migration histories does not just revolve around questions of representation. While interrogation of the cultural politics of photography and the representation of migration continues to be of critical importance in the current geopolitical climate of nation-state responses to the crisis of global migration, the contributions to this book approach the relations of photography, migration, and America from a different perspective. Of more interest to the essays in this volume are questions such as how migration experience configures photography as a culturally distinctive way of seeing or looking; how photographs are mobilized as forms of agency within and between migrant communities and the homeland; how photographs allow migrants to self-fashion identities fractured by geographical and cultural dislocation; the ways photography operates as manifestations of migrant assimilation and adaptation to new physical and cultural environments; the role of photographs in maintaining familial and cultural bonds across time and space; and how photography, activated in forms of exhibition, publication, and display, mediate migrant histories, memories, and experiences.

Migrants rarely travel empty handed. They bring with them material objects, images, ideas, beliefs, and forms of cultural imagining, a luggage that helps them to navigate and express their experiences of life in America, and their longing for home. This luggage often includes photographs. As Marianne Hirsch reminds us, "in lives shaped by exile, emigration and relocation, … where relatives are dispersed and relationships shattered, photographs provide even more than usual some illusion of continuity over time and space."[27] Migrants bring not only photographs but also cameras through which culturally differentiated practices of looking at the world are materialized. They also take with them culturally diverse and distinctive practices of making and doing photography, which are assimilated into

cultural norms of American life. Photographs migrate from one geographical location to another, traveling in suitcases and family albums brought with migrants on
the journey to America or following letters home. Photographs also travel through
time, migrating either from one generation to the next, or from familial archives
to public spaces such as museums, archives, and online auction sites. The photographs from these familial and institutional archives also migrate into the work of
artists and photographers who explore and appropriate the histories and cultural
legacies of migration and America. The essays in this book address many of these
practices of photography and migration through specific case studies that are oriented around what we conceptualize in this volume of essays as photography's
contact zones.

The term *contact zone* is drawn from Mary Louise Pratt's contribution to postcolonial literature in her analysis of European travel and exploration writing from
the mid eighteenth century, and its role in colonial expansionism in Africa, the
Caribbean, and South America. Borrowing the term from linguistics, in which a
contact language is a language improvised to allow speakers of different tongues to
communicate with one another, Pratt introduces the term *contact zone* to describe
the spaces of colonial encounter through which cultural exchange and transformation takes place. In her analysis of literary forms that "gave European reading pub-
lics a sense of ownership, entitlement and familiarity with respect to distant parts
of the world that were being explored, invaded, invested in, and colonized" (15),
Pratt utilizes the concept of the contact zone to frame processes of transculturation
that emerge out of the cultural encounters between subjugated peoples and their
colonizers.[28] In *Imperial Eyes*, she develops the concept to

> invoke the spatial and temporal copresence of subjects previously separated by
> geographic and historical disjuncture's, and whose trajectories now intersect. By
> using the term "contact" I aim to foreground the interactive, improvisational
> dimensions of colonial encounters so easily ignored or suppressed by diffusion-
> ist accounts of conquest and domination. A "contact" perspective emphasizes
> how subjects are constituted in and by their relations to each other. [It stresses]
> copresence, interaction, interlocking understanding and practices, often within
> radically asymmetrical relations of power.[29]

Pratt further expands her understanding of the concept to define contact zones as
"social spaces where disparate cultures, meet, clash, and grapple with each other."[30]

Pratt's concept of the contact zone has proved to be a malleable theory that has
allowed the concept to be reconfigured to provide innovative and novel inquires
of colonial and postcolonial culture. The most notable example of this reconfig-
uration is James Clifford's essay "Museums as Contact Zones," published in his

study of cultural mobility, migration, and diaspora, *Routes: Travel and Translation in the Late Twentieth Century*.[31] Clifford's analysis seeks to undermine assumptions of the museum as a sort of frontier through which the collections of items can only be seen from the perspective of the institutional custodianship and salvage of the material culture of "Others." As Pratt notes, "the frontier is a frontier only with respect to Europe," and Clifford's work draws attention to the contact zone as a polyvocal site of multiple contexts and meanings that will not be understood in the same way by peoples in asymmetrical relations of social power.[32] Clifford's interpretation of the contact zone can be extended to photography in its capacity to envision heterogenous, polyvocal migrant histories and memories. In addition, Clifford's understanding of the contact zone as undermining conceptualizations of culture as a frontier provides a framework to shift the perspective of photography, migration, and the United States away from narratives of departure and arrival (the frontiers of migrant experiences) to photography's ongoing role in visually articulating transgenerational and trans-locational experiences that continue to shape American migration histories.

Pratt's concept of the contact zone has also found its way into photography history and colonial and postcolonial visual culture. Engaging with diverse geographical and historical contexts, several studies of colonial photography have drawn on Pratt's theorization of spaces of cultural encounters as sites of transculturation. Contact zones have been understood as the geographical locations or social spaces in which the act of taking photographs facilitates processes of transcultural negotiations. In this way contact zones can also refer to the cultural encounters between photographer and subject. On another level, photography, in its multiple material forms, has been identified as a zone of contact between viewers as political subjects, and the image itself as an agent of cultural transformation.

In his study of Dutch national tourist imagery in the twentieth century, Remco Ensel identifies contact zones as public spaces in which travelers and locals meet in mutual interest in the production of photographs that project performances of folklorist ethnic and national identity.[33] In an earlier study, he employs the concept to encompass the social spaces of face-to-face contact between photographer and subject where "physical contact, cultural exchange and negotiation took place."[34] A slightly more nuanced articulation of the spatial relations of photography and contact zones is Steven Hoelscher's study of nineteenth-century photographer H. H. Bennett's representation of Native Americans in the Wisconsin Dells. In his discussion of Bennett's stereoscopic cards, landscape views, and portraits of Native Americans, Hoelscher describes photography as a medium that documents and envisions contact zones as regional geographical spaces of the uneven power relations of subjugated peoples and colonizers. Photography pictures the physical zones of contact between Native Americans and photographers while simultaneously producing marketable pictures adapted to catering to tourist imaginaries. However, they are also spaces of negotiation between Native Americans and photographers that envision Native American agency in absorbing and transforming the technology and culture of photography.[35] Katrien Pype, in a study of the political urban visual culture of Kinshasa, identifies photographs themselves as constituting "a particular zone of contact." Drawing on the work of Pratt, through Uli Linke's analysis of the embodied, sensual concrete forms of the state, Pype explores political billboards as zones of contact for political actors that "set in motion as sensuous connection between the body of the perceiver and the image perceived" (190).[36] In her study of the commercial photography studios of the Himalayas and the production of images for imperial pleasures, Clare Harris mobilizes the notion of contact zones as an analytical tool to identify how photography operates as a form of indigenous agency. Highlighting concepts such as copresence, transcultural self-fashioning, and negotiation of "European aesthetics imposed on [a] subaltern subjects" in studio portraiture, Harris argues that photographic contact zones are not merely about unequal power relations; in their production, display, and afterlives, they can also be explored as modes of indigenous auto-ethnography and colonial interaction.[37]

Much of this literature addresses itself to colonial, postcolonial, and ethno-national identity formation that is oriented around the contact zone as a space in which colonizers, indigenous peoples, and other marginalized groups negotiate social relations of power and cultural transformation through photography. This volume, however, focuses on the concurrent nature of the histories of photography and migration. It proposes that photography, similarly to the travel books that Pratt explores, works as a mediator in historical processes of US migration as well as in the present American settler coloniality, as the "spaces where cultures meet, clash and grapple with each other." Recalling the fundamental ideas in Pratt's theory, each of the contributors discusses photography's role in processes of transculturation. Inspired by how Pratt challenged the notion of culture as something that could be expressed through a common language, the chapters engage with photography and the photographic image's intermediary potential in exploring the medium's relationship with migration and the United States. These explorations may simply entail looking at how photography is employed, both by migrants and Americans, as a way of exposing oneself to new cultures. But they also involve studies of how photography is used in meetings between migrants as a marginalized group and the predominant culture of settler coloniality.

This volume addresses not only the photographic image's variegated forms of repository, display, and distribution but also the archive, the family album, the exhibition, and social media as part of this transcultural process. It also takes into consideration how photography, rather than acting as a fixed and stable entity within a specific contact zone, forms part of a series of fluid and overlapping contact *zones.* Consequently, we use the phrase contact zones—the plural form rather than the singular *contact zone*—to emphasize the polymorphic or multiple forms in which photography emerges in contact spaces. Moreover, photography's positionality in contact zones is thus not just related to photographer and subject but also to the photographer's engagement with technology or practices of aesthetic codification, or the viewers encounter with the photograph in the family album, archive, or museum. Indeed, the photograph can be situated within multiple contact zones in different geographical locations and across time. The mass reproducibility and simultaneous distribution of photographic imagery allows individuals to both experience other cultures and to maintain, establish, and articulate cultural bonds, forge imagined communities, and share cultural experiences across and between nations. In this sense, photography's role in cultural encounters as we conceive them can be as a discrete space shaped by a specific historical context or entangled within various contexts of communication which reflect the ongoing production and reproduction of migrant histories and memories identified by Stuart Hall as core to the formation of diasporic identities.[38] In this expansion of the concept of contact zones, we seek to align it more closely with Pratt's intention to "invoke the spatial and temporal copresence of subjects previously separated by geographic and historical disjunctures," and to emphasize the "interactive and improvisational dimensions" of cultural encounters that allow migrants to creatively fashion photography's shared materials, and modes of distribution and circulation to communicate diverse cultural experiences.[39]

About this book

In the first section of this volume, "Photographies, Representations, and Migrations," David Bate discusses what he terms "The Figure of Migration." Bate's essay engages with a general historiographical pattern that has recently been brought to attention by migration scholars. As mentioned above, they have pointed to the way histories of migration and settler colonialisms have been dominated by ideas of "newness."[40] Bate points to how photography forms part of this historical struggle to enunciate something new, to establish a new discourse on what it means to be modern. By engaging in a historiographical discussion centered around Allan Sekula's reading of Alfred Stieglitz's iconographic photograph *The Steerage* (1907), he argues that neither Sekula nor Stieglitz, in his own writings, confront the "implicit politics" involved in images of this kind, particularly with regard to the "figural forms of representation and affect in which they are encoded."[41]

This volume's second section, "Vernacular Photographies and Migration," engages with other aspects of the photographic culture of European migrants in America. Ireland is a country estimated to have a larger share of its population migrate to the United States than any other European nation. The two chapters in this section explore how photographs worked as contact zones, not only in the large transatlantic exchange of photographs between immigrants in America and their relations back home in Ireland. It also discusses the current position of this vernacular photographic heritage in public and private albums and archives.

In Chapter Two, Orla Fitzpatrick analyzes an early twentieth-century photo album created by an Irish emigrant to the United States. While the dominant narrative of Irish migration characterizes the typical Irish emigrant as Catholic and male, the album visualizes the post-famine period migrant as a younger female. More specifically, it traces the migration of a single female nurse from a Protestant and Quaker Society of Friends family to a rural setting in the American Midwest. Fitzpatrick shows how the album's photographs contain references both to the migrant's new life and her country of origin, while also including political affiliations of transatlantic nationalism. She also points to how the album's many joyful images counter the established narrative of the Irish emigration as an experience of painful exile.

The next chapter, by Justin Carville, addresses the codification and narrative formation of the Irish American diaspora through the circulation of vernacular photographs as image-objects between Irish immigrants and their families back in Ireland. The chapter studies the affective resonances of what he terms the photo-remittance in disrupted familial relations, memories, and histories of the Irish American diaspora. Carville argues that contact spaces of circulation of photographs among diasporic communities allowed polyvocal histories and imaginaries of migration experiences to be visually articulated.

The volume's third section, "Diasporic Imaginations," exclusively engages with works by professional emigrant photographers. In Chapter Four, Helene Roth writes about how three exiled European photographers, Josef Breitenbach, Lisette Model, and Hermann Landshoff, perceived New York through the camera shortly after their arrivals in the 1940s. Analyzing their work, the chapter holds that photography in this sense worked as a contact zone. Roth identifies photography as a visual medium that émigrés could access without the anxieties of language barriers and problems of understanding as they were distanced from their homeland. These photographers produced images in the United States that spoke to their positions in exile as well as articulating their own aesthetic ideals. It thus created links between the art and culture of the abandoned homeland, the new homeland, and not least between emigrated artists themselves.

In Chapter Five, Aleksandra Idzior explores the work of another European artist and immigrant, Teresa Żarnower. As a Pole of Jewish descent, Żarnower was forced to take flight after Nazi Germany's invasion of Poland in 1939. Idzior presents a study of the Dadaist photomontages that this renowned Polish constructivist avant-garde artist produced while exiled in Montreal and New York during World War II. She demonstrates how these works worked as zones of contact, as they were aimed at directing the viewer's attention to the enormity of the loss and suffering inflicted on the inhabitants of Poland, Europe, and Canada during World War II.

While the immigrant photographers discussed in the above-mentioned chapters all came from a Europe in distress, the section's last chapter addresses the work of a photographer with a Caribbean background, the Dominican American Winston Vargas. In this chapter, Leslie Ureña writes about Vargas's photographs of the northern Manhattan neighborhoods of Washington Heights and Inwood, taken from the 1960s to the 1990s. She argues, based on her own personal experiences and familiarity with this area and its people, that Vargas presents "evocative portraits of people far from home, caught 'between two islands'—the Dominican Republic and Manhattan."

The essays in the third section, "Exhibiting Migrations," address how photographs used in exhibitions confront histories of migration. In Chapter Seven, Sandra Križić Roban examines the Croatian Museum of Emigration in Zagreb, which maintains numerous photographs related to the conditions in which Croatian immigrants lived prior to their emigration, as well as to their travel experiences and their new homes. In addition to critically examining this material, the chapter discusses the different curatorial strategies and use of photographs in three different exhibitions dedicated to Croatian migration processes. Roban concludes that photographs in such contexts have the potential to bring forth the ephemeral and everyday aspects of migration history, and thus also the many previously untold emigrant narratives.

In Chapter Eight, Alexandra Irimia uses her own personal experiences as a migrant in 2017 as a point of departure for a discussion of that brings into dialogue Georges Didi-Huberman's Didi-Huberman, *Passer quoi qu'il en coûte*, a response to Niki Giannari 2016 documentary *Spectres Are Haunting Europe* on migration and the exhibition *Out of Many – Stories of Migration* by the Pittsburgh-based collective *The Documentary Works*. Through the juxtaposition of these works, Irimia poignantly states that "photographs and migrants alike concern us, they are objects of sight that return our gaze, and they are moved by a desire to pass through our subjectivity and affects the way they find their ways through historical epochs, walls and borders to survive."[42]

The chapters in the volume's final section, "Documenting Migrations," are dedicated to photographic projects that address migration to the United States in a contemporary documentary vein. In Chapter Nine, Sigrid Lien discusses an experimental documentary project by the Italian photographer Giulia Mangione. In this project, Mangione searched for the photographic traces of an exceptional part of the Norwegian history of migration: the legendary failure of the internationally renowned Norwegian violinist virtuoso, Ole Bull, to establish a Norwegian colony in the forest area of Potter County, Pennsylvania. Lien adapts Pratt's concept of contact zones to explore what she conceives to be a tension in Giulia Mangione's series of photographs between the settler-colonial utopia and its bleak, dystopian counterpart. While Pratt analyzes literature to understand how Europeans came to feel so "naturally" entitled to the non-European places in the world that they explored and invaded, Lien argues that Mangione similarly used photography in an effort to grasp a specific part of this larger pattern—the Norwegian settlers' sense of entitlement to certain areas in the United States.

Bridget Gilman's chapter presents two case studies of documentary photographic practices on migration. The first is Janet Delaney's documentation of the social and spatial pressures of gentrification and their impact on the local immigrant population in San Francisco's South of Market (SoMa) neighborhood. The second is Ingrid Hernández's documentary work in Tijuana's Nueva Esperanza (New Hope) neighborhood, where the residents are mainly women working in local maquiladoras, assembly factories owned by foreign companies that rely on comparatively cheap Mexican labor and duty-free trade agreements. Gilman argues that, while Delaney and Hernández are both dedicated to documenting urban regions defined by the movement of people, goods, and capital, their work also aims to illuminate the personal costs of global migratory powers.

The personal costs of contemporary migration are also confronted in the following chapter by Sarah Bassnett. She points not only to the neglect of the United States in raising public awareness about how government policy affects experiences of undocumented migration, but also to the way mainstream media relies on a limited series of tropes to represent migration. Bassnett's chapter examines the outdated motifs that are used in the representation of people trying to cross the southern border. As a contrast to this public preservation of the status quo, she explores the work of the Mexican photojournalist Moysés Zuñiga Santiago, which is explicitly directed to expose human rights violations.

This connects the final chapter, in which Erina Duganne discusses the *X post facto* series (2009) by immigrant artist and photographer Muriel Hasbun. While Hasbun, in other works, has explored her own multicultural family history through the inclusion of family photographs and documents, the *X post facto* series is made up of X-rays discovered in her father's dental archive in El Salvador. Duganne writes about how the artist, through this material, brings forth the collective trauma of her family's migratory history and the experiences of the Salvadoran Civil War.

Finally, to return to the notion of the photograph as a contact zone in histories of migration and exile: it is our opinion that every chapter of this book demonstrates the potential and complexity of photographs as sites of multiple contact zones in different geographical locations and across time.

Notes

1. For a discussion of this in reference to the history of the Norwegian migration to the United States, see Sigrid Lien, "Ragnhild's Images: Migration, Settler Colonialism and Photography," *International Journal for History, Culture and Modernity*, 2020, 1–22. DOI: https://doi.org/10.1163/22130624-00801003

2. Diana Brydon, Peter Forsgren, and Gunlög Fur, "What Reading for Concurrences offers Postcolonial Studies," in Diana Brydon, Peter Forsgren, and Gunlög Fur (eds.), *Concurrent Imaginaries, Postcolonial Worlds Toward Revised Histories* (Leiden: Brill, 2017), 10.

3. Gunlög Fur, "Concurrences as Methodology for Discerning Concurrent Histories," in Diana Brydon et al. (ed.), *Concurrent Imaginaries, Postcolonial Worlds Toward Revised Histories* (Leiden: Brill, 2017), 39–40.

4. Fur, "Concurrences," 34.

5. Miles Orvell, *American Photography* (Oxford: Oxford University Press, 2003), 9. The historiography of photography and the United States throughout the twentieth century has pursued the thesis that photography is a distinctly American art. With the exception of analysis of the influence of the European avant-garde on early modernist photography, relatively little in the survey histories of American photography focus on the influence or effect of migration on the development of the medium in the nineteenth and twentieth centuries. Mick Gidley, *Photography and the USA* (London: Reaktion, 2011), does observe that photography's cultural signifiers and effects have contributed to projecting both the mundane and celebratory migrant experiences of absorption into the American way of life (19–20). For an early examination of the links between European and American modernism in photography, see Abigail Solomon-Godeau, "The Armed Vision Disarmed: Radical Formalism from Weapon to Style," *Afterimage* 11, No. 6 (January 1983), 9–14.

6. Orvell, *American,* 17.

7. Anthony Moran, "As Australia Decolonizes: Indigenizing Settler Nationalism and the Challenges of Settler / Indigenous Relations," *Ethnic and Racial Studies* 25, No. 6 (2002), 1015–1016. DOI: https://doi.org/10.1080/0141987022000009412

8. Moran, "As Australia," 1016.

9. Lien, "Ragnhild's Images," 10.

10. Patrick Wolfe, "Settler colonialism and the elimination of the native," *Journal of Genocide Research* 8, No. 4 (2006), DOI: 10.1080/14623520601056240

11. Janne Lahti, *The American West and the World. Transnational and Comparative Perspectives* (New York/Abingdon: Routledge 2019), 46.

12. Williams, Carol J., *Framing the West: Race, Gender and the Photographic Frontier in the Pacific Northwest* (Oxford/New York: Oxford University Press, 2003).

13. Anna Pegler-Gordon, *In Sight of America: Photography and the Development of U.S. Immigration Policy* (Berkeley: University of California Press, 2009), 10.

14. Robin Kelsey, *Archival Style: Photographs and Illustrations for U.S. Surveys, 1850–1890* (Berkeley: University of California Press, 2007); Martha A. Sandweiss, "Photography, the Archive and the Invention of the American West," in Constanza Caraffa and Tiziana Serena (eds.), *Photo Archives and the Idea of Nation* (Berlin: De Gruyter, 2015); Martha Sandweiss, *Print the Legend: Photography and the American West* (New Haven: Yale University Press, 2006); Don D. Fowler, *Myself in the Water: The Western Photographs of John K. Hillers* (Washington, DC: Smithsonian Institution Press, 1989); James D. Horan, *Timothy O'Sullivan: America's Forgotten Photographer* (New York: Bonanza Books, 1966).

15. Sigrid Lien, *Pictures of Longing: Photography and the Norwegian-American Migration* (Minneapolis: University of Minnesota Press, 2018).

16. Lien, "Ragnhild's Images," 1–22.

17. Gisela Parak, *Photographs of Environmental Phenomena* (Bielefeld: Transcript Verlag, 2015), 97.

18. See Maren Stange, *Symbols of Ideal Life: Social Documentary Photography in America, 1890–1950* (Cambridge: Cambridge University Press, 1989), 1–46.

19. Robert Frank, *Les Américains* (Paris: Robert Delpire, 1958); Robert Frank, *The Americans* (New York: Grove Press, 1959).

20. James Guimond, *American Photography and the America Dream* (Chapel Hill: University of North Carolina Press, 1991), 232–239.

21. On the legacy of Frank's *The Americans*, see Sarah Greenough and Alexander Stuart, *Looking In: Robert Frank's* The Americans (Washington, DC: National Gallery of Art, 2009) and Jonathan Day, *Robert Frank's 'The Americans': The Art of Documentary Photography* (Bristol: Intellect, 2011). On photography and road trips, see David Campany, *The Open Road: Photography & the American Road Trip* (New York: Aperture, 2014)

22. There is a growing body of excellent work on photography, migration and diaspora visual cultures in America. See in particular; Thy Phu, *Picturing Model Citizens: Civility in Asian American Visual Culture* (Philadelphia: Temple University Press, 2012); Bakirathi Mani, *Unseeing Empire: Photography, Representation, South Asian Empire* (Durham & London: Duke University Press, 2020) and Elizabeth Ferrer, *Latinx Photography in the United States: A Visual History* (Washington: University of Washington Press, 2021). See also several contributions in Tanya Sheehan (ed.) *Photography and Migration* (London: Routledge, 2018).

23. See Sarah Greenough, *Modern Art and America: Alfred Stieglitz and His New York Galleries* (Washington, DC: National Gallery of Art, 2000) and Dorothy Norman, *Alfred Stieglitz: An American Seer* (New York: Aperture, 1990).

24. Mildred Constantine, *Tina Modotti: A Fragile Life* (New York: Bloomsbury, 1993), 19–57.

25. For a discussion of the Chicago Bauhaus, see Hall Foster, "The Bauhaus Idea in America," in Achim Borchardt-Hume (ed.), *Albers and Moholy-Nagy: From the Bauhaus to the New World* (New Haven: Yale University Press), 92–100. For a broader overview of the transnationalism of modernism, Europe and America, see Serge Guilbaut, *How New York Stole the Idea of Modern Art: Abstract Expressionism, Freedom, and the Cold War*, trans. Arthur Goldhammer (Chicago: Chicago University Press, 1983). See also John Pultz and Catherine B. Scallen, *Cubism and American Photography* (Rochester: George Eastman House, 1981).

26. A notable example is the exhibition *Points of Entry*, organized by the Museum of Photographic Arts in San Diego, which was also part of a series of exhibitions on immigration held in conjunction with the Jimmy Carter Presidential Library in Atlanta in 1995. See the catalog: *Point of Entry: A Nation of Strangers* (Albuquerque: University of New Mexico Press, 1995).

27. Marianne Hirsch, *Family Frames: Photography, Narrative and Postmemory* (Cambridge: Harvard University Press, 1997), ix.

28. Mary Louise Pratt, *Imperial Eyes: Travel Writing and Transculturation*, 2nd edition (London: Routledge, 2008), 3.

29. Mary Louise Pratt, *Imperial Eye: Travel Writing and Transculturation*, 1st edition (London: Routledge, 1992), 7.

30. Pratt, *Imperial*, 1st edition, 4.

31. James Clifford, *Routes: Travel and Translation in the Late Twentieth Century* (Cambridge: Harvard University Press, 1997), 188–219.

32. Pratt, *Imperial*, 1st edition, 7; Clifford, *Routes*, 192–193, 204.

33. Remco Ensel, "Knitting at the beach: tourism and the photography of Dutch fabriculture," *Journal of Tourism and Cultural Change* 16, No. 4 (2018): 379–399.

34. Remco Ensel, "Going Native: Besnyö's Zeelandish Girl and the Contact Zone of Dutch Photography," *Depth of Field*, 4, No. 1 (January 2014), https://depthoffield. universiteitleiden.nl/0401a02/.

35. Steven D. Hoelscher, *Picturing Indians: Photographic Encounters and Tourist Fantasies in H. H. Bennett's Wisconsin Dells* (Madison: The University of Wisconsin Press, 2008), 12–13.

36. Katrien Pype, "Political Billboards as Contact Zones: Reflections on Urban Space, the Visual & Political Affect in Kabila's Kinshaa," in Richard Vokes (ed.), *Photography in Africa: Ethnographic Perspectives* (Suffolk: James Curry, 2012), 187–204; Uli Linke, "Contact Zones: Rethinking the Sensual Life of the State," *Anthropological* Theory 6, No. 2 (2006): 205–225.

37. Clare Harris, "Photography in the 'Contact Zone': Identifying Copresence and Agency in the Studios of Darjeeling," in Markus Viehbeck (ed.), *Transcultural Encounters in the Himalayan Borderlands: Kalimpong as a "Contact Zone"* (Heidelberg: Heidelberg University Publishing, 2017), 118. See also Clare Harris, *Photography and Tibet* (London: Reaktion, 2016), 38.

38. Stuart Hall, "Cultural Identity and Diaspora," in Patrick Williams and Laura Chrisman (eds.), *Colonial Discourse and Post-Colonial Theory: A Reader* (Columbia: Columbia University Press, 1994), 392–403.

39. Pratt, *Imperial*, 1st edition, 7.

40. Anthony Moran, "As Australia Decolonizes: Indigenizing Settler Nationalism and the Challenges of Settler / Indigenous Relations," *Ethnic and Racial Studies*, 25:6 (2002), 1016.

41. See Bate 'The Figure of Migration' in this volume.

42. See Irimia 'What Moves You?' in this volume.

Photographies, Representations, and Migrations

The Figure of Migration

David Bate

*The theatre of emigration must start again at the beginning, not
just its stage, but also its plays must be built anew.*[1]
Walter Benjamin

In 1938, Walter Benjamin argued that, in new situations, the old ways of doing
things must be changed, not only in their content but also in their very form,
they should be "built anew." Times of transition demand a transformation in cultural form, at least, this is the thesis that Benjamin advances in relation to Bertolt
Brecht's theatre:[2] drama must be adequate to the new realities being confronted, to
become contemporary in meaning (even if the material of the play is historical). It
is a thesis equally at home in other new situations, not only in the dramatic form of
theater but also across other forms of representation. All this, it seems to me, is the
kind of setting in which we should locate a critical history of photography, that is
to say, a view of photography as part of a historical struggle to enunciate something
relating to new conditions, to establish a discourse on what it means to be modern.[3]

How and where is the experience of migration located, and in what representations? What cultures and histories are encoded there, and how are these included
or excluded in the multiple discourses within which photographic images circulate? What effects do these representations have, and what are their ethical and
aesthetic *affects*? What relations do these images have to the body of the migrant,
the migrant's location and place, the migrant's social status and situations? Such
are the questions that should inform a history of photography concerned with
migration.

Migration is one of the most critical social, political, and economic issues in
culture today, central to all our lives and cultures. Indeed, the "management"
of migration is central to the politics of every nation-state. One way or another,
migration affects us all and has done so for centuries: colonialism, slavery, war,
persecutions (religious, ethnic, political, and sexual), social and cultural beliefs, and
economic discriminations have all played their part in the gathering and scattering
of diasporic groups and their identities. As refugees, exiles, émigrés, emigrants,
immigrants, "foreigners," strangers, and the newly displaced, there is a vast canvas,

with literally millions of stories and situations that, told or untold, have constantly shaped who we are today. This *we* is multiple, not singular. I want to insist on this multiple history of migration, because the speaking of any one story is inevitably a singularity among the many multiple histories of migration, diaspora and exile. What must be acknowledged here is that any story is sometimes faced with that unspoken look: "but that is not *my* story." In this respect, the contemporary term most often used today, *migrant*, does little justice to the multiple vicissitudes of all the different *we*s that constitute the global migrations and all their diverse hybrid effects in and on human culture. I am reminded here—speaking from Dublin— of James Joyce, the Irishman who wrote in English, was sometimes criticized for using the language of the colonizer, and yet, in doing so, also changed it.[4] Or the opening of the National Museum of Migration in Paris in 2007 at the instiga- tion of an Algerian immigrant, Zaïr Kedadouche, supported by French histori- ans and the (right-wing) President Chirac, who officially announced and publicly endorsed France as "a nation of immigrants." Yet, of course, emigration from one place to another also means the depopulation of the point of departure, "the old place," which also has another set of social, economic, political, and cultural effects. Ireland, for example, lost half its population between 1841 and 1911.[5] As Eric Hobsbawm has noted, the statistics of migration from Europe to the United States in the period between 1860 and 1914 are staggering, some fifty-two million people left different parts of Europe for the continent of America.[6]

What kinds of representations have come to embody that experience? Whose experiences are represented in photographs? How and where are these experiences of the migrant located in any discourse? What discursive spaces do these photo- graphic images enable or constitute? What kinds of people are included or excluded as subjects or objects of these discourses? And what effects do these images have? What role has photography played in producing spaces for migratory meanings? If a history of the relations between photography and migration is not fully artic- ulated, or does not even exist yet, the traces of migration are nevertheless to be found everywhere in photography and its archives. Look carefully and the figure of migration can be found almost anywhere. I use this word *figure* in its most open and plural meaning: a figure is a statistic, the shape of a human body, a rhetorical form, an image; or something that features (*figures*) in a situation. Each of these overlapping senses relates to the question: What is the figural space of migration in photography? The answer to this question is not just a matter of collating pho- tographic images of migrants and arranging them into chronological order (or some other taxonomic logic), but to consider the way that migration is encoded, embodied, rendered meaningful, or even uncoded in photographic images. That is to say, what, where, how, and why are the implicit and explicit figures of migration present in photography historically?

Departure

My particular concern here is with the image of a passage between Europe and America. More than what happens *before* the departure, *after* the arrival of the migrant, or in the *beyond* of a "somewhere else" of settlement, it is the journey itself that signifies as a traumatic passage, from one culture to another. Even afterward, it is the journey that leaves its mark, its impression on those who made that journey. The passage is a journey, a temporal and spatial process of transition. Such moments of transition are already present in the history of photography, made perceptible, notably by the social photographs of Lewis Hine, pictures that he made during the first decade of the twentieth century (Fig. 1).

Hine's early social portrait photographs signify the arrival of a new wave of migrants in the United States, and the dream of "America." In these "interpretive photographs," as Hine called his pictures, already acknowledging his intervention as a photographer, we are shown individuals, families, and small groups at "the" moment of their arrival.[7] The photographs, famously taken at the port of arrival on Ellis Island, New York, show us the faces, bodies, clothing, demeanors, and place of arrival of these migrants. These elements establish a key photographic trope of migration, productive of the figure of the migrant, their visibility as they "arrive." In the very repetition of these different scenes, the pictures insist on the veracity of their identity, in representing what the viewer might expect to see. Such figures "arriving," as individuals, families, and small groups, begin to establish an early twentieth-century photographic trope: the photograph as a document. The term *figure* here operates in its open and plural sense: a figure is a numerical statistic (this is one among many migrants), a rhetorical form (the cluster of faces, bodies, clothes, and spaces of transition, e.g., the port), and the actual figure of a person (the shape of the human body). The figure is an image, thus something that features (*figures*) the situation of migration. In each of these overlapping senses, the formative figure of the migrant image is at the heart of a whole discourse on migration and its visibility. What do we expect to see figured (Fig. 2)?

In Hine's work is a repertoire of facial expressions: a direct stare at the camera (and thus to the imagined viewer); a cursive glance at the camera (perhaps as much in fright or apprehension of the camera as any shock of arrival in America); a look of dignity and apprehensiveness, mixed with the mutable expressions of fear, resignation, defiance, a smile (a modern photographic convention), or resistance to it. Hine's figures are burdened with bundled clothes and possessions, hats, suitcases, and bags in their pause for the camera, sometimes with a clutched piece of paper in hand. A weary posture, a wary expression, a focused stare, the happy display of a baby, children lined up as if in a military parade, women burdened with heavy baggage: these images show a multiplicity of postures, exposed to the photographer's

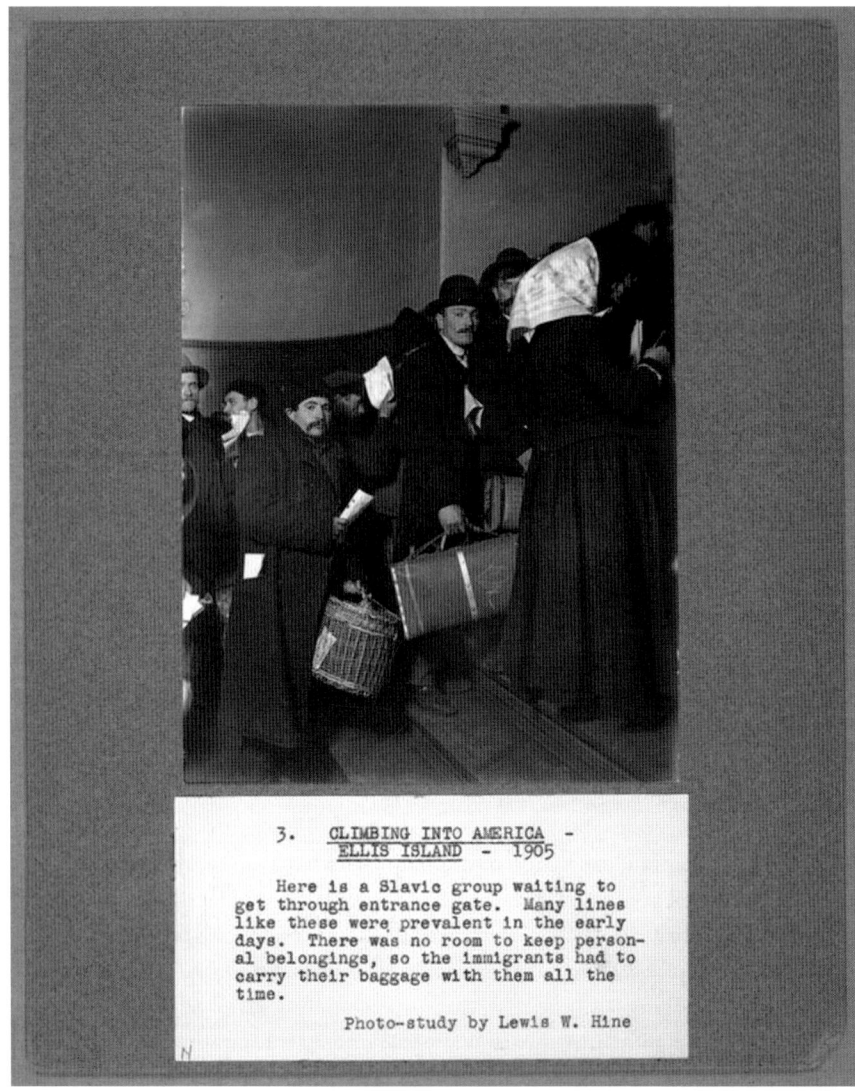

Figure 1: Lewis Hine, *Climbing into America, immigrants at Ellis Island*, 1905. The Miriam and Ira D. Wallach Division of Art, Prints and Photographs: Photography Collection, The New York Public Library. *Climbing into America, immigrants at Ellis Island*, New York Public Library Digital Collections. Accessed August 2020. http://digitalcollections.nypl.org/items/510d47d9-4e76-a3d9-e040-e00a18064a99

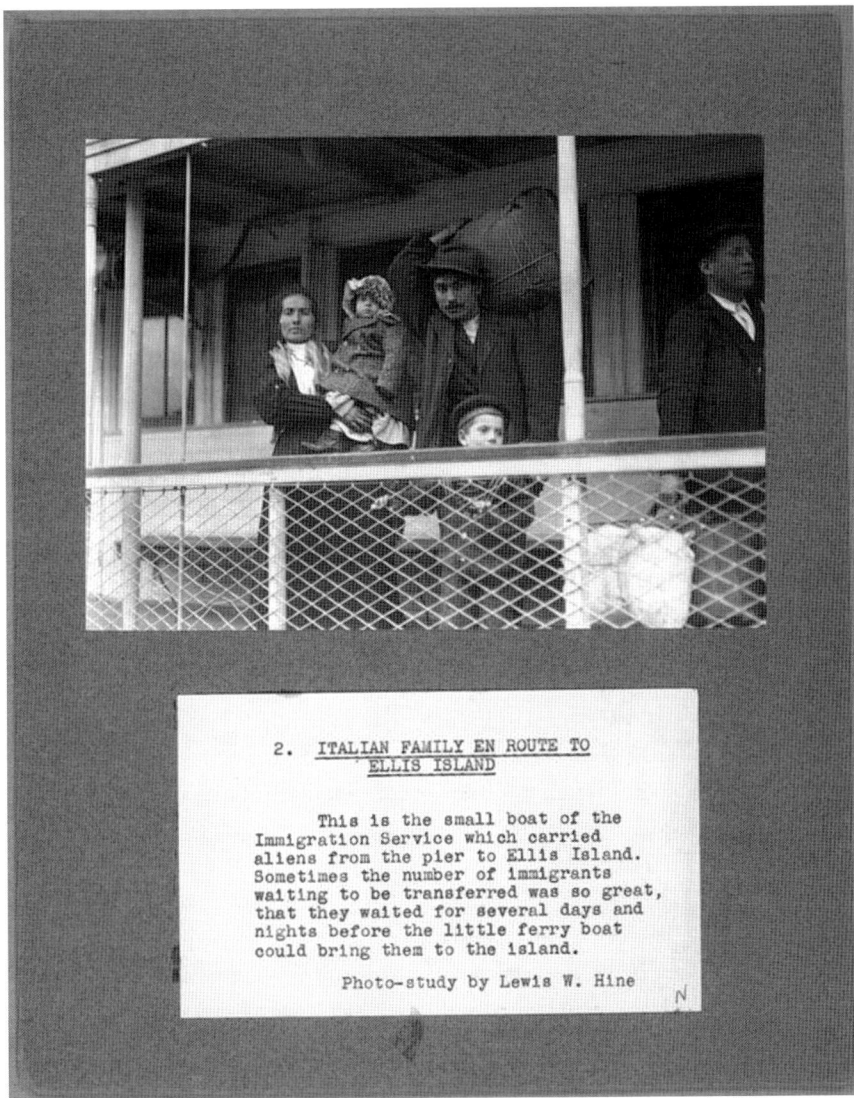

Figure 2: Lewis Hine, *Italian family enroute to Ellis Island*, (1905). The Miriam and Ira D. Wallach
Division of Art, Prints and Photographs: Photography Collection, The New York Public Library.
"Climbing into America, Ellis Island, 1905" New York Public Library Digital Collections.

camera at their "moment" of arrival. A process is turned into a moment, an image. These figures are illuminated in Hine's photographs by either his harsh frontal flash or the natural light filtered through the skylights of the Ellis Island station buildings (now a migration museum).

What is not in question here is the status or the dignity of the figures or their incidental arrangement before the camera, but rather the effects of these pictures in their dissemination: as foundational of a certain image of Ellis Island and the immigrant peoples who passed through there. Of the millions who came through the Ellis Island port of entry, it is these pictures that establish the who, what, where, and why of the figures of arrival in migration photography. The pictures bestow a certain look, appearance, and legitimacy to the image of the European migrant arriving in America. Hine's photographs open up an affective space of loss and belonging, or of yearning for an identity to which every person can feel as their experience too, especially those who have moved from one place to another. The disjunctive space of these images offers the spectator a place for the figures of migration to matter. These migrant figures, marked by the moment of arrival, show their determined movement toward somewhere else. These are not nomadic global travelers, at home in the restless homelessness of the wandering soul, seeking refuge in adventure and travel. No, these are the faces of a committed transition, a gritty displacement, as the move from one place to another (Fig. 3).

Historically, Hine's work occupies a role as the de facto truth of things in photographic discourse. It is through this route of veracity that Hine's early photographic work is established as canonical in the history of photography.[8] The historian of photography Alan Trachtenberg suggests that the recognition of Lewis Hine's work "depends upon an institutionalized community capable of conferring prestige upon photographers."[9] This occurred, according to Trachtenberg, when Hine's work was "rediscovered" later by a younger generation of American photographers, such as Berenice Abbott and Walker Evans, and the historian-curator Beaumont Newhall in 1938.[10] Trachtenberg argues, "Hine's 'rediscovery' occurred":

> just at the moment when a quasi-official history appeared side by side with the introduction of photographs into museums of art. How to explain and justify this new public role of the photograph in exhibitions of art? To guide public responses and help cultivate public taste, categorical distinctions were in order, and Hine conveniently fit one of the bills.[11]

Trachtenberg claims Hine's work "fitted the bill" for photography in art museum exhibitions. Hine himself called his work "Social Photography" as a form of "social document," in which the use of photography was to be concerned with matters of social record.[12] Hine's social photography work is constructed and given a place as

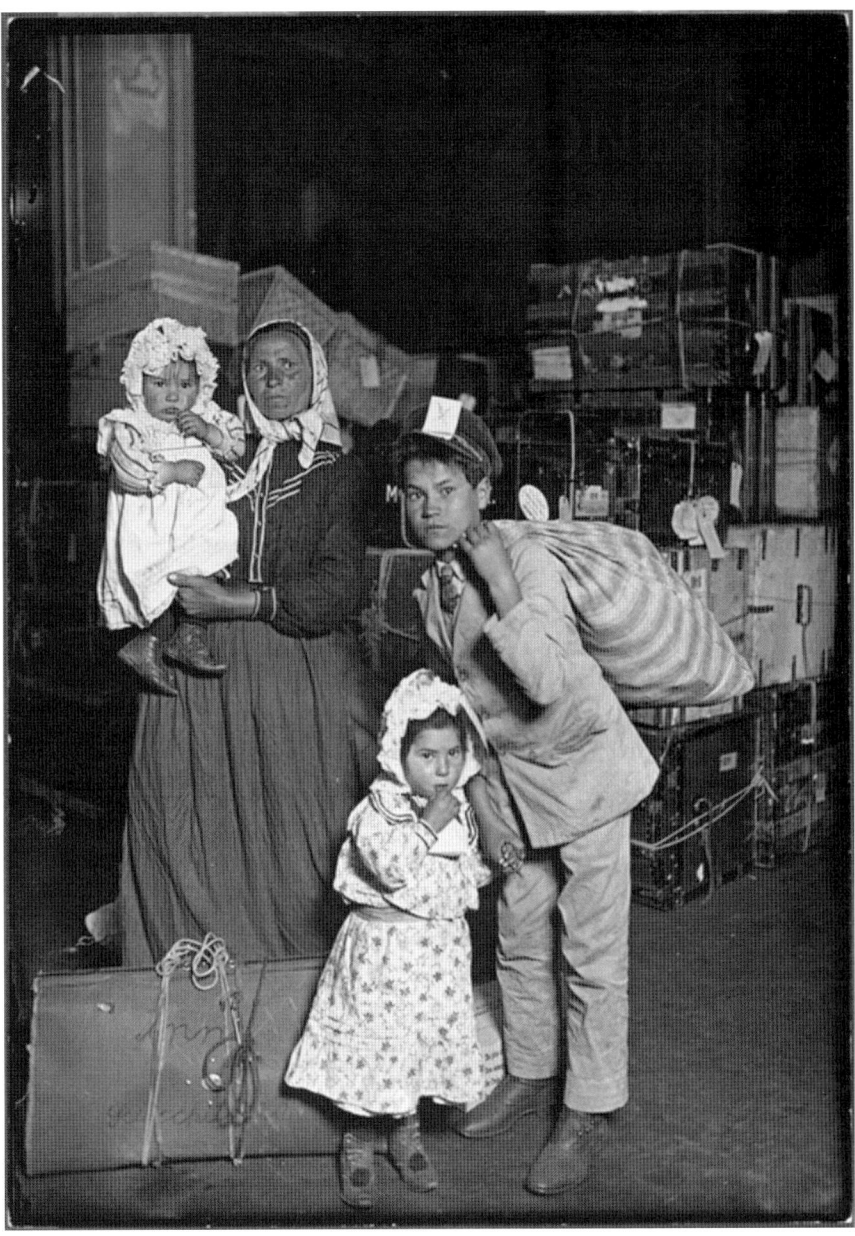

Figure 3: Lewis Hine, *Immigrant family looking for lost baggage, Ellis Island*, 1905. The Miriam and
Ira D. Wallach Division of Art, Prints and Photographs: Photography Collection, The New York
Public Library. *Immigrant family looking for lost baggage, Ellis Island*. New York Public Library Digital
Collections.

a practice in the United States' history of photography within the art museum and within the general category of documentary. Lewis Hines's image-text-based social photography is re-situated within a tradition of art and documentary photography, and that is where it has rested ever since. The effect of this positioning within the history of photography is twofold. First, the images are colonized by a discourse on photography named *history*, in which the images establish a mode for the recognition of reality, the immigrant, child poverty, and so on, and which confers on them a certain type of veracity. Second, the culturally affective dimension of these photographic images is subjugated to the studiously thematic fact of *arrival*. We can surely now recognize a certain emotive force around these photographs, which remains suppressed in discourses surrounding them. We should admit here that alongside their relation to the perception of migration, the figure of the migrant also carries an emotive aspect, a dimension that is interlinked implicitly with what would conventionally be called its representational power. The critical discourse that surrounds a photographic image needs to interrogate the links between representation and affective power. Hine's migrant photographs are thus framed by these respective discourses of representation and affect, documentary and art.

Since Roland Barthes's *Camera Lucida*, it has been possible to recognize that an aspect of the affective, emotional dimension of any photograph, Barthes's *punctum* (or private affect), is both predicated on the photograph's initial social function, what Barthes calls its *stadium*, and yet may be separated from it too.[13] Thus, the personal affective dimension of a photograph cannot be determined in advance. It requires a spectator's glance, look, or stare at an image and even then, the affect may remain unprocessed verbally, or even unconscious. In other words, the meaning of a still photograph is not passive or fixed inside the image rather, the meanings come partly from the way an image is animated by the spectator, who interacts with it to make a personal "cinema" out of the image. (As the French say about children acting out: *fait du cinéma*, they make their own film about something.) From the theoretical frame of *stadium/punctum*, the role of representation and emotional affect is intertwined in the cultural space of an image and engagement with it. These issues of an affective relation within the power of representation are central to the question of migration.

Passage

I want to consider these issues here within the space of transition itself, of travel from Europe to the Americas. It is the image of the ship, as Paul Gilroy suggests in his study *The Black Atlantic*, that relates to the "middle passage" of migration, the ship as a "living micro political system in motion."[14] The ship offers a beautiful

metaphor and tragic metonymy for the very threshold of transition and migration, the passage that highlights the contradictions in time and space that are the
condition of all narratives of migration. That is to say, the ship is a space in which
someone has not yet arrived, nor have they quite left the departure point.

The ship that I have in mind, or at least the photograph taken on it, is a famous
photograph by Alfred Stieglitz, known as *The Steerage* (1907), a classic picture in
the history of photography and photographic criticism. As it happens, the year
Stieglitz took this photograph, 1907, was statistically the peak year of all European
migration to the United States.[15] According to archive records, 1,200,000 emigrants
were admitted to the United States that year, all carried on ocean liners.[16] What
does this picture bring into being in its presence? What is the now of this picture
then, that can mean something in our present *now* today (Fig. 4)?

In the history of photography, the account given of *The Steerage* (1907) is more
or less the same one, repeated everywhere. It relates Stieglitz's heroic struggle to
achieve a status for photography as a new *modern* art in the new-world metropolis
of New York City at the beginning of the twentieth century.[17] *The Steerage* was
Stieglitz's own favorite photograph, such that he later claimed: "If all of my photographs were lost and I'd be represented by just one, *The Steerage*, I'd be satisfied."[18]
I will take him at his word and consider this one photograph.

A critical account of *The Steerage* in photographic criticism comes from a different axis, one that examines this picture's credentials as "art." Here, it is Allan
Sekula who took up *The Steerage* as a basis for a critique of "the relationship between
photography and high art."[19] Sekula's text is itself an influential one in photography
theory; it was first published in *Artforum* in 1975, then in Victor Burgin's 1982 book
Thinking Photography, and later referred to again by dozens of others.[20] Stieglitz's
own written account of the photograph is cited by almost everyone in discussion
of this picture. I will not deviate from this since his commentary is crucial for my
subsequent discussion. It is worth quoting at length because it gives his version of
"How *The Steerage* Happened." Stieglitz recounts:

> Early in June 1907, my small family and I sailed for Europe. My wife insisted
> upon going on the Kaiser Wilhelm II – the fashionable ship of the North German
> Lloyd at the time. Our first destination was Paris. How I hated the atmosphere of
> the first class on that ship. One could not escape the *nouveaux riches*.
> […]
> On the third day out I finally couldn't stand it any longer. I tried to get away
> from that company. I went as far forward on deck as I could. […] As I came to
> the end of the deck I stood alone, looking down. There were men and women
> and children on the lower deck of the steerage.
> […]

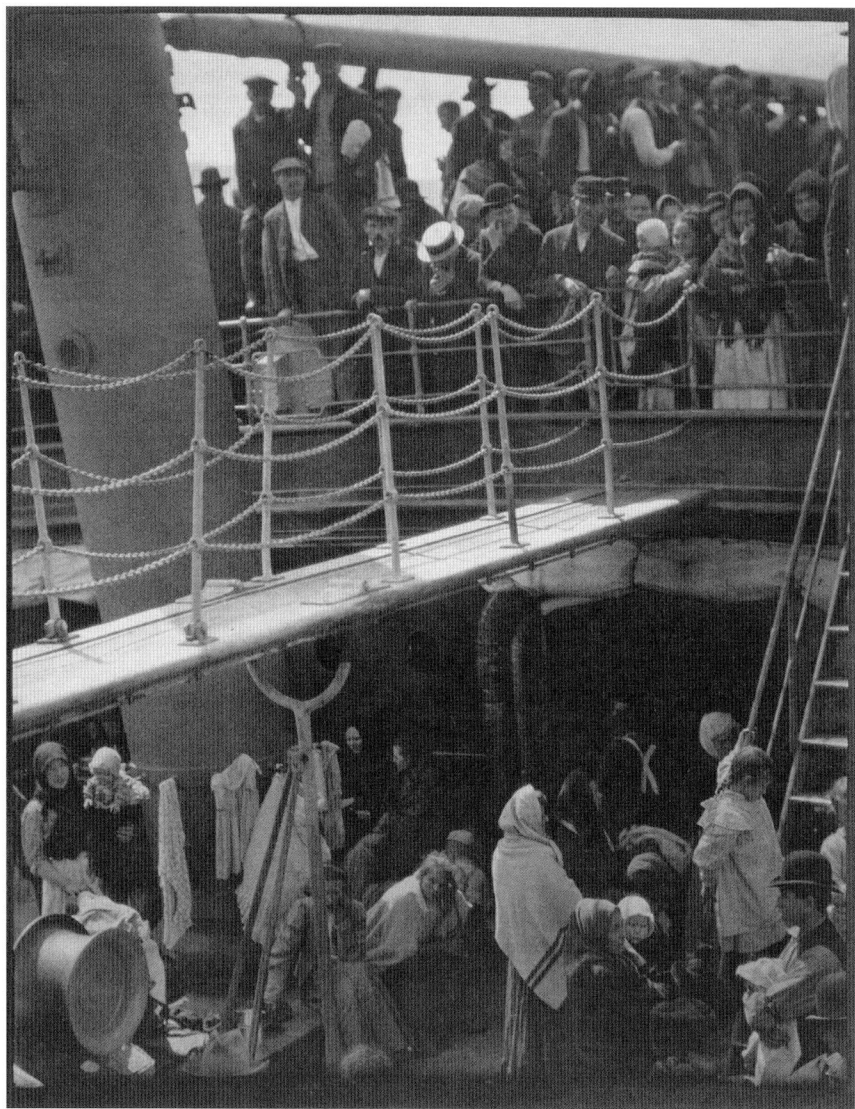

Figure 4: Alfred Stieglitz, *The Steerage*, 1907 (Plate 1, p. 329). National Gallery of Scotland, presented by Mrs. Elizabeth Uldall in memory of her sister, Ruth Anderson, 1998.

On the upper deck, looking over the railings there was a young man with a straw hat. The shape of the hat was round. He was watching the men and women and children on the lower steerage deck. Only men were on the upper deck. The whole scene fascinated me. I longed to escape from my surroundings and join those people.

[…]

A round straw hat, the funnel leaning left, the stairway leaning right, the white draw-bridge with its railings made of circular chains-white suspenders crossing on the back of a man in the steerage below, round shapes of iron machinery, a mast cutting into the sky, making a triangular shape. I stood spellbound for a while, looking and looking. Could I photograph what I felt, looking and looking, and still looking. I saw shapes related to each other. I saw a picture of shapes and underlying that the feeling I had about life. And as I was deciding, should I try to put down this seemingly new vision that held me – the common people, the feeling of a ship and ocean and sky and the feeling of release that I was away from the mob called the rich – Rembrandt came into my mind and I wondered would he have felt as I was feeling.[21]

At this point, Stieglitz reports, he rushed back to his cabin for one of his Graflex film cameras (five-by-seven-inch plate) and returned to take the photograph of this scene. From his account, the scene was still exactly as it had been when he left it earlier. A few days after his arrival in Europe, he successfully developed the plate at a photographer's darkroom in Paris (the photographer was recommended by a Kodak laboratory).[22]

Four months later, on 24 September 1907, Stieglitz was back home in New York with a negative of *The Steerage*. Four years later, *The Steerage* first appeared in public, in a portfolio of his pictures in *Camera Work* magazine, accompanied by a text describing all the pictures as snapshots, mostly taken in New York and its harbor. *The Steerage* then began to appear repeatedly in exhibitions, publications and as a photogravure in *291* (1915). It was also printed as a separate 500 deluxe edition of prints on Japanese tissue, which did not sell well, and most were destroyed.[23]

The scene of the picture and what it represents for Stieglitz is well established in his text. Stieglitz has explicitly expressed his wish to escape his class and first-class status (although he unkindly blames his wife for this) and to be separated from this world. The title he gives to the photograph, *The Steerage*, refers directly to the cheapest and literally lowest class of travel on a ship. He found his own alienation expressed in the scene before him. Excitedly, he wanted to represent this scene as a photograph. The photograph that he then made thus also expresses this feeling, or at least, this is what his text says. Yet oddly, despite the title he gave the picture, this is not what he really *sees*. According to his text, he saw only "shapes related to each other."[24] It is as though Stieglitz has a special filter for his vision, which translates objects and people into symbols, as he calls them, or forms, as figures that signify his state of mind. How did Stieglitz come to be able to formulate such statements, and what are the conditions of this discourse that he initiates? What sense does it make?

Metonymical meaning

Stieglitz understands the visible scene as a translation of his subjective feelings: "I saw a picture of shapes and underlying that the feeling I had about life."[25] It is such a description of the photograph by Stieglitz that Allan Sekula regards as "pure symbolist autobiography."[26] Sekula argues that, for Stieglitz, "the photograph is imagined to contain the autobiography."[27] In Stieglitz's discourse, Sekula suggests:

> The photograph is invested with a complex metonymic power, a power that transcends the perceptual and passes into the realm of affect. The photograph is believed to encode the totality of an experience, to stand as a phenomeno-logical equivalent of Stieglitz-being-in-that-place. And yet this metonymy is so attenuated that it passes into metaphor.
> [...]
> Instead of the possible metonymic equation "common people = my alienation", we have the reduced, metaphorical equation "shapes = my alienation". Finally, by a process of semantic diffusion we are left with the trivial and absurd asser-tion: shape = feelings.[28]

The straw hat and the funnel in the picture are metonymic substitutions in Stieglitz's discourse, for man and ship respectively. These metonymical figures are then read as poetic metaphors for Stieglitz's personal separation/alienation. Sekula demonstrates the rhetorical transition of meaning from the photograph to the writ-ten discourse of Stieglitz's autobiographical text, which is then projected back on the photographic image as its meaning.

In Sekula's view, Stieglitz's writing constitutes a metalanguage, a type of dis-course to speak *about* photographs without speaking photographically. Stieglitz's "language" about seeing symbols, shapes, and feelings is precisely a manner of *not* describing the picture itself in terms of its content. This modernist (meta-) language of symbols constructs a theory of vision that is rhetorical; in other words, it replaces the visual codes of the photograph with another type of figurative language, literary synonyms that imply another language (for lack of a better word) that speaks about the photograph indirectly. In this division between picture and words, Stieglitz "speaks" the photograph within the features of North American modernism, oth-erwise called Western formalism.[29]

Allan Sekula's essay is a sophisticated critique of the closure given to photography as art (or as art for art's sake) in this discourse, and he demonstrates this by considering what different kinds of information and knowledge certain photographs provide, through quality, artfulness, or narrative capacity, and the effect on their positioning within a discourse.[30] To make this point clear, Sekula contrasts *The Steerage* with a photograph by Lewis Hine, taken two years earlier at Ellis Island, the New York port of entry for emigrants to the United States. The picture, from Hine's early social photography, shows two migrants on a gangplank (Fig. 5).

A contrast is made between Stieglitz's artful, aesthetic approach to photography, and the literal description of Lewis Hine's picture, which, Sekula argues, refuses to elevate itself much beyond the theme of arrival: a theme reiterated in the simple declarative title, *Immigrants on a Gangplank* (1905).[31] From this juxtaposition, Sekula sets up a series of more general binary differences between Stieglitz and Hine as two different approaches to photography, of art and documentary, respectively.

Lewis Hine's social photography belongs, Sekula insists, to a social-political discourse aimed at mobilizing public opinion, and at changing people's minds and legislation; in contrast, the high-minded aesthetics of Stieglitz's work is aimed at the spectator's imagination: social documentary evidence on one side and formalist aesthetics of art on the other. Sekula's essay culminates in a general summary of this "binary folklore" as a "misleading but popular" argument about "photographic communication."[32] We can list these binary categories by Sekula as: art/documentary, symbolism/realism, viewer/witness, expression/reportage, imagination/empirical truth, affective value/informational value, metaphor/metonymy. Sekula argues that "Stieglitz's reductivist compulsion is so extreme, his faith in the power of the image so intense, that he denies the iconic level of the image and makes his claim for meaning at the level of abstraction."[33] This was the idea Stieglitz presented when he says that what you see is not the depicted (literal) object, because it is nothing but "shapes in relationship to one another," and these shapes give rise to feelings. In Sekula's argument, it is precisely this type of linguistic discourse that provides the frame for Stieglitz's distinction between art and documentary photography. Yet, in his critique of this distinction, Sekula also appears to suggest these opposing values are embedded and intrinsic to the actual photographs:

> While the Steerage is denied any social meaning from *within*, that is, is enveloped in a reductivist and mystical intentionality from the beginning, the Hine photograph can only be appropriated or 'lifted' into such an arena of denial. The original discourse situation around Hine is hardly aesthetic, but political. In other words, the Hine discourse displays a manifest politics and only an implicit aesthetics, while the Stieglitz discourse displays a manifest aesthetics and only an implicit politics.[34]

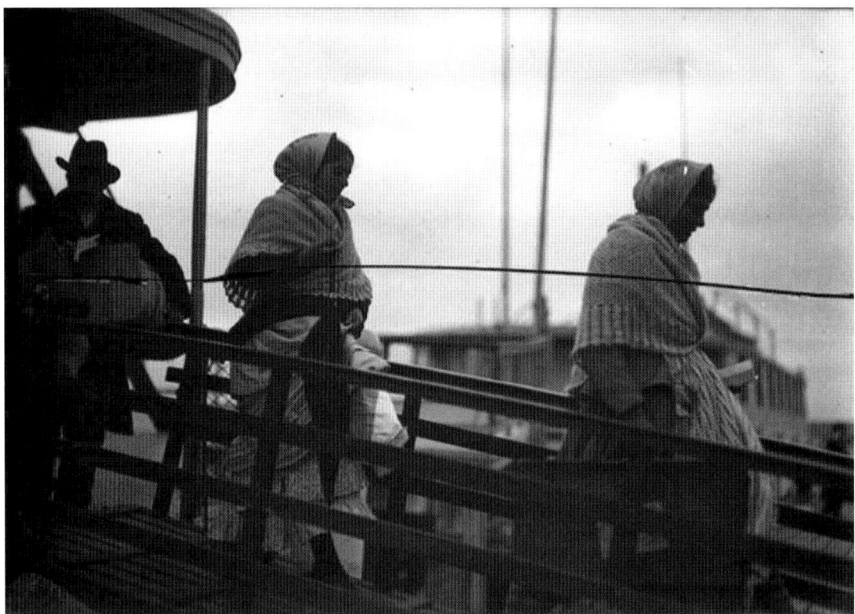

Figure 5: Lewis W. Hine, *Immigrants on a Gangplank*, 1905. Gift of the Photo League, New York: former collection of Lewis Wickes Hine, George Eastman House, Rochester, New York, United States.

So although a documentary photograph may be treated by art criticism as *aesthetic* (i.e. as formal, without its content), or an art photograph can be given a political critique, these photographs are, for Sekula, already positioned and limited by the original discourse in which they were produced.[35] Yet if we follow this path along the significations already set out by Stieglitz (or Hine), we are condemned to tread the same weary path of photography criticism, the eternal cul-de-sacs of meaning as *modernism* versus *realism*. Curiously, Sekula's own reading is in a manner that itself seems unable or unwilling to explore the path of rhetorical substitutions of meaning, of one thing for another, which he himself introduced. Sekula's discourse of criticism in effect fetishizes the authorial producer so that Stieglitz *is* the source of meaning for the image, resulting in a critical position that more or less inevitably condemns Stieglitz's photograph to the same values and reading as Stieglitz's own reading as author and, as a consequence, *fixing* the image's meaning.[36] It is no longer adequate, as it perhaps was in 1975 when Sekula wrote his article, to simply condemn the photograph as "mystical," for it is indeed within the nature of visual rhetorical figures such as metaphor and metonymy for shapes to slide along chains of signifiers to signified meanings that are not necessarily via the rational thought processes of consciousness.[37] My aim here is not specifically to critique Sekula's argument and analysis, which did much to disinvest photographic criticism of its romanticism, but more to reconsider what we can do with such a celebrated photograph today, given its obvious yet suppressed reference to migration.

What would it mean to return to the photograph, not as the matter of its provenance as an art object, but precisely as an *image*, symbolically trapped by its own place in photographic history and discourse? What might be the *implicit* politics— that neither Stieglitz nor Sekula mention—involved in this image, whether considered via the affective intention of its author or the social-historical context of the picture? It is worth pausing here to take up these points of authorial intention and social history, because they both impinge on the discussion of the picture in intersecting ways.

Historical narratives

Firstly, the authorial account that Stieglitz gives of *The Steerage* was written long after the picture was made. Stieglitz's text was published in 1942, some thirty-five years after he actually took the photograph.[38] What took him so long? Why wait? (Stieglitz was never known for his shortness of words.) Then it is also clear that Stieglitz's text, poured over by historians, is full of inaccuracies. Anyone can see the obvious discrepancy between the actual photograph that he describes in his text and what we can see with our eyes. For instance, he claims that "[o]nly men were on the upper deck." This is patently wrong. Even in a poor reproduction of the picture, women are clearly visible on the right side of the upper deck. Why does he not see or remember this? Then, what he claims to be a "funnel" is actually a mast. This boom arm acts like a visual border, a line that hems in the people at the top of the frame to visually separate them from the sky. Why does Stieglitz make such basic errors in his text?[39] After all, if this is the one photograph he claimed meant so much to him, why would he have forgotten the very formal components that make it the image that it is, an iconography that he would surely have known by heart? One obvious answer would be that Stieglitz had simply made a mistake, accounted for perhaps by old age or a foggy memory. Whether these are errors in Stieglitz's memory or alterations he made in his mind about the picture we cannot know. Memory has a habit of leaving out details of a scene less relevant to the specific valued memory. Perhaps the duration of time is a factor in the memory, or not, but let's leave this question of memory errors in abeyance; it may return later within a different frame. Nevertheless, this text does something that Sekula does not really remark on. Stieglitz's text *narrates* the photograph; it animates the image and turns it into a story. The text links the scene of the picture to Stieglitz's *before* and *after* what the photograph depicts and adds his feelings about all this (as *discontent* and *satisfaction*), which locates the image squarely within the temporality of his experience. Stieglitz weaves his personal feelings into the narrative context, which has come to determine how the photograph is seen. Thus, the image turns us to the second question about its moment in history: What might the photograph have to say about this?

As a matter of history, we know *The Steerage* photograph was taken on a ship, whose destination was Europe, the journey departing from New York. Although this fact is obvious from Stieglitz's account of the picture, since he says he is traveling from the United States to Europe, no one seems to have noticed its significance. It means the people in his photograph, those of the steerage class, are all returning to Europe, not migrants on their way to the United States. (It has been suggested that the photograph was likely taken while docked in Plymouth, England where it had stopped en route to France.[40]) If these people had once intended to migrate to the United States, they were now certainly on their way back to Europe. Strangely, the discursive myth of the picture has always inverted this idea, so the figures in the photograph appear to be new migrants to the American continent. As was customary at that time, the steerage-class passengers were brought up on deck at that moment in the day—everyday—when all the steerage passengers were herded up to the well decks so that their quarters could be cleaned.[41] The scene that Stieglitz photographed is what was called the third-class promenade. As one account puts it:

> If it was cold they brought with them the grey company blankets that were, by the turn of the century, included in the price of their fare. They perched on winches or in the lee of the hatches, the old people huddled about the steam pipes. Sometimes there were impromptu concerts or dances on the hatch covers that would attract a gallery of spectators from the second cabin. Slumming from above, they would lean over their promenade deck railing and throw candy and pennies down to the steerage children.[42]

It was the privilege of first-class passengers such as Stieglitz to have the luxury of a *choice* on such trips about whom they mixed with in their leisure time. The upper-class passengers could choose to join "common people" in the steerage class, in what was called "slumming."[43] *Slumming* meant going down and actually mixing with the steerage passengers, as portrayed, for example, in James Cameron's 1997 love disaster film, *Titanic*, a Hollywood version of the actual Titanic disaster of 1912.[44] "Slumming from above" meant to just *look* down at the steerage class, as Stieglitz did for his photograph. As an upper-class passenger, he could have joined them, as many did.

Robert Louis Stevenson, the Scottish novelist and travel writer, for example, had traveled by steerage class to immerse himself in their ways, to research for his writings and infuse his writing with a sense of authenticity for his readers. He published a book on the different "Steerage Types," recounting with enthusiasm his negative racist stereotypes, for example, of the Irish American as "for all the world like a beggar in a print by Callot," and so on.[45] This period spawned new literature about Atlantic migration and a new language about everyone in it, even about first-class passengers. The word *posh*, for instance, is popularly linked to the acronym of "Port Out, Starboard Home" (POSH), assumed to describe the best location and most desirable preference for (first- or second-class) cabins on outward and return stages of the journey.[46]

In this view, Stieglitz was a posh person who slums from above. The photographer, from his position on the upper deck, can see those below as a whole scene, a bird's-eye view of these other classes. It is this viewpoint of Stieglitz's camera that every viewer also inherits as the primary point of view, a position that, when looking at his photograph, invites us to also look down at these same people below: we are given this experience of slumming from above. From the first-class passenger's privileged viewpoint, the picture gives a visibility to these steerage migrants who make up the cheapest ticket of steerage passage.

Steerage-class immigration was a massive economic component of the shipping industry until the First World War. The Cunard Line even paid a fee to the then Austrian-Hungarian government for a regular supply of migrants to transport to the United States.[47] In this way, emigrants became a kind of commercial freight, a human commodity, to be transported from one place to another. Over time, the big German companies built small villages, with "emigrant buildings" as collection points where they would disinfect, cleanse, and check the health of emigrants entering on one side, before allowing them through and on board a ship.[48] Such were the improvements to healthcare on these routes and ships that, it was rumored, poor emigrant families would try to time a child's birth to coincide with their travel, so as to have the best possible conditions for the birth.[49] The port area of Hamburg, Germany became a massive gathering point for emigrants, gathered from different parts of Europe, to migrate to the United States. Areas such as this one in Hamburg were like small towns with their own railway stations, separate churches (for different religions), and various facilities for processing emigrants to make sure they met the strict Ellis Island medical and immigration checks. (Medical inspections were automatically *not* applied to first or second-class passengers.[50]) These precautions directed at steerage migrants were instrumental to ship owners, to avoid the expense and trouble of dealing with them as "returned cargo," because the shipping companies were held responsible if emigrants were refused entrance. Advance medical inspections were also aimed to avoid outbreaks of disease on the ship, which risked spreading across all the classes and crew during the seven to eight-day voyage across the Atlantic Ocean.[51] Despite all these improvements to the conditions of steerage travel, the trip was far from romantic, even by 1907.

The liner that Stieglitz and his family traveled on was one of the fastest ships of the period,[52] the German-owned *Kaiser Wilhelm II*. Built in 1903, it was one of four new Atlantic-crossing ships with a capacity of some fifteen hundred passengers, four hundred and sixty-eight in first class and almost double that, eight hundred, in steerage.[53] The first-class facilities were opulent; the spaces and quality among different classes of travel were far from equal. The garish first-class dining room, designed by Johann Poppe, was derided as "Bremen Baroque."[54] In effect, the luxurious spaces of the first-class passengers, who were smaller in number, were financed and subsidized by the larger numbers of people in steerage class, who were all squeezed into much smaller and lower deck spaces with minimal facilities allocated to them—in a fraction of the space allotted to the upper decks.

Such information on the history of migration is not contained in *The Steerage*, but this photograph opens out onto that history, as a historical referent of the picture. We might say that the value of this picture as a historical image is its depiction of these people from the steerage class during 1907, shown as they are returning to Europe for whatever reason, whether they were refused entry to the United States (for supposed poor health, undesirable characters, etc.) or they were returning voluntarily to Europe to live. However, the picture is structured around these first-class–steerage-class relations, of a first-class passenger looking at the steerage-class people depicted in the photograph.

We might say that the old modernist art discourse imposed on this photographic image could be undone by returning it to a social-historical framework, to a discussion of shipping and migration, and to a discourse on social history, from which Stieglitz clearly wished to hide or distance this image. Yet this would be to repeat and simply reverse the binary opposition set out by Sekula between art and documentary discourses, rather than to undo them. I want to argue that these two discourses are not mutually exclusive, but are intertwined. One of the key features of photography is that it can offer both a point of social identification, and also a space for subjective imagination (whether as a dream or as a nightmare). In other words, it is not that an art photograph has to be simply put back into a historical context to fulfill its "full" social, cultural, historical, political, or economic meaning, but to consider and acknowledge that the emotive productivity of the image is part of these other dimensions too. These so-called contextual meanings (what, in semiotics, would be called the connotations) of an image are themselves produced, informed, and understood through the aesthetic *affect* and imagination involved in the social production of the image. How might such a process proceed?

Affective memories

We know that images can evoke feelings, even abstractly. This is indeed the direct aim and ambition stated by Stieglitz in his essay on making the photograph. It is the man's straw hat, Stieglitz says, that triggers a feeling in him, although he does not say what this feeling actually is. What feeling, what was it about? The hat catches the light. If the hat is a symbol, what is its meaning? The man who is wearing this hat (which is singular among the cloth and bowler hats of the other men) is looking down to the deck below. In a sense, he is doing exactly what Stieglitz is himself doing: looking down at the people below. The figure in the straw hat thus offers a point of identification for Stieglitz (and the viewer of the photograph). This man, who inhabits the same position and point of view that we do, acts as a kind of witness inside the scene. He looks down on the people below him, just as we look down on him. The light shines down on this man in the hat, although this same light also touches other things too, notably the baby to his left (on the viewer's right), the gangplank, and, importantly, the women and children on the deck below—where he seems to be looking. In fact, this scene is at the apex of Stieglitz's camera viewpoint given to us. Like Stieglitz we also look at the young man who looks at women and children below. There is a chain of formal signification: the hat, the man, his look, the gangplank, and the mothers/women figures below. (This associative chain might also explain why Stieglitz's written account of the scene erases the women on the upper deck in his essay on the image.) On the lower deck, the lighter tones of the clothes hanging there help to pick out the women's heads and shoulders, especially the woman standing with a company blanket, worn like a shawl, and the seated woman next to her. This seated woman with light hair and light falling on her shoulder is directly in line with the look of the man in the straw hat. The light dances across these figures—mothers, babies, and children in the lower part of the scene—to form a rhythm of light tones. Like vertical marks, figures are picked out against the darkness by the light falling on them. The viewer's eye is led across this lower part of the picture and back up the staircase on the right-hand edge, which takes us back to the upper deck again.

The gangplank cuts across our vision of this look, if not that of the man in the straw hat, and it offers a dynamic intervention in the design of the picture. A gangplank enables passengers to go from one place to another, from land to ship, from ship to land, and thus from one continent to another. The gangplank metaphorically marks the moment and space of transition, a passage from one place to another, but here it also links one deck to another. Yet the gangplank also clearly divides the picture into two parts, splitting the people in it into two groups, even though they are all steerage class. This is perhaps also why Stieglitz was so offended when he first showed a print of the picture to his friend Joseph Keiley, who responded by saying "you have two pictures there, Stieglitz, an upper one and a lower one."[55] Stieglitz privately noted that Keiley had not understood the picture. Thus, for Stieglitz, the gangplank in the steerage picture figures not to *separate*, but to *link* one part of the ship in the photograph to the other, to join one deck to the other. Perhaps Stieglitz's affront at his friend's remark of this as a separation of two parts of the image is because the idea of division in the picture reminds him of his own alienated separation, his own longing, that he might belong down there too. Either way, Keiley and Stieglitz are both right; their viewpoints are two sides of the same coin: the gangplank graphically divides the two parts of the image, but also links them together like a bridge. Curiously, the chain railing on the gangplank curve in a wave pattern along the length of the plank, echoing the poetic idea of waves of the sea, the gangplank as a figurative metaphor for the whole voyage from one place to another. Stieglitz makes no attempt to offer any interpretation of the picture; he is content with the suggestion of feelings and separation from his own class. Yet why would he wish to belong to this crowded deck, to be jostled among these poor people crammed into these decks below his own first-class one? Is it not curious that a man expressing claustrophobia at being in first class, which was completely spacious, should nevertheless, in his essay at least, wish to be amid this crowded space, full of poor people? Is his wish a literal one to actually be among this crowded multitude? Is it a metaphorical yearning, linked to this scene by what it triggers, something as already in his mind? It is tempting to suggest a different biographical reading of this scene.[56]

Stieglitz, fed up with his lot and stuck in the dreary first class, wanders out on the balcony and sees this scene. Does he not see himself here as this young man, distinguished by his boater hat, as an identification with someone clearly looking down at the young women, babies, and children there? Does he, perhaps, see himself, in another time and space, as this younger man? Does he imagine himself as this younger man journeying to Europe like these passengers are? What other space and time is populated by these people below, apparently unfettered by the woes of his own position, his family, his class, his world? We know from Stieglitz's biography that he had traveled to Europe many times before. A child of first-generation German Jewish immigrants to the United States, Stieglitz had been taken by his parents to be educated in Germany at the age of seven. He had then returned again frequently, in numerous voyages to Europe, doing the grand tour route to Italy, Vienna, Venice, Sicily, and so on. It was on these trips to Europe that he had learned, practiced, and refined his eloquent pictorialist art photography, before returning to live and work in New York.

We can begin to imagine a complex temporality involving personal memory and various different times in this snapshot photograph taken in 1907 on a ship—a trip he had already made many times before. Stieglitz was forty-three when he took

The Steerage and seventy-eight when he published the essay (in 1942) and finally had his photography exhibited at the Museum of Modern Art in New York. The work of memory is often seen in its "afterwardness."[57] In going back over the past by Stieglitz, we can recognize the implicit migratory experience in its disjunctive temporal form, the to-and-fro of the past in the now of the photograph. The youthful man in the hat, the potential of his future before him, the future of these women and children: a multitude of different narratives. The past intrudes into the present, the photograph, at once a spectacle and a juxtaposition of different movements, can be oriented toward questions of the experience of migration.

Stieglitz does not own the memory of this photograph because the very image opens out—literally—onto the history of other migrations, the transitional space of the migrant, and myriad multiple memories. Stieglitz acknowledges this much in the naming of the picture as *The Steerage*, a class and category linked to migration, yet his discourse around it, like that of Sekula, in effect also disavows the figures of migration. I suggest this silence is linked to the ambivalence at the heart of migration, sometimes perceived as a threat to the very stability of knowing oneself. It is this push and pull of belonging and loss, presence and absence that the history of photography has to be attentive to in the question of migration. Such questions are important, not as a form of nostalgia or politics (migrants as victims or active agents of their own doing), but of the very figural logic in visual forms of representation and their unspoken affects, whether they are encoded or uncoded. Walter Benjamin was right, we must start again at the beginning to rethink here again the writing of the history and criticism of photography.

Notes

1. The emigration that Benjamin refers to is that of the refugees from the Third Reich in Nazi Germany. Brecht's plays were called *Terror and Misery of the Third Reich*. See Walter Benjamin, *Understanding Brecht* (London: New Left Books, 1977), 37.

2. See also John Willett (ed.), *Brecht on Theatre* (London: Methuen, 1964) and Walter Benjamin, *Understanding Brecht* (London: New Left Books, 1977).

3. To be *modern* is to invoke a term here that many may be suspicious of, in that many today would probably wish to be *contemporary*. The contemporary here would mean being "out of joint" with time, as Georgio Agamben proposes, though I see no real fundamental difference from the term *modern*, as I use it here in this sense. See Georgio Agamben, "What is the Contemporary?," in *What is an Apparatus? And Other Essays* (Stanford: Stanford University Press, 2009).

4. Colin McCabe argues that James "Joyce is very much the prototype of the post-colo-
    nial artist." Colin McCabe (ed.), *Futures for English* (Manchester: Manchester Univer-
    sity Press, 1988), 12.

5. Eric Hobsbawm, *The Age of Empire* (London: Weidenfeld & Nicolson, 1987), 41.

6. *Encyclopedia of European Social History*.

7. The reverses of Lewis Hine's Ellis Island photographs were stamped with the label
    "INTERPRETIVE PHOTOGRAPHY."

8. In Beaumont Newhall's foundational book, *The History of Photography*, for example,
    Lewis Hine's work features in Chapter Ten, which is simply called "Documentary."
    See Beaumont Newhall, *The History of Photography* (London: Secker & Warburg, 1964).

9. Alan Trachtenberg, *Reading American Photographs: Images as History, Mathew Brady to
    Walker Evans* (New York: Hill & Wang, 1989), 165.

10. Trachtenberg, *Reading American Photographs*, 190–191.

11. Trachtenberg, *Reading American Photographs*, 190–191.

12. See Lewis Hine's description of his work in his essay "Social Photography," reprinted
    in Alan Trachtenberg (ed.), *Classic Essays on Photography* (New Haven: Leete's Island
    1980), 109–113.

13. Roland Barthes, *Camera Lucida* (London: Fontana, 1980).

14. In his text, Paul Gilroy is talking more generally about the historical passage of arti-
    facts and ideas, cultural traditions and values between continents and places, and not
    just people or the early trade and traffic in slave exploitation. The point made is that
    it is *the ship* that is the transport for all these things. See Paul Gilroy, *The Black Atlantic,
    Modernity and Double Consciousness* (London: Verso, 1993), 4.

15. As is often the case, the influx of "foreigners" to the United States caused anxiety
    about them and their impact on the existing (immigrant) populations. The Dillingham
    Commission (1907–1910) and the US Immigration Commission helped to put a cap
    restricting immigration during the 1920s, with laws such as the Emergency Quota Act
    of 1921. In the earlier 1900s and 1910s, the bulk of passengers on ocean liners were
    migrants.

16. "About 52 million migrants left Europe between 1860 and 1914, of whom roughly
    37 million (72 per cent) travelled to North America, 11 million (21 per cent) to South
    America, and 3.5 million (6 per cent) to Australia and New Zealand. About one third
    of the emigrants to North America returned home." *Encyclopedia of European Social
    History*, Volume 2, ed. Peter Stearns (New York: Charles Scribner, 2001), 137.

17. See for example: Beaumont Newhall, *The History of Photography* (London: Secker &
    Warburg, 1980), 111–113; Mary Warner Marien, *Photography: A Cultural History*, 2nd
    edition (London: Lawrence King, 2006), 182–183; Jean-Claude Lemagny and Andre
    Rouille, *A History of Photography: Social and Cultural Perspectives* (New York: Cambridge
    University Press, 1987), 106–108.

Elizabeth Anne McCauley has recently added a more historical contribution to the literature in her essay "The making of a Modernist Myth," in a finely detailed forensic account of the picture. See The Steerage *and Alfred Stieglitz* (London: University of California Press, 2012).

18. Alfred Stieglitz, "How *The Steerage* Happened," *Stieglitz on Photography: His Selected Essays and Notes*, ed. Richard Whelan (New York: Aperture, 2004), 197. This remark supersedes the earlier one made by Stieglitz in 1899, when he was still a Pictorialist, that his "favourite picture" was his own *Mending Nets*, 1894. Also see *Stieglitz on Photography*, 60–61.

19. Allan Sekula, "On the Invention of Photographic Meaning," in Victor Burgin (ed.), *Thinking Photography* (Basingstoke: Macmillan, 1982), 88.

20. Allan Sekula, "On the Invention of Photographic Meaning," *Artforum* 13, no. 5 (1975); *Thinking Photography*, ed. Victor Burgin (Basingstoke: Macmillan, 1982); and *The Contest of Meaning*, ed. Richard Bolton (London: MIT Press, 1986). Sekula's essay was central in banging a final nail into the theoretical coffin of modernist photography, even if it has taken the corpse longer to accept death. In 1984, Abigail Solomon-Godeau noticed a renewed interest in Stietglitz, which she dubbed it a "Stieglitziana." See Abigail Solomon-Godeau's essay on the Stieglitz myth, "Back to Basics: The Return of Alfred Stieglitz," *Afterimage*, vol. 12, nos. 1 & 2 (Summer 1984), 21–25. See also Katherine Hoffman, *Stieglitz: A Beginning Light* (London: Yale University Press, 2004), 237–238.

21. Alfred Stieglitz, "How *The Steerage* Happened," *Stieglitz on Photography: His Selected Essays and Notes*, ed. Richard Whelan (New York: Aperture, 2004), 194–195.

22. The photographer is unnamed in Stieglitz's account, but he adds, in a typically immodest comment: "I wanted to pay the photographer for the use of the darkroom, but he said, 'I can't accept money from you. I know who you are. It's an honor for me to know you have used my darkroom.'" See Alfred Stieglitz, *Stieglitz on Photography: His Selected Essays and Notes*, ed. Richard Whelan (New York: Aperture, 2004), 196.

23. See Sarah Greenough, *Alfred Stieglitz: The Key Set, Volume One: 1886–1922* (Washington, DC: National Gallery of Art/Harry Abrahams, 2002), 190–194. Stieglitz's account of the 291 prints can be found in his essay "The Magazine 291 and *The Steerage*," reprinted in Alfred Stieglitz, *Stieglitz on Photography: His Selected Essays and Notes*, ed. Richard Whelan (Aperture, 2004), 215–221.

24. Stieglitz, "The Magazine 291 and *The Steerage*," 215–221.

25. Stieglitz, "The Magazine 291 and *The Steerage*," 215–221.

26. Allan Sekula, "On the Invention of Photographic Meaning," *Thinking Photography*, 99.

27. Sekula, *Thinking Photography*, 100.

28. Sekula, *Thinking Photography*, 100.

29. *Formalism* here is to be distinguished from Russian formalism, for instance, which developed a different relation of form to content, in which one is not subordinated

to the other, but they are instead mutually productive. See, for example, Abigail Solomon-Godeau, "The Armed Vision Disarmed: Radical Formalism from Weapon to Style," *Photography at the Dock* (Minneapolis: University of Minnesota Press, 1991), 52–84; Victor Burgin, "Looking at Photographs," *Thinking Photography*, ed. Victor Burgin (Basingstoke: Macmillan, 1982).

30. Allan Sekula, "On the Invention of Photographic Meaning," in *Thinking Photography*, ed. Victor Burgin (Basingstoke: Macmillan, 1982), especially 90–92.

31. Sekula uses the phrase "mindless straightforwardness" to describe Hine's photograph. Sekula, *Thinking Photography*, 91.

32. Sekula, *Thinking Photography*, 108. Alan Trachtenberg has since made a similar comment: "Largely through Stieglitz's influence, a polarised language entered photography criticism: factual reporting versus personal expression, art versus document." Alan Trachtenberg, *Reading American Photographs* (New York: Hill & Wang, 1990), 174.

33. Sekula, *Thinking Photography*, 100.

34. Sekula, *Thinking Photography*, 103, original emphasis.

35. To put the argument in semiotic terms, Sekula argues that the signified discourse of the photographer begins to determine not only the reading of the signifier (the picture) but also the actual production of photographs.

36. A similar criticism can be made of Alan Trachtenberg's essay argument on Stieglitz and Hine, "Camera Work/Social Work," in his book, *Reading American Photographs* (New York: Hill & Wang, 1990).

37. In linguistics, the figures of metaphor and metonymy constitute two poles for the selection and combination of units of meaning. Metaphor is based on notions of similarity, one thing is connected to another, while metonymy is based in contiguity; both can be found interacting in semantic systems other than that of language. See, for example, the now classic essay by Roland Barthes, "Rhetoric of the Image," in *The Responsibility of Forms* (Los Angeles: University of California Press, 1991). In Roman Jakobson's famous paper on the topic, Cubism is a "manifestly metonymic orientation," whereas Surrealist painting is predominantly a "metaphoric attitude." Eisenstein's cinema uses synecdoche "close-ups and metonymic setups, which are 'overlayed by a novel, metaphoric montage.'" See Roman Jakobson, *On Language*, eds. Linda R Waugh and Monique Monville-Burston (London: Harvard University Press, 1990), 130–131.

38. Stieglitz died four years later, in 1946.

39. Elizabeth Anne McCauley has pointed to other errors, for example, relating to the dates of Stieglitz's voyage. See her "The Making of a Modernist Myth," in Anthony W. Lee, *The Steerage and Alfred Stieglitz* (London: University of California Press, 2012), 21–22.

40. The presumption is that there is no wind, so the ship was not sailing mid sea. See Beaumont Newhall, "Alfred Stieglitz: Homeward Bound," *Art News*, 87, no. 3 (March 1988), 141–142.

41. John Maxtone-Graham, *The Only Way to Cross* (London: Patrick Stephens, 1983), 159.

42. Susanne Wibourg and Dr. Klaus Wibourg, *The World is Our Oyster, 1847–1997* (Hamburg: Hapag-Lloyd, 1997), 159.

43. Cited in R.A. Fletcher, *Travelling Palaces* (London: Sir Isaac Pitman, 1913), 159.

44. In *Titanic* the character called Rose, played by Kate Winslet, goes slumming with her steerage-class friend to experience the "community" down there.

45. Robert Louis Stevenson, "Steerage Types" [1895], *The Works of Robert Louis Stevenson*, vol. XVI (London: William Heinemann, 1925), 30.

46. Lee Server, *The Golden Age of Ocean Liners* (New York: Todtri, 1996), 10. The origin of this term is disputed but nevertheless often assumed as right in the literature on the period.

47. The Cunard line paid a stipend for the government to supply twenty thousand emigrants to the port annually. See Susanne Wiborg and Klaus Wiborg, *The World is Our Oyster: 150 years of Hapag-Lloyd* (Hamburg: Hapag-Lloyd, 1997), 155–156.

48. Wiborg and Wiborg, *The World is Our Oyster*, 151–152.

49. Wiborg and Wiborg, *The World is Our Oyster*, 155–156.

50. Rob McAuley, *The Liners* (London: Macmillan, 1997), 62.

51. See Wiborg and Wiborg, *The World is Our Oyster*, 152.

52. According to this author, the ships of this class were already built with military purposes in mind. See P. Ransome-Wallis, *North Atlantic Panorama, 1900–1976* (London: Ian Allen, 1977), 178.

53. The *Kaiser Wilhelm II* ship, built in 1903, had 1535 passengers in total: 468 first-class passengers, 268 second-class passengers, and 799 third-class or steerage passengers. The crew numbered 650. See Arnold Kludas, *Record Breakers of the North Atlantic Blue Riband Liners, 1838–1952* (London: Chatam, 2000), 87; Wiborg and Wiborg, *The World is Our Oyster*, 145–146.

54. Wiborg and Wiborg, *The World is Our Oyster*, 145.

55. Alfred Stieglitz, *Stieglitz on Photography: Selected Essays and Notes*, ed. Richard Whelan (New York: Aperture, 2000), 196–197.

56. Of the various attempts at this, Elizabeth Ann McCaulay's more recent historical discussion of the picture broaches this in a surprising concluding comment on Stieglitz's sexuality: "The impotence that he often commented upon in his letters found its compensation in the 'feeling of release' that he got from photographing." Elizabeth Ann McCaulay, *The Steerage and Alfred Stieglitz*, 65.

57. *Afterwardness* is the term used to translate Freud's concept of "Nachträglichkeit," as found in the work of French psychoanalyst Jean Laplanche. See Jean Laplanche, "Notes on Afterwardness," *Essays on Otherness* (London: Routledge, 1999), 260–265.

Vernacular Photographies and Migration

From Cavan to Kansas

A Photographic Album of Family Migration from Ireland to North America

Orla Fitzpatrick

An early twentieth-century photographic album created by a female Irish emigrant to the United States references both her new life and her country of origin. It presents a rare opportunity to analyze and explore how the contact zones created by Irish migration were visualized photographically and narrated through the format of the album. This snapshot album was compiled by Anna Whitfield (1884–1956), who emigrated to the United States from her home in the border county of Cavan, Ireland, in 1916.[1] The album allowed her to visually negotiate her complex Irish identity, as a Protestant Ulster woman, and also her later one as a naturalized American citizen.

Histories of Irish emigration

The scale of Irish emigration to the United States in this post-famine period is outlined by Kerby A. Miller:

> Thus, in 1856–1921 Ireland lost between 4.1 and 4.5 million inhabitants, of whom perhaps 3.5 million ended their travels in North America, primarily the United States. Indeed, by 1900, more Irish men and women (including second-generation Irish-Americans) were living in the United States alone than in Ireland itself.[2]

Although the numbers going to the United States had begun to decline by the start of the twentieth century, America was still the main destination for Irish emigrants. A considerable population of Irish-born and Irish American families retained strong bonds with Ireland and an interest in Irish affairs. Miller also traced demographic changes to Irish emigration, noting that those leaving the country were younger and increasingly more likely to be female than were earlier cohorts.[3] The dominant narrative of Irish migration in the nineteenth century, and indeed much of the twentieth, characterized the typical Irish emigrant as Catholic and male. They were the younger sons of small tenant farmers and agricultural laborers, who moved from rural holdings on the west coast of Ireland to the large cities of North America. As Hasia R. Diner notes in her work *Erin's Daughters in America: Irish Immigrant Women in the Nineteenth Century*, studies have concentrated on the experiences of Irish males "ignoring the data on women, who composed more than half the group."[4]

However, the work of scholars such as Emma Moreton, Margaret Lynch-Brennan, and Ruth Ann M. Harris has done much to redress this position.[5] Indeed Harris recognizes that, in order to tell the story of these women, "historians must be innovative in identifying and using nonconventional sources. Personal documents like letters are an especially appropriate source for research on immigrant and ethnic women, whose lives are so often hidden."[6] Photograph albums such as Anna's represent another valuable potential source for migrant history and its visualization.

Family albums can lose meaning and relevance once all those depicted have died and faded from memory, and it is at this moment in time that they often leave the domestic setting and become a commodity. Anna's album took such a journey. After migration, images taken in Ireland were pasted into the album alongside newer snapshots of American life. At some stage, the album returned to Ireland before eventually moving out of the family's ownership. I bought it in a Dublin antique, bric-a-brac store in 2015. As an interesting example of female migration and also its rarity as a depiction of the movement of a Protestant family from the Ulster province, the album provides an opportunity to address a gap in our understanding of Irish photographic and migrant history.

In general, Irish emigration has not been considered as a visual history and the emphasis has been placed on written sources. This is in keeping with the observations made by Sigrid Lien in relation to Norwegian migration and photography; she notes that photographs were sometimes used as illustration but rarely as historical interpretation themselves.[7] The vernacular album falls outside of the collecting remit of major cultural institutions whose emphasis, for the most part, is placed upon depictions of the famous or the topographical. Recent scholarship by Justin Carville and a project entitled the Irish Family Album led by Dublin's Gallery of Photography have done much to highlight this area.[8] Nonetheless, the absence of a large publicly held collection of twentieth-century vernacular Irish photography means that analysis of this album is undertaken somewhat in isolation. Likewise, the role of the photograph in representing and facilitating Irish migration remains an under-examined aspect of Irish history. Anna Whitfield's album counters the male and rural-to-urban narrative as it traces the migration of a single female nurse from a Protestant and Quaker/Society of Friends family moving firstly to the Irish capital Dublin and then to a rural setting in the American Midwest via Kansas City. Anna Whitfield was the eldest of five children, born in 1884, to Edward (1850–1924) and Mary (née Irvine) (1859–1917) Whitfield. The family farmed a small holding of twenty-nine acres, in the townland of Donge, County Cavan,[9] and paid rent to the local landlord, Richard Coote. By 1911, Anna had left Cavan to work in a Dublin drapers' store, where she lived along with dozens of other single female employees.[10] She later worked as a nurse at a city sanatorium in Ringsend, Dublin, before emigrating from Ireland in 1916—firstly to nurse in Kansas City and, following her marriage to farmer and senator Walter Harrison Bradbury (1893–1952) in 1923, to a farm in rural Jasper, Missouri. Following this relatively late marriage, her unmarried sister Janie came to live with Anna and her husband on their farm, where all three remained until their deaths in the 1950s.

Traces of Anna's Cavan and Dublin life can be found through census documents and her detailed captions in the album. Local newspapers such as the *Anglo Celt* provide information on the Whitfield family through notices of births, deaths, and marriages, alongside detailed listings for the sale of land and houses. Her life in Missouri was also uncovered through the local press, namely in the notices of community life that appeared in publications such as the *Joplin Globe*. These homely and chatty articles paint a vivid picture of the interconnected rural community in which Anna, her husband, and her sister played an active role through hosting parties and picnics at their home and through their attendance at church.

Created after her migration, the album contains images of her life in Ireland and America. She has attempted to counter the fragmentation caused by emigration by gathering together images representing family members on both sides of the Atlantic Ocean. As Deborah Chambers notes, in relation to her own family's use of photography, emigrant families often "reconnected through visual narratives of connected kinship."[11] Albums acted as social objects, performing a role in the maintenance of relationships and in the remembrance of home countries and in celebration of new identities.

Whitfield's album contains 290 images spread over 102 pages. Of these images, 261 are captioned and, unlike many such albums, in which the compiler loses interest in the project, each page of Anna's album has been populated. Its creation represents a considerable investment of time and energy. These photographs are enclosed in a mass-produced album whose cover imitates more expensive leather-bound volumes, and it is embossed with the word *Photographs*. Easily held and transported, this album is typical of millions manufactured between 1900 and 1920. The captions throughout the album are written in white ink, which contrasts strongly with the dark brown paper used in photo albums. It is clear that Anna has taken considerable pains to write a narrative around most of the images. Although not strictly chronological, it is divided loosely into themes relating to female kinship, work, migration, and education.

Although the images span between 1904 and 1929, the majority date from the late teens and early 1920s—when Anna and her sisters were young women. It includes their attendance at Mrs. Wingham's Academy in Dublin;[12] her period of employment at the Douglas Draper's Shop, Wexford Street, Dublin; her nursing career; and her married life in Missouri. Some pre-date Anna, and Jane's emigration to America and her brother John Henry's to Canada although the ratio between Irish and American images is fairly equal.

The image arrangements adhere to the tropes and conventions of snapshot album production.[13] Freed from the rigidity of Victorian albums, with their pre-assigned slots for carte de visite portraits, this period of album-making practice allowed for dynamic layouts and sequencing. Stephanie Synder notes that these hybrid objects performed many functions:

> Within these albums – crafted primarily by women – one encounters war, industrialization, immigration, family life, and public rituals (such as World's Fairs and tourism) interwoven into idiosyncratic narratives that are highly personal yet reflect and embody the culture. Equal parts visual diary, lay ethnography, family history, and reportage the vernacular photo albums […] are sites where art, culture, history, and private life intersect.[14]

Upheaval and change: Protestant life in newly independent Ireland

The album was created in an era that saw not only the First World War (1914–1918) but also the Easter Rising of 1916, the War of Independence (1919–1921), and the Irish Civil War (1922–1923). Before looking at the album in detail, it is necessary to outline how these political upheavals had particular implications for non-Catholic families such as Anna's, who lived alongside the newly created border. Anna's home county of Cavan was part of the nine-county province of Ulster. Following the partition of the country in 1921, a mainly Protestant, unionist, six-county state of Northern Ireland remained part of the United Kingdom while a predominantly Catholic twenty-six-county Irish Free State formed an independent jurisdiction. Cavan (Anna's home county) is one of the three Ulster counties that did not become part of the new state of Northern Ireland when the country was partitioned in 1921.[15] The introduction of the border cut Anna's family off, not only from a shared Ulster Protestant community but also from the marketplaces for their produce.[16] Between 1911 and 1926, the Protestant population in the twenty-six counties declined by 32.5 percent.[17] Some crossed the border to Northern Ireland while others emigrated. Did migrants such as Anna leave because they felt that there was no place for them in the new Catholic state, or was this exodus another phase in the decline of small tenant farmers? Perhaps her emigration was a reaction to the harsh realities of rural life in the border county? Or was it her impending role as a dependent, unmarried sister on a farm that her elder brother would inherit? In relation to the post-partition reduction in the Free State Protestant population, Graham Dawson notes that "the cultural memory of this migration and the wider effects of partition on Three Counties Protestants has been rendered largely private and invisible, and its history is still to be written."[18]

Anna's photographic album provides some clues as to the family's political allegiances while also facilitating her self-representation as a modern young woman. It is a rare visualization of Three Counties Protestant life and migration in the first half of the twentieth century and, as Campt notes with regard to similar African diasporic material,

regardless of whether these images succeeded in presenting their' subjects aspirations or intentions with greater or lesser accuracy – the photographs nevertheless represent expressive cultural texts that are of abiding historical significance for the insights they offer into the process of diasporic cultural formation.[19]

Anna's images announce her desires and ambitions and allow us to trace her gradual acclimatization to American life. Depicting modernity in the form of the innovative Kansas City hospital where she worked, and consumerism in the guise of a new automobile, telephone, and radio set, she highlights new facets of her post-migration life and offers a contrast to her rural place of origin. Campt recognizes that we cannot be certain that migrants succeed in accurately representing their ambitions photographically nor in controlling how these images were received. Nonetheless, the snapshots in Anna's album form part of a process of assimilation and change that is ongoing, and photographing oneself with the trappings of the new culture can play an early and sometimes entirely aspirational and anticipative part in this continuing identity formation. Lien refers to such images as "bragging photographs," which were sent back home to illustrate migrants' progress in the new country.[20]

The phase of Irish history in which Whitfield produced her album coincided with an exponential growth in the use of photography by the general public. Generated by advances in camera technology such as Kodak's Box Brownie, this democratization saw photography playing a greater role in the recording of family and community life. Gathered together into albums, these photographic objects often traverse both the public and the domestic sphere; this intersection is especially evident during periods of political turmoil.

Just as photographs cannot be considered in isolation from their historical and political context, this study will also regard the manner of their display within the album format. This material culture approach echoes the work of Elizabeth Edwards and Geoffrey Batchen; their study takes into account not only the image content but also the means of display, production, and circulation.[21]

Whitfield, as the compiler of the album, places herself as the central character and this in keeping with Batchen's observations on the snapshot album format:

> These albums were a vehicle for storytelling, often conveying a bio-epic starring the maker of the album (who we know, from ink captions, only as "me"). Roughly chronological, this narrative usually located its principal actor within a web of familial and social events and settings, allowing the depiction of an idealized life in pictorial form (snapshots rarely capture moments of tension or unhappiness).[22]

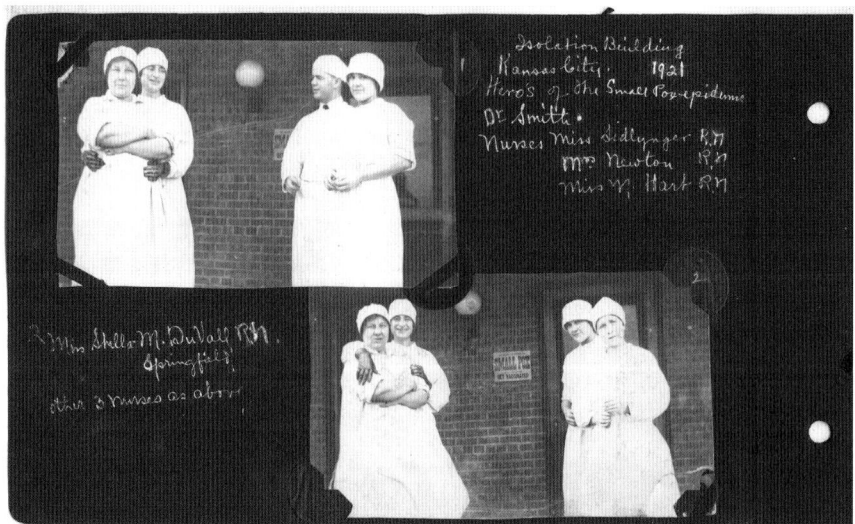

Figure 1: Kansas City Hospital, Smallpox epidemic, 1921 (Plate 2, p. 330). Page from Whitfield album, snapshots on craft paper, ink captions. Source: Author's collection.

Family, work, and friends in Anna's album

Anna was obviously proud of her nursing profession and includes several spreads showing her in this role both at the Ringsend Sanatorium in Dublin and at the Kansas City General Hospital. These jobs and her stint at the draper's store were live-in positions with her colleagues acting as de facto family and, as such, depict a communal, gendered existence that departs from a life based on familial associations. In Kansas City, she worked during the 1921 Small Pox Epidemic (Fig. 1). The latter shows her as part of a team in a modern city hospital and the collegiality and friendship of nursing colleagues is evident. This self-portraiture is a conscious attempt at positive self-representation. She has playfully captioned this sequence and, despite the seriousness of the disease, the photographs show camaraderie and bravado in the face of an epidemic. The album pre-dates Anna's marriage and that of her sister Mary Amelia.[23] As only one of the three sisters had children, there is an obvious dearth of imagery showing conventional family units; in other words, a mother, father, and young children. Instead, the emphasis appears to be on female kinship and friendship, with nursing colleagues, cousins, aunts, and sisters displayed predominantly (Fig. 2). In this way, it mirrors the album compiled by the Chinese American teenager, Frank Jue, which is analyzed by Attewell. She notes that "while it depicts families and kin networks, it does not tell a story of nuclear family formation or chart the development of one family over a time."[24]

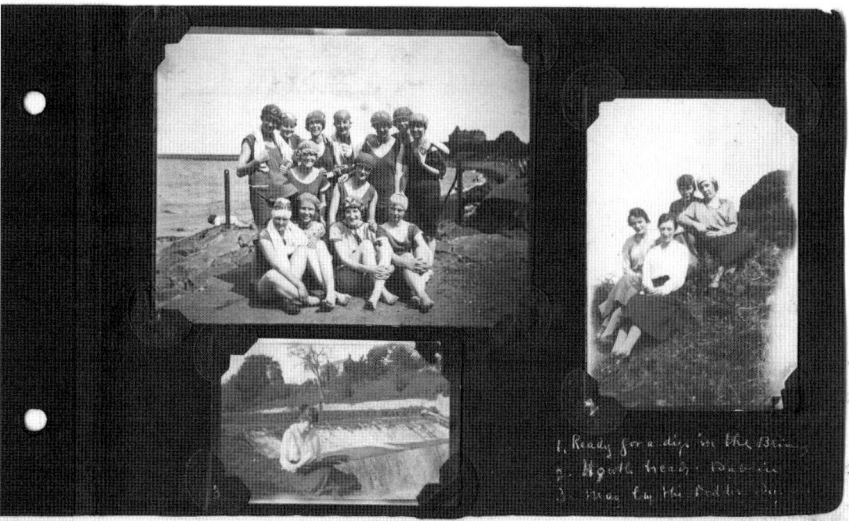

Figure 2: Whitfield sisters and friends, Dublin, ca. 1916. Page from Whitfield family album, snapshots on craft paper, ink captions. Source: Author's collection.

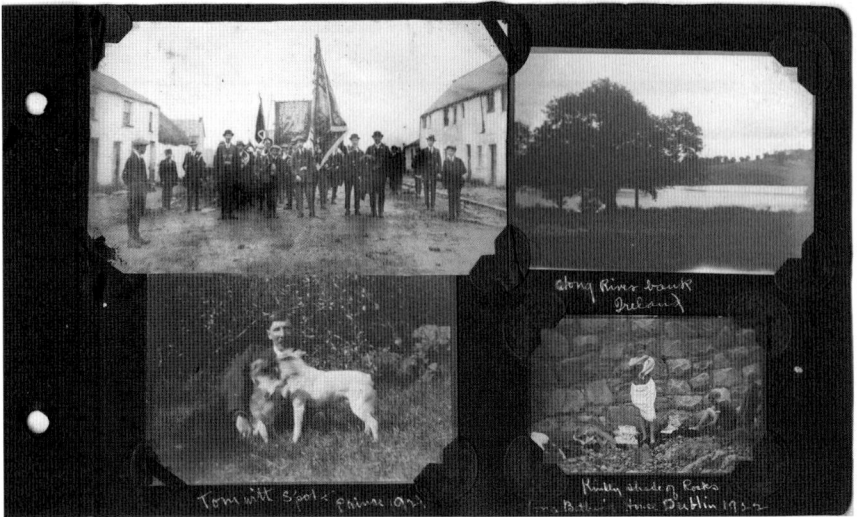

Figure 3: Royal Black Preceptory group, Cootehill and various family scenes in Dublin and Cavan, ca. 1922. Page from Whitfield family album, snapshots on craft paper, ink captions.
Source: Author's collection.

Whitfield's album represents the intersection of the political and the private. One page includes snapshots of young women in fashionable two-tone bathing suits on Killiney beach, Dublin, while another pictures the parading of an all-male Protestant fraternal society, the Royal Black Preceptory (Fig. 3). Anna's album includes set pieces typical of the snapshot album showing events such as picnics, sightseeing, field-day high jinks, gymnastic competitions, annual club outings. In many ways, it conforms to the attributes and tropes of this genre. Although purporting to depict the everyday, in reality the concentration is on special occasions, avoiding the routine and banal obligations of the everyday. In her examination of the albums created by Dorothy Stokes, a music teacher at the Royal Academy of Music in Dublin during the 1920s, Erika Hanna remarks upon the physicality and lack of reserve displayed in the seaside and bathing snapshots of Stokes and her circle of female friends. These photographs are similar to those in the Whitfield album, and both albums counter a rigid narrative that views Irish women's experience of life in the early Free State as dour and conservative. The physicality is evidenced in Anna's album, both in her photographs of Irish and American life. Anna and her circle of friends knew how to behave in front of the camera; they had likely internalized the advertisements created by Kodak and other firms. In many ways their demeanor and attitudes mirror those observed by Nadine Attewell in her discussion of Chinese diasporic practices of photography:

The photographs of Jue and his male intimates are suffused with ease, revealing their comfort not just with one another but with the camera, whose presence seems integral to the way in which they negotiate their being together.[25]

Images from picnics on Howth Head, County Dublin in 1916 show that several of Whitfield's companions also owned small box cameras, and advertisements in the local and national press show that photographic kits were available at many locations in Dublin.[26]

Anna's Cavan home

The playfulness of the snapshot medium is also evident in several of the staged images. Figure 4 shows the sisters Anna and Mary engaged in the same activity, captioned "Mary Amelia Whitfield, picking curly greens for dinner, Oct 1919" and "Anna E. in Cootehill, Ireland," these two images show the young women reenacting an agricultural and domestic chore, both laughing and dressed in similar attire. It conveys a sense of fun and their connection to their birthplace. Indeed, many of the captions include a particularity and geographic specificity relating to the Cavan farmstead, which the images alone do not reveal: "Happy party in the old farm cart, 1920," "Old Bob in the far rock, 1919," "Family group in Lower

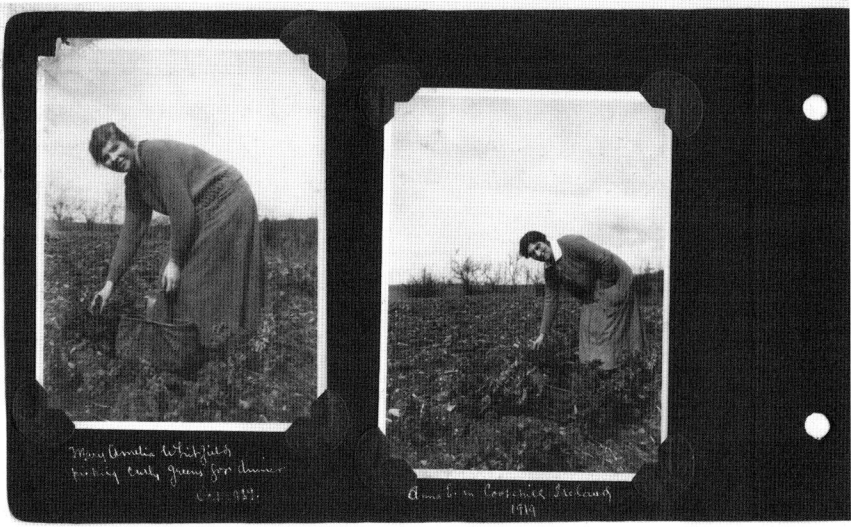

Figure 4: Anna and Mary Whitfield, Cavan, 1919. Page from Whitfield family album, snapshots on craft paper, ink captions. Source: Author's collection.

Garden," "Here we are in the flower garden," "May & Anna by the Laurel hedge at home, Cootehill, Ireland." In-jokes refer to family rituals and routines and this can make the narrative within such domestic albums difficult to decipher and decode for an outsider. Anna's detailed captioning offsets the loss of oral commentary that usually accompanies the viewing of such albums within the domestic setting, although not everyone is named within the album. This is not unusual, as photo albums were generally examined and shared among a closed circle of family and friends: people who were often personally acquainted with the sitters. A high level of familiarity is usually required when decoding family albums. As Chambers states, "the family album is therefore located in oral interaction."[27] We can infer from other sources such as newspaper accounts, obituaries, and census documents what the narrative within the album is trying to say. Some pages are themed around Irish branches of the family; some are based on gender; others mix location and format but reveal no discernible theme or link, the logic behind their collation having been lost to the outsider over the decades. As Barbara Levine notes, "it is the maker of the album – the one who has presented it and woven moments together – that created an illustrated story."[28] This album was purchased from a secondhand shop in Dublin in 2015, which is in itself evidence of the loosening of familial ties.

The images of farming in Cavan reveal the lack of mechanization and, in many ways, Anna's emigration was no different from that of other rural Irish women seeking to escape the drudgery of life without electricity and modern conveniences. Nonetheless, images showing both Jane and Anna's Missouri homestead (and that of their brother Henry, who settled in Canada) do not hide the hard work associated with their lives. The album places an emphasis on hard work and thrift, as demonstrated through photographs of agricultural activities, and this is very much highlighted in the captioning. There is definite pride in their old and new homesteads and possessions with images showing interiors and farming equipment.

Memory and loss

Memory and loss are represented through images of the Whitfield parents. Their mother died in 1916; their father in 1924. As the mother's passing pre-dated the bulk of the snapshots in the album, Anna chose to represent her through the only studio portrait in the album, which is one of the earliest images. Captioned "Mother and Myself, 1904," its inclusion is an attempt to unify the original family unit within the album. Likewise, a photograph of the patriarch is fondly captioned "Dear Father, 1920."

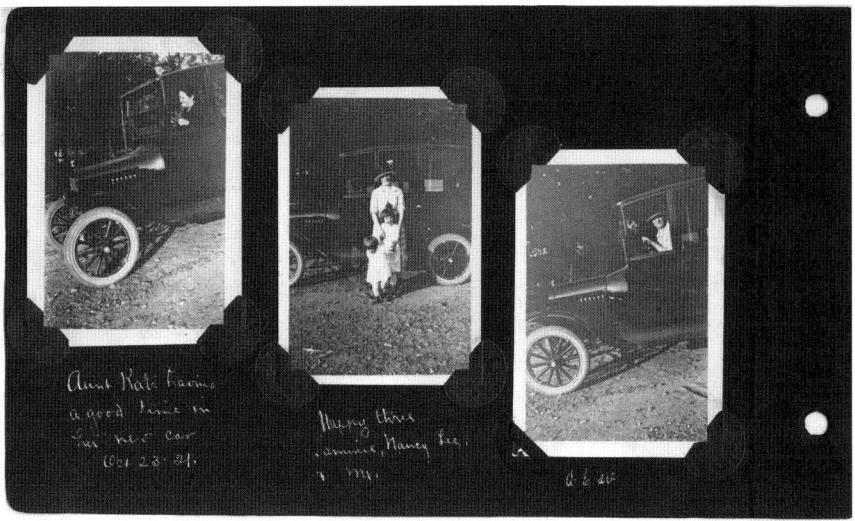

Figure 5: Aunt Kate and her new car, 1922 (Plate 3, p. 330). Page from Whitfield family album, snapshots on craft paper, ink captions. Source: Author's collection.

Female financial independence is alluded to in the figure of Aunt Kate (Fig. 5). An image showing a farmstead is captioned to indicate her ownership of property: "Aunt Kate's House, 1920." Another image shows levity and humor while also revealing her independence of spirit: "Aunt Kate having a good time in her new car, Oct. 23. 1921." The repetition and changing scale of these three images conveys movement and has a cinematic effect. This impact of cinema upon vernacular photographic practices is noted by Dahlgren, who references the term "book-film," a term in common usage in Sweden, when discussing photo albums.[29] Anna is confident and modern in her engagement with the photographic medium, using humor and visual tricks to create a personal narrative, dictating how the images within the album were to be viewed.

The aforementioned Aunt Kate was part of an earlier wave of Irish emigrants in the late nineteenth century. The causal factors for the decline of the Protestant population in the newly independent state can also be seen as part of this continuum. Indeed the Whitfields were part of a process of chain migration. Several of Anna's aunts and uncles had emigrated to Canada and the United States of America in the 1880s as the following death notice reveals:

Mr. Nesbitt, who had been in failing health for some time, attended work around the house this morning. He was born in Cootehill, Cavan county, Ireland. He and his wife and son, Fred Nesbitt, a member of the city council from the Third Ward; came to America about forty years ago, settling in New

York State, from where they moved here about five years later. Mr. Nesbitt was a member of the First Presbyterian church and of the Modern Woodmen lodge.[30]

A group portrait of the previous generation of female migrants opens the album and acts as a placemaker. Scholars have noted the importance of letters in maintaining bonds, sending remittances home, and encouraging further emigration.[31] This correspondence often enclosed photographs (such as the one pictured in Anna's album), which were exchanged between emigrants and their families in an attempt to bridge the distance. This exchange of photographs is acknowledged by historians of Irish America, with particular reference to those images sent by emigrants to the home country:

> In addition, Irish-Americans not only sent home enormous sums of money but also deluged relatives with presents such as clothes and with consumer-oriented materials: newspapers, glossy magazines, mail-order catalogues, and even photographs of themselves proudly attired in stylish new garments.[32]

Indeed, such was the influence of these photographs that the reformer, editor, poet, and nationalist George Russell felt impelled to write about the phenomenon in a 1910 issue of his journal *The Irish Homestead*. In an editorial "Photographs and Emigration," he cites the photographs sent by emigrant girls to their sisters as a major impetus in encouraging further emigration. Somewhat facetiously, he maintains that the glamorous fashions featured in these studio portraits came to symbolize the possibilities that America offered.[33] Of course, Russell is writing of a slightly earlier generation and refers to the more typical female emigrant coming from a subsistence farming background on the periphery of the country. Anna appears to have had a modicum of agency in her life: switching careers and attaining financial independence and a social life in Dublin prior to her move to the United States. Nonetheless, it is highly likely that the previous generation of Whitfield emigrants, including Anna's aunts, sent photographs back to Cavan illustrating their new lives in America, and that these in turn influenced and impacted Anna's decision to move to Kansas.

Generally, Irish emigrants settled in large urban centers, and the Whitfields' patterns of belonging and integration took a different form to that of most Irish. A perusal of the 1920 census returns for the state of Missouri reveals that the Irish-born population of the state numbered at 15,022 and constituted 9.1 percent of the total population.[34] The statistics for the more popular and typical destination of New York show that, while the percentage of the overall state was not dissimilar to that of Missouri, the numbers by far exceeded it. The 1920 census shows that

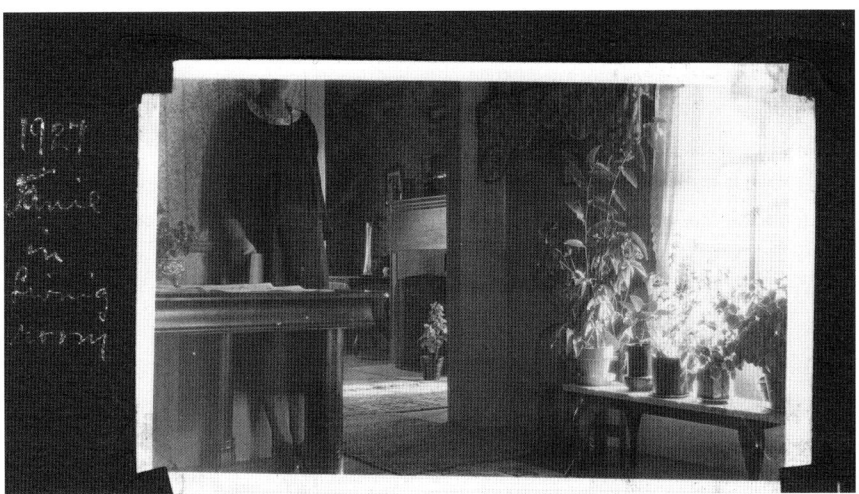

Figure 6: Interior of Whitfield/Bradbury farmhouse, Jasper, Missouri, 1927 (Plate 4, p. 331). Page from Whitfield family album, snapshots on craft paper, ink captions. Source: Author's collection.

284,747 Irish-born people lived in the state of New York. Their participation in Irish Republican political groups and in organizations such as the Ancient Order of Hibernians and the Gaelic League expediated their assimilation into their new country, as did their patronage of the Irish bars and clubs. The parishes of Catholic churches formed the hub of the Irish districts in large cities such as New York, Boston, Philadelphia, and Chicago and were, for many, integral to adaptation to life in the United States. In contrast, Anna, her sister, and her aunts appear to have replicated their rural Cavan lifestyle with attendance at bible school while fraternal societies based on the Protestant religion provided a similar role for her brother in Canada and her uncles in the United States. Local newspapers' society columns reveal that they were part of a lively social scene that centered around voluntary and religious groups. Gatherings took place in homes or halls with many suppers and prayer meetings. Anna's husband was a state representative and this important role, no doubt, generated a ready-made cohort of connections. His obituary and the tone of the local newspaper articles place an emphasis upon thrift, sobriety, and godliness. This emphasis on the homestead generated some of the more evocative and telling images in the Whitfield album such as one which shows the interior of the Bradbury farmhouse and the consideration and pride in their domesticity (Fig. 6). Taken when the couple and sister-in-law were middle-aged, these images, bathed in diffused light, show them at leisure amid houseplants, chintz, a stove, and modern conveniences such as a phone and a radiogram. Despite the emphasis within the album upon the farm and farmyard, theirs was not an experience of rural isolation and austerity as the following notice describing a gathering at the Bradbury/Whitfield home reveals:

Society News – Miss Janie Whitfield, who makes her home with her sister, Mrs. W.H. Bradbury, northeast of Carthage, was pleasantly surprised Thursday night by about 40 friends who assembled at the Bradbury home to bid her farewell. Miss Whitfield will leave Sunday morning for New York where she will sail June 18 for Dublin, Ireland, for an extended visit. Miss Whitfield was born in Dublin. She came here 13 years ago. She will be accompanied to New York by her sister, Mrs Bradbury, who will visit relatives there. C.L. Plummer acting as an expressman, came to the door during the evening with a number of packages for the "lady going to Ireland." These proved to be gifts suitable for one going on a long journey. Among them was a beautiful travelling bag presented by the Madison Sunday School of which Miss Whitfield is a member. Refreshments of ice cream and cake were served.[35]

Within this album is a broader meaning of family, as the album's narrative extends beyond the nuclear family to include the wider community. It is perhaps closer to what Anderson considers an "imagined community," which, in this instance, includes not just those living in Ireland but also the wider community. Membership of organizations was especially important for immigrants as they provided ready-made social circles and facilitated adaptation to the new country:

Fragmented by generation, class, and culture, torn between the New World's opportunities and the Old World's real or imagined securities, Irish-America in the late nineteenth and early twentieth centuries expressed its needs for community and identity in diverse but inter-related patterns of social interaction and institutional affiliation which linked past and present, communal ideas and divergent realities, in tenuous yet creative resolution.[36]

However, as Miller notes in the following lengthy quotation, it would be incorrect to surmise that homesickness and a sense of exile were the overriding emotions felt by the emigrant. Indeed it would appear that certain occasions, for example Christmas, birthdays, and national holidays, ignited these feelings. At various points in an emigrant's life, this identification with Irishness was also accentuated:

Although a significant proportion of Post-Famine emigrants thus embraced American opportunities and either consciously rejected or gradually abandoned Irish habits, outlooks, and loyalties, the surviving evidence indicates that a very large number still regarded themselves as homesick, involuntary exiles. For most individuals that self-perception was not consistent, but neither was it invariably situational – sometimes reflecting, but often conflicting with, objective circumstances – and it stemmed from complex interactions between transplanted Irish outlooks and American experiences. For many late-nineteenth and early twentieth-century emigrants, the exile imagery was merely rhetorical or ceremonial, a label of communal identification but not personally internalized. For others, probably the majority, it was a personalized but transitory image, deeply felt at certain stages of the emigrants' life cycle or on particularly emotive occasions, but otherwise suppressed or irrelevant.[37]

The above quotation could be seen as applicable to Anna and her sister. Despite their unionist sensibilities, Anna retained an identification as Irish, as evidenced in her annual St. Patrick's Day suppers:

St. Patrick's party. Irish games and stunts were played, green prizes being given the winners. Favors were given each one present. Mrs. Walter Bradbury, gave an interesting talk on "Farm Life in Ireland as She Knew It." Refreshments were of sandwiches, salads, cake and coffee.[38]

Indeed many of the joyful images in the album counter the narrative of emigration as an experience of painful exile. The concept of enforced exile is hotly contested by historians of Irish migration, both in relation to notions that Catholic emigrants left due to persecution by the Protestant landlord class in the nineteenth century and that the post-partition decline of the Protestant community in the newly independent Ireland was due to a form of ethnic cleansing, an opinion put forward by Hart.[39] Indeed both views deny the existence of emigration motivated by mundane economic reasons rooted in the dynamics of their own society, and as in the case of the Whitfields, the impartible inheritance system, which meant that the land went directly to the eldest son, the only member of the family to stay in the county. As Harris remarks, it was not usually the most impoverished who emigrated but rather those "who saw their opportunities declining and sought to re-create in the New World what was slipping from them in Ireland."[40] The loss of the shared Ulster community cannot be underestimated and indeed it is highly likely that the album played a role in the remembrance and sustained memory of a homeplace that she did not visit for many decades. As the following local notice shows, Anna returned to Ireland for the last time in 1953, the year following the deaths of her husband and sister Janie:

Mrs W.H. Bradbury of northeast Carthage, will leave 24 March for New York and from there will go to Ireland for an extended visit with relatives. She is making the entire trip by plane. Mrs Bradbury will visit a sister, Mrs Fred

Walker, in Dublin. She has not seen the sister in 33 years. She will also visit a brother, Thomas Whitfield, in County Cavan, Ireland and cousins in New Brighton, England.[41]

Canada, the commonwealth, and Ulster migrant allegiances

In a page from the album two snapshot photographs depictict Anna's brother Henry in Ontario, Canada (Fig. 7). One was taken upon the occasion of her brother Tom's visit from Ireland and shows the two brothers, both attired in suits, standing in a quintessential suburban North American setting with telegraph poles in the background. It marks a special occasion—the rare transatlantic visit of a sibling—and represents continuity and familial cohesion. A second snapshot, captioned "Henry and Cowdrey," shows Anna's brother and his young son, who is around seven or eight years of age, and the family pet. The child is well dressed, wearing knickerbocker shorts, a black top, and a white tie. The background reveals a sizable brick homestead with similar dwellings visible in the background. The young boy represents the future and the putting down of roots in Canada. He is part of a new generation that will identify as Canadian rather than Irish. British imperial destinations such as Canada accounted for a greater number of Protestant emigrants than the United States between 1911 and 1926. This difference from the

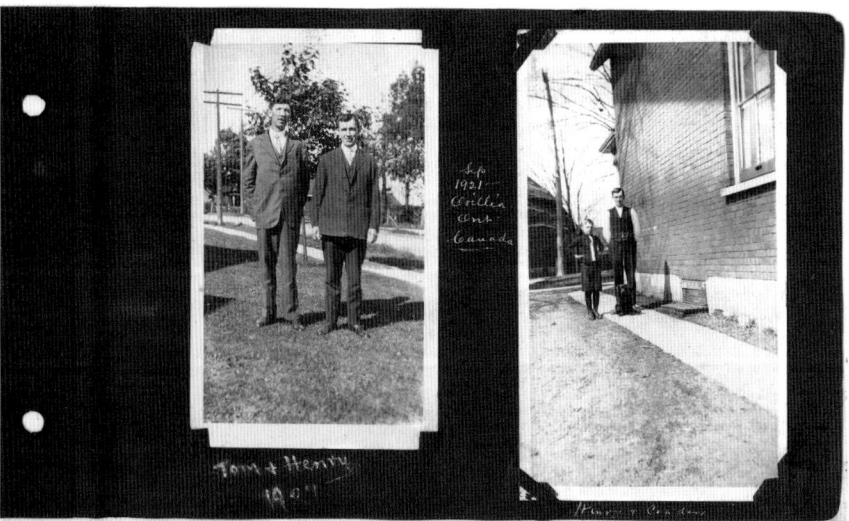

Figure 7: Whitfield family members, Canada, 1920s. Page from Whitfield family album, snapshots on craft paper, ink captions. Source: Author's collection.

long-established Irish preference for the United States is just one of a number of characteristics of minority emigration in this period that does not fit the prevailing pattern since the mid nineteenth century. The attraction of Canada for men such a Henry was not unprecedented, as "over the twentieth century, Canada was the popular destination for migrants from Northern Ireland," and its place within the commonwealth undoubtedly impacted the political allegiances of the Whitfield family.[42] How they felt about the new Irish state is hinted at by the inclusion of photographs of the annual twelfth of July parades in Cootehill. Another page from the album includes a photograph of members of the Black Preceptory lodge (R.B.P) in Cootehill, County Cavan in 1920 (Fig. 8). Also known as the Royal Black Institute, it is a Protestant fraternal society (non-Protestants cannot become members unless they agree to adhere to the principles of Orangeism and convert). To join the R.B.P., one must already be a member of an Orange Order Lodge. The photograph in the top right-hand corner of the page shows the group gathering on the outskirts of the town, complete with banners and flags. Some wear sashes adorned with what appear to be military medals. Orangemen are members of the Loyal Orange Institution, a sectarian fraternal organization founded in Armagh in 1795, whose members are sworn to maintain Protestant dominance. The term was synonymous, for some, with a certain type of bigotry and intolerance. While the organization was not as active in the United States as it was in Northern Ireland, Scotland, nor indeed Canada, it did maintain several lodges in these countries. In

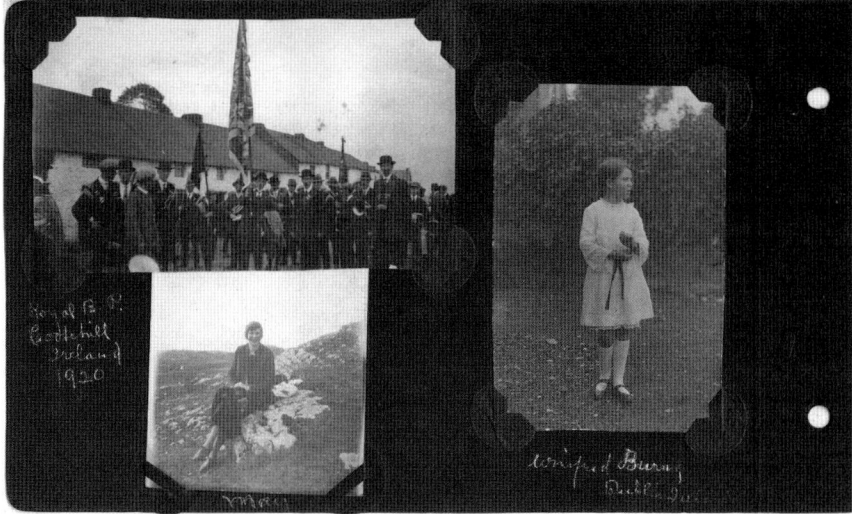

Figure 8: Scenes from Ireland, including Royal Black Preceptory March, n.d. (Plate 5, p. 331). Page from Whitfield family album, snapshots on craft paper, ink captions. Source: Author's collection.

this instance, the term might well have been used to refer to an individual adhering to anti-Catholic sentiments who may or may not have been member of the lodge or some other masonic society

A further indicator of their inclinations is given in the fact that both Janie and her brother Edward signed the Ulster Covenant in 1912. This document was made in protest against the Third Home Rule Bill introduced by the British government in the same year. Totaling nearly half a million signatures, 237,368 men signed the Covenant and 234,046 women signed the corresponding women's Declaration.

The wording for the women's declaration leaves one in no doubt as to where the Whitfield allegiances lay and, as such, it is highly probably that living in the new Irish state and being governed by Dublin would have been unpalatable for Anna's sisters and brothers. I include the text of the Ulster Covenant here to give some inkling as to the social and political backdrop to the Whitfield album:

> We, whose names are underwritten, women of Ulster, and loyal subjects of our gracious King, being firmly persuaded that Home Rule would be disastrous to our Country, desire to associate ourselves with the men of Ulster in their uncompromising opposition to the Home Rule Bill now before Parliament, whereby it is proposed to drive Ulster out of her cherished place in the Constitution of the United Kingdom, and to place her under the domination and control of a Parliament in Ireland. Praying that from this calamity God will save Ireland, we hereto subscribe our names.

Conclusion

Through an examination of the album format within an Irish American context, this essay has attempted to rectify the dearth of scholarly writing on Irish photography and migration and fill a gap in our understanding of the Irish diaspora. While also addressing wider notions of identity and placing the images within their cultural and political context, it is in keeping with the approach to familial photography outlined by Levitt, which:

> does not allow readers to take comfort in any simple reading of the family anywhere as a respite from history or politics. There is no such thing as 'the family' in postwar America, nor is home easily found in the promises of European cultural inclusion or class mobility. These ambivalent legacies demand that we see 'the familial gaze' as self-contradictory. Like identity, it too is inflected by nationality, ethnicity, race and history. Despite and because of this, this collection asks us not to give up on community.[43]

Anna's album reveals a complex self-fashioning that reflects a process of adaptation from life in Ireland to that in America. It acts as a contact zone accommodating the cultural differences she encountered in her various migrations: starting in a small rural homestead in Ireland before moving to the country's capital and then documenting her transatlantic years in Kansas City and rural Missouri, where she was to spend the majority of her life. These images sustained Anna and her sister through many decades away from their native land, and its nuanced depiction of Anna's life reveals her editorial and curatorial vision. Its narrative is fluid and like the process of assimilation has the capacity to celebrate and represent both the Irish and American aspects of her biography. This migration story concludes with the discovery of a photograph showing the headstone of Anna's sister Jane in Jasper, Missouri. This image appears on the popular website "Find a Grave," and it reveals that this woman who had signed the Ulster Covenant, and lived for forty years in the United States, chose to highlight not her position as a subject of the British Empire nor that as an American citizen but rather the fact that she was born in Cootehill, Ireland.

Notes

1. Travel and census records show that Anna left Ireland for the first time in 1916, returning home for a period in 1920 before finally settling in the United States.
2. Kerby A. Miller, *Emigrants and Exiles: Ireland and the Irish Exodus to North America*, (Oxford: Oxford University Press, 1985), 346.
3. Kerby A. Miller, *Emigrants and Exiles: Ireland and the Irish Exodus to North America*, (Oxford: Oxford University Press, 1985), 581.
4. Hasia R. Diner, *Erin's Daughters in America: Irish Immigrant Women in the Nineteenth Century*, (Baltimore: Johns Hopkins University Press, 1983), xiii.
5. Ruth Ann M. Harris, "Come you all courageously: Irish women in America write home," *Éire-Ireland*, 36, 1 & 2 (Spring/Summer 2001), 166–184; Margaret Lynch-Brennan, *The Irish Bridget: Irish Immigrant Women in domestic service in America, 1840–1930* (Syracuse: Syracuse University Press, 2009); Emma Moreton, "Never could forget my darling mother: the language of recollection in a corpus of female emigrant correspondence," *The History of the Family*, 21, 3 (2016), 315–336.
6. Harris, "Come you all courageously," 166.
7. Sigird Lien, *Pictures of Longing: Photography and the Norwegian-American Migration* (Minneapolis: University of Minnesota Press, 2018), 20.
8. See the following for a consideration of the photographic albums compiled by Dublin native Dorothy Stokes in the 1920s: Erika Hanna, "Reading Irish Women's Lives in Photograph Albums," *Cultural and Social History: The Journal of the Social History Society*,

11:1 (2014), 89–109. Justin Carville has examined photographic albums created by Irish soldiers during the First World War. See Justin Carville, "The Postcard Album will tell my name, when I am quite forgotten: Cultural Memory and the First World War Soldier Photograph Albums," *Modernist Cultures*, 13.3 (2018), 417–444.

9. The other Whitfield siblings were Thomas (1886–1959); John Henry (1887–1962); Jane (1895–1952); and Mary Amelia (1898–1976).

10. The listing for John Douglas and Sons, 18 Wexford Street, Draper's, on the 1911 census, shows Anna Whitfield, then twenty-six years of age, as a Draper's Assistant, who lived over the shop with nineteen other apprentices or assistants, nearly all of whom give their religious denomination as "Society of Friends."

11. Deborah Chambers, "Family as Place: Family Photograph Albums and the Domestication of Public and Private Space," in Joan Schwartz Joan and James R. Ryan (eds.), *Picturing Place: Photography and the Geographical Imagination* (London: I.B. Taurus, 2003), 105.

12. According to a blog post on the Quaker Meeting House on Strand Street, Dublin, Edith M. Wigham ran a "drilling association for women, which included activities like gymnastic classes." See Wide and Convenient Streets, "Friends on Strand St." https://wideandconvenientstreets.wordpress.com/tag/edith-m-wigham/

13. See Richard Chalfen, *Snapshot Versions of Life* (Bowling Green, Ohio: State University Popular Press, 1987); Julia Hirsch, *Family Photographs Content, Meaning and Effect* (Oxford: Oxford University Press, 1981); Catherine Zuromskis, *Snapshot Photography: the Lives of Images* (Cambridge: MIT Press, 2013); and Mattie Boom, *Everyone a Photographer: The Rise of Amateur Photography in the Netherlands, 1880–1940* (Amsterdam: Rijksmuseum, 2019).

14. Stephanie Snyder, "The Vernacular Photo Album: its origins and genius," in Barbara Levine and Kirsten M. Jensen, *Around the World: The Grand Tour in Photo Albums* (New York: Princeton Architectural Press, 2007), 25.

15. See Robin Bury, *Buried Lives: The Protestants of Southern Ireland* (Dublin: History Press, 2016) and Ian d'Alton and Ilda Milne (eds.), *Protestant and Irish: The minority's search for place in Independent Ireland* (Cork: Cork University Press, 2019).

16. For a detailed study of the impact of partition upon the region, see: John Anthony Donohue, *The Impact of the Partition Crisis on Cavan-Monaghan, 1914–1916*, unpublished MA thesis presented to NUI Maynooth, 1999.

17. Andy Bielenberg, "Exodus: The Emigration of Southern Irish Protestants during the Irish War of Independence and the Civil War," in *Past and Present*, 218, 1 (2013), 201.

18. "The Ulster-Irish border, Protestant Imaginative Geography and Cultural Memory in the Irish Troubles," in Maurizio Ascari and Adriana Corrado (eds.), *Sites of Exchange: European Crossroads and Faultlines* (Amsterdam: Rodopi, 2006), 237–251.

19. Tina M. Campt, *Image Matters: Archive, Photography, and the African Diaspora in Europe* (Duke University Press, 2012), 17.

20. Sigrid Lien, *Pictures of Longing: Photography and the Norwegian-American Migration,* (Minneapolis: University of Minnesota Press, 2018), 165–169.

21. Geoffrey Batchen, *Each wild idea: Writing Photography History* (Cambridge: The MIT Press, 2002) and Elizabeth Edwards and Janice Hart, "Introduction: Photographs as Objects," in Elizabeth Edwards and Janice Hart (eds.), *Photographs objects histories: on the materiality of images* (London: Routledge, 2004), 2.

22. Geoffrey Batchen, "Snapshots: Art history and the ethnographic turn," *Photographies,* 1. 2. (2008), 135.

23. Anna's youngest sister, Mary Amelia, married Frederick Samuel Walker in August 1924 in Dublin. They remained residents of that city and it is perhaps through this branch of the family that the album came to return to Ireland.

24. Nadine Attewell, "Intimacy out of doors: landscape, labor and Chinese diasporic practices of looking," in Tanya Sheehan (ed.), *Photography and Migration* (London: Routledge, 2018), 199–216 (205).

25. Attewell, "Intimacy," 205.

26. See Orla Fitzpatrick, "Photography, Dublin and 1916," *Reflecting 1916* (Dublin: Gallery of Photography, 2016).

27. Chambers, "Family as Place," 97.

28. Barbara Levine, "Collecting Photo Albums – Musings on," in Stephanie Snyder and Barbara Levine (eds.), *Snapshot Chronicles: Inventing the American Photo Album* (New York: Princeton Architectural Press, 2006), 19.

29. Anna Dahlgreen, "The ABC of the Modern Photo Album," in Jonathon Carson, Rosie Miller, and Theresa Wilkie (eds.), *The Photograph and the Album: Histories, Practices, Futures* (Edinburgh: MuseumsEtc., 2013), 76–108.

30. "Nesbitt Funeral," *Joplin Globe*, November 30, 1929, 5.

31. See Arnold Schrier, *Ireland and the American Emigration 1850–1900* (Chester Springs: Dufour Editions, 1997).

32. Miller, *Emigrants and Exiles*, 425.

33. Henry Summerfield (ed.), *Selections from the Contributions to The Irish Homestead by G.W. Russell – A.E. Volume I* (Atlantic Highlands: Humanities Press, 1978), 214. On the relationship between photographs and remittances see; Carville's essay " A Letter From Pat in America" in this volume.

34. *Fourteenth Census of the United States taken in the year 1920, Volume III, Population 1920,* (Washington, DC: Government Printing Office, 1922), 549.

35. "Society Notes," *Joplin Sunday Globe,* June 13, 1937, 3.

36. Miller, *Emigrants and Exiles*, 520.

37. Miller, *Emigrants and Exiles*, 512.

38. "Additional Farm News," *Joplin Globe*, Sunday, March 25, 1934, 18.

39. Peter Hart, "The Protestant Experience of Revolution in southern Ireland," in Richard English and Graham Walker (eds.), *Unionism in Modern Ireland: New Perspectives on Politics and Culture* (London: Macmillan, 1996), 81–98.

40. Ruth Ann M. Harris, "Come you all courageously: Irish women in America write home," *Éire-Ireland*, 36, 1 & 2 (Spring/Summer 2001), 183.

41. "To Visit Ireland," *Joplin News Herald*, March 6, 1953, 7.

42. Johanne Devlin-Trew, *Leaving the North: Migration and Memory, Northern Ireland 1921–2001* (Liverpool: Liverpool University Press, 2013), 159.

43. Laura Levitt, "Blurring the Familial: An Afterword," in Marianne Hirsch (ed.), *The Familial Gaze* (Hanover: University Press of New England, 1999), 345.

A Letter from Pat in America

Photo-remittances and the Irish American Diaspora

Justin Carville

As an Irish immigrant growing up in Chicago in the mid 1970s, a regular feature of family life was having to pose for photographs on weekends. During family outings on Saturdays and on public holidays, my brother and I would be instructed to pose alongside one of our parents as the other took photographs with the latest family camera. These photographs were often taken beside the new family car, outside the first family home when we moved from an apartment in the city to the suburbs, or on the steps of the local Catholic church on the rare occasions we were brought to Sunday Mass. Frequently, we were posed wearing clothes sent from family members back in Ireland or in outfits that reflected the latest fashion trends in America.

Although the taking of these photographs remains a distinct memory, the actual photographs are not. The photographs were only fleetingly seen by anyone other than my parents in our immediate family, and rarely found their way into family albums. Only when we traveled back to Ireland for summer holidays or after we had returned home permanently in the mid 1980s did we get to see the photographs that had preoccupied much of familial social life in the United States.

The responses to photographs received by relatives varied from appreciation of the vibrant colors produced by the Kodacolor II, and later the Kodacolor VR film taken with my father's Asahi Pentax camera, to the importance of the photographs in maintaining familial relations across the Atlantic. Often, relatives made observations on how our posing in the photographs seemed to express the family's newly acquired American cultural values that marked our difference upon remigration back to Ireland. They would point to photographs displayed on sideboards or hanging on living-room walls, and comment on how much we had changed in physical appearance, disposition, and attitude. They spoke to these photographs as if they somehow evidenced our bicultural transformation as a result of being Irish immigrants in America, and returned "Yanks" upon our remigration back home.[1]

The narratives of technology, "lowbrow" vernacular aesthetics of popular photography, consumerism, and familial anxieties of separation and belonging

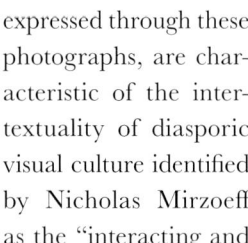

Figure 1a:Lawrence Lindsay
Statter Carr and Katherine
Statter Carr, Harris Photo,
Daytona, Florida, 1903.
Edward Chandler Collection/
Author's collection.

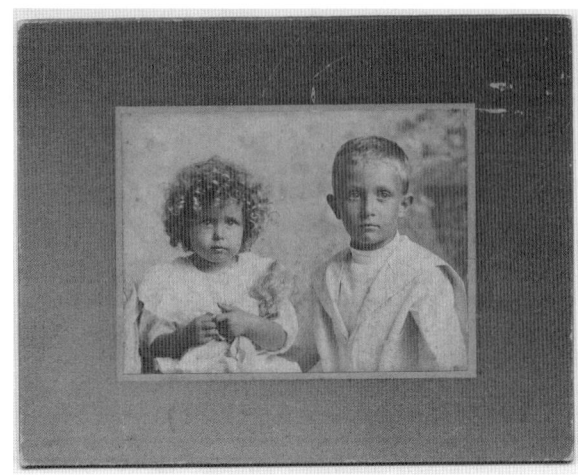

expressed through these photographs, are characteristic of the intertextuality of diasporic visual culture identified by Nicholas Mirzoeff as the "interacting and interdependent modes of visuality."[2] In what he terms "intervisuality," Mirzoeff argues that intertextual narratives of history and memory are intertwined with various modes of visual culture to generate diverse diaspora imaginaries. Processes of intervisuality filter the multiple viewpoints and polyvocal associations generated by an image, which may be at variance to the original intention of the photograph.[3] In diaspora visual cultures, photographs are not only intertextual through the enunciations and narratives that make sense of the image, they also have the capacity to engender multiple imaginary and epistemological associations through the content and material form of the image-object. The visual content of the photograph is responsible for much of the work photography does in facilitating the production of multiple perspectives of diasporic epistemologies, imaginaries, and histories. However, photographs as image-objects also generate multiple associations of knowledge and affect through their circulation. As Elizabeth Edwards demonstrates, the circulation of photographs through networks of exchange has long been a feature of the social and natural sciences, and like the more formal scientific exchange of photographs, the availability of cheap studio portraits and, later, family snapshots facilitated the movement of photographic images between diasporic communities in the United States and relatives back home.[4] The epistemologies of the photograph, and their emotional affects, do not reside objectively in the codes and codifications of the photograph, but rather, to borrow a phrase from Sara Ahmed, "are produced only as an effect of its circulation."[5]

In this essay, I discuss the circulation of vernacular photographs as image-objects between Irish immigrants and their families back in Ireland as culturally salient forms of intervisuality, which contribute to the self-fashioning of diasporic identities. However, rather than treating vernacular photographs as cultural representations that are mono-directional, I am interested in how they transmit shared,

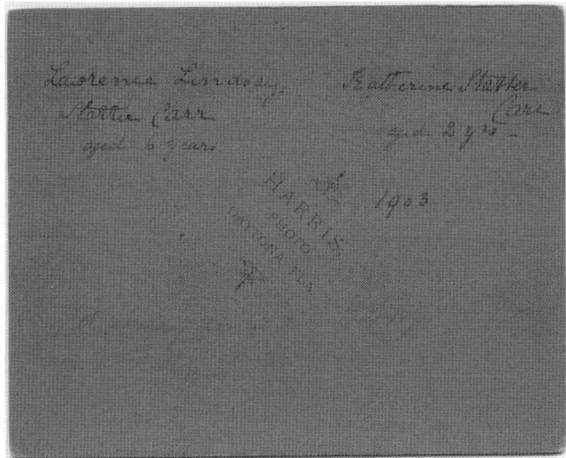

Figure 1b: Verso of Lawrence Lindsay Statter Carr and Katherine Statter Carr, Harris Photo, Daytona, Florida, 1903.
Edward Chandler Collection/Author's collection.

discrepant, and novel forms of cultural experience to families and communities at home or scattered across the United States. Taking as a point of departure photography and the narrative formation of Irish American diasporic identity, I explore the circulation of vernacular photographs among diasporic communities as forms of what anthropologists Peggy Levitt describes as "social remittances" and Juan Flores as the "cultural remittances" of counter-streaming.[6] Discussing ubiquitous, vernacular forms of commodity portraiture as what I term photo-remittances, I am interested in the affective resonances of the photo-remittance not only in disrupted familial relations, memories, and histories of the Irish American diaspora, but also in racial formations, and political and religious identities. Photo-remittances are complex contact zones that "invoke the spatial and temporal copresence of subjects previously separated by geographic and historical junctures" while also providing material visual forms that become intertwined with narrative memories of migration.[7] It is through the contact spaces of circulation of photo-remittances among diasporic communities that polyvocal histories and imaginaries of migration experiences are visually articulated (Fig. 1).

Framing photo-remittances

Scholarly work on photography and diaspora has largely focused on first or multi-generational experiences of exile and displacement of migrants as generating novel, transcultural aesthetic forms of creativity. Through what Appadurai identifies as the "complex, overlapping, disjunctive order" of cultural flows, new cultural practices and forms emerge within diasporic communities and artists.[8] These cultural practices facilitate communities fractured and dispersed through migration and exile to imaginatively rediscover shared histories, articulate emerging cultural identities, and meliorate collective experiences of geographic and cultural dislocation.[9] The spaces where cultural flows intersect in the production of new material conditions for emerging diasporic cultural practices have predominantly been identified as those of the host country, by and large the cosmopolitan centers of the United States, North America, Central and Western Europe. Mirroring perspectives of migration historiography, ethnography, and cultural production, analysis of photography and diaspora has largely been skewed toward the cultural practices, epistemologies, and resources that are carried by migrants to the host country. These practical, aesthetic, and conceptual resources are brought to bear on their negotiations and transformations of cultural identity, which are expressed through the knotty entanglements of transcultural visual cultures emanating from specific locales, those where migrant communities have established "positions of *enunciation*," to borrow Stuart Hall's phrase, from which to visually articulate diasporic cultural identities.[10]

The work of Leigh Raiford on photography and the Pan-African diaspora, and Tina Campt on the African diaspora in Europe, have done much to shift this geographically skewed perspective of photography and diaspora. In what she calls the "photographic practice of diaspora," Raiford identifies "photography's capacity to build or envision community across geographical locations, its capacity to engage its viewers on both critical and emotional registers," as compatible with the affective registers of diasporic imaginings of transnational belonging.[11] Campt, in her discussion of vernacular studio portraits of the British Afro-Caribbean diaspora, observes that:

> The seriality of these visual performances thus function as an ensemble of diasporic calls and responses between people elsewhere and "back home", and as improvisational versions that register complex and competing iterations of the poses, posturing, and enunciations of diasporic belonging.[12]

The condition of diaspora, of course, is one that is always calling into question conventional ideals of belonging. As Hall so eloquently puts it, diasporas "will never be *unified* in the old sense, because they are irrevocably the product of several interlocking histories and cultures, belonging at one and the same time to several 'homes' (and to no one particular home)."[13] Diaspora consciousness of belonging and of the return home are thus always imaginaries of cultural longing that are never fulfilled but can be enacted through photography: in the terms identified by Raiford, through the labor and shared cultural resources that mobilize photography as a practice to shape collective and individual imaginings; and by Campt, the repetitive conventions of vernacular portraits and subjective reflexivity of bodily deportment, which are reflected back to the homeland through the photograph.[14]

Vernacular photographs also enact imaginaries of belonging and of the return home through their circulation as material objects. Transported by migrants in their luggage, exchanged within and between diasporic communities, shared with extended families, and sent to the homeland as expressions of familial bonds, self-fashioning, and aspiration, circulating photographs have the potential to displace the positions from which diaspora imaginaries are spoken, and to where and to whom they speak. Vernacular photographs follow routes of migration; however, as much as they are carried along with the paltry possessions of immigrants, they also return home. They are material forms of what Flores describes as the "diasporic 'countersteam,'" the assemblage of knowledge, values, images, and imaginings that flow back against the waves of migration from the homeland.[15]

Vernacular photographs maintain contact between diasporas and communities of origin through their simultaneous temporal presence of a family member's likeness, but they are also forms of social and cultural remittance. As a distinction from financial remittances, Levitt describes social remittances as the "ideas, behaviours, identities and social capital that flow from receiving to sending-country communities."[16] Building on Levitt's concept, Flores extends what he identifies as the limited scope of her conception of culture to incorporate the collective, ideological, and creative dimensions of nonmonetary forms of remittance.[17] Vernacular photographs are modes of transmission and also express ideological, creative, and symbolic images and imaginings of ethnic and familial values, religious and political identities. I draw on elements of both Levitt and Flores to conceptualise what I call *photo-remittances.*

Vernacular photographs are highly specifiable, individualized, and direct filters of cultural diffusion; as forms of expressing personal-political agency, they speak directly between families and diaspora communities.[18] The continual circulation of vernacular photographs as material expressions of familial inheritance or as collective visual migration histories interweave shared customs, cultural practices, and novel forms of imagining into the fabric of diaspora communities through familial and communal conduits of formal information exchange. It is through these personal filters of cultural transmission that the photo-remittance may have a broader impact on the culture of communities in the homeland. Photo-remittances, as I conceive them in the context of the Irish American diaspora, have different modes of transmission and material forms, which emerge at specific historical junctures, not all of which will be discussed in this essay. However, in the form of vernacular studio portraits, photo-remittances have two main characteristics that contribute to their mobilization as social and cultural remittances: the photographic and extra-photographic.

The photographic characteristics are those of the material form of the photograph. Commercial studio portraits, in their various styles and repetitive poses, emphasize shared or sometimes discrepant cultural norms of self-fashioning. The hierarchy of fashionable commercial studios also project aspiration, wealth, and social status. Even the introduction of the studio portrait into familial and social relations through their remittance can initiate new cultural expressions of marking or celebrating customs, rituals, and rites of passage.

Extra-photographic characteristics are those oral and textual narratives, memories, and descriptions in the forms of letters that accompany the vernacular photograph, and are brought to bear on their interpretation by those who receive it. The extra-photographic has the capacity to shape, influence, accentuate, or diminish the photograph's impact as a form of social or cultural remittance. This characteristic also involves the codes and codifications of the subjects in their self-fashioning of their cultural identity through the photograph, and how these may be interpreted by the receiver: physical appearance, fashion, bodily deportment, and the projection of the self, for example, are all open to interpretation, which may determine the cultural impact of the photo-remittance. The photographic and extra-photographic characteristics of the photo-remittance become intertwined through their circulation, opening them up to the type of intervisuality identified by Mirzoeff. They become spaces of cultural contact through which multiple experiences, narratives, and affective responses are negotiated and find expression.

The photo-remittance was a salient feature of the formation of the Irish American diaspora in the nineteenth and first half of the twentieth century. As numerous historians of Irish migration in general, and to America in particular, have observed, the culture of remittances back to the homeland was a well-established characteristic of the Irish diaspora from the mid nineteenth century. Letters from emigrants were much anticipated within families and communities as evidence of social status and financial success.[19] As Kirby Miller observes, in addition to money, consumer goods including photographs displaying Irish American prosperity and self-fashioned modernity also accompanied letters home.[20] The commodity form of remittances not only evidenced the wealth of Irish Americans, they also materially reconfigured the social life of the receivers as families emulated or rejected the cultural norms of America refracted through social and cultural remittances such as photographs. Although little attention has been paid to social and cultural remittances in the histories of Irish migration, photo-remittances in the form of vernacular commercial studio portraits are an early example of the mediated counter-streaming of the Irish American diaspora. Photo-remittances were not only modes of information exchange between Irish immigrants in the United States and the homeplace, they also had affective value. They were "sticky objects" of affect, to borrow Ahmed's term, the anticipation of which could generate positive or negative responses.[21] Remittances, monetary and cultural, and their social and political affects, were wedded to cultural representations of the Irish American diaspora from the nineteenth century, reflecting what Miller has identified as the real and imaginary exile motif in a range of cultural representations of

Irish immigrants in America.[22] I want to turn to an example of this cultural formation to set out the ways in which photography, migration, and remittances became
intertwined in the cultural formation of the Irish American diaspora.

Photography and narratives of Irish American diaspora

The title of this essay, "A Letter from Pat in America," is borrowed from a popular stereoview card originally published by the Keystone View Company in the
late nineteenth century (Fig. 2). Keystone periodically published versions of "A
Letter from Pat in America" as part of its numerous themed series and boxed
sets of stereoviews, which depicted indigenous peoples and geographic locations
from around the world as late as the 1930s. For the best part of three decades,
from the turn of the nineteenth century, this particular stereoview, along with
Keystone's other depictions of Irish life, was circulated by the company in print
runs of tens of thousands of copies. During this period, "A Letter from Pat in
America" became a prominent if somewhat atypical representation of Ireland.
Throughout the last decade of the nineteenth century, and for three decades of
the twentieth, the dominant representations of Ireland published by Keystone
focused on tourist views and romanticized or jocular visions of peasant life and
folk industries. In the series "A Tour of the World," the multivolume set *A Trip
Around the World Through the Telebinocular*, and various editions of the *Visual
Education Teachers' Guide*, published between 1906 and 1933, Keystone stereoviews contributed to the geographical imagining of Ireland for the American

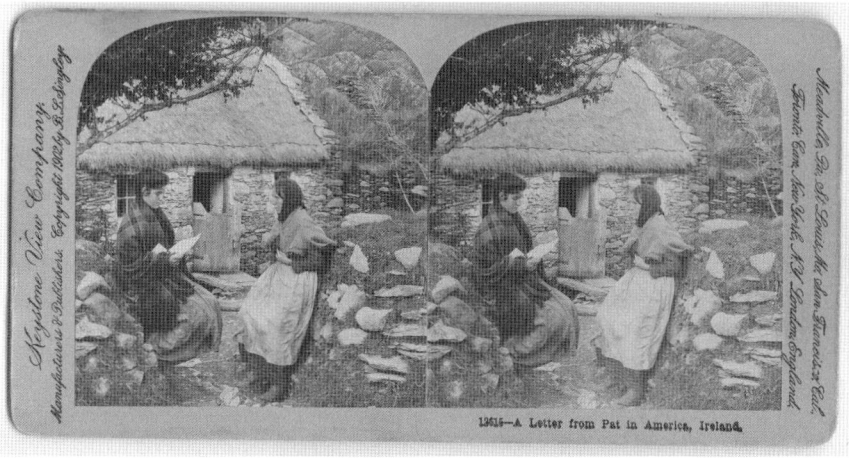

Figure 2: "A Letter from Pat in America," Keystone View Company, 1902. Author's collection.

public.[23] "A Letter from Pat in America" is distinctive within the company's image repertoire of Ireland for its explicit appeal to the transatlantic relations between Ireland and America through the narrative framing of the photograph.

The stereoview depicts a young peasant woman dressed in a woolen shawl, seated on a low stone-cut wall across from an older peasant woman who is presumably the woman's mother. Seated in front of the backdrop of a stone-built, thatched cottage and rocky hills, the young woman is pictured intently reading a letter from the visually absent figure of Pat. The visual sceneography of the thatched-roof stone cottage projecting an Arcadian vision of rural peasant life had long been a recurring visual trope of stereoviews of Ireland before "A Letter from Pat in America" was published in the late nineteenth century.[24] The photograph draws on this familiar codification of Irish peasant life as an idealized rural existence through its picturesque backdrop. However, the stereocard also supplements the visual imaginary with extratextual information. As with most Keystone stereoviews packaged into their various published series and visual teacher's guides for American schoolchildren, the photograph is accompanied by descriptive and imaginative textual material, which mobilizes the card as an educational or instructional visual mode of forging geographical imaginings of the subject for the viewer. On the verso of the stereoview a textual narrative not only informs the reader of historical details of Irish migration, but invites the viewer to imagine the diasporic consciousness of the Irish through the transatlantic relations between the young woman reading the letter and its absent author, Pat. The significance of this short text to the shaping the stereocard's configuration of Irish migration is such that it is worth quoting in its entirety:

There are as many Irish out of Ireland as in it. Two-thirds of the Irish emigrants come to the United States; the others go chiefly to Canada and Australia. The strong ties of family affection, so characteristic of the Celt, strengthened in Ireland by centuries of poverty and oppression, and intensified at last by famine. The Millions now beyond the seas are tenderly and practically reminded of their impoverished kinsfolk at the old home. The homeward letters do not go empty; a million dollars a year go with them, from the brothers and sons and daughters and husbands and lovers, who have found prosperity in far off Australia or America, the land of the free. In this letter we may fancy, Pat is telling Nora that he has the cottage nearly finished and that he will send a ticket to come to him before Christmas. Then Nora will bid her friends and dear old Ireland good-bye, as we now do.[25]

In alternative versions of "A Letter from Pat in America," reproduced in the "Tour of the World" series, the verso text emphasizes even further the affective bonds between migrant and homeland by proclaiming, "Wherever they [the Irish] go the heartstrings hold to the kindred at home." Similarly invoking the centrality of American prosperity to the narrative of Irish migration by identifying Boston as a destination for the country's emigrants, one alternative version states:

> The Letter from Pat is seldom empty. The home going letter is rich not only in sincere affection but also in that practical love which does not end with words. It is historic fact that tens of millions of dollars have been thus remitted by Irish emigrants to their parents, wives, sisters and sweet-hearts in the lovely mournful isle.[26]

There is much to unpack in the short pithy texts printed on the verso of the various iterations of "A Letter from Pat in America," not least the narrative's eliding of several hundred years of Irish colonial and migration history, which normalizes the economic and cultural motivations for Irish emigration across the globe.[27] In many respects, the narrative projected through the stereoview of the tight-knit familial bonds, and attachments to the homeland, prefigures the motifs of much popular culture portraying Irish American consciousness from the mid twentieth century to today.[28] Tourist promotional material, novels, memoires, and Hollywood cinema have all drawn on the actual and psychic return home for narrative direction in representation of Irish America.[29] However, for the sake of brevity, I want to draw out how "A Letter from Pat in America" narratively frames the relations between remittances and photography as an expression of the entwined economic and affective bonds between the Irish American diaspora and their families back in Ireland.

The representation of Ireland in "A Letter from Pat in America" is notable for its benign portrayal of the Irish immigrant as a clearly marked and defined migrant group within American society, yet exemplary in that the Irish are assimilable into the strata of that society as productive and prosperous citizens who share in the nation's cultural values. Much like the ambivalence of Homi K. Bhabha's theorization of colonial mimicry, the Irish immigrant is portrayed as "almost the same, but not quite."[30] This ambivalence is significant in its formation of Irish Americans as a socially acceptable ethnic group, which emerged through the longue durée of the racialized transformation of the Irish from a European non-white race, to a fully integrated white ethnic group in the melting pot of America.[31] For those Irish diaspora whose descendants had emigrated to America prior to 1850, this transformation marked a significant turn toward social integration, cultural acceptance, and political respectability. To borrow a phrase from Noel Ignatiev's description of this section of the Irish diaspora, "a racial (but not ethnic) line invented in Ireland was recreated as an ethnic (but not racial) line in America."[32]

The racialization of the Irish as non-white was most starkly marked in forms of cultural representations from England throughout the nineteenth century, especially during periods of anti-colonial revolution and political agitation for emancipation from imperial rule.[33] However, the visual tropes of the simianized Celt as the figurative portrayal of the Irish throughout the nineteenth century were transnational, also appearing in US popular visual culture.[34] The origins of this racialized representation of the Irish as non-white are unclear, but can be found in Victorian racial science (in references to dark-haired and dark-eyed Irish whose ancestry were speculated to originally be Iberian or Spanish), political discourse, and in much popular culture addressing Irish political affairs.[35] In nineteenth-century America, the use and meaning of anti-Irish stereotypes had morphed to incorporate the Catholic, peasant, poor, and destitute Irish who had emigrated in the period of the famine.[36] The effect of these representations led to the kind of stereotypes and anti-Irish discrimination that has been the focus of much discussion of the Irish experience of migration to America by historians, sociologists, and cultural theorists.[37] However, the experience of Irish emigration to the United States also contributed to a sort of racial rehabilitation in that "America has thus literally whitened (that is to say, civilized) the Irish Celt."[38]

Various forms of visual culture, such as "A Letter from Pat in America," contributed to this reforming of the racialization of the Irish, not only by representing the Irish as a benevolent, socially assimilable ethnicity to Americans, but also by projecting this representation back across the Atlantic to the families and communities of Irish migrants in the homeland.[39] The accompanying text to the verso of "A Letter from Pat in America," with its references to economic remittances, familial ties, and the geopolitical liberalism of America as the "land of the free," was entwined with the distant topography and romantic vision of Irish rural life depicted in the photograph to configure a sentimental imaginary of the Irish immigrant and, with it, the formation of an Irish American diaspora. Keystone's stereoviews, it is important to note, were not produced as frivolous forms of visual entertainment that transported viewers through armchair travel to distant geographical locations: they were highly codified modes of visual instruction with imperialist intent.[40] As a mode of visual instruction, stereoviews positioned viewers within a mobile imperialistic gaze that refracted American cultural values. The viewer was always caught between the relationships of home and abroad, invited through the intervisuality of the steroview to imagine the connections between distant topographies and races, and their own subjective experiences of nation, race, and class.

Through the combination of the inter- and extratextual imaginings of the Irish and Irish American migrant and their kinship relations, "A Letter from Pat in America" places the American viewer at the center of these sentimental "domesticated visions"—to borrow Laura Wexler's term—of the new emerging relations and ethnic formation the Irish American diaspora.[41]

Photo-remittances and the Irish diaspora

The representation of a benign Irish American migrant community with affiliations to American values of ethnic and cultural assimilation, combined with strong kinship ties to the homeland in "A Letter from Pat in America" is significant for two main reasons. Firstly, it demonstrates a process of repositioning the Irish within the cultural politics of race in the U.S.. Secondly, the references to remittances and strong bonds to the homeland goes against the grain of conventional perceptions, that immigrants from the nineteenth century and the first half of the twentieth century severed ties with the homeland in the process of assimilating into the various strata of American society.[42] What is of interest here is the centrality of remittances in both demonstrating the prosperity and social mobility of the Irish migrant in the context of the discourse of American immigration and race, and in the projection of the familial bonds with the homeland. More significantly for the discussion I pursue in this essay is that in "A Letter from Pat in America," remittances are not portrayed as solely economic. Remittances also represent affective expressions which maintain familial and kinship relations disrupted through migration. They are objects to which affect sticks.[43]

Studies of remittances have predominantly focused on their financial form and role in the economic relationships between migrants and their home countries.[44] However, in addition to having affective qualities through their circulation, remittances also have social and cultural forms, which contribute to the exchange of "ideas, values and beliefs" from migrants to families and communities back in their country of origin.[45] They are also collective, ideological, and imaginative cultural forms "remitted from diaspora to the homeland," which contribute to the formation of diasporic consciousness.[46]

Photographs are an effective form of social remittance in maintaining familial relations disrupted by migration. As Marianne Hirsch reminds us, in familial histories fractured by exile and migration, photographs provide "some illusion of continuity over time and space."[47] However, as forms of remittance, or what I term *photo-remittance*, their circulation also has the potential to convey variegated expressions of self-fashioning by diasporic communities, and to, in turn, generate multiple affective responses among the recipients of the remittance at home. Indeed, as a cultural form that mediates the relationship between two communities—the Irish American diaspora and the "kinsfolk at home"—to invoke the sentiment of "A Letter from Pat in America," the photo-remittance can produce both positive and negative responses from the families and communities who receive them. As Ahmed sets out in her discussion of the affective configurations of happiness, families provide "a shared horizon in which objects circulate, accumulating positive affective value."[48] Photographs, and the letters that transmitted them across the Atlantic, were received with anticipation and excitement as they extended the shared horizon for the continuity and maintenance of familial relations fractured by migration. However, the dread of the empty letter, one that contained no money, could generate negative responses to objects with which they were associated. As observed in a quote from a letter cited by Miller in his discussion of the expectations and jealousy of families of Irish immigrants back in Ireland, photo-remittances became objects of unhappy affect, the father of emigrants from Roscommon exclaiming, "They might not have bothered sending their pictures, for we know well what they look like. The pictures I would like to see are a few Abraham Lincoln's."[49] Photo-remittances thus involve precisely the processes of inter-visuality identified by Mirzoeff in the generation of multiple interacting modes of diaspora viewpoints.[50] Through its material forms and circulation, the photo-remittance thus speaks to the intentions and desires of how the Irish American diaspora wished to be perceived, while generating the ungoverned responses by families and communities that received such self-crafting back in Ireland.

The dominant form of photo-remittance throughout the nineteenth and first three decades of the twentieth centuries were vernacular, commercial studio portraits. Studio portraits have a formal repetitive familiarity. Poses, format, and scenography vary little between one portrait and the next. However, studio portraits project social status and refract cultural values both through their material form as commodities and in the content of the photograph. As Tina Campt observes in her study of vernacular photography and the black European diaspora, it is "the familiarity and seriality reproduction of these compositions and conventions that, in large part, make them register so widely and evocatively."[51] Although there are other forms of photo-remittance, such as vernacular family snapshots and social media imagery, in addition to expressing prosperity and social status, studio portraits have specific modes of transmission as material objects through the exchange of letters between diaspora communities.[52] A number of Irish migration histories have identified the exchange of letters between migrants and their families as frequently requesting or containing photographs.[53] As a commodity, studio portraits also involve organized systems of image production and exchange—a visual economy of the diasporic photo-remittance, to borrow Deborah Poole's concept of the transatlantic exchange of image-objects.[54] It is through such visual economy that affective responses to photographs' expression of political, cultural, and familial relationships can be accentuated or suppressed. Indeed, photo-remittances in the form of commodity portraits continue to play a role in the familial repositories of migration histories of the Irish diaspora, through which their entwined registers of geographic dislocation and cultural belonging still carry emotional resonance. Rather than draw on personal family archives of vernacular photographs, however, I want to turn to orphaned photographs to identify a number of material forms of the photo-remittance.

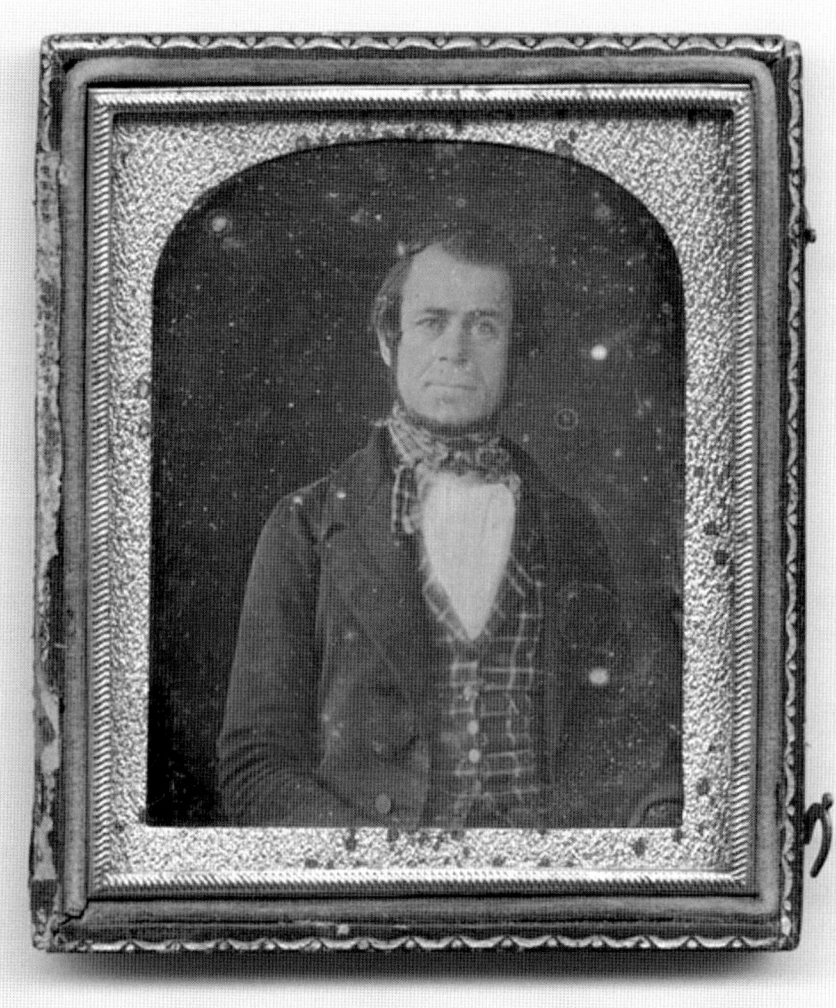

Figure 3: Anonymous, Irish American Daguerreotype, ca. 1850 (Plate 6, p. 332). Author's collection.

Daguerreotype portraits were an early form of photo-remittance, particularly for wealthy immigrants and skilled artisans from Europe, the latter using occupational portraits to not only display their professional skills and artisanship but also their social status within the strata of American society.[55] However, the exchange of daguerreotype portraits between Irish diaspora and their families is rare, in large part because the majority of immigrants during the height of popularity for daguerreotype portraits in America were poor, unskilled laborers. The prohibitive cost of having a daguerreotype portrait taken meant that many early portraits of

Irish immigrants were cheaper tintypes taken in small studios, or increasingly by itinerant photographers. However, a daguerreotype portrait of an unknown man from the 1850s, which was sent to recent Irish immigrants in America, demonstrates that photographs were exchanged between Irish migrants from an early stage (Fig. 3). The anonymous daguerreotype is accompanied by an unsigned letter, which discusses people known to both the author and addressee of the letter from their home place in Kerry, with the author exclaiming:

> Two days since I have the pleasure of receiving your present. I have never seen so exquisite a Daguerreotype and judging of the fidelity of your wife's portrait from that of your own … I congratulate you most warmly upon having the good fortune to coin the affection of me whose face is not only worth prizing for itself, it is more to be appreciated as the reflex of a gentle benevolent disposition.[56]

In addition to the references to the exchange of daguerreotypes, the letter also discusses the author's personal affiliations with other migrants in America. The exchange of this daguerreotype suggests that photographs were not only circulated between immigrants and Ireland, but also within Irish and Irish American communities within the United States. While migrants from Ireland frequently congregated together to form communities, particularly in the urban centers along the eastern coast of the United States, many extended families were dispersed across the country or neighboring Canada.[57] A cabinet card portrait from 1888–1889 provides another example of this exchange of photographs within Irish immigrant communities (Figs. 4 & 5). Produced by the John S. Clime Studio based in St. John, New Brunswick, the portrait is of a Catholic priest in a formal studio setting.[58] On the verso of the cabinet card is a hand-draw Catholic cross with a graphic inscription, "Erin Go Brag," on one side, and on the other, "Cedi Mille Fail the!" The inscription below reads: "Presented to Miss Maggie McCauley of Hartford, Conn. U.S. By Her Cousin 'E. J. McCauley', N. Ireland, N. B., 'Albert, Co. Albert' April – 1888 – and 1889." The photograph is most likely of Edward J. McCauley (the author of the handwritten inscription), the parish priest of New Ireland, a small settlement of mostly Catholic Irish immigrants established in 1816 and abandoned in the 1920s. During the wave emigration that accompanied the famine years, many of the poorest Irish immigrants landed in Nova Scotia and New Brunswick.[59] Those who remained established small parish communities such as New Ireland, but many of these communities increasingly became depopulated as residents relocated to larger rural or urban areas of Canada or, more often, traveled onward to Boston.[60]

These two forms of portraiture, the daguerreotype and the cabinet card, function as photo-remittances on a number of intertwined levels. As commodity forms of portraiture, they are, on one level, a type of property, an object whose ownership is transferred as a social remittance. However, while the commercial studio portrait's value is symbolic of prosperity and wealth, the photo-remittance cannot be reduced to crude economics of its commodity form. As physical objects with "volume, opacity, tactility and a physical presence," the daguerreotype and cabinet card portraits were affective objects to be possessed and exchanged between family members: ownership could be fleeting and transient, as could their social and cultural value.[61] The commercial studio portrait was, on another level, "a sign whose purpose is both the description of an individual and the inscription of a social identity."[62] The appeal for likenesses and their exchange among the Irish diaspora and their families back home are a feature of letters that traveled across the Atlantic.[63] The portraits sent by the anonymous figure in the daguerreotype and E.J. McAuley thus fulfill a sort of obligation to maintain a connection to dispersed familial relations through their physical appearance and rematerialized presence in the form of the photographic portrait.

Before the introduction of mass popular photography and informal family snapshots, formal commercial studio portraits were the dominant form of photo-remittance exchanged by the Irish diaspora. While the Irish diaspora and their families may have appealed for such portraits for their likeness, the commercial studio portrait was more than a mere description of a family member's physical appearance or indeed a material object of familial remembrance. As photo-remittances, commercial studio portraits are, on a social level, material forms of exchanging what Levitt identifies as normative structures, "ideas, values, and beliefs," which incorporate behaviors, familial responsibilities, communal relations, and "aspirations for social mobility."[64] They portray to the home country established norms of behavior and adherence to shared values, and at the same time are potential models for the transformation of self-fashioning cultural identity.

In her discussion of portraiture among the Javanese, Karen Strassler observes that

In adopting a pose, people conform themselves (both consciously and unconsciously, willing and unwilling) to a set of available models of appearance. This bodily molding anticipates being seen by others and is a bid to be recognized in particular way. As subjects of photographs, people both appropriate available image-repertoires to stake claims to particular identities and social positions and, at the same time, are subjected to ideologies and narratives attached to these visual appearances that are never entirely of their own making.[65]

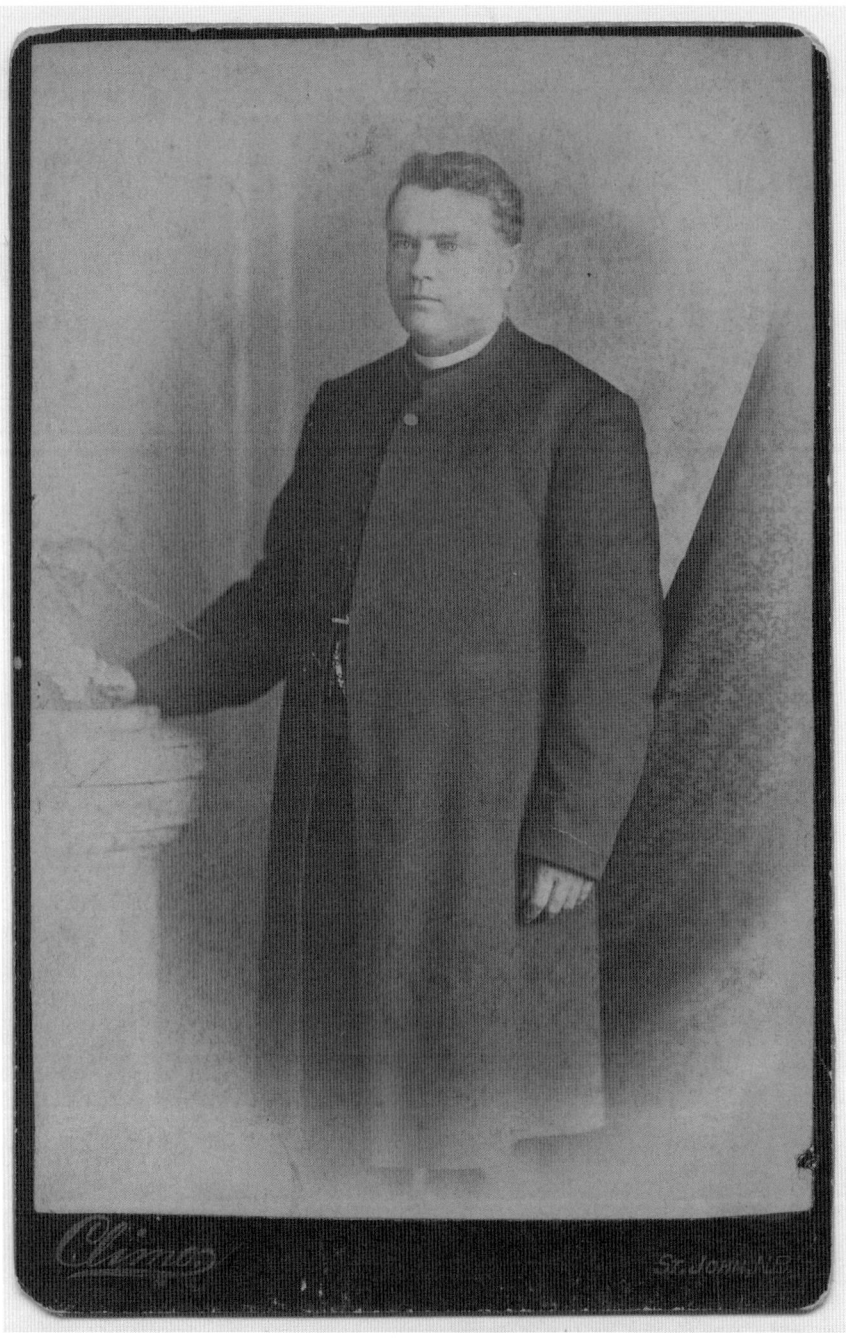

Figure 4: Edward J. McCauley, Cabinet Card, John S. Clime Studio, St. John, New Brunswick, 1888–1889. Author's collection.

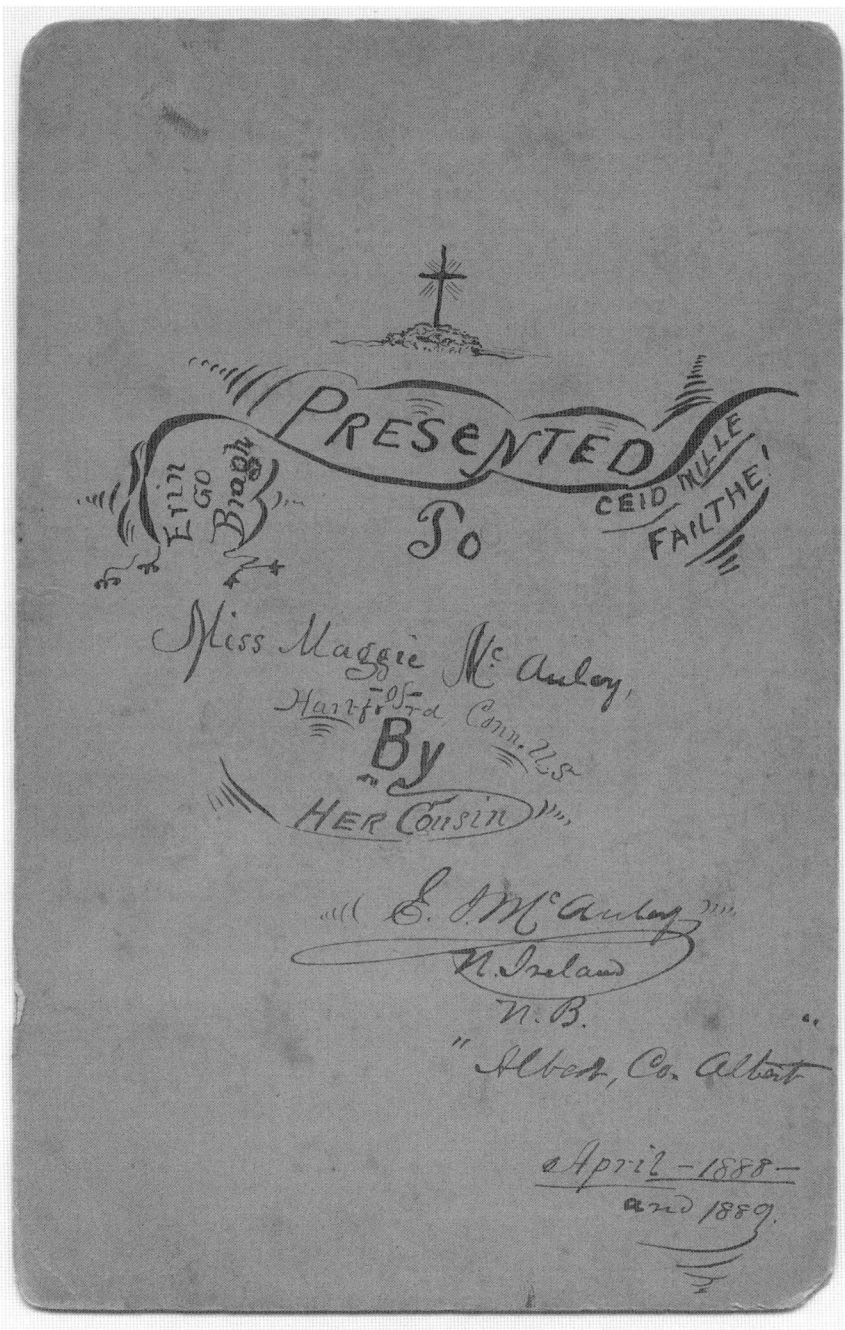

Figure 5: Verso, Cabinet Card, John S. Clime Studio, St. John, New Brunswick, 1888–1889. Author's collection.

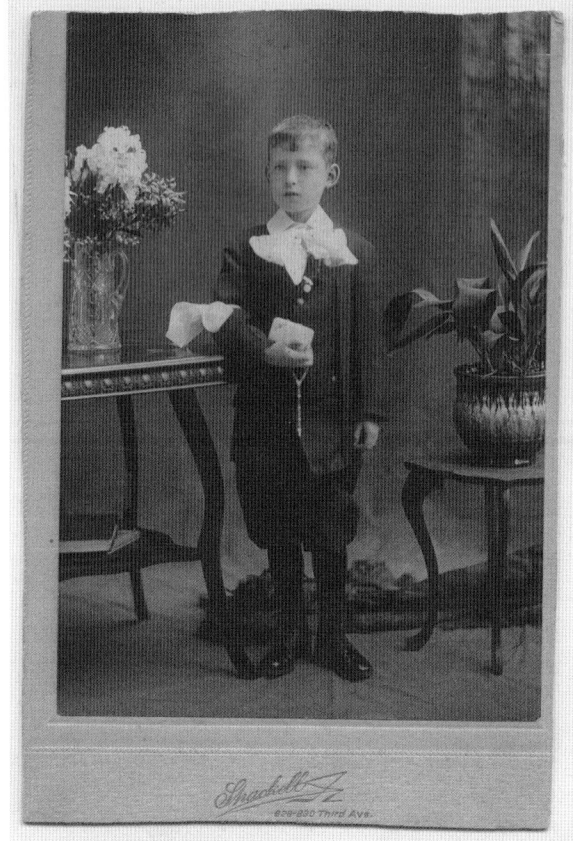

As a number of commentators have observed, social and cultural formations of diaspora are forged through the tensions of continuity and change, the inheritance of cultural traditions and their rupture, and the conforming to established customs and their disjuncture through the absorption or rejection in new cultural environments.[66] These tensions are materialized in the ubiquitous form of the studio portrait as the diasporic subject conforms to the repetitive normalization of posing in standardized studio settings while mobilizing the portrait to envision their own sense of subjectivity. As Campt observes such "portraits performatively invoke and produce respectable and accomplished diasporic subjects within their photographic frames" for the "consumption of intimate and extended relations."[67] Traditional costume, modern fashions, religious symbols, and bodily deportment can all be activated by the diasporic subject in an assemblage with the repetitive conventions of the commercial studio portrait to convey to family members the adherence to shared social norms, at the same time as crafting a self-image that reflected their aspirations to social status in America. They could also be highly personalized in the form of accompanying letters, as in the case of the daguerreotype, or as with the McAuley cabinet card, through handwritten inscriptions and messages on the photograph itself.

The understanding and effects of such portraits, however, were not solely determined by the aspirational projection of the diasporic subject. As photo-remittances, they also introduced their recipients, in specifiable and individualized

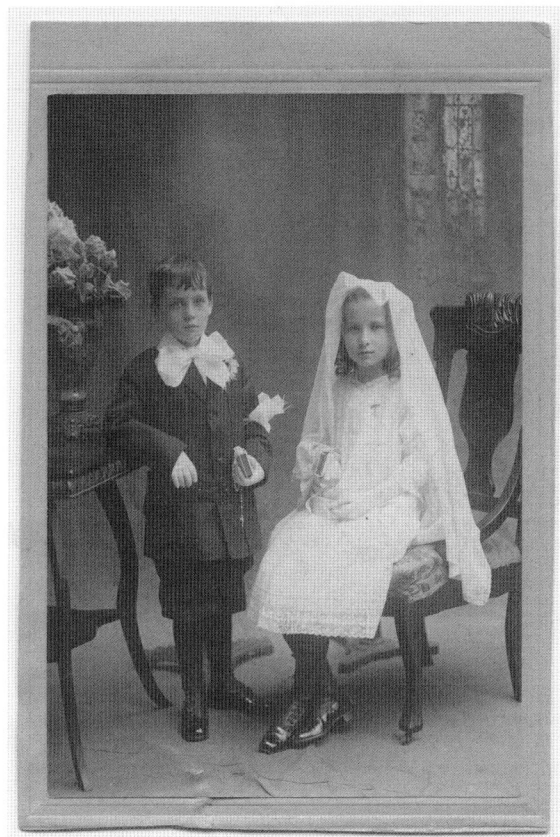

Figure 7: Anonymous, Francis Shackell Studios, n.d. (Plate 7, p. 333). Edward Chandler Collection/ Author's collection.

forms, to novel ideas, styles, and cultural processes of self-fashioning. Indeed, for many Irish families in rural Ireland or poorer areas of large provisional towns and cities, the introduction of the commercial studio portrait into the sociability of familial relations significantly transformed the routines of communal and religious rites of passage.

Anonymous vernacular photographs of Irish immigrants in America from the former collection of antiquarian historian of Irish photography Edward Chandler, include a number of studio portraits of children commemorating their First Holy Communion (Figs. 6–8). Mass migration to America was perceived as a double threat to Catholic institutions at home and in America, both through depopulation in Ireland and the fear that Irish immigrants would drift away from the cultural and political influence of the church as they sought to assimilate into American society.[68] The Catholic Irish in America were caught between loyalties to the church and the liberal, democratic system of their adopted country, yet maintained loyalty to Catholicism as a symbolic marker of their ethnic cultural identity.[69] The photographs of the children would have been remitted to family members to demonstrate the continuation of rituals of Catholicism and to visually demonstrate their faith and loyalty to the church. One portrait is from the photography studio at Bloomingdale Brothers, New York; the others from the Francis Shackell studio on Third Avenue in New York City.[70] The portraits depict boys dressed in black communion suits with traditional white armbands; the girls in white dresses with veils. Clutching rosary beads and bibles,

Figure 8: Anonymous, Francis
Shackell Studios, n.d.
Edward Chandler Collection/
Author's collection.

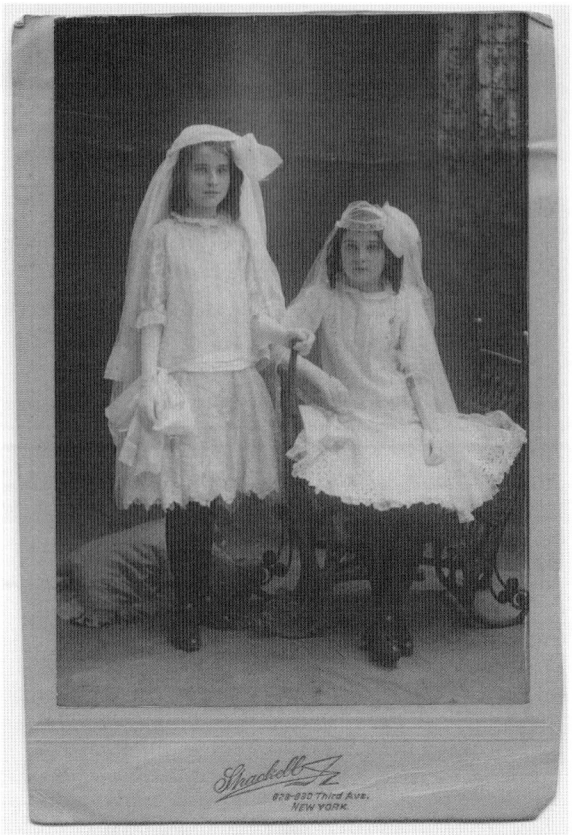

the children in the por-
traits perform adher-
ence and continuation
of shared Catholic val-
ues and communal
childhood rites of pas-
sage (rosary beads and
bibles are traditional
familial gifts to chil-
dren to mark their First
Holy Communion).
However, the elabo-
rate studio settings of
upmarket New York
commercial studios are
also an expression of
social status. The intro-
duction of formal studio
portraiture into the rituals of Holy Communion would have demonstrated new
cultural practices of commemorating communal religious milestones and photographic self-fashioning of religious identities among the Irish diaspora. For all but
the wealthiest rural and urban Catholic families back in Ireland, the incorporation
of formal studio portraits into the rituals of religious practice would have been rare.
As a form of photo-remittance, the First Communion studio portrait would have
thus introduced new material realities for the expression of religious identities to the
families and communities of the diaspora at home. Such new cultural practices of
photography eventually become so normalized in the home country as to become
inseparable from the social routines of religious events and ceremonies, with many
Irish families, by the mid twentieth century, incorporating commercial studio portraits into commemorations of religious activities.

Such photo-remittances had wider social influence outside the family, but not
all were positively appreciated for their potential transformation of self-mediation.
In his "Notes of the Week" column for the newspaper of the Irish Agricultural
Organization Society, *The Irish Homestead*, the editor, writer George William

Russell, decried the influence of returned photographs from America on young Irish women. Under the subtitle "Photographs and Emigration," Russell proclaimed that stemming the tide of migration of women from rural Ireland was futile against what he described as the secret, occult-like lure of the returned image of the migrant Irish woman in the form of the photograph. Declaring that, above all, a woman in her youth wants to beautify herself, Russell states that the "Irish girl who has gone to America sends home photographs of herself. It is these photographs that do all the mischief with her remaining sisters."[71] The period in which Russell was writing saw Irish women take a central role in the transatlantic diasporic relations as they sought greater independent lives, employment opportunities, and world experience.[72] From the 1890s, single Irish women migrated in greater numbers and figured predominantly in the remittance culture and letter-writing home. Remitted portraits, such as those from the McNabb Studio on Broadway in New York City and the Gray Studio in Boston, regularly accompanied letters home (Figs. 9–11). These photographs, according to Russell, were evidence of an authentic Irish femininity that was lost to migration as Irish immigrants turned to the contrived appearances of the self-configured through migration: "The girl who is remembered without a hat, with bare feet, with short red petticoat, is seen as a duchess in her American transformation."[73] Moreover, Russell identifies such photographs as both culturally transformational of the Irishwoman's self-reflexive mediation of herself and as potential imaginaries that will lure away future generations: "Irish girlhood sees itself reflected in American photographs and trembles with longing and delight."[74]

Russell's remarks on the remitted photograph are notable against the backdrop of the increased migration of women from the 1890s, reflecting how the photo-remittance could generate particular responses through its appearance at certain historical junctures. It also demonstrates how the photo-remittance, as an individualized form of transmitting cultural practices of self-fashioning, became a filter for the wider transcultural diffusion of photography as a tool of mediating oneself "renewed and once removed."[75] As forms of photo-remittance, vernacular studio portrait photographs could thus be experienced both as affective objects through their circulation within the intimate shared horizon of the family and as conduits of transmitting social and cultural remittances within the wider sphere of the diaspora community, within which they accumulated negative affective value.[76] In the counter stream of waves of migration, the transcultural photo-remittance thus suggests a more discrepant imagining of the Irish American diaspora: an imagining that could bring together the meliorating affects of photography in lives fractured by migration and the anxieties of cultural transformation of the diaspora through the self-mediation of the remitted vernacular photograph.

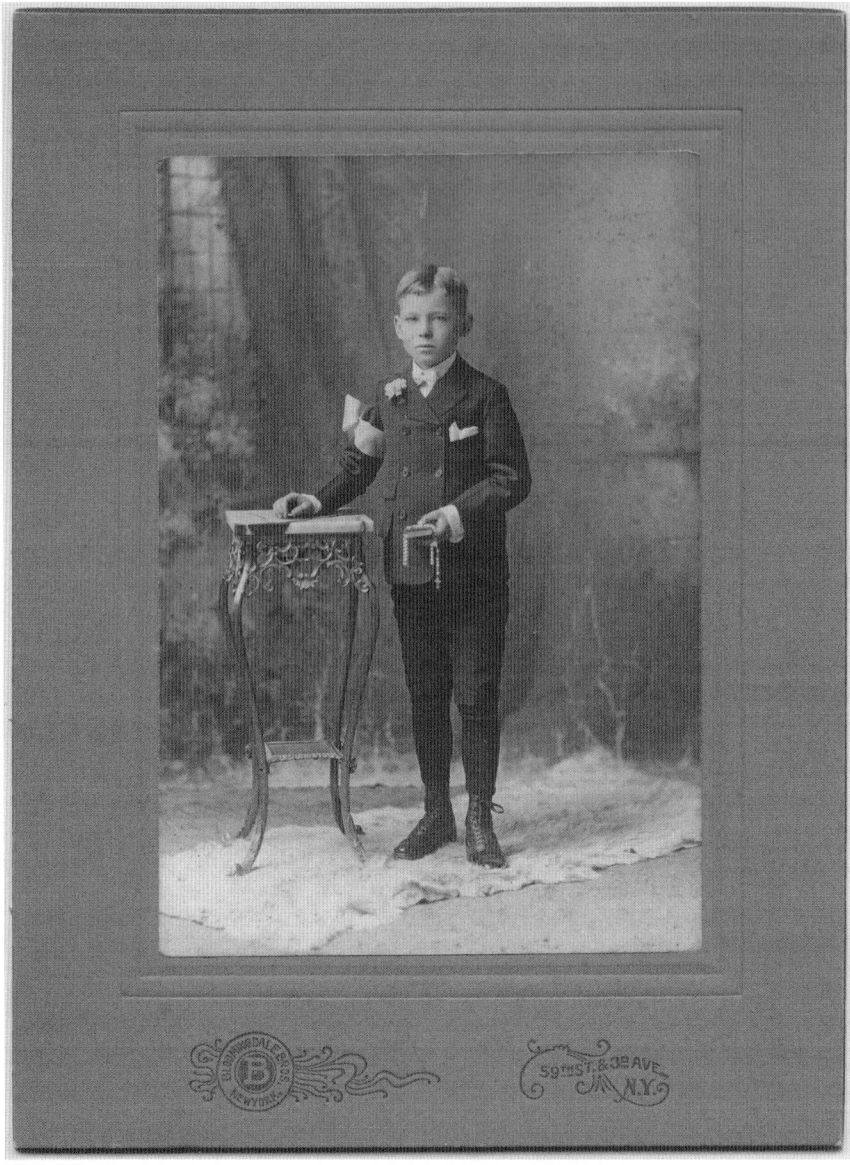

Figure 9: Anonymous, Bloomingdale Bros., New York, n.d. (Plate 8, p. 334). Edward Chandler Collection/ Author's collection.

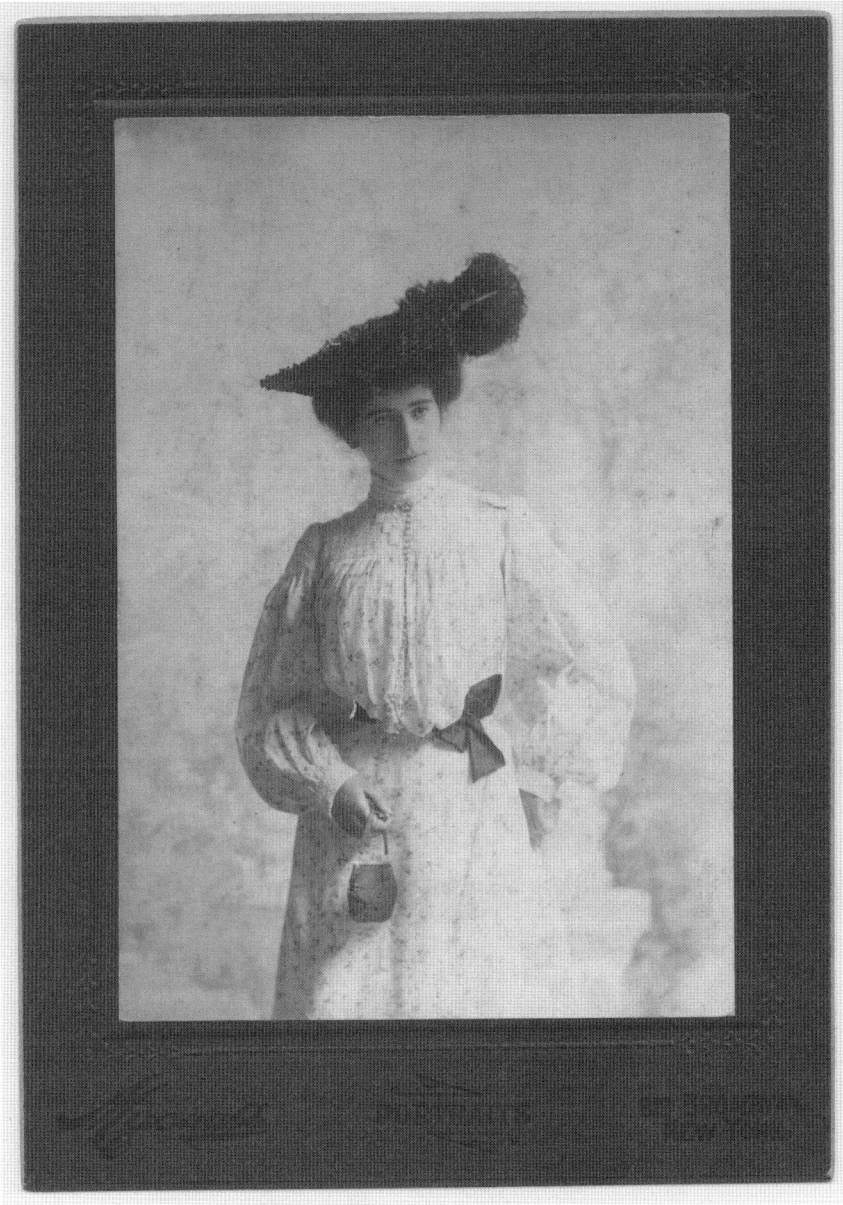

Figure 10: Anonymous, McNabb Studio, New York, n.d. Edward Chandler Collection/ Author's collection.

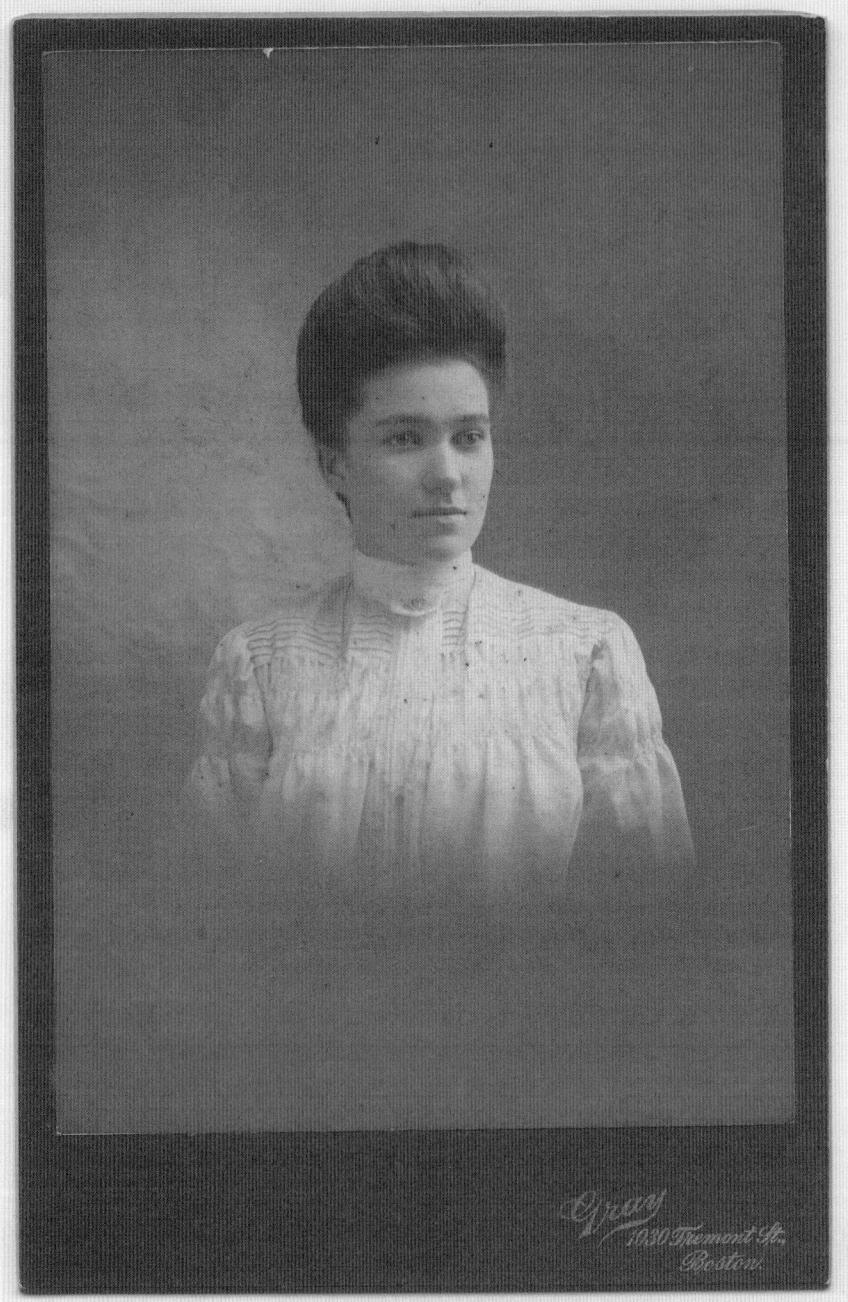

Figure 11: Anonymous, Gray Studio, Boston, n.d. (Plate 9, p. 335). Edward Chandler Collection/ Author's collection.

Notes

1. On the figure of the returned yank in Irish culture see; Sinéad Moynihan, *Ireland, Migration and Return Migration: The "Returned Yank" in the Cultural Imagination, 1952 to Present* (Liverpool: Liverpool University Press, 2019) and Ann Schofield. "The Returned Yank as a Site of Memory in Irish Popular Culture," *Journal of American Studies*, 47 (2013): 175-195.

2. Nicholas Mirzoeff, "Introduction, The Multiple Viewpoint: Diasporic Visual Cultures," in Nicholas Mirzoeff (eds.), *Diaspora and Visual Culture: Representing Africans and Jews* (London: Routledge, 2000), 7.

3. Mirzoeff, "Introduction," 5–6.

4. Elizabeth Edwards, "Exchanging photographs: preliminary thoughts on the currency of photography in collecting anthropology," *Journal des Anthropologues* [Online], 80:1 (2000), http://journals.openedition.org/jda/3138; DOI: 10.4000/ jda.3138

5. Sarah Ahmed, "Affective Economies," *Social Text*, 79, 22, No. 2 (Summer 2004), 120.

6. Peggy Levitt, "Social Remittances: Local-Level Forms of Cultural Diffusion," *International Migration Review*, 32, No. 4 (1998), 926–948; Juan Flores, *The Diaspora Strikes Back: Caribeno Tales of Learning and Turning* (New York: Routledge, 2009), 44–47.

7. Mary Louise Pratt, *Imperial Eyes: Travel Writing and Transculturation* (London: Routledge, 1992), 7.

8. Arjun Appadurai, "Disjuncture and Difference in the Global Economy," *Public Culture* 2, No. 2 (1990), 3.

9. Stuart Hall, "Cultural Identity and Diaspora," in Jonathan Rutherford (ed.), *Identity: Community, Culture, Difference* (London: Lawrence & Wishart, 1990), 222–237.

10. Hall, "Cultural Identity," 222.

11. Leigh Raiford, "Notes Toward a Photographic Practice of Diaspora," *English Language Notes* 44, No. 2, (2006), 213.

12. Tina Campt, *Image Matters: Archive, Photography, and the African Diaspora in Europe* (Durham: Duke University Press, 2012), 168.

13. Stuart Hall, "The Question of Cultural Identity," in *Modernity and its Futures* (London: Polity Press, 1992), 310, emphasis in original.

14. Campt observes, for example, that for the British Afro-Caribbean diaspora, the studio and style of portrait were chosen for their similarity to those from the homeland. *Image Matters*, 162.

15. Flores, *The Diaspora*, 52, 4.

16. Levitt, "Social Remittances," 927.

17. Flores, *The Diaspora*, 9.

18. Levitt, "Social Remittances," 936–937.

19. Arnold Schrier, *Ireland and the American Emigration, 1850–1900* (Minneapolis: University of Minnesota Press, 1958); Kirby Miller, *Emigrants and Exiles: Ireland and the Irish*

Exodus to North America (Oxford: Oxford University Press, 1985); Geraldine Meaney, Mary O'Dowd, and Bernadette Whelan, *Reading the Irish Woman Studies in Cultural Encounters and Exchange* (Liverpool: Liverpool University Press, 2013).

20. Miller, *Emigrants and Exiles*, 425.

21. Sarah Ahmed, "Happy Objects," in *The Affect Theory Reader* (Durham: Duke University Press, 2010), 29, 41.

22. Miller, *Emigrants and Exiles*, 4–8.

23. For brief discussions on the stereoscope as an aid in education, and of Keystone and visual literacy, see W.S.T., "The Stereoscope as an Educational Instrument," *The Massachusetts Teacher*, 12, No. 12 (1859), 467–469; Everett L. Getchel, "The Picture in Education," *The Journal of Education*, 79, No. 12 (September 1912), 321; Michael Lesy, "Visual Literacy," *The Journal of American History*, 94, No. 1 (June 2007), 145.

24. As early as 1859, Oliver Wendell Holmes, in his essay "The Stereoscope and the Stereograph," concluded his caution to investors in stereoscopic views not to purchase groups of viewcards, lest they became weary of looking at them by exclaiming, "all have agreed in admiring Irish Views, as those about the lakes of Killarney, for instance which are beautiful alike in general effect and nicety of detail." Oliver Wendell Homes, "The Stereoscope and the Stereograph," *The Atlantic Monthly*, 3 (1859), 747.

25. Keystone View Company, "12615 – A Letter from Pat in America," "Tour of the World" series (16), c. 1892–1933.

26. "A Letter from Pat."

27. This motif was perpetuated well into the twentieth century through a range of media and popular culture. For a discussion in relation to photography, see Justin Carville, "A Sympathetic Look: Documentary Humanism and Irish Identity in Dorothea Lange's 'Irish Country People'," in James P. Byrne, Padraig Kirwan, and Michael O'Sullivan (eds.), *Affecting Irishness: Negotiating Cultural Identity Within and Beyond the Nation* (Oxford: Peter Lang, 2009), 197–217.

28. See Stephanie Rains, *The Irish-American in Popular Culture* (Dublin: Irish Academic Press, 2007).

29. Luke Gibbons, "Romanticism, Realism and Irish Cinema," in Kevin Rockett, Luke Gibbons, and John Hill (eds.), *Cinema and Ireland* (London: Croom Helm, 1987).

30. Homi K. Bhabha, *The Location of Culture* (London: Routledge, 1994), 123.

31. There is not space here to go into the history of Irish race formation as white or non-white within American racial politics. See Noel Ignatiev, *How the Irish Became White* (New York: Routledge, 1995); Matthew Frye Jacobson, *Whiteness of a Different Color: European Immigrants and the Alchemy of Race* (Cambridge: Harvard University Press, 1999); Theodore W. Allen, *The Invention of the White Race, Volume I: Racial Oppression and Social Control*, 2nd ed. (London: Verso, 2012); Peter D. O'Neill, *Famine Irish and the American Racial State* (New York: Routledge, 2017); and Hidetaka Hirota, *Expelling the Poor: Atlantic Seaboard States & the 19th-Century Origins of American Immigration Policy* (Oxford: Oxford University Press, 2017).

32. Ignatiev, *How the Irish*, 39.

33. See L. Perry Curtis, *Apes and Angels: The Irishman in Victorian Caricature*, revised edition (Washington, DC: Smithsonian Institution Press, 1997); Michael de Nie, *The Eternal Paddy: Irish Identity and the British Press, 1798–1882* (Madison: The University of Wisconsin Press, 2004).

34. Curtis, *Apes*, 58–67. John J. Appel, "From Shanties to Lace Curtains: The Irish Image in *Puck*, 1876-1910," *Comparative Studies in Society and History* 13 (1971): 365-375.

35. Steve Garner, *Racism in the Irish Experience* (London: Pluto, 2004), 91–113. The English race theorist John Beddoe, for example, speculated that the Irish had African origins and described certain portions of the population as "Africanoid Celts." Curtis, *Apes*, 20.

36. On anti-Irish discrimination of poor Irish immigrants, see Hirota, *Expelling*, 122–125.

37. Ignatiev, *How the Irish*; Hirota, *Expelling*; Garner, *Racism*.

38. Garner, *Racism*, 94.

39. Garner, *Racism*, 106–107.

40. Established by B.L. Singley in 1892, Keystone set up an education department in 1898, the same year that one of its versions of "A Letter from Pat in America" was published. For a brief overview of the Keystone view company, see Paul Rubinstein, "Keystone View Company, Meadville Pennsylvania – New York – Toronto – London – Sydney," https://www.yellowstonestseroviews.com/publishers/keystone.html.

41. Laura Wexler, *Tender Violence: Domestic Visions in an Age of U.S. Imperialism* (Chapel Hill/London: The University of North Carolina Press, 2000).

42. Levitt, "Social Remittances," 927.

43. Ahmed, "Happy Objects," 29.

44. Vinder S. Kalra, Raminder Kaur, and John Hutnyk, *Diaspora and Hybridity* (London: Sage, 2005), 23–25.

45. Levitt, "Social Remittances," 933.

46. Flores, *The Diaspora*, 44–47.

47. Marianne Hirsch, *Family Frames: Photography, Narrative and Postmemory* (Cambridge: Harvard University Press, 1997), xi.

48. Ahmed, "Happy," 38.

49. Kirby Miller and Bruce D. Boling, "Golden Streets, Bitter Tears: The Irish Image of America during the Era of Mass Migration," in *Journal of Ethnic American History*, 10, No. 1 & 2 (Fall 1990–Winter 1991), 31; see also Miller, *Emigrants and Exiles*, 487.

50. Mirzoeff, "Introduction," 6.

51. Campt, *Image Matters*, 14.

52. Levitt, "Social Remittances," 936–937.

53. David Fitzpatrick, *Oceans of Consolation: Personal Accounts of Irish Migration to Australia* (Ithaca: Cornell University Press, 1994).

54. Deborah Poole, *Vision, Race and Modernity: A Visual Economy of the Andean Image World* (Princeton: Princeton University Press, 1997), 9–13.

55. Little scholarly research has been undertaken of occupational daguerreotypes or of their role within immigrant communities in America. For a brief overview of the occupational daguerreotype, see Harry R. Rubenstein, "With Hammer in Hand: Working Class Occupational Portraits," in Howard B. Rock, Paul A. Gilje and Robert Asher (eds.), *American Artisans: Crafting Social Identity, 1750–1850* (Baltimore: The Johns Hopkins University Press, 1995), 191–198. A more substantial account can be found in Brooks Johnson, "The Progress of Civilization: The American Occupational Daguerreotype," in John Wood (ed.), *America and the Daguerreotype* (Iowa City: Iowa University Press, 1997), 109–117.

56. Unsigned and undated letter accompanying anonymous daguerreotype, c. 1850–1860. Collection of the author.

57. As Miller has observed, British passenger acts and cheaper passage redirected many Irish emigrants to Nova Scotia and New Brunswick. While some settled in Canada, if only for brief periods, many sailed on to America. Miller, *Emigrants and Exiles*, 193–197.

58. The John S. Climo Studio was established in the early 1970s and operated in St. John's, New Brunswick, until the 1960s. See Jim Burant, "A Written Portrait: Saint John Photographers and their Studios in the 1871 Census," *Archivaria*, 17 (Winter, 1983–1984), 276–277.

59. Miller, *Emigrants and Exiles*, 292.

60. Gerard P. Moran, *Sending Out Ireland's Poor: Assisted Emigration to North America in the Nineteenth Century* (Dublin: Four Courts Press, 2013), 116.

61. Geoffrey Batchen, *Photography's Objects* (Albuquerque: University of New Mexico Press, 1997), 2.

62. John Tagg, *The Burden of Representation: Essays on Photographies and Histories* (London: Macmillan, 1988), 37.

63. See Fitzpatrick, *Oceans*, 246.

64. Levitt, "Social Remittances," 933–934.

65. Karen Strassler, *Refracted Visions: Popular Photography and National Modernity in Java* (Durham: Duke University Press, 2010), 26.

66. Appadurai, "Disjuncture"; Hall, "Cultural Identity," 222–237.

67. Campt, *Image Matters*, 163, 162.

68. Miller, *Emigrants*, 129, 329–330.

69. Lawrence John McCaffery, *The Irish Catholic Diaspora in America* (Washington, DC: The Catholic University of America Press, 1997), 146, 129.

70. The studio of Shackell & Clauss operated out of 828 and 830 Third Avenue from the 1880s to circa 1906, after which time Francis Shackell was established, until its closure circa 1915.

71. George William Russell, "Photographs and Emigration," in Henry Summerfield (ed.), *Selections from the Contributions to the Irish Homestead by G.W. Russell – A.E.: Volume I* (Atlantic Highland: Humanities Press, 1978), 213–214.

72. Meaney, O'Dowd, and Whelan, *Reading*, 93–100. For an account of vernacular photography and the experience of women migrants to the U.S. see Orla Fitzpatrick's essay "From Cavan to Kansas" in this volume.

73. Russell, "Photographs," 214.

74. Russell, "Photographs," 214.

75. William Mazzarella, "Culture, Globalization, Mediation," in *Annual Review of Anthropology*, 33 (June 2004), 357.

76. Ahmed, "Happy," 38.

Diasporic Imaginations

"First Pictures"

New York through the Lens of Emigrated European Photographers in the 1930s and 1940s

Helene Roth

Prelude

In 1932, the magazine *Berliner Illustrirte Zeitung* (BIZ) published a photo reportage by the German Jewish photographer Erich Salomon; this reportage was taken during his trip to New York and titled "Die Gefangenen der Weltkrise – Bei den unerwünschten Einwanderern und Deportierten auf Ellis Island im Hafen von New York" ("The prisoners of the world crisis – The unwanted emigrants and deportees on Ellis Island in New York's harbor") (Fig. 1). In a series of six pictures, Salomon revisits the emigrants' and deportees' situation on Ellis Island from different perspectives, capturing with his camera the life of the prisoners on the island.[1] The text in the reportage informs that the island not only served as a deportation processing center where mostly European, Asian, and African emigrants were held before they were granted entry into the United States, but also as detention center where emigrants who had been living in New York for several years were arrested because they had not fulfilled all legal requirements at the time of immigration.[2] In a photograph directly to the right of the headline, Salomon focuses on the emigrants' view, through the barred windows, of New York. The skyline of Manhattan was considered by many arriving ship passengers to be a symbol of freedom and hope, which they first saw and had in mind after days on the open sea when they entered the harbor.[3] In Salomon's photograph, however, the skyline and the view of the skyscrapers is subdivided into the fine rectilinear structure of the barred windows, and moves into the distance, behind the delicate grid of gray areas. The deserted photograph forms a counterproposal to a happy life of freedom and with hope that the emigrants expected from the new life in America. In its strict and matter-of-fact composition, it conveys the image of the distanced, unreachable goal

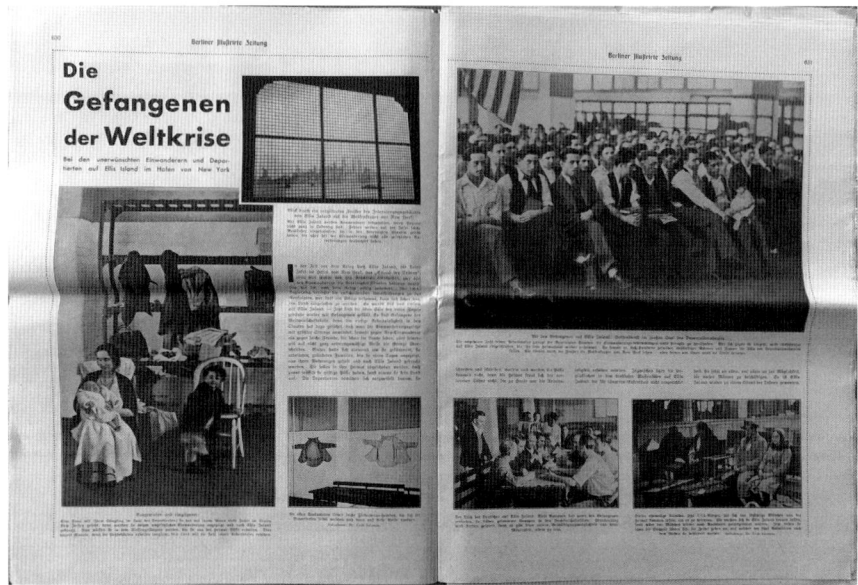

Figure 1: Anonymous, "Die Gefangenen der Weltkrise," photographs by Erich Salomon, in *Berliner Illustrirte Zeitung*, vol. 41, no. 20 (22 May 1932), 630f. © Private archive Helene Roth.

of emigration. When Salomon made the reportage on Ellis Island in 1932, he could not have guessed that, in 1933, when the National Socialists came to power in Germany, the island would again gain importance for emigration from Europe in the following years.[4] This was the case for many of his European colleagues who emigrated to New York in the 1930s and 1940s.

"First pictures": Through New York with the camera

When the National Socialists came to power and major private and professional restrictions were imposed in Germany, Great Britain and neighboring France, especially in their capitals London and Paris, offered a first place of refugee for persecuted photographers. A second wave of emigration with destinations overseas and to the United States of America, especially to New York, began with the occupation of France during World War II.[5] The entry to the harbor of New York City was one of the most commonly desired destinations at this time—it was the symbol for the "New World" and a new home for the émigrés. Erwin Blumenfeld, a German Jewish photographer, who also emigrated to New York in the 1940s, describes this important moment of arrival in the harbor of Manhattan in his autobiography *Eye to I*:

On the seventh day, after passing the Ambrose lightship, the steamer slowed down. Seagulls screeched, passport officials, pilots and reporters clambered on board. For the second time I watched excited the passengers jostle each other impatiently with their binoculars on the rails, each watching to be the first to spot the first skyscraper. As the veils of the Gulf stream mist thinned, a strip of land emerged, silvery green in the distance, a line of dunes rising from the Atlantic: the New World! Roofs of disappointingly pretty-pretty toy houses began to appear, one beside the next in childish old lady's colours: pink, mauve, light blue, beige, all alike. Behind them rose pointless iron constructions from some gigantic Meccano set: Coney Island, New York's amusement park. […] Only at the very last, under the watchful eye of the verdigris Miss Liberty, did the immense backdrop of the Manhattan skyscraper with their greyish-mauve glaze (every city has its own colour, New York has a purplish tinge), rise up into the inhuman August sky […].[6]

After successfully arriving in New York City, the paths of European emigrant photographers took different directions. In many cases, the photographers already had contacts with other emigrated family members, friends living in New York, or American colleagues. Mostly without employment, commissions for magazines, or their own photography studios, the exiled photographers undertook this urban exploration in private. They were overwhelmed and impressed by the spatial dimension of skyscrapers, vanishing points, light conditions, and the big avenues of the metropolis. While emigrated writers and journalists were often confronted with professional problems caused by the new language, photographers could use their cameras as a transnational and universal medium. In the period after their arrival, many explored their new hometown by taking pictures of this fascinating metropolis.[7]

This phase of arrival represents an interesting topic and starting point for an analysis: on the one hand the escape from Europe was only a short time ago, but on the other hand the physical arrival on American soil had already begun with the docking of the ship. The transcultural oscillation between the old, familiar, and the abandoned and the new, future, previously unknown country becomes particularly clear in the first visual impressions of the metropolis. The camera served as a medium to articulate a new urban vision and the personal feelings of exile. It is remarkable that also European fashion and portrait photographers focused their first pictures of New York on urban and architectural views.

Although many of these images can be classified as modern street and city photography, there remains a lack of analysis of these images in the context of emigration movements from Europe in the 1930s and 1940s, and in migration and photography studies.[8] It is in this framework that I will put a particular focus on the photographic productions of New York by the Jewish European photographers Josef Breitenbach, Hermann Landshoff, and Lisette Model.[9] These three photographers are connected by their self-taught access to photography, as well as their first experiences of exile in Paris in the 1920s and 1930s. In Paris, Breitenbach had his own portrait studio, Landshoff specialized in fashion photography, and Model studied music and voice before she recommitted herself to studying visual arts and photography. Due to their Jewish descent, they were forced to leave Europe and emigrated from France via different routes to New York in the late 1930s and early 1940s.[10] In 1939, Lisette Model emigrated with her husband, the painter Evsa Model, to New York; Hermann Landshoff and Josef Breitenbach arrived in 1941.[11] After their arrival in New York, they took their first divergent, experimental, and creative approaches to the process of encountering the metropolis through photography. Each of the three emigrants photographed first impressions and encounters with the metropolis in a unique artistic language, utilizing different techniques and compositions.[12] In this essay I therefore want to discuss the significance of these first pictures of Landshoff, Breitenbach, and Model in the context of exile, migration, and photography studies. Can photography serve as a visual medium for ameliorating exilic experiences and approaching new homelands and cultural encounters? To what extent do these first pictures of artist émigrés negotiate personal emotions and cultural exchanges? What image of the metropolis do these photographs convey? Building on Vilém Flusser's analyses of the creativity of exile and Marie Louise Pratt's concept of contact zones, my paper will analyze in a second step if the first pictures can be examined as creative results of their emigration within urban and cultural contact zones.[13]

We New Yorkers: Josef Breitenbach's experimental skyline visions

In 1942, Breitenbach made a photogram-photomontage titled *We New Yorkers* (Fig. 2). Two skyscrapers were photographed at night and combined with a colorful diagram of the human nervous system. The diagram is represented in red and refers to the blood circulation system of veins and arteries. The bright red color in the foreground contrasts with the darkened city and appears like a red signal of an electric light sign or billboard. At first glance, this photogram perhaps seems peculiar and unapproachable. Breitenbach made this photogram during his first year in New York.[14] It symbolizes the symbiotic and mutual relationships between the city and its inhabitants. Breitenbach refers to the vibrant life in the city, where people move in the labyrinth of skyscrapers while the mechanisms of the city allow them a dynamic and vivacious life. The picture illustrates the atmosphere of New

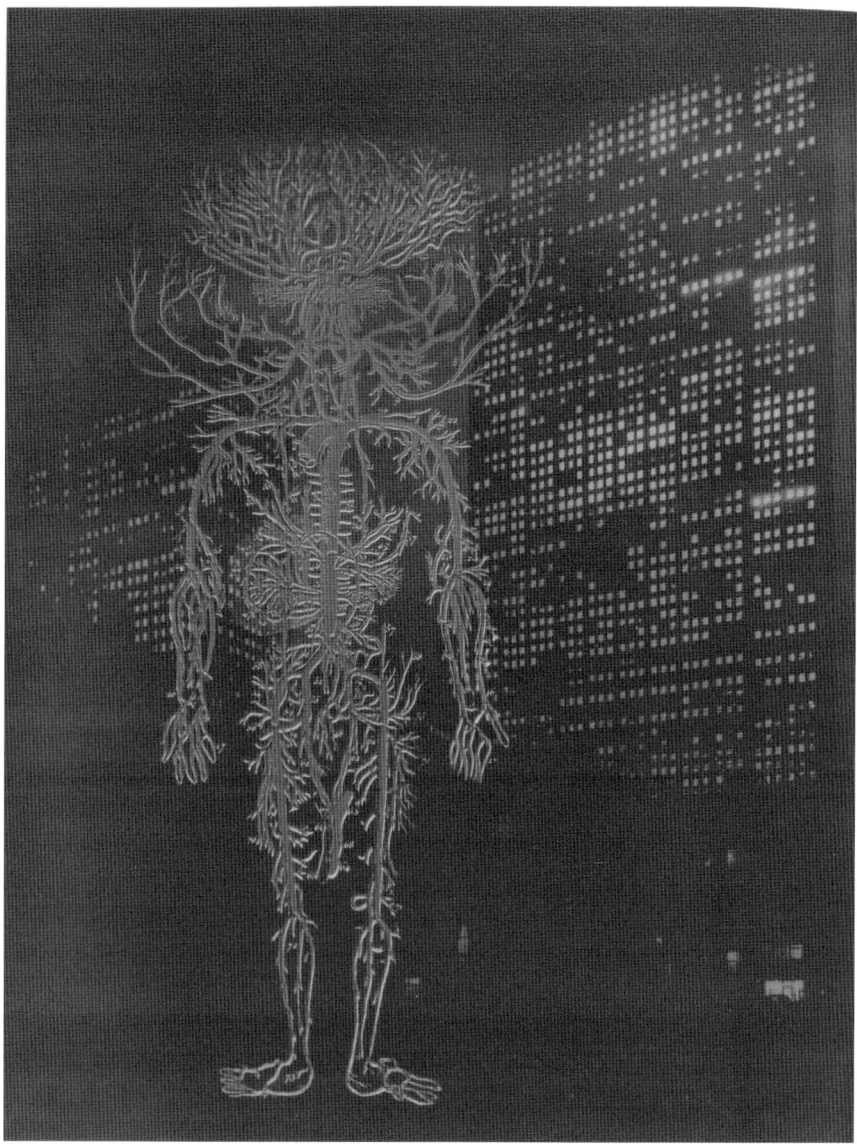

Figure 2: Josef Breitenbach, *We New Yorkers*, 1942, 38.4 × 30.5 cm (Plate 10, p. 336). inv.-no. FM 96/3-33 © The Josef and Yaye Breitenbach Charitable Foundation, Courtesy of the Munich City Museum.

York, which probably overwhelmed and impressed the photographer upon his arrival. Instead of crowded streets, he shows blood circulation, which generally represents human life. The key to this photomontage lies in the title and the word *We*. It indicates that Breitenbach already felt settled in New York in the first year

Figure 3: Josef Breitenbach, *Victory Day Parade*, New York, 1945, 35.3 × 28 cm. inv.-no. FM 93/346-6 © The Josef and Yaye Breitenbach Charitable Foundation, Courtesy of the Munich City Museum.

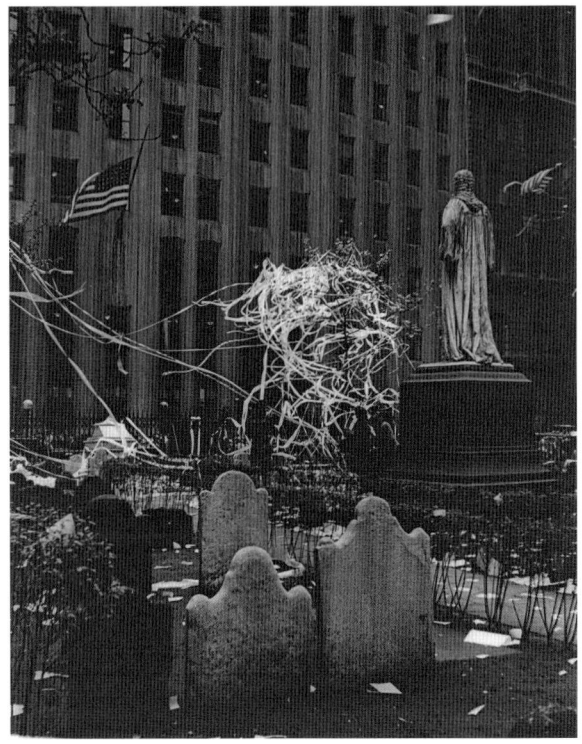

after his emigration—and consequently saw himself as an American. Instead of speaking of a certain group such as *The New Yorkers*, Breitenbach underlines his affiliation with the city through the word *We*.[15] Therefore, the picture can be read as a manifestation of his readiness to identify with the metropolis of New York and with American society. At the same time, the image also reproduces the impression of anxiety by losing the individuality in the anonymity of the city. "Surrounded by night, the skyscrapers take on a disquieting presence. Man, facing these, appears highly vulnerable. He is skinned alive, so to speak, disrobed of his individual identity, reduced to a mere network of lines."[16]

In addition to *We New Yorkers,* further photographs of the artist's first years in the metropolis exist, which also show complex experimental perspectives on his new home and can be read as a reference to surrealism. During his time in Paris, Breitenbach had contact with Surrealist artists and photographers (such as Man Ray) and was able to collect and implement inspirations for his own photographic work.[17] On May 8, 1945, he took several images on the occasion of the Victory in Europe Day (V-E Day).[18] On the same day, the photographer Alfred Eisenstaedt also created a series of images of cheering and kissing people in Times Square; Breitenbach, however, stayed away from the crowded avenues and turned his attention to the traces of the festivities amidst the skyscrapers from a city graveyard (Fig. 3). A guidebook of the Trinity Church describes that the cemetery is one of the few places in central Manhattan that retains the original and historic character of old New York: "Here in fair weather the office workers come at noon to rest in the green and sunlight of God's Acre. Strangers to the city stroll about the paths trying to identify the great names of the past."[19] Breitenbach thus stood at a historical site in American history and referred to this fact by integrating the national flag and the statue into the image motif. Due to the combination with the waving paper flags and ticket ribbons, this photograph has a dynamic moment as well as an aesthetic quality.[20] The photo theorist Kelly George wrote that "even if the image is realistic in the sense that the scene is not manipulated or constructed, it can be classified as surrealistic."[21] In Breitenbach's image, as in much surrealistic photography mostly constructed by photograms, the paper strips of light buzz weightlessly across the paper. This impression is reinforced by the choice of the remarkable location. By using photographic techniques or collage-like compositions of several elements (as in *We New Yorkers*), different levels of reality and multilayered experimental perspectives on the cityscapes of New York arise in one of Breitenbach's first pictures. Characterizing both of Breitenbach's photographs is a lack of people captured in the city views; rather, the artist represents them in symbolic forms through diagrams and surrealist techniques.

Going with the flow: movement and dynamics in Lisette Model's *Running Legs*

The network of European emigrated photographers also included Lisette Model, who arrived in New York in 1938, and who was a colleague of Breitenbach at the New School of Social Research as of 1951.[22] Lisette Model was also struck by her new home and the vibrant urban life in the city. This fascination can be seen in two series created in the first years after her emigration. Until 1939, Model explored the city and photographed urban shop windows in a modernist aesthetic. The photographs produced for the series *Reflections* were taken either inside or outside of shop windows and reflected the comings and goings of passersby as well as the architecture of the skyscrapers and shops. The result is a multilayered picture in which the window display and the street scenes reflect and represent the complex urban life that overwhelmed her. Simultaneously, the inside and outside of this dynamic street scene becomes visible to the viewer in an entangled palimpsest. One can feel the fascination for the wide avenues, skyscrapers, billboards, and shop windows where the pedestrians pass by. In contrast to the window displays of the photographer Eugène Atget or Bernice Abbot, Model sought a creative and artistic image. She deliberately works with different levels of reality and experiments with light, shadows, angles, and perspectives, depending on which objects are more or less pronounced. In her series *Reflections*, the viewer and the observed passersby flow together into one image, whereby the gaze can be directed from inside to outside or vice versa. The images are also reminiscent of a collage of photographs, which "were all on the same plane, showing the bustle and the commercial activity, and at the same time the grandeur and the chaos of the city."[23]

After her emigration, Model started a second series that also articulates these experimental and creative ways of seeing and her first impressions of this metropolis. From 1940 on, for at least two years, she followed the hectic and dynamic life of the newly experienced city with great perseverance and consistency in a series named *Running Legs* (Fig. 4). In close-up pictures, the photographer focused her camera on the passersby. Instead of a full portrait, she decided to take only the view of the running legs. In these pictures, we can see high heels, shoes of business men, and groups or individuals rushing by as quickly as possible. The dynamic moments are also captured in the blurred and fuzzy photographic technique. The cropping of the subjects as well as the blurring evokes a dynamic movement extending beyond the edge of the photograph.[24] The series of photographs has a cinematographic rhythm and gesture to the anonymous and crowded life of the metropolis, which expressed Model's own anxieties about New York urban life. In this context, it is important to explain the artist's photographic technique and camera type. Model used a Rolleiflex camera, which hangs in front of the upper body.[25] To frame a picture, the photographer uses the finder on the top of the camera. Therefore, Model must have been very flexible and mobile to capture the running legs and must have held her camera in a very unique position—perhaps squatting on the edge of the sidewalk next to a building. It is remarkable how the photographs were taken, and the process also feels somewhat mysterious as nobody appears to have noticed her actions—again underlining the anonymity of the big city. Consequently, Model has visually not only captured the perceived dynamics of the street, but also operated dynamically herself in active photographic gestures behind the camera as well as in movements such as stooping, bowing, and lowering her gaze.

For Model it was crucial, she explained in an interview, "that a photograph must be a product of the present, not of the past. It must refer to everything that holds meaning for us in life at this time."[26] For her, the camera was therefore "an instrument for detection: it shows us not only what we know, but also explores new aspects of a world in constant change." In the context of exile, which can also be read as a state of liberated existence, these images also reflect moments of the fugitive, the unstable, and the overwhelming.[27] Thus, Model used patterns that can also be transferred to life immediately after the arrival in the new home. In contrast to Breitenbach, who photographed the monumental and architectural framework of the metropolis, Model stood in the midst of the metropolitan, documenting microcosms of New York. Model's special and unusual point of view also aroused great interest among American photo experts.[28] Finally, through the contact and

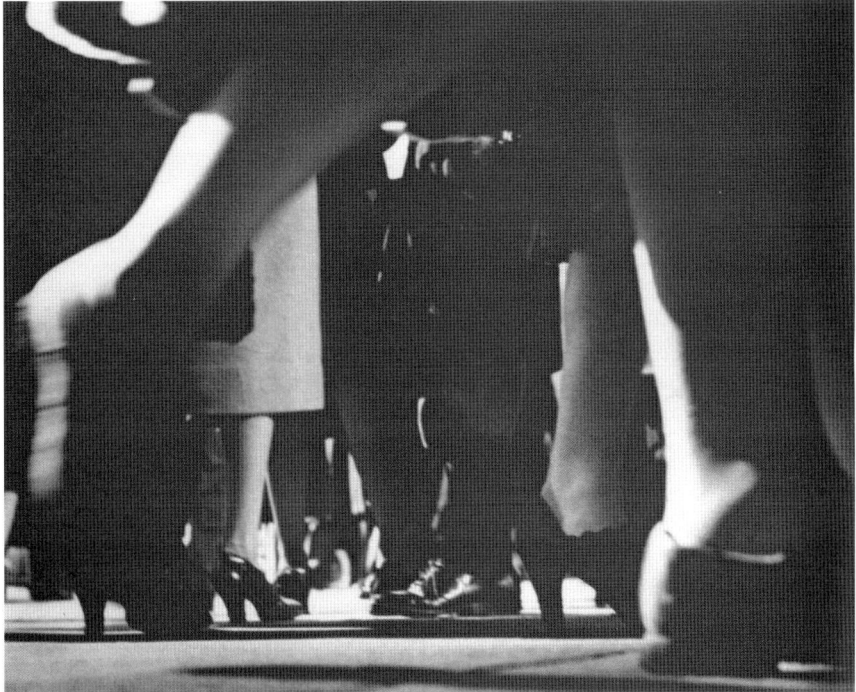

Figure 4: Lisette Model, *Running Legs*, New York, 1940, 81 × 101.6 cm. © The Lisette Model Foundation, Inc. (1983). Used by permission.

help of the art director Alexey Brodovitch, an image of the *Running Legs* series was published in *Harper's Bazaar*.[29]

Day or night? The infrared photographs of Hermann Landshoff

Hermann Landshoff is also connected with the previous two photographers by a similar emigration route to New York.[30] Likewise, Hermann Landshoff wrote about this important moment of arriving securely in New York in his autobiography: "Great desire to pass the Statue of Liberty at the entrance to New York Harbor. It has once again become a living symbol for many inhabitants of the Old World, something concrete, a lifestyle."[31] Because he was unable to immediately find work as a fashion photographer, he dedicated himself to documenting urban architecture in his first months of exile in New York, creating photographic portraits of the city. Although he limited his work to the glamorous side of New York and its impressive high-rise architecture, he also explored the city with a creative way of seeing. In his archive, I found three pictures taken during his first year in New York. With their high black-and-white contrast and detailed clear depth of field, these pictures differ from Landshoff's later works. In one picture, the edges on the right and left side are framed by two high-rise buildings (Fig. 5). The middle is framed by the cityscape and a cloudy sky. By broaching the two buildings at the top and the side, Landshoff evoked and emphasized the impressive height of these monuments, which extend beyond the picture. The artist wasn't standing in the middle of nowhere or on the outskirts of the city, but in the center of Manhattan. The building on the right side is St. Patrick's Cathedral, and the building on the left side is probably Rockefeller Center. He took this picture from a slightly raised perspective, perhaps standing on a rooftop terrace. This very dense and heterogeneous picture is underlaid by the special technique of infrared photography, a complex photographic process in which infrared-sensitive recording material and a special filter are used.[32] Through this technological feature, the film, which is normally sensitive to visible light, can block the visible light spectrum with the filter, making possible a new way of seeing. The artist and photographer Raoul Hausmann explains that

> a photographer [must] be different, more comprehensive and more specialized at the same time than before. He has to get to know many things and materials in their effect on the photochemical layers. […] Here, above all, the photographer has to learn: the best means of representation is the detailed contrast range.[33]

In addition to application in science and medicine, this photographic technique is also used for cityscapes. Because of the special filter and the red light, disturbing effects such as fog and haze can be converted into a detailed, clear picture. This example of Landshoff's first picture and urban vision can be seen as a very good result of this infrared process. The photo also meets the criteria described by Hausmann for a high-contrast image that also achieves a graphic character through backlighting. It can be claimed that Landshoff not only experimented with cutting-edge technologies but also evoked a new way of urban seeing in this new home and a different perspective to visualize the fascinating skyscrapers. The "new" New Yorker Hermann Landshoff opted for a photographic process through which he could feel his new hometown in a different way. He tried to emphasize the vertical architecture of the metropolis while focusing on the ambivalence between modern and historical buildings. It seems interesting that Landshoff used infrared technology only in his first pictures in New York. In this respect, the terms of arrival and experiment should be considered interrelated.

During his first two years in his new home, Landshoff took pictures not only street scenes but also portraits, which originated in private settings. Until now, these portraits have received little attention in art, photography, and exile studies and represent a little-recognized research topic. This area also includes the extensive portrait series

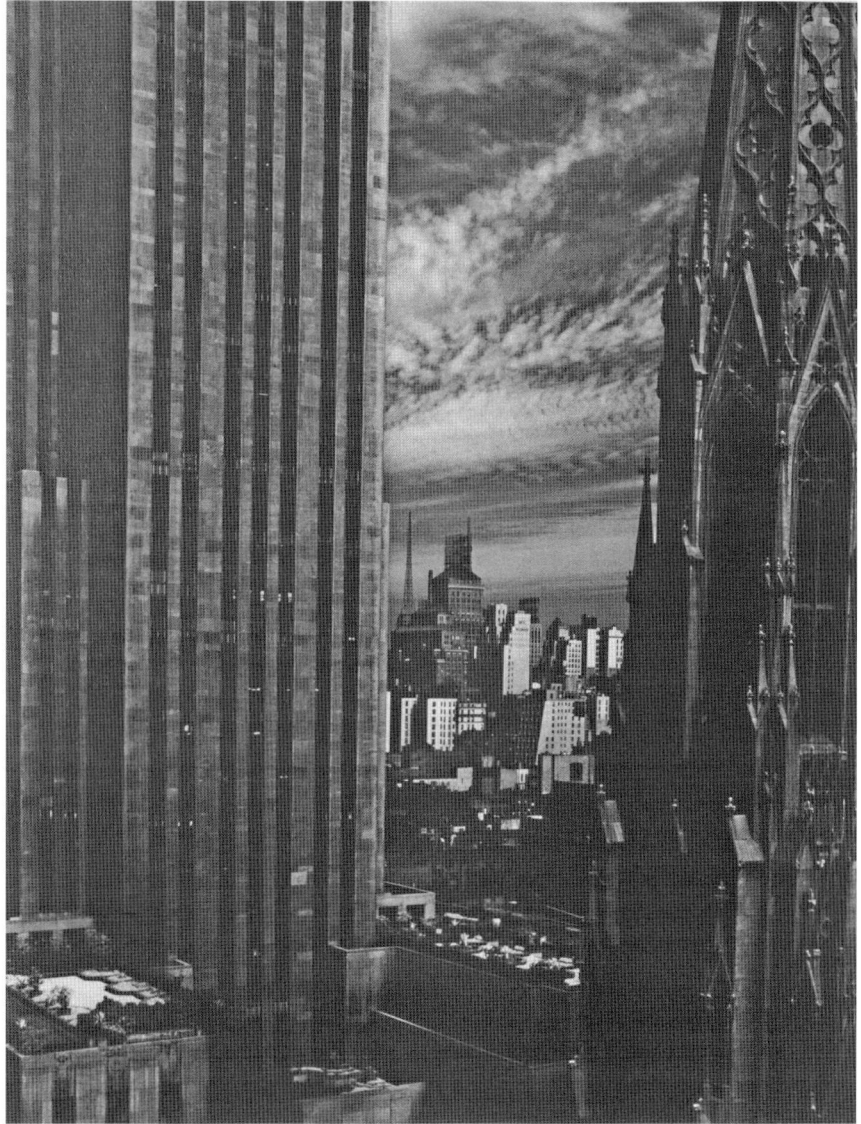

Figure 5: Hermann Landshoff, *New York*, 1941, 29.4 × 24.2 cm (Plate 11, p. 337). inv.no. FM-2012/200.99 © bpk, Münchner Stadtmuseum, Sammlung Fotografie, Archiv Landshoff.

of various predominantly European exiled artists who, after emigrating, attempted to reestablish themselves in the New York art scene and to get in touch with American colleagues. In 1942, Landshoff created a photo series of the exiled Surrealist art scene in New York. He took two group portraits and several individual portraits in Peggy Guggenheim's house, which was a meeting point for the Surrealist circle.[34]

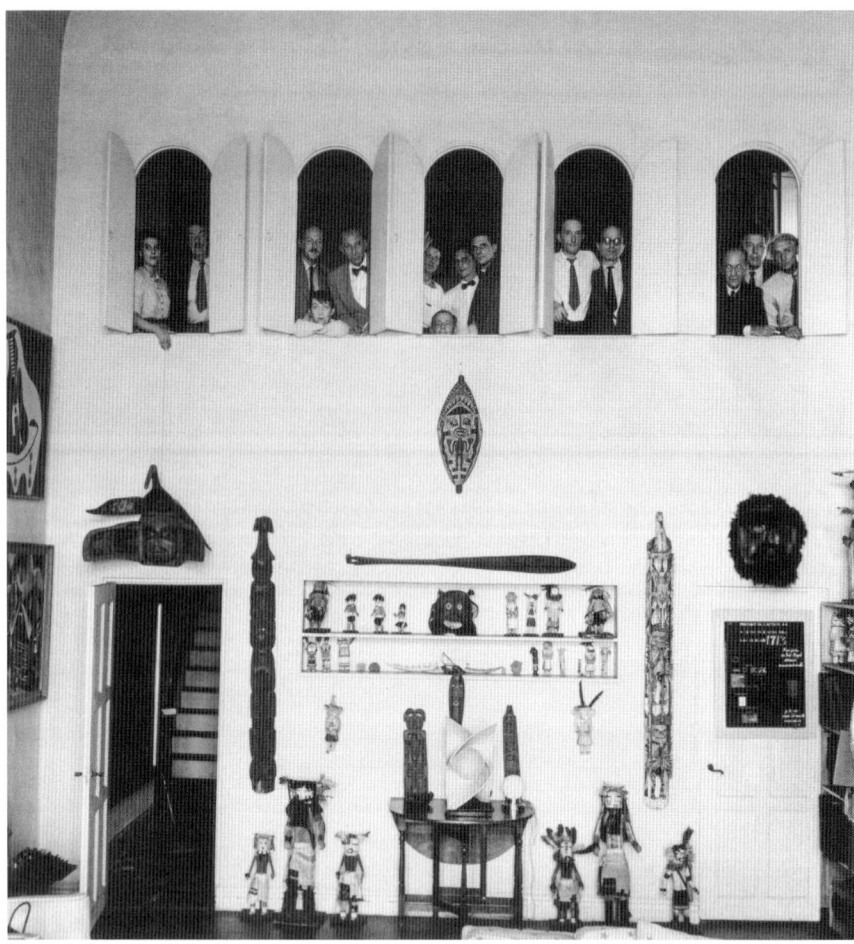

Figure 6: Hermann Landshoff, *Die Surrealisten in den Balkonfenstern im Haus von Peggy Guggenheim*, New York, 1942. inv. no. FM-2012/200.191 © bpk, Münchner Stadtmuseum, Sammlung Fotografie, Archiv Landshoff.

In one of these group portraits, Landshoff chose a staged arrangement in which the space and the dimensions of size also includes Peggy Guggenheim's convoluted collection of art objects, masks, and paintings (Fig. 6). The members of the Surrealist community are poised on the gallery in the balcony windows, looking straight into Landshoff's camera, Landshoff standing in the living room below. From left to right, we see Leonora Carrington, Fernand Léger, John Ferren, Berenice Abbot, Amédée Ozenfant, Peggy Guggenheim, Frederick Kiesler, Jimmy Ernst (Max Ernst's son from his first marriage), Stanley William Hayter, Marcel Duchamp, Kurt Seligmann, Piet Mondrian, André Breton, and Max Ernst. Surrounded by artifacts and collected masks from Africa and North America, the creative art scene of the Surrealists is positioned above. They are standing more or less above the art and give the image of a lofty and pseudo-spiritual touch. With the exception of Guggenheim, John Ferren, and Berenice Abbot, this photograph shows only European emigrants who had recently arrived in their new American home—the metropolis of New York. But even Ferren, Guggenheim, and Abbot were familiar with Europe, as they themselves had lived on the continent for many years: Abbot lived in Berlin from 1921 to 1929, and had later lived in Paris, where she worked as an assistant to the photographer Man Ray and had even portrayed numerous intellectuals of the Parisian art and culture scene of the 1920s.[35] Thanks to Peggy Guggenheim, Abbot opened her first studio in Paris in 1927. Guggenheim also spent the 1920s and 1930s in Paris, where she had close contact with famous artists such as Man Ray and the Surrealists. Because of her Jewish descent, she fled to New York in 1941 with her complete art collection.[36]

Apart from the two prominent group portraits attesting to the Surrealists' meeting in New York, other Landshoff recordings made in Peggy Guggenheim's townhouse testify to the community connection, such as portraits of Max Ernst or Leonora Carrington.[37] In the following years, Landshoff not only portrayed emigrated artists and creative networks but also photographers.[38] All images share common traits in that the caption refers to the job title and full name of each person. Notably, the subjects were not shot in a photographic studio, but in their personal environments at home or at their places of creative work. Landshoff precisely identifies each individual in a professional setting, thus acknowledging each as an artist.

The infrared photograph and portrait photography of Hermann Landshoff can be seen as a connecting element to his emigration, accompanying the photographer on his life journey from Munich via Paris to New York. It can therefore be assumed that the photographs illustrate his own personal examination of the forced change of location and exile in New York and also depict his attempt to establish himself professionally as well as privately in his new home.[39] The portraits can be read as a testimony and contemporary document of a very close network of emigrated artists in New York exile, and can also be read as the first pictures—the first portraits—of their new home.

Photography as a creative medium in the context of exile

This essay analyzes how European emigrant photographers captured their first visual contacts shortly after their arrival in New York. In the works of Josef Breitenbach, Lisette Model, and Hermann Landshoff in the 1940s, American street photography was subjected to a reinterpretation of the arriving émigrés, which is also seen in the context of their exile experiences. These first pictures are examples of creative and experimental first visual interpretations of the metropolis. Breitenbach, Model, and Landshoff chose their own photographic languages and styles and transferred their visual emotions into artistic images. It is crucial to remember that the experience of displacement and exile as an existential experience of crisis also carries with it the potential of failure and the stagnation of creativity and artistic expression. However, the media philosopher and photo theorist Vilém Flusser suggests a positive assessment of exile and seeks to refute the hypothesis that exile can only be evaluated negatively. In his 1984 essay "Exil und Kreativität," he argues for a more positive revaluation and defines exile as a breeding ground for creative acts, for the new.[40] In his subsequent book *The Freedom of a Migrant* (German version published in 1994), Flusser dedicates a whole chapter to this topic of exile and creativity, in which he views "exile as a challenge of creativity"[41] and clarifies his reasons for this hypothesis. In exile, the émigrés were torn from their accustomed surroundings, customs, and habits, which they had known in their lives before emigration. Exile is, to them, "an ocean of chaotic information," in which "the lack of redundancy does not allow the exile to receive this information."[42] To be able to live in their new homes, the émigrés must first transform the new information into meaningful messages and "must produce data."[43] According to Flusser, processing data is synonymous with creation and therefore the émigrés must be creative.

> One can therefore speak of creation of a dialogue process, in which either an internal or external dialogue takes place. The arrival of expellees in exile evokes external dialogues and a beehive of creativity spontaneously surrounds the expellee. He becomes the catalyst for the synthesis of new information. If, however, he becomes aware that his dignity resides in his rootlessness an inner dialogue develops that consists of an exchange between the information that he brought with him and the ocean of waves of information that wash about him in his exile. At this point he attempts to make creative sense of what he brought with him as well as of the chaos that surrounds him in the present. When such internal and external dialogues resonate with each other, not only the world but the settled inhabitants and expellees as well are transformed creatively.[44]

Flusser argues that the new work in exile is created through creative dialogues, which can be characterized by a "cracking of the self and an opening to the other."[45] These statements can certainly be applied to the examples of Josef Breitenbach, Lisette Model, and Hermann Landshoff presented in this paper. Combining familiar and appropriated photographic techniques, working methods, and genres, these three photographers created new creative and experimental views and articulations of the city in their examination of urban life in exile. In his images *We New Yorkers* (Fig. 2) and *Victory Day Parade* (Fig. 3), Josef Breitenbach refers to surrealism, which he already knew from his years in Paris, although the urban architecture of New York and life in the big city also gave him new photographic impulses. As already demonstrated in her photographs of the beach promenade in Nice, Lisette Model chooses unusual perspectives and cutouts. Like Breitenbach, she visualizes the dynamics and anonymity of big-city life in the excerpts of the passing passersby in *Running Legs* (Fig. 4). Hermann Landshoff, on the other hand, attempts to visualize the parables of modern metropolitan photography and the architectural contrasts in Manhattan between modern and Gothic architecture through the use of infrared technology in his image *New York* (Fig. 5).

In a second step, these first pictures of Breitenbach, Model, and Landshoff can also be analyzed through Mary Louise Pratt's concept of contact zones. Pratt's concept of contact zones is defined as a term "to refer to social spaces where cultures meet, clash, and grapple with each other, often in context of highly asymmetrical relations of power, such as colonialism, slavery, or their aftermaths as they are lived out in many parts of the world today."[46] From a methodological-theoretical point of view, her concept, which originates from the field of postcolonial studies, could be transferred to migration and exile studies. Therefore, the social and urban spaces of emigrants could also be read as contact zones where different cultures, traditions, languages, as well as different artistic and photographic aesthetics, coincide. The photograph of Landshoff showing the gathering of exiled Surrealists at the home of Peggy Guggenheim clearly shows a social contact zone—the contact zone and network of emigrated artists in New York and, at the same time, referring to Flusser, the creative dialogue between the European and American art and art market characterized in the circle around Peggy Guggenheim (Fig. 6). Therefore, Hermann Landshoff, by taking this photograph, was also included in this social, cultural, and intellectual contact zone in exile. Beside networks and social groups as contact zones, which can be experienced through images by émigré photographers, the metropolis itself and urban life can be seen as a contact zone where modern aesthetics, architecture, and the social life were explored and visualized in different modalities. The photographs of Breitenbach, Model, and Landshoff are therefore examples of these varieties of urban contact zones (Figs. 2–5). In contrast to Peggy Guggenheim's home, which can be seen as a more private contact zone, the streets and architecture of New York City can be interpreted as a public contact zone, in which the exile life in the metropolis is expressed in photographs. For Breitenbach, Model, and Landshoff, New York as a city was itself a contact zone where they could express their first impressions by using different photographic techniques, cameras, and aesthetic modes of view. Consequently, they were also able to transform and manifest parables of metropolitan life such as anonymity, mass accumulation of city crowds, and the specific architecture of New York. In a broader understanding of the concept of contact zones, the examples of Landshoff, Model, and Breitenbach reveal the close interdependence of European emigrants and their American colleagues; in the 1940s, these European emigrant artists were instrumental in establishing new artistic principles and interacted in new contact zones visualizing these encounters in their first pictures. Additionally, in the years following their arrivals, all three protagonists actively participated in the photography scene in New York both privately and professionally, establishing new photographic contact zones, such as working at the New School for Social Research, for the Photo League, or for magazines such as *Harper's Bazaar*.[47]

In the context of the conference "Photography, Migration and Cultural Encounters in America," this essay will contribute to a broader and new understanding of photography in the field of migration studies: even though forced emigration particularly leads to a turning point in artwork, the exilic career of these three photographers could also instigate new forms and techniques.[48] Above all, the modern urban space and the metropolitan life of New York opened up new creative photographic approaches, which they visualized in their first pictures. To conclude, photography can be read as a visual medium that émigrés could access without language barriers and problems of understanding as they were far away from their homeland; photography is also both linked to exile and articulates the artists' own artistic ideas. Photographer Andreas Feininger, who emigrated to New York in 1939, describes this as follows in his essay *A Philosophy of Photography*: "Photography – the language of vision – is my medium. Bridging the barriers of speech and alphabet, it is understood by everybody anywhere, making it the ideal means of universal communication, each picture a self-contained statement, short, precise and true."[49] Nevertheless, it should be pointed out that not all emigrated photographers could quickly reestablish themselves in the professional field in their exile in New York. They could not always manage to prevail against the competition and start a productive career in their new home. In other cases, due to financial problems, they had to earn money in other areas or often their partners were the main earners. Finally, it should be emphasized that the work and life of many emigrants, apart from the photographic canon, is still inadequately researched.[50]

Notes

1. In addition to the reportage on Ellis Island, from 1929 to 1932, Salomon spent several months in New York and the United States. For example, he was the first photographer who was allowed to take pictures in the White House and the Supreme Court in Washington, DC (see digitized photos in the estate of Erich Salomon, Berlinische

Gallerie, Berlin). During the years of the Weimar Republic, he was considered one of the most famous photographers, who repeatedly succeeded in capturing well-known personalities from politics and society in unobserved moments. See *Erich Salomon. "Mit Frack und Linse durch die Politik und Gesellschaft." Photographien 1928–1938*, eds. Janos Frecot et al. (Berlin: Berlinische Galerie, 2004), catalogue of an exhibition at Berlinische Galerie. Berlin.

2. Anonymous, "Die Gefangenen der Weltkrise. Bei den unerwünschten Einwanderern und Deportierten auf Ellis Island im Hafen von New York," in *Berliner Illustrirte Zeitung*, vol. 41, no. 20 (May 22, 1932), 630; Barry Moreno, *Images of America. Ellis Island* (Charleston: Arcadia Publishing).

3. Roland H. Bayor, *Encountering Ellis Island. How European Immigrants Entered America* (Baltimore: Johns Hopkins University Press 2014), 22ff.

4. Salomon, who was Jewish, fled Germany for the Netherlands in 1932 and continued to work as a freelance photojournalist, traveling in England, France, and Switzerland until the Nazis occupied Holland in 1940. In 1943, he was imprisoned and deported; he died at Auschwitz in 1944.

5. For further publications on New York as an arrival city and emigration destination, see Claus Dieter-Krohn, "Vereinigte Staaten von Amerika," in Claus Dieter-Krohn (ed.), *Handbuch der deutschsprachigen Emigration 1933–1945* (Darmstadt: Wissenschaftliche Buchgesellschaft, 1998), 446–466; Michael Winkler, "Metropole New York," in Claus Dieter-Krohn et al. (eds.), *Exilforschung. Ein internationales Jahrbuch. Metropolen des Exils*, Vol. 20 (Munich: Edition text + kritik, 2002), 178–198. For publications in the context of exile and photography, see Claus-Dieter Krohn et al., *Exilforschung. Ein internationales Jahrbuch, Film und Fotografie*, Vol. 21 (Munich: Edition text + kritik, 2003); Hanno Loewy, "Fotografie," in Dan Diner et al. (eds.), *Enzyklopädie jüdischer Geschichte und Kultur, Band Co–Ha 2* (Stuttgart: J. B. Metzler, 2011), 362; Sybil Milton, "The Refugee Photographers, 1933–1945," in Helmut F. Pfanner (ed.), *Kulturelle Wechselbeziehungen im Exil – Exile across Cultures* (Bonn: Bouvier, 1986), symposium on German and Austrian Exile Literature at the University of New Hampshire March 7–March 10, 1985, Bonn 1986, 279–293; Irme Schaber, "Fotografie," in Claus Dieter-Krohn et al. (eds.), *Handbuch der deutschsprachigen Emigration 1933–1945* (Darmstadt: Wissenschaftliche Buchgesellschaft, 1998), 970–983, here 978.

6. Erwin Blumenfeld, *Eye to I. The Autobiography of a Photographer. Erwin Blumenfeld* (London: Thames & Hudson 1999), 233. This edition of his autobiography accompanies photographs taken at various stages of Blumenfeld's emigration, such as a still life with self-portrait in Paris, and a view through the slats of blinds on the New York skyline in 1939; see 229, 351. In 1922 Blumenfeld opened his leather goods shop, the Fox Leather Company, in the Kalverstraat in Amsterdam; the company failed in 1935. During this time, he taught himself photography. Deciding to become a professional photographer, he moved to Paris in 1936, where his images were published in mag-

azines such as *Vogue*. After the outbreak of WWII, he was placed in an internment camp. In 1941, he was able to emigrate to the United States, where he lived in a flat at the Hotel des Artistes (67th street) and shared a studio with the emigrated photographer Martin Munkácsi.

7. Photographers who emigrated to New York included, for example, Alfred Eisenstaedt, Andreas Feininger, Martin Munkácsi, Ilse Bing, Erwin Blumenfeld, and André Kertész. See *Und sie haben Deutschland verlassen ... müssen. Fotografen und ihre Bilder 1928–1997*, ed. Klaus Honnef (Bonn: Rheinisches Landesmuseum Bonn, 1997), catalogue of an exhibition at Rheinisches Landesmuseum Bonn, Bonn 1997. Many of these photographers found work in the field of photojournalism, as well as in fashion and portrait photography.

8. For photography in the context of the city of New York, see: Quentin Bajac, et al., *Photography at MoMA: 1920–1960* (New York: Museum of Modern Art, 2016); Max Kozloff (ed.), *New York Capital of Photography* (New York: The Jewish Museum, 2002), catalogue of an exhibition at The Jewish Museum, New York 2002; Ortrud Westheider et al. (ed.), *New York Photography 1890–1950. Von Stieglitz bis Man Ray* (Hamburg: Bucerius Kunst Forum, 2012), catalogue of an exhibition at Bucerius Kunst Forum, Hamburg 2012; Jane Livingstone, *The New York School Photographs 1936–1963* (New York: Stewart, Tabori & Chang, 1992).

9. This article is based on research by the author and is part of her dissertation project on New York as an exilic photographic city within the ERC Consolidator Grant "Relocating Modernism: Global Metropolises, Modern Art and Exile (METROMOD)" at the LMU Munich (2017–2022), www.metromod.net.

10. It is not clear if Breitenbach, Landshoff, and Model knew each other in Paris. See: Larisa Dryansky (ed.), *Josef Breitenbach, 1896–1984. Une photographie impure* (Paris: Musée Nicéphore Niépce, 2001), catalogue of an exhibition at Musée Niépce de Chalon-sur-Saône, Paris 2001; Monika Faber et al. (eds.), *Lisette Model. Fotografien 1934–1960* (Vienna: Kunsthalle Vienna, 2000), catalogue of an exhibition at Kunsthalle Vienna, Vienna 2000, 12; Ulrich Pohlmann: "I owe everything to Landshoff", in Ulrich Pohlmann et al. (eds.), *Hermann Landshoff. Portrait, Mode, Architektur. Retrospektive 1930–1970*, (Munich: Stadtmuseum München, 2013), catalogue of an exhibition at Münchner Stadtmuseum – Sammlung Fotografie, Munich 2013, 15–45.

11. Lisette married Evsa Model, a Jewish Nicéphore Painter of Russian origin, in 1937 in Paris. See Marianne Le Pommeré, *Evsa Model. Peintre Américan* (Paris: Éditions Norma, 2010).

12. After their ship passages from France to New York, each of these photographers could restart,—although each in a different way—their careers as photographers. Landshoff continued after a short break to take fashion photographs for well-known magazines such as *Harper's Bazaar*. Breitenbach succeeded in opening his own photo studio near Central Park and gave lectures at the New School for Social Research, where Lisette

Model was his colleague. Besides teaching at the New School and the Photo League, Model also worked for magazines and was very well connected in the American photography scene.

13. Vilém Flusser, "Exil und Kreativität," in *Spuren – Zeitschrift für Kunst und Gesellschaft*, 7, (Dec./Jan. 1984–1985), 5–9; Mary Louise Pratt, "Arts of the Contact Zone," in *Profession* (1991), 33–40.

14. Kelly George, "Josef Breitenbach," in *Und sie haben Deutschland verlassen ... müssen*, 23; Imke Wartenberg: "Die Straße neu gesehen," in *New York Photography 1890–1950*, 234f.

15. The image, and Breitenbach's attribution to American society, can be interpreted as an alternative to Hannah Arendt's reflections as an emigrant. In 1943, she published the article "We Refugees," in which she wrote about the political self-understanding of the terms refugee, emigrant, and exile in the context of their own Jewish exile experiences. Hannah Arendt, "We Refugees," *Menorah Journal*, 31, no. 1 (1943), 69–77.

16. *Josef Breitenbach, 1896–1984. Une photographie impure*, 101.

17. See Ludger Derenthal, "Paris 1933–1941. Porträts und Experimente," in T.O. Immisch et al. (eds.), *Josef Breitenbach. Photographien zum 100. Geburtstag* (Munich: Staatliche Galerie Moritzburg, 2001), catalogue of an exhibition at Staatliche Galerie Moritzburg Saale, Munich 1996, 76–83; Keith Holz and Wolfgang Schopf, *Im Auge des Exils: Josef Breitenbach und die Freie Deutsche Kultur in Paris 1933–1944* (Berlin: Aufbau Verlag, 2001), 138.

18. The Victory in Europe Day (V-E Day) denotes the end of WWII in Europe on May 8, 1945.

19. Corporation of Trinity Church (ed.), *A Guide Book to Trinity Church and the Parish of Trinity Church in the City of New York* (New York: Corporation of Trinity Church 1944/1950), 53ff., here 54.

20. Quite similar shots exist from the emigrated photographer Robert Haas, who also took an image of the festivities from of his window and on the streets of New York together with photographer and friend Trude Fleischmann. See Anton Holzer et al. (eds.), *Robert Haas. Der Blick auf zwei Welten* (Berlin: Wien Museum, 2016) catalogue of an exhibition at Wien Museum 2016, 176ff.

21. Kelly George, "New York 1941–1984," in T.O. Immisch et al. (eds.), *Josef Breitenbach. Photographien zum 100. Geburtstag*, 120. English translation (original German quote: "Auch wenn das Bild in dem Sinne realistisch ist, daß die Szene nicht manipuliert oder konstruiert ist, kann man es als surrealistisch klassifizieren").

22. Josef Breitenbach was employed at the New School from 1949 to 1975. See George, "New York 1941–1984," 125f. As a liberal institution, the New School was an important professional hub for European exiles in the arts and sciences. See Claus-Dieter Krohn, *Intellectuals in exile: refugee scholars and the New School for Social Research* (Amherst: University of Massachusetts Press, 1993).

23. Christina Zelich (ed.), *Lisette Model* (Madrid: Fundación Mapfre, 2009), catalogue of an exhibition at the Fundación Mapfre, Madrid, 2009, 19. Model started her professional carrier in the studio of the photographer Florence Henri in Paris, where she also came in contact with the stylistic techniques of the Surrealists and the Bauhaus.

24. Monika Faber et al. (eds.), *Lisette Model. Fotografien 1934–1960*, 24.

25. Since 1929, the medium format twin lens reflex camera, Rolleiflex, which was also equipped with a roll of film, was available in Europe. During the 1930s, it was a popular user-friendly reportage camera for many photographers. See Walther Heering, *The Golden book of the Rollfleix* (Harzburg: Heering-Verlag, 1936); Fritz Henle, *Fritz Henle's Guide to Rollei Photography* (London: Thames & Hudson, 1956).

26. Lisette Model, "Pictures as Art. Instructor Defines Creative Photography As Scientific Eye That Captures Life," *The New York Times*, December 9, 1951, 143.

27. See Stephanie Barron, "European artists in exile," in Stephanie Barron et al. (eds.), *Exile + emigrés. The flight of European artists from Hitler* (New York: Los Angeles County Museum of Art 1997), catalogue of an exhibition at Los Angeles County Museum of Art 1997, Los Angeles 1997, 11–29; Sabine Eckmann, "Exil und Modernismus: Theoretische und methodische Überlegungen zum künstlerischen Exil der 1930er- und 1940er-Jahre," in Burcu Dogramaci (ed.), *Migration und künstlerische Produktion. Aktuelle Perspektiven* (Bielefeld: Transcript Press, 2013), 23–42; Megan R. Luke, "The trace of transfer," in Frauke V. Josenhans (ed.), *Artists in Exile. Expressions of Loss and Hope* (New Haven: Yale University Art Gallery, 2017), catalogue of an exhibition at Yale University Art Gallery, New Haven 2017, 129–141.

28. From 1941, the photographs of Lisette Model were shown in exhibitions at MoMA. See George Steeves (ed.), *Lisette Model. A Performance in Photography* (Halifax: Mount Saint Vincent University Art Gallery, 2011), catalogue of an exhibition at Mount Saint Vincent University Art Gallery, Halifax 2011, 23ff.

29. Alexey Brodovitch also emigrated to New York in 1934 and worked as the art director for the magazine *Harper's Bazaar*, which received a new design under his direction. See Kerry William Purcell, *Alexey Brodovitch* (New York: PRESS, 2002); Livingston, *The New York School Photographs*, 289–295.

30. T.O. Immisch et al. (eds.), *Joseph Breitenbach. Photographien zum 100. Geburtstag*, 210.

31. Hermann Landshoff, *Autograph* (n.p.: unpublished, 1939/1949), 327. Located in the estate of Hermann Landshoff in the Photography Collection at the Munich City Museum. Original German: "Große Sehnsucht, die Freiheitsstatue am Eingang des New Yorker Hafens zu passieren. Sie ist von neuem für viele Bewohner der Alten Welt zum lebendigen Sinnbild erwacht, zu etwas Konkreten, zu einem Lebensstil."

32. According to Ulrich Pohlmann, the director of the Photography Collection at the Munich City Museum, the infrared photography technique could be verified by restorative examinations. For a detailed explanation of infrared photography, see Eastman Kodak Company (ed.), *Applied infrared photography* (Rochester: Eastman Kodak

Co, 1987); Joseph Paduano, *The Art of infrared photography: a comprehensive guide to the use of black & white infrared film* (Amherst: Amherst Media, 1995). In the American photography magazine *Popular Photography*, there are also more articles about the technology and practice of infrared photography in the 1940s. Therefore, when Landshoff arrived in New York, this photographic process was not an unknown technique in America; it's possible that the existing practice may have even have inspired him. See *Popular Photography*, 3, no. 1 (July 1939), 30f; *Popular Photography*, 6, no. 5 (May 1940), 24f, 99–103; *Popular Photography*, 12, no. 5 (May 1943), 30f, 82f; *Popular Photography* 21, no. 3 (September 1947), 59f, 145–149.

33. Raoul Hausmann, *Fotografisches Sehen. Schriften zur Photographie 1921–1968* (Paderborn: Wilhelm Fink, 2016), 395. The English translation of Hausmann's original German quote is by the author (original quote: "Photograph anders, umfänglicher und spezieller zugleich geschult sein [muss] als bisher. Er muss viele Dinge und Materialien in ihrer Wirkung auf die photochemischen Schichten kennen lernen […] Hier vor allem hat der Photograph zu lernen: das beste Mittel der Darstellung ist der detailreiche Kontrastbereich"). Raoul Hausmann wrote his own book on infrared photography, which was not published during his lifetime. In 1939, he transferred the rights to László Moholy-Nagy, hoping to establish an institute for infrared photography at the School of Design in Chicago. However, the plans, as well as the emigration, failed, see Bernd Stiegler, "Nachwort. Fotografisches Sehen," in Raoul Hausmann, *Fotografisches Sehen. Schriften zur Photographie 1921–1968* (Paderborn: Wilhelm Fink, 2016), 509–540, here 540.

34. Ulrich Pohlmann et al. (eds.), *Hermann Landshoff. Portrait, Mode, Architektur. Retrospektive 1930–1970*, 73ff.

35. Gaëlle Morel, "New York-Paris-New York. The photographic Modernism of Berenice Abbott", in *Berenice Abbott (1898–1991)*, ed. Gaëlle Morel et al. (New Haven: Jeu de Paume de Paris, 2012), catalogue of an exhibition at Jeu de Paume de Paris, Ryerson Image Center at the Art Gallery of Ontario, 2012, 10–52.

36. Peggy Guggenheim, *Confessions of an Art Addict* (London: André Deutsch, 1960), 95–137. The dates of Hermann Landshoff's individual and group portraits coincide with the opening of Peggy Guggenheim's gallery museum Art of this Century in the fall of 1942.

37. Ulrich Pohlmann et al. (eds.), *Hermann Landshoff. Portrait, Mode, Architektur. Retrospektive 1930–1970*, 76ff.

38. Ulrich Pohlmann et al. (eds.), *Hermann Landshoff. Portrait, Mode, Architektur. Retrospektive 1930–1970*, 137–169.

39. Franziska Dunkel, "Hermann Landshoff – Karrierebrüche eines Photographen," in *Zu Unrecht Vergessen. Künstler in Munich des 19. und 20. Jahrhunderts,* Präsidenten und Direktorium der Bayerischen Akademie der Schönen Künste (ed.), (Göttingen: Wallstein Verlag, 2009), 105–123.

40. Flusser, "Exil und Kreativität," 9.

41. Vilém Flusser, *The Freedom of the Migrant: Objections to Nationalism*, trans. Kenneth Kronenber (Urbana/Chicago/Springfield: University of Illinois Press, [1994] 2003), 81–87, here 81.

42. Flusser, *The Freedom of the Migrant*, 81.

43. Flusser, *The Freedom of the Migrant*, 81.

44. Flusser, *The Freedom of the Migrant*, 86.

45. Flusser, "Exil und Kreativität," 9 (English Translation by the author of the original quote: "ein Aufknacken des ,Selbst' und ein Öffnen hin zum anderen")

46. Pratt, "Arts of the Contact Zone," 34.

47. Hermann Landshoff worked as a fashion photographer at *Harper's Bazaar, Junior Bazaar*, and *Mademoiselle*. Lisette Model and Josef Breitenbach also executed commissioned works for these magazines. All three protagonists also achieved artistic recognition in exhibitions at Helen Gee's Limelight Gallery and the Museum of Modern Art, for example, in 1944 in the exhibition *Art in Progress*. See Ulrich Pohlmann et al. (eds.), *Hermann Landshoff*, 15–47; Livingston, *The New York School Photographs*, 298–302; *New York Photography*, 53–61.

48. Burcu Dogramaci (ed.), *Netzwerke des Exils. Künstlerische Verflechtungen, Austausch und Patronage nach 1933* (Berlin: Gebr. Mann Verlag, 2011), 14.

49. Andreas Feininger, *A Philosophy of Photography* (n.p.: unpublished, 1992), Andreas Feininger Archive, Center for Creative Photography, The University of Arizona Library, AG 53:13.

50. Some indications of the lack of research on émigré photographers can be found, for example, in the publications of Holzer, *Robert Haas;* Dieter-Krohn, *Exilforschung;* Milton, *The Refugee Photographers* as well as in the exhibition catalogues *Artists in Exile. Expressions of Loss and Hope; Exiles + émigrés;* and *Und sie haben Deutschland verlassen müssen.*

Migrating Images of War and Dislocation

From War Zone to Contact Zone and from Photography to Photomontage

Aleksandra Idzior[1]

Adolf Hitler's ascendancy to power in 1933, and Germany's invasion of Poland on September 1, 1939, led to the outbreak of World War II, which gave rise to unprecedented forced displacements, deportations, expulsions, and mass evacuations of millions of peoples. Compelled into migratory routes, they were forced to relocate, carrying with them the memories of families left behind in the homeplace. Seeking safe ground, migrants from Europe traveled with limited personal possessions holding on to few objects, including photographs. The photographic medium has played an important role in recording the human crossing of geographical, cultural, and national borders. As observed by Hong Zeng, exile is prefigured in photography, which functions as "emblem of exile" because every photograph is "a reservoir of the destroyed past," which represents a "nostalgia for dying culture."[2] At the same time, escalation of military conflict, including its impact on civilians in the ever-growing theaters of war, was widely documented on camera.

Teresa Żarnower, a Polish artist born into an assimilated Jewish family, led a life marked by war and dislocation. The story of her life in exile is representative of an emigrant, who became an immigrant, then a war refugee. She was one of the many émigrés to move across different geographical, national, and political environments before settling in the United States in 1943. However, for Żarnower, exile was not only a mental and physical state but also a catalyst for creativity in imaginative utilization of photographs for political ends. To continue her artistic practice as a war refugee, she had to overcome a great many additional obstacles. While adapting to often changing circumstances, she needed to seek networks for securing art commissions and new audiences. At the same time, the artist had not only to obtain material for her works but also to generate energy to create them.

Żarnower's art reminds us how modern Western culture, in the words of Edward Said, "is in large part the work of exiles, émigrés, refugees."[3] Scholarly attention has often focused on the unprecedented impact on the American art world by male exiled artists.[4] However, women immigrant artists have been often overlooked.[5] To recover one such story, I concentrate on Żarnower's migration and her photomontages published in New York in 1942. The entire series was included in a booklet, with personal accounts by a Polish socialist activist, Zygmunt Zaremba, of the siege of Warsaw entitled *Obrona Warszawy: lud polski w obronie stolicy (wrzesień, 1939 roku)* [The defense of Warsaw: people of Poland in defense of their capital (September 1939)] (Fig. 1). Recognizing the artist's constant relocations, I investigate how migration and the war impacted Żarnower's oeuvre, while taking into account a number of photographs made by an American photojournalist, Julien Bryan, which, in turn, the artist used as "building blocks" to construct her photomontages. However, for the purpose of this study, I am concerned with more than Żarnower's production of a series of photomontages by appropriating photographic images as a means of creating overtly political art. I reevaluate the photographic images of war and dislocation gathered, cut, and rearranged by the artist through the framework of contact zone and translation, keeping in mind that the meeting of cultures and exchange of objects never occurs in spaces void of power.

Because of transcultural displacement during World War II, America became a site of multicultural artistic ferment and reciprocal cultural influence as well a scene of contradictions, a place of various contact zones. While contact zones, as defined by Mary Louise Pratt, refer to certain regions, they also describe primarily social spaces, or constructs, where different cultures clash, collide, or maintain relationships with each other.[6] According to Pratt, contact zones take into account the ongoing impact of exposure to political violence. Although Pratt originally coined the term in the context of the seventeenth-century Spanish colonial conquest of the New World, this term can be applied to investigate modern wartime and military occupations. The long epoch of political violence during the past century culminated in the Second World War—the brutal conflict par excellence resulting both in forced displacement, deportation, expulsion, mass evacuation, intercontinental migration, horrific ruination, and death. The production and migration of photographic images of war cannot ignore the political conditions of such trajectories.

James Clifford, deriving from Pratt's concept, emphasized multi-directorial processes of cultural borrowing, appropriation, exchanges, and translation aligned by relations of dominance and resistance.[7] Indeed, the process of translation is part and parcel of relocation—after all, moving from one place to another, from a native language to a foreign one, or more than one, as was the case for Żarnower, involves translation. During her exile, the artist moved between places while situated within sites that Emily Apter calls "the translation zones," in which *zone*, constitutes a "broad intellectual topography […] of critical engagement that connects the 'l' and the 'n' of transLation and transNation."[8] Although much can be lost in translation,

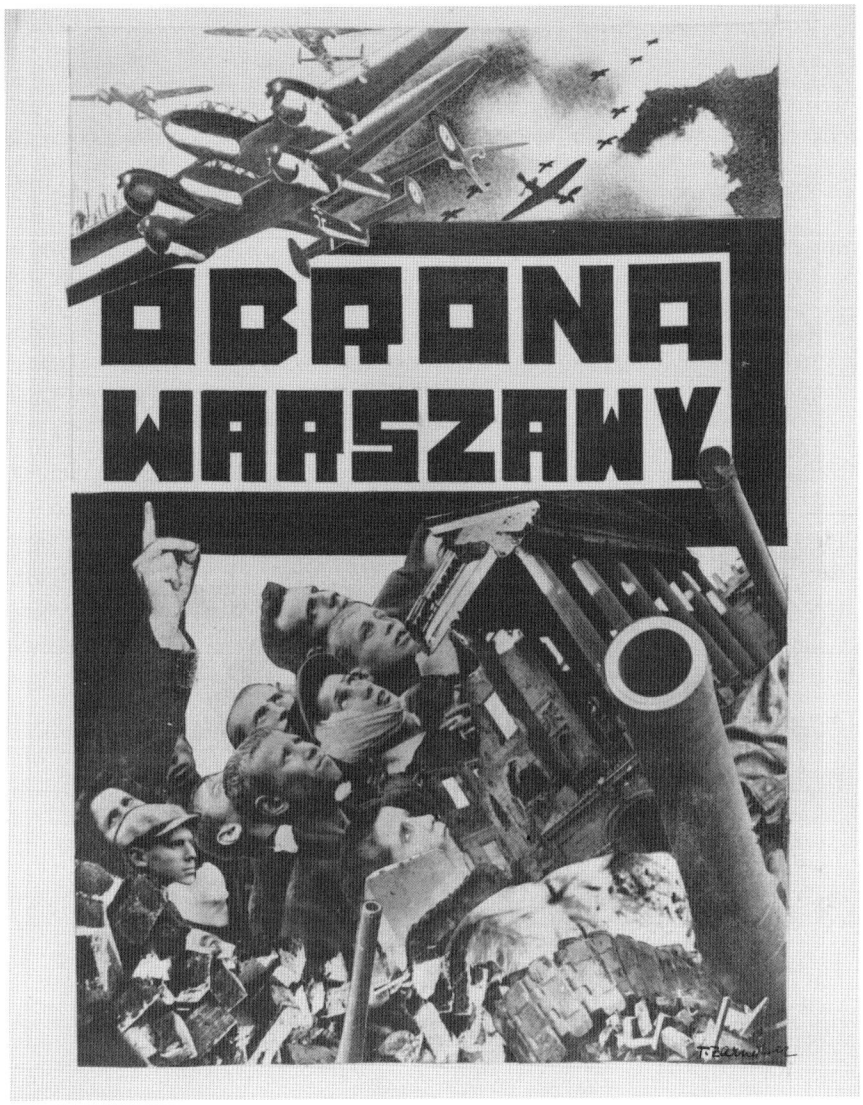

Figure 1: Teresa Żarnower, *Obrona Warszawy: Lud polski w obronie stolicy (wrzesień 1939)* [The Defense of Warsaw: People of Poland in Defense of the Capital (September 1939)], 1942, signed maquette for a front cover with title, photomontage (Plate 12, p. 338). The New York Public Library, New York

as Eva Hoffman has claimed, what, if anything, did the artist gain through the processes of transformed rendition, conversion, and interpretation?[9] When concentrating on Żarnower's exilic experience and art production, we must recognize that, before crossing the Atlantic, she was once an established multimedia artist well recognized for incorporating photographs into her works.

Photography's social and political role

Born in 1897, Żarnower, after graduating in 1920 from the Warsaw School of Fine
Arts, became a pioneer of radical avant-garde art in Poland, linked to the Russian
Constructivism and the Dutch De Stijl movements. Between the wars, the avant-
garde movement as a whole was based on international exchange and communication between artists, constantly eliminating political and national borders while
seeking international contexts. During the 1920s and 1930s, working together with
Mieczysław Szczuka, her artistic collaborator and partner in life, Żarnower, having
left-wing political views, privileged "sztukę utylitarną" [utilitarian art], including
posters, book covers, newspaper layouts, architectural projects, and photomontages
that addressed explicitly sociopolitical issues of the day. Familiar with Marxist ideology via her art, she actively promoted revolutionary ideas. Żarnower's utilization
of photographs in collages, as a visual syntax synonymous with modernity, followed
the model of anti-aestheticism and anti–fine-art model established by the German
Dadaists (John Heartfield, Raoul Hausmann, Max Burchartz, Hannah Höch) and
the Soviet revolutionary artists (El Lissitzky, Aleksandr Rodchenko, Gustav Klutsis).
In both countries, montaged photographs were popular in commercial culture and
as powerful tools vested with political significance. In Europe, the medium of photomontage gained in relevance in the politically charged atmosphere of the 1930s.[10]

 Although during the 1930s and 1940s, photomontage was a popular practice in
Europe and Latin America, in the United States photomontage was rarely a vehicle
for social criticism and examination. As Sally Stein observes, American artists were
typically skeptical, if not outright dismissive, of photomontage before World War
II.[11] When the method was adopted for sociopolitical ends, it was done on a limited
basis. However, in the United States, photomontage was often used in the increasingly sophisticated practice of modern advertising, which made heavy use of photographic material. On the other hand, although modern photojournalism started in
Germany, it was in America that employment of candid photographs in magazines
reached new levels. Soon after the suppression by the Nazis of German photo
magazines, many of the photo magazine editors came to the United States, where
a similar type of photo reporting quickly gained recognition and popularity. The
growing role of photojournalism in the United States would be unthinkable without the contributions of many refugee photo-magazine editors and photographers.

Żarnower's exilic life

Żarnower's expatriation began in 1937 when she decided to leave Poland for Paris.
Ten years earlier, in 1927, she lost her partner, Szczuka, to a mountaineering

accident in the Tatra Mountains. Grief-stricken, she experienced a growing crisis leading to the diminution of her artistic practice. At the same time, the political climate in Poland also encumbered her activity—during the early 1930s, right-wing radicalization must have caused the artist to be doubly isolated and marginalized, as a Jewish Pole and as a communist sympathizer. By the time Żarnower reached Paris, repressions and a sense of dread spread throughout Europe, with fascism in Italy and Spain, Stalin's purges in Moscow, and the Nazis' escalating assault within Germany. There is no record of what Żarnower produced while living in Paris—all her works from this period have perished. We know that soon after the Second World War broke out, her talent and skills as a graphic designer were appreciated by the Government of the Republic of Poland in exile, the legitimate institution established after the fall of Poland, and the ruling body of the structures of the Polish Underground State and its military arm. According to Żarnower, she was "[c]alled upon to collaborate" with the Information and Documentation Bureau under the Department and Ministry of Propaganda of the Polish government-in-exile and "recorded the war in Poland and the tragedy of the nation in a series of photo-montages […] [and] designed the graphics of the upcoming book on Warsaw in ruins."[12] It is through this network that the artist came into contact with photographs documenting atrocities committed by Germany in Poland, which the Polish government-in-exile used for exposing Nazi violence through the press and through diplomatic channels. Most likely, Żarnower was able to preserve some of the material from that project and include it later in *Obrona Warszawy*. Before Paris surrendered to the German army on June 22, 1940, the Polish government-in-exile, for security reasons, destroyed its archive, together with any of Żarnower's works, and evacuated its headquarters to London. Żarnower could not go there, as she did not obtain an entry visa. Aware of potential danger if she remained in Vichy France—as a Jew and as a left-leaning artist—she began her lengthy exile via Madrid, Spain, to Portugal.

The route from Paris to Lisbon was just the beginning of Żarnower's long and taxing escape from war. She reached the Portuguese capital in October 1940. Although Żarnower hoped for a short asylum there, her stay in Lisbon lasted fourteen months. Finally, in December 1941, she received proper documentation to cross the Atlantic. Leaving Europe, Żarnower aimed, as so many emigrants and war refugees before her, for New York. The artist reached Ellis Island on December 16, 1941, just nine days after the Japanese attack on Pearl Harbor, which forced America to enter the war. However, because of a five-day "special inquiry," she did not receive permission to enter. Żarnower then went to Montreal, Canada, arriving there on December 31, 1941, where she hoped for a short stay while applying for American residency. She remained in Montreal for more than seventeen months. Żarnower finally received permission to go to New York and landed there on June 11, 1943.

First in Nazi-occupied Europe, and later in North America, Żarnower knew about the ongoing tragedy in Poland from personal, written, and photographed accounts. She turned to the newest medium to comment on her experiences with powerful anger and artistic talent. Distant from her native country at the outbreak of the war, while working for the Polish government-in-exile, the artist learned from and made use of the ghastly images as a source of ethical reflection and material for her art. Żarnower used photographs from the domain of journalistic or documentary information, retaining their formal attributes: print raster and monochromatic tones. But her interventions—the magnification and multiplication of the images—restored to the depicted events their original tragic character often lost in mass press news.

Migration and photography: speaking of/from exile

For Żarnower, diaspora was a very trying experience. Her own journey, her multiple displacements and constant moving from site to site, from one country to another, and finally crossing the Atlantic, is conveyed by the artist at the outset. The first photomontage *Dni grozy (1)* [Days of terror (1)] (Fig. 2)—of the second edition of *The Defense of Warsaw*—contains a scene that shows large crowds of people who are waiting to board an ocean liner, not unlike the one that brought Żarnower to North America. The artist herself took the route from Lisbon boarding the SS Excalibur, an American passenger cargo liner, which was instrumental in the success of the wartime Emergency Rescue Committee, transporting thousands of refugees from Nazi-occupied Europe to the United States.

The image of a throng of people in front of the ship hovers above the rest of the montaged photographs in a literal and formal sense—at the top of the page and as a stylistic device and extended metaphor—symbolizing the dislocating experience of a refugee. It serves as an epigraph, an overture that opens the story that follows, which is the visualization of the grave fate of those left behind in Warsaw. Placed among the many fragments of photographs showing violated, terrified, and humiliated people amidst total ruin, this picture of people crammed together in an attempt to escape danger by boarding the vessel reveals the only means available to some, including the artist, to flee from the Nazi occupation. Thus, this singular representation of amassed escapees stands for the artist's new identity as a refugee. It is a testimony to Żarnower's own situation beginning in 1937, as a nomad, who traveled from place to place without a permanent home, and who was alienated and constantly positioned on the margins. Indeed, her own war-induced exile takes on the symbolical connotations of the Wandering Jew. Although the journey to North America offered the artist relative safety—which she would not have enjoyed by staying put in Poland, France, or elsewhere in Europe—the exile positioned

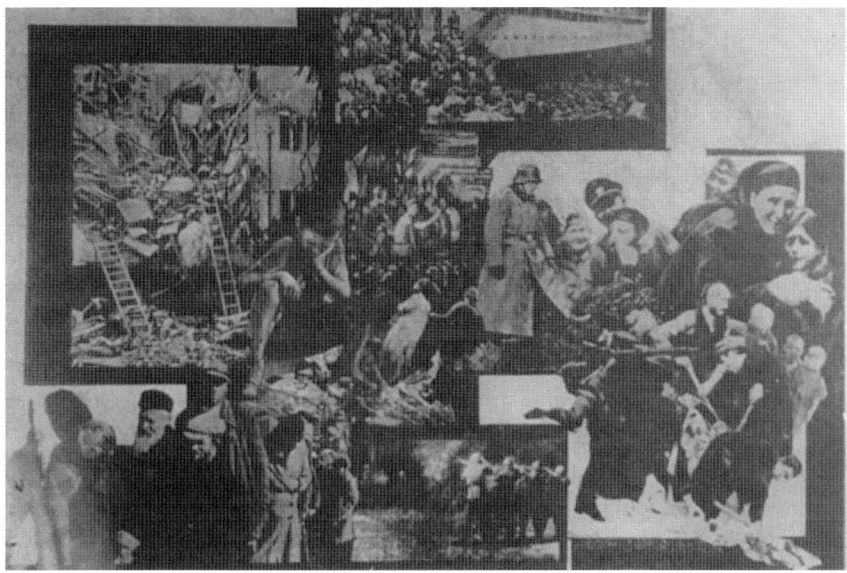

Figure 2: Teresa Żarnower, *Dni grozy (1)* [Days of terror (1)] in *Obrona Warszawy: Lud polski w obronie stolicy (wrzesień 1939)* [The Defense of Warsaw: People of Poland in Defense of the Capital (September 1939)], 1942, photomontage. The New York Public Library, New York

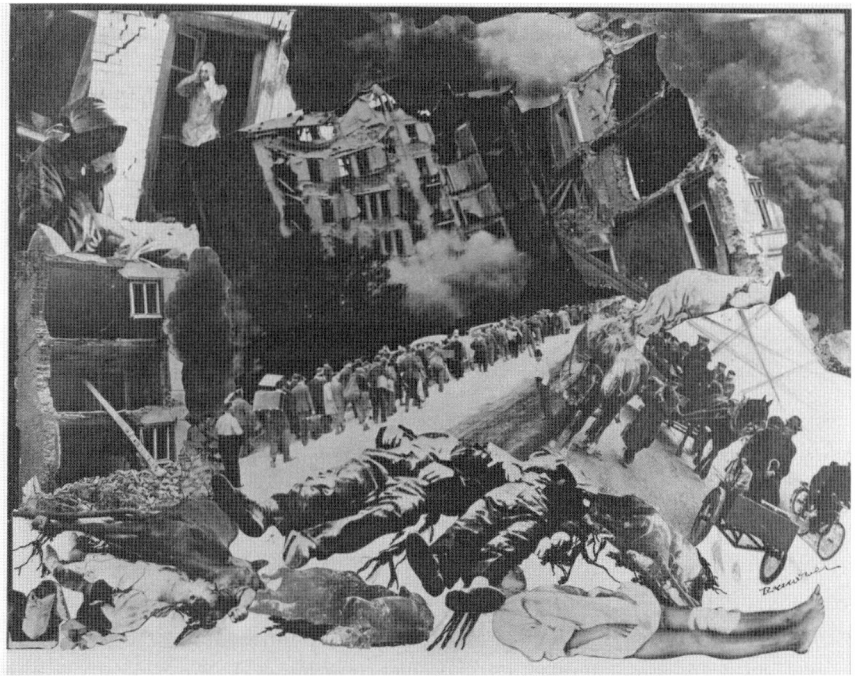

Figure 3: Teresa Żarnower, *Droga śmierci* [The road of death] for *Obrona Warszawy: Lud polski w obronie stolicy (wrzesień 1939)* [The Defense of Warsaw: People of Poland in Defense of the Capital (September 1939)], 1942, signed maquette, photomontage. The New York Public Library, New York

Żarnower at a physical distance not only from, the theater of war, but also from her loved ones. It created a sense of despair and helplessness, and most likely caused a sort of "survival syndrome." Sharing this experience with the majority of refugees, she had lost friends and family.

Within the entire series of photomontages in *The Defense of Warsaw*, there is yet another trace of forced relocation and displacement caused by the war. Two different photographs included in *Droga śmierci* [The road of death] (Fig. 3) show long lines of countless refugees who appear marching in and out of the picture plane as in a circular motion without any respite. The first scene—on the left, with an endless stream of walking people seen from behind—shows Polish civilians fleeing the Germans on the orders of Polish authorities for planned evacuation on September 11. The other picture—on the right, with people walking, riding bicycles, and riding in horse-drawn carts, all moving toward a picture plane—depicts civilians returning to Warsaw on September 25, as the Poles understood that, after September 17, when Stalin's army attacked eastern Poland, they had nowhere to flee to as Germany and the Soviet Union overran the country. These two photos, while conjuring up a perpetual movement with no end in sight, bear witness both to the repetitive relocations of the Polish population in September of 1939, as well as to Żarnower's own peregrinations forced by the war. The artist signed the maquette by placing the initial of her first name, followed by her last name, next to the second photograph, positioning herself in company with the migrating Warsovites.

Photographic documentation of war

Throughout the entire Second World War, photography in Poland became a crucial weapon for the resistance movement, whose aim was to capture on film the devastating effects first of the German invasion and then of the occupation: human and material carnage, arrests and executions, persecution of Poles, and systematic extermination of Jews. In moments of silence, in which victim's lives are brutally taken and their stories cannot be heard, photography can function as a trace of memory by intervening as a witness. Within months of Germany's attack on Poland, large numbers of photographs were taken. Some of them were shot by military photographers, others by photojournalists, freelance reporters, members of the Polish and Jewish underground, anonymous individuals, and, not least, the Nazi propaganda machine and the Nazi "soldier tourists."[13] The functions and use of the pictures were manifold, stretching from secretly taken snapshots to official assignments. Most of the photographers were risking their lives; many of them were killed on the front or inside the war zone. Some of them, however, were lucky enough to complete their task and return home.

When Germany attacked Poland, the United States was holding to its isolationist policy and nonintervention established after World War I. America entered the global conflict only on December 8, 1941, by declaring war on Japan. The experience of the war in the United States was very different from that of populations in Europe and elsewhere. No battles or civilians were killed on the American mainland, though families endured thousands of military casualties. Instead, the distant war was experienced primarily through media and popular culture—often in print form: newspapers, magazines, and books, with some visual information conveyed via newsreels. Thus, the pictorial means by which most people engaged with news about the war were mainly through photography. In April 1942, when *The Defense of Warsaw* was published, the United States was just a few months into the war when the photographs, predominantly portrayed soldiers vigorously and enthusiastically training for battles, were disseminated publicly. Up to 1943, media photographs, newsreels, and posters had uniformly spared American viewers the horrific reality of seeing war casualties, especially their own. Only over time did the increasingly violent sequence of the war's images progress with more prominent displays of death.[14] Still, when Hitler invaded Poland, this information was publicized in America on the first pages of the printed press with, however, only a limited number of photographs. There were just a few foreign photojournalists in Poland, who captured the beginning of the war and the country's consecutive occupation;[15] among them was Julien Bryan, an American photojournalist and documentary filmmaker.

Before World War II, Bryan was known for his travelogues and educational films about mundane life in many countries worldwide.[16] Although he never received formal training as a photographer, Bryan learned the craft during the course of his many travels. In the summer of 1939, he had been working in Western Europe. Upon learning about the invasion of Poland, he decided to travel to Warsaw. By the time he arrived there on September 7, the city was already in ruins, destroyed by heavy shelling and incendiary bombing raids. He then decided to record the events with his three Leica cameras and his two 35mm Bell and Howell Eyemo motion-picture cameras, approaching the story with an eye to the market at home. Bryan was what Susan Sontag identified as a "professional, specialized tourist known as journalist."[17] Credited as the only foreign correspondent at that time in Warsaw, Bryan was in the midst of a war zone for two weeks, witnessing the German *Blitzkrieg*. On September 21, during a brief truce negotiated to allow citizens of neutral countries to leave the city, Bryan relocated via Königsberg in East Prussia back to the United States. Overall, he took hundreds of photographs and shot many reels of film.

Bryan's photographs shot in Warsaw were taken often at eye level or from a higher vantage point reminiscent of the "magisterial gaze," the strategy and attitude that signified the nineteenth-century American expansionism, coupled with the desire to master the land and a national will to power. His elevated stance—standing atop a street barricade or directing his camera down from the window of the American embassy and taking pictures from its roof—allowed him to feel the process "exciting and thrilling,"[18] while the views from above conveyed control and dominance. Bryan's photographs also appear to express an "observational position." He focused on the victims in a series of devastating portraits, some close-up. Many of the photographs were medium-long shots that captured the persons, often in the foreground, in a certain environment, such as the street, a hospital, or a church, most of which were damaged or ruined. He documented people caught by tragedy—some are killed, many are wounded, and most are in shock. Finding themselves in new horrific situation, the citizens of Warsaw try to carry on. A number of images feature the devastation of the city fabric with private scenes of reclaiming normalcy among the destroyed houses. Other photographs make visible the brutality he witnessed.

Migration of photographs: from photographs to photomontage

After arriving home, Bryan provided the American audience with the devastating effects the Luftwaffe brought upon Warsaw and its citizens. He shared his experience through various illustrated magazines and traveling lectures.[19] Later, in early 1940, he published a book called *Siege*, and RKO Radio Pictures used some of his film footage to produce a ten-minute newsreel *Siege of Warsaw*.[20] From early September 1939 throughout 1940, a number of Bryan's photographs of besieged Warsaw also appeared in various European publications.[21] Many of the photographs Bryan published in the United States were explained by captions—Walter Benjamin noted that, in the age of mass-produced photographic imagery, it had become obligatory for photographs to be accompanied by explanatory text[22]—however, when the same pictures circulated in Europe, at times the written information was partial or even misleading, as the unstable, changing nature of the photographs' identification was the norm during the war, not the exception.[23]

One snapshot made by Bryan, from a sequence of nine, was extensively disseminated from the early days of the war. It is of a young Polish girl, Kazimiera Kostewicz-Mika, in a field, beside the blood-stained body of her fourteen-year-old sister Anna (the identification of this child Bryan would be able to gain only in 1958 when he visited Poland to find the people he had documented in 1939).[24] Bryan caught the girl's utter despair and horror, as she had never before seen death and could not understand why her sibling did not respond to her. Although, as Errol Morris pointed out, "it is impossible to capture the horror of war in a single image,"[25] this was one of the most widely publicized photographs to come from the European war

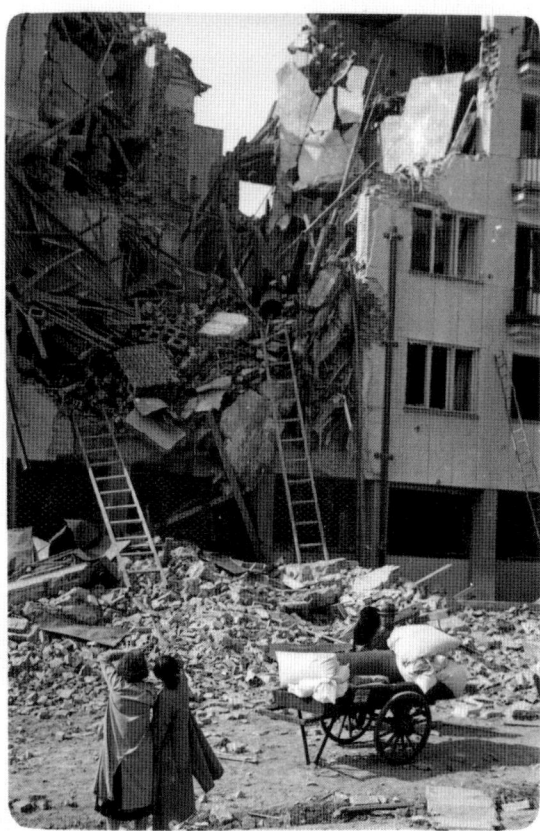

Figure 4: Julien Bryan, *Two Polish women look at the destruction of an apartment building in besieged Warsaw*, 1939, photograph.
US Holocaust Memorial Museum, Washington, DC, gift of Julien Bryan Archive.

zone and belongs to the "iconic" photographs of World War II.[26] When in 1940 the Ministry of Information of the Polish government-in-exile published in Paris *L'Invasion Allemande en Pologne* [The German Invasion of Poland],[27] this photograph— slightly cropped—was placed on its front cover, while on its back there was another picture taken by Bryan, of two women in front of destroyed houses (Fig. 4), the same one that Żarnower, after cutting it, incorporated in her photomontage *Days of terror (1)* (Fig. 2).

The photographs utilized by the artist were of distinct provenance and all of them migrated from the war zone to diverse geopolitical locations, as images do not know boundaries. During the Second World War, photographs migrated widely— they were exchanged, copied, reformatted, cropped, traced, drawn on, annotated, mounted, then remounted, and often published. As mentioned above, the same happened to Bryan's photographs of Warsaw. Looking closely at Żarnower's series of photomontages for *Obrona Warszawy*, we can recognize fragments of many more of Bryan's pictures. Indeed, working on *The Defense of Warsaw*, the Polish artist relied on many shots taken by the American photojournalist, whose works were archived by the Polish government-in-exile. Recognizing some of the images utilized by the artist, it is certain that she had access to photographic sources in possession by the Polish Armed Forces in the west, with whom, as already stated, she had contact in France and for whom she was working producing photomontages during the war.[28]

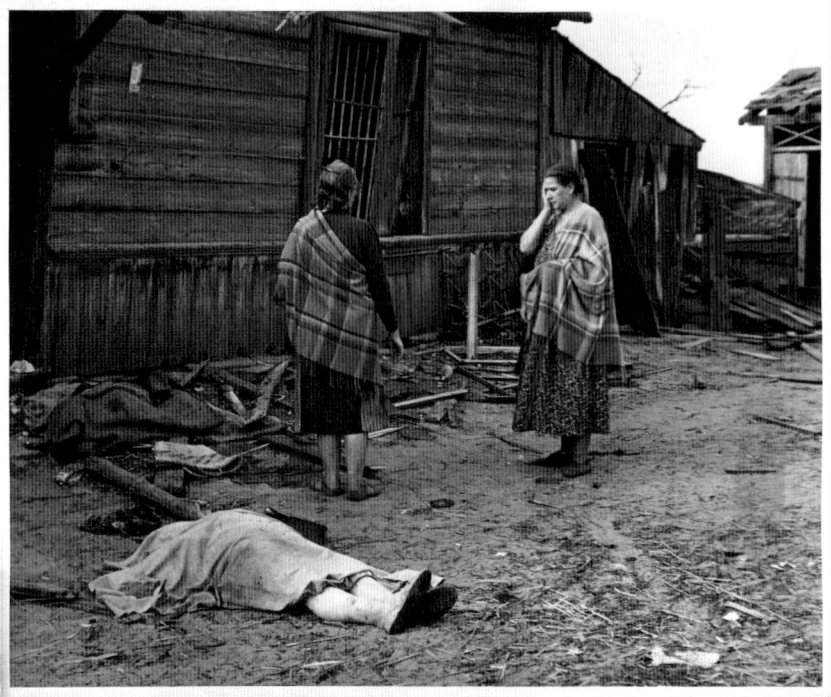

Figure 5: Julien Bryan, *Two Polish women stand horrified after the destruction of their homes by the Germans – in the foreground is the corpse of one of the women killed in the air raid*, 1939, photograph. US Holocaust Memorial Museum, Washington, DC, gift of Julien Bryan Archive.

In a sequel to the previously mentioned *The German Invasion of Poland*, the Polish government-in-exile compiled a collection of contemporary accounts of Nazi crimes committed in Poland between the invasion in September 1939 and the occupation from October 1939 to June 1941, and published, in 1942, *The Black Book of Poland*.[29] Among the photographs included in this 750-page book, a few are, again, Bryan's. Of Bryan's photographs in *The Black Book of Poland*, Żarnower included a fragment of one (Fig. 5)—a detail showing the shrouded body of a dead woman—in *The road of death* (Fig. 3). In the lower foreground of the last photomontage, she also inserted among the dead and injured people a number of dead horses, killed during the German air raids on Warsaw, remains of which the starving population of the city used as a food source during a siege. One of the details chosen by the artist is, once again, a fragment of one of Bryan's photographs, documenting two carcasses lying on a street in Warsaw (Fig. 6).

As already mentioned, in composing her photomontages, Żarnower relied on many other photographs by Bryan. She incorporated a fragment of one twice. When in Warsaw, the American photojournalist took two shots of a nine-year-old

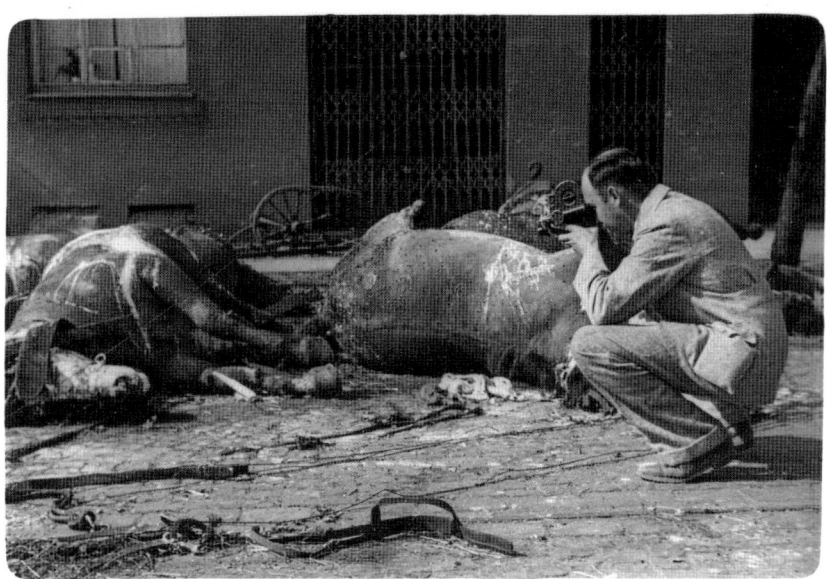

Figure 6: Julien Bryan, *Julien Bryan films dead horses on the streets of besieged Warsaw*, 1939, photograph. US Holocaust Memorial Museum, Washington, DC, gift of Julien Bryan Archive

Ryszard Pajewski among the ruins. In the first photograph, Bryan noticed the boy from some distance before capturing him with his camera. The shot is composed horizontally (Fig. 7), as to include the environment with the remains of a pulverized home, on which the little boy is sitting with his hunched back and lowered head resting on his left hand. The slouched, thin, small body of the young boy, with a pensive expression on his face, embodies a fragile figure bearing world's weight on his tiny shoulders. Despite the boy's small frame, and because of his stillness and concentrated introspection, the scene is monumental. Bryan made another version of the them same scene by arranging it vertically (Fig. 8). In this shot, the photographer came nearer and approached the boy not from the side but frontally. In the second version, the boy occupies the lower-left foreground and is larger and closer to the viewer than in the previous take. The sequence of both images conveys zooming technique and movement, animating the documented moment. Seeing both photographs, we can appreciate Bryan's interest in film.

It is the second image, the same one that ended up in the archives of the Polish government-in-exile in London, of which Żarnower included a fragment two times in *Obrona Warszawy*. For *Days of terror (1)* (Fig. 2), she cut out the boy's figure and placed it at the center of the composition, surrounding it with harrowing scenes such as depiction of ruined homes, acts of execution, and German soldiers humiliating an elderly Jew. This boy is one of many child casualties that Żarnower included in

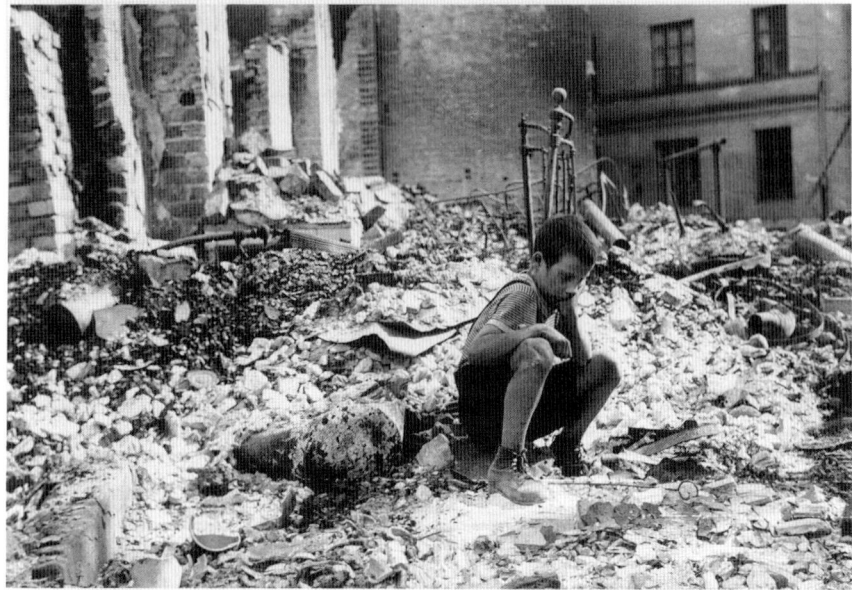

Figure 7: Julien Bryan, *A young boy sits among the ruins of his home in Warsaw after it was destroyed during a German air raid*, 1939, photograph. US Holocaust Memorial Museum, Washington, DC, gift of Julien Bryan Archive.

the series, here, however, he is superimposed over images of victims and aggressors. It seems this sorrowful young boy hovers among the horrific scenes in pensive stupor as the cataclysm around him is too overwhelming. For a second time, the artist included a fragment of the same photograph in the photomontage used as the back cover (Fig. 9). There, in the lower-left foreground, a cropped and enlarged figure of the little boy seems to step out of the entire arrangement by breaking the black line that frames the composition—the well-established device to reach the spectator by breaching the "fourth wall"—and the boy moves forward toward the viewer. The youngster's saddened face is also reinforced twice on this cover. Crossing diagonally through the picture plane, in the upper-right corner, Żarnower placed the lowered faces of two emotionally distressed women, who hold their hands to their cheeks while wiping away their tears, here amplifying another motif employed throughout the series, that of crying women and mothers. The entire composition is layered with dynamic rendition of depth in space. Again, as Bryan created effects of motion and animation with two shots of the boy, likewise Żarnower in her photomontages offered strong, dynamic, and amplified filmic effects, especially of the montage techniques characterizing avant-garde films—the fascination she expressed already in 1923. Indeed, cutting out photographic images and recombining them, a practice as old as photography itself, had acquired a new relevance in the era

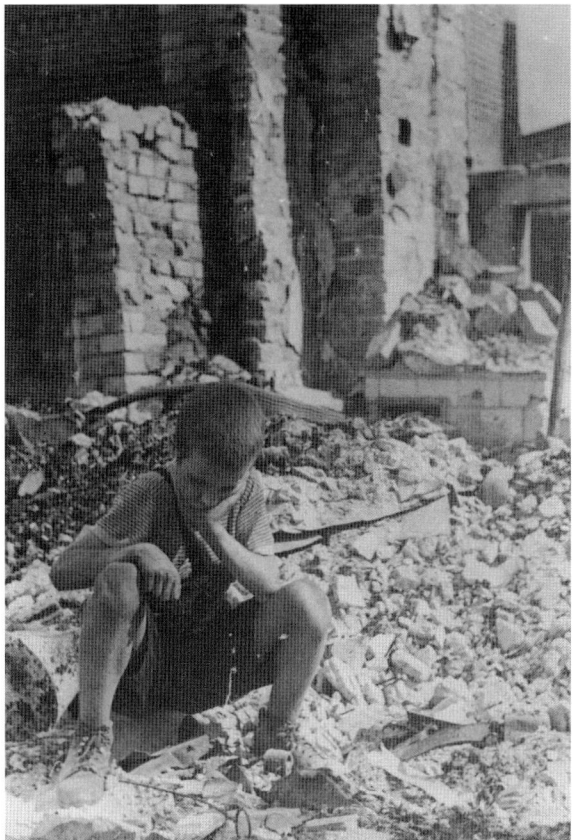

Figure 8: Julien Bryan, *A boy sits among the ruins of his home after it was destroyed during Luftwaffe air raid*, September 1939, Warsaw, Poland, photograph. The Polish Institute and Sikorski Museum in London/ Ośrodek KARTA, Warsaw.

of film and illustrated magazine. Last, but not least, this maquette once again bears in its lower-right corner a discreet artist's signature. Written in black ink, it is placed on the photographic rendition of a desolated, scorched landscape. Żarnower's name, standing in for her, is juxtaposed and connected with the boy in the opposite corner of the closing composition of the entire series. While he is depicted among Warsaw's ruins in Poland, she, through her name, presents herself as occupying a barren piece of land—a *terra incognita*. When *Obrona Warszawy* was published, the grieving artist was in limbo, waiting in Montreal for her American visa. The two figures/ elements of the ensemble, innocent victim in Warsaw and Żarnower in exile, are separated, distanced, and, at the same time, paired together in mourning.

Photomontage, or photographic fragments as resistance

The artist employed photomontage as praxis to construct a political narrative. Her approach was similar to the Dadaists' strategy, who, since the Great War, utilized photomontage not only as anti-art but also as a means to oppose the military conflict in which modern technology was employed for killing. The photomontages executed by the artist during World War II, however, not only acted

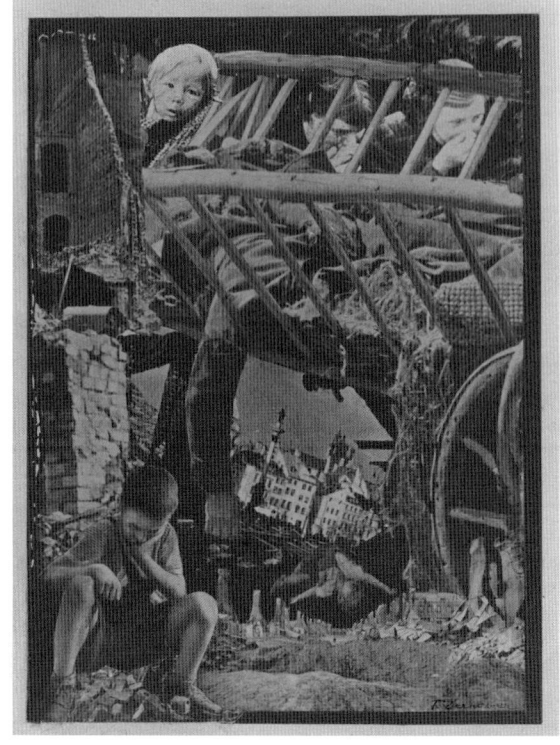

Figure 9: Teresa Żarnower, *Obrona Warszawy: Lud polski w obronie stolicy (wrzesień 1939)* [The Defense of Warsaw: People of Poland in Defense of the Capital (September 1939)], 1942, signed maquette for a back cover, photomontage (Plate 13, p. 339). The New York Public Library, New York

as artistic expression but also were used to change the mimetic illusion of the real into a cognitive problem (not unlike Bertolt Brecht did in his war montages). Montage, according to Georges Didi-Huberman, has the capacity to intensify and transform the impact of the image by bringing together disparate materials into unpredictable juxtapositions. It entails more than just the proper sorting and amassing of the images—it is a creative and critical engagement with each individual photograph. Żarnower, as other artists affected by war, rendered the historical world in such a manner that it became a *"haunting memory, a scourge of imagining."*[30] For Żarnower, photomontage was not so much a medium for self-expression, but rather a method and a tool to direct the viewer's attention to the enormity of the loss and suffering already inflicted on the inhabitants of, first, Poland, the assault of which, by 1942, had continuously escalated.

While the titles of Bryan's documents—his book and the newsreel—underscored siege, or an act of surrounding and blockading of Warsaw by the Germans, and indeed the agency and force of the attackers, Żarnower's title of the entire series of her photomontages (via Zaremba, *The Defense of Warsaw*) stressed resistance and the heroic struggle of Warsaw's inhabitants in defending the invaded capital. At the same time, as effective instruments of protest, her photomontages seem to be a plea for protection and a cry for help for Warsaw and its citizens. Her response to frustration and despair was channeled into the production of the photomontages that represented the other side of the military conflict: the price paid by civilians, the euphemistic "collateral damage," including her own life.

In Żarnower's entire oeuvre, the montaged photographs of the human cost of war and the resulting total ruination project a sense of discomfort and despair so intense as to be almost palpable. The densely collaged images create a sensation of *horror vacui*, or "a fear of emptiness," with packed fragments of photographs that seem to overflow the crowded compositions. She constructed the montaged composition not unlike the composition of the photographs. More than any other medium, photomontage's character and nature depend on the evocative quality of its materials.

The medium allowed the artist to express extreme emotions such as anger, fear, helplessness, and sense of injustice. The instrument—shears, scissors, and/or a knife—enabled her to heighten the affective impact of her chosen imagery, while both masking and highlighting the results of her cutting and pasting. Using photographs and relying on the mimetic nature of the material, she conveyed empathy toward victims and ire against perpetrators. In her project, she acknowledges the power of the fragment as a means of seeing and of recuperation. In this way she manages to render and criticize current political and military phenomena—she makes them visible. In addition, her fragmentary compositions echo the type of experience and manner of perception determined by modernity, which according to Zygmunt Bauman, was one of the conditions of the Holocaust.[31]

Unfortunately, there is not much information about the reception of Żarnower's photomontages during the 1940s and later. In 1944, Irena Piotrowska, writing in English for a Polish publication in New York, in her essay surveying depiction in Polish art throughout the centuries of "Warsaw's fight for freedom," mentions *Obrona Warszawy*, naming Żarnower a "creator of excellent photomontages."[32] We may assume that limited distribution of the booklet played a role in diminished recognition of the artist's project. The fact that the publication was written in Polish language, thus a foreign one for the typical American, would further restrict its reach. In addition, if confronted with the content of Żarnower's works in 1942, audiences in the United States would not have been accustomed to seeing images of victims of conflicts. Finally, those who did see the photomontages may have found it difficult to comprehend the enormity and scale of tragedy, which was represented in fragments.

Mediating affect

The photographic image, from its inception, introduced a radical new proposition about representation by offering an isolated moment captured from the flow of time and events. Photomontage, on the other hand, not unlike drawing, painting, and printmaking, requires prolonged contemplation of the subject and the composition.

Both mediums provided new aesthetics and new ethical considerations. The use of photography in photomontage generates problems other than formal ones, and it is not just the issue of translating one medium into another. When Żarnower's work is compared with Bryan's photographs, there are some similarities, but the differences are more striking. His images published in America by major illustrated magazines had a different function, meaning, and impact than those constructed by the Polish artist. In each publication, Bryan showcased photographs from the war zone on a few pages that were sandwiched between other articles on a constellation of divergent topics that were all embellished with a myriad of pictures. In addition, Bryan's photographs were competing for attention with advertisements of quotidian products and other breaking news akin to capitalist commodity. The artist's photomontages, as a part of the entire booklet *Obrona Warszawy*, are in a company of five photographs of Warsaw by unknown photographers during the siege depicting the wounded city marked by fires and graves.

Although her work had a limited circulation and reach, she aimed at a wide public. These works were not displayed on the gallery walls as unique, private works of art, but as repeatable images on the cover and on the pages of a publication independently produced outside of the mainstream circulation that could be easily reproduced and distributed. They were to be consumed on a very intimate level—by holding the book in one's hands and looking at them closely among the pages with Zaremba's text narrating the story of the defense of Warsaw. The method of display and the process of viewing Żarnower's photomontages were not very different from the way Bryan's photographs were issued to the reading/viewing public; however, the context and the overall format was distinct.

Although Żarnower signed her maquettes, the final published prints do not display her name; she is, however, credited by name on the verso of the title page as the designer of the cover and of the photomontages. On the other hand, authorship of Bryan's photographs published in the American magazines is displayed in multiple ways. First, he is indicated as the author of both the text and the images. Then, many of the published photographs are of Bryan, who is shown equipped with a camera and/or in the process of documenting the besieged city. Finally, the two-part reportage in *Popular Mechanics*, for example, underscores the photographer's significance with the headline, "Cameraman at the Front"; additionally, twelve of the twenty-two pictures included in the reportage depict Bryan. At the same time, only a few of his photographs (eight out of seventy) published in the American illustrated magazines depict a dead person, while Żarnower saturated her project with images of the carnage inflicted on Warsaw. The display of trauma was to disrupt and defy it.

I argue that Żarnower created an alternative to Bryan's optics and offered a more nonnormative practice of seeing and showing war. The artist exposed the viewer the intensely compiled photographs of destruction and death to make a timely and critical judgment on the practices and effects of war. She assaulted the viewer with intense fragments of densely montaged images to mobilize against the ongoing—by then already global—war and the continuous occupation of her native country. The artist wanted the viewers in the United States to recognize their own proximity to the conflict. She used the medium as a way to draw attention to the horror of the war raging overseas.

Bryan's photographs were part of the American publishing industry, and they could not be freed from their institutional background; they were immersed in the politics and ideology of the Franklin Delano Roosevelt government, a larger order that John Taggs calls "a structure of relations of domination and subordination."[33] Żarnower was likewise entangled within specific politics, ideologies, institutional backgrounds, and networks: the Polish Labor Group was a New York publishing agent of the Polish government-in-exile, whose *modus operandi* was to document and disseminate numerous accounts and reports about Nazi persecution and oppression of population in Poland—Poles and Jews—and to mobilize allied foreign governments. The main goal was to be impactful, especially in the United States, to devise an information policy plan for the American public "in order to educate it about Polish war aims, a plan that would make use of various propaganda tactics."[34] The graphic nature and intensity of the fragments of photographs gathered and reassembled by Żarnower was unique in 1942—the first full year of the war for the United States—not only among the publications supported by the Polish government-in-exile; more generally, her photomontages pre-dated grisly depictions of casualties in America during World War II.

From war zone to contact zone

We cannot escape an important observation about the distinction between living through war and witnessing it via the mechanism of photography. As Sharon Sliwinski reminds us, "seeing dead people on the streets is not the same as seeing them in photographs."[35] This reflection concerns not only us—the viewers of Żarnower's photomontages, and we who are currently exposed to a plethora of circulating images of ongoing wars—but also the artist, who was forced to flee war-ravaged Europe before becoming a victim herself. Although Żarnower did not literally witness the scenes represented in her photomontages, the images she incorporated in her project are brought forth and made visible, akin to a testimony given by an observer, acting as an "artistic document" of the Nazi atrocities.[36] This testimony is mediated by memory itself and by the affective force of its transmission. The victims captured in each shot as appropriated by Żarnower present a corporeality constituting a visible evidence of engaged presence of the person with a camera. Actually, it was Bryan, and the other anonymous photographers, who were on the ruined sites with dead bodies around them. It must be emphasized that Żarnower most likely did not know Bryan's name, nor the names of the other photographers, their nationalities, or their backgrounds. Likewise, she was probably not aware who the people in the photographs were, whose images she included in her photomontages. Consequently, the identities of the people in the photographs were also unknown to the viewers. Nonetheless, Żarnower's project went against historical oblivion or political disempowerment.

The Second World War resulted in an unprecedented number of dislocated people and in horrific carnage, but it also facilitated a range of meetings and interactions—direct and indirect, personal and mediated. The conflict indeed created new spaces and opportunities for various encounters of people, ideas, and objects, including photographs. Wartime produced a large number of photographs. Not unlike the migrants, the photographic images moved across time and space crossing geographical and cultural borders; they migrated throughout local, regional, national, and global contexts, becoming themselves a part of a diaspora. The shots selected by the artist documented not only hardship and displacement, experienced by many refuges, but also the ultimate price—life lost during the war. The photographs chosen and arranged by Żarnower, which were meant to document events at the time the pictures were taken, were later transformed by Żarnower into both emblems of memory and objects of art. The artist navigated between "realistic" representations of war by various photographers, including the American photo-reporter, and her own visions of war and dislocation.

Holocaust and trauma

After reaching America in 1943, war haunted Żarnower, and she continued to visually represent the Holocaust by creating subsequent projects, among them another photomontage entitled *Getto warszawskie* [The Warsaw Ghetto], published in 1945 by the *Freie Arbeiter Stimme* [The Free Voice of Labor] in New York.[37] Despite the fact that this photomontage was issued in June of 1945, one month after the official end of war in Europe, there is not a celebratory tone, not even a sense of formal cessation of oppression and violence. Instead, there are faces of victims marked by pain and terror—and again many of them are the faces of women and children, as in *Obrona Warszawy*. In 1945, the occupation of Poland by the Third Reich was just over. It was also more than two years after the beginning of the Warsaw Ghetto uprising (April 19, 1943) and its bloody suppression (May 16, 1943), yet Żarnower continued to confront the victims and their perpetrators. Publishing *The Warsaw*

Ghetto in a Yiddish paper testifies to the need for commemoration and to keep the memory of the Holocaust alive. Perhaps Żarnower and *Freie Arbeiter Stimme* attempted to reproduce the traumatic event as, to use Michael Rothberg's terms, "an object of knowledge," with the purpose of "transform[ing] its readers [and viewers] so that they are forced to acknowledge their relationship to posttraumatic culture."[38]

The following year, Żarnower hoped for a greater chance to make inroads in the emerging American art scene by abandoning photomontage and changing artistic medium. However, regardless of producing paintings and showing them at the Peggy Guggenheim gallery, and despite the backing of Barnett Newman, her work did not sell, nor was it promoted by the critics.[39] Although she had achieved a level of professional acceptance and was appreciated by some members of the avant-garde milieu in America, success never came and she was untouched by wider recognition. Paraphrasing Joseph Brodsky, it seems that America offered Żarnower physical safety but rendered her socially and culturally insignificant.[40]

Searching for and wishing to find a place of respite from war and its cruelty, uprooted Żarnower suffered from isolation and depression. After reaching her desired destination, resolution escaped her. Having moved from one place to another, for many years, Żarnower must have felt increasingly isolated and exhausted. Changing places, countries, and continents, she was required—as many immigrants are—to adjust to a new milieu, yet another language, and different cultural and social customs. Displaced from one site to another, she experienced various adversities, including economic hardship. Indeed, her lengthy peregrination was compounded by numerous and persistent financial difficulties and ceaseless economic misery.

War, its cruelty, and the images that captured it did not leave Żarnower after she arrived in the United States. Atrocities committed by the Germans in Poland seemed to occupy the artist. The subject haunted her and, ever obtrusive, it did not disappear. Once burdened by it, she could not get rid of the images of it. Branded by war, Żarnower continued to visually represent the Holocaust by creating subsequent projects. The subject of diaspora and longing appeared among the titles of her works shown at Peggy Guggenheim's gallery in 1946—*Exile*—and a year later, at the San Francisco Museum of Art—again *Exile*, and *Nostalgic Memory*. Even when Żarnower abandoned photomontages, the photos she appropriated, or rather what they represented, terrified the artist. Żarnower was not able to absorb the Nazi genocide, perhaps because of her relative proximity to the Holocaust or perhaps due to the intensity of experienced loss. The constant mourning never left her, consuming time and creative energy until the artist could bear it no more. In May of 1949, Żarnower was found dead in her apartment. Allegedly, she committed suicide, electing what Hannah Arendt called "negative liberty."[41] In the case of Żarnower, especially poignant is Henryk Grynberg's observation that people who take their own life become refugees *par excellence*.[42] Undeniably, for some, exile offered a new life, a chance for reinvention, and a "land of opportunities" from which many artists drew a renewed energy and inspiration; however, for many, it proved to be intolerable.[43] Zones of contacts and translations where processes of interaction, appropriation, and exchange occur are filled with uneven relations, hierarchies, and anxieties, and they can become, for some displaced people, too overwhelming. As Madelaine Hron observes, "In our age of multiculturalism and globalization, we often prefer to extol the 'difference,' 'hybridity,' and 'mobility' of the nomadic, cosmopolitan hero rather than fixate on the sufferings of the unhappy immigrant."[44] To curb such effects of compassion avoidance, Stanley Cohen suggests getting closer to subjects in pain—by learning more about their stories.[45] Teresa Żarnower deserves attention and recognition for both her creative contribution and for her pain and struggle as a refugee.

Notes

1. This paper stems from my earlier research on Żarnower: Aleksandra Idzior, "Fighting for the Same Cause," in Milada Ślizińska and Andrzej Turowski (eds.), *Teresa Żarnower (1897–1949). An Artist of the End of Utopia* (Łódź: Muzeum Sztuki, 2014), 75–95; "Response to a Catastrophe: Cultural Memory in Teresa Żarnower's Photomontages *The Defense of Warsaw*," in Ślizińska and Turowski, *Teresa Żarnower (1897–1949)*, 111–137. I thank the editors, especially Justin Carville, and reviewers for their careful reading of the manuscript and thoughtful comments.

2. Hong Zeng, *The Semiotics of Exile in Literature* (New York: Palgrave MacMillan, 2020), 2–3, 7, 10.

3. Edward W. Said, "Reflections on Exile," *Reflections on Exile and Other Literary and Cultural Essays* (London: Penguin Books, 2001), 173.

4. Kobena Mercer (ed.), *Exiles, Diasporas, and Strangers* (Cambridge: MIT Press, 2008); Frauke V. Josenhans (ed.), *Artists in Exile: Expressions of Loss and Hope*, exh. cat. (New Haven: Yale University Art Gallery and Yale University Press, 2017).

5. Linda Nochlin "Art and the Conditions of Exile: Men/Women, Emigration/Expatriation," *Poetics Today*, 17:3 (Fall 1996), 327.

6. Mary Louise Pratt, *Imperial Eyes. Travel Writing and Transculturation* (London: Routledge, 2007 [1992]), 7.

7. James Clifford, *Routes: Travel and Translation in the Late Twentieth Century* (Cambridge: Harvard University Press, 1997.

8. Emily Apter, *The Translation Zone: A New Comparative Literature* (Princeton: Princeton University Press, 2006), 5.

9. Eva Hoffman, *Lost in Translation: A Life in a New Language* (New York: E.P. Dutton, 1989). For analyses of translations between visual art mediums, see Mieke Bal and Joanne Moora (eds.), "Acts of Translation," Special Issue *Journal of Visual Culture*, 6, No. 1 (2007).

10. David Evans and Sylvia Gohl, *Photomontage: A Political Weapon* (London: Gordon Fraser, 1986).

11. Sally Stein, "'Good Fences Make Good Neighbors': American Resistance to Photo-montage Between the Wars," in Matthew Teitelbaum (ed.), *Montage and Modern Life, 1919–1942* (Cambridge: MIT Press, 1992), 133–134.

12. "Teresa Żarnower CV (16 January 1941)," trans. Krystyna Mazur, in Turowski, *Teresa Żarnower (1897–1949)*, 14–15. Unfortunately, conducted searches have failed to yield any results—no works or projects have been found, nor have any references been located.

13. As pointed out by Janina Struk, in occupied Poland, Poles and Jews were not allowed to own cameras, buy film, or take photographs. Taking pictures became a clandestine, underground task. See *Private Pictures: Soldiers' Inside View of War* (London/New York: I. B. Tauris, 2011), 79.

14. James J. Kimble, "Spectral Soldiers: Domestic Propaganda, Visual Culture, and Images of Death on the World War II Home Front," *Rhetoric and Public Affairs* 19, No. 4 (Winter 2016), 535–569.

15. The photojournalists and documentary filmmakers who recorded the break of war in Poland were: from the United Kingdom, Clare Hollingworth (1911–2017), Douglas Slocombe (1913–2016), and Eric Calcraft (active 1930s–1940s); from Germany, Hugo Jaeger (1900–1970), the personal photographer of Hitler, who shot color photographs; and from the United States, Harrison Forman (1904–1978), Herbert Kline (1910–1999), and Julien Bryan (1899–1974). Eric Calcraft, who worked for Planet News, sent from Warsaw to the United States three photographs with captions that were published as "Civilian Suffering Shown Behind Lines in Poland," *Lancaster New Era* (September 16, 1939), 5. Harrison Forman published a text, "Filming the Blitzkrieg," including nine photographs; see *Travel* magazine 74, No. 2 (December 1939), 18–22, 49. Forman also captured in Warsaw the "Crowds of Polish people cheering after Britain and France declared war on Germany on September the 3rd, 1939"; however, this image, as with most of his ninety photographs shot in Poland in September 1939, was never published.

16. For Bryan's biographical information, see "Julien Bryan," United States Holocaust Memorial Museum, https://encyclopedia.ushmm.org/content/en/article/julien-bryan; and his obituary, "Julien Bryan, Film Maker, Dies; Honored for His Documentaries," *The New York Times*, October 21, 1974, 39.

17. Susan Sontag, *Regarding the Pain of Others* (New York: Farrar, Straus and Giroux, 2003), 18.

18. Julien Bryan, *Die Farben des Krieges: Die Belagerung Warschaus in den Farbfotografien von Julien Bryan / The Colors of War: The Siege of Warsaw in Julien Bryan's Color Photographs*, bilingual edition (Berlin/Munich: Deutscher Kunstverlag, 2011), 115.

19. In the United States, Bryan's photographs first appeared in *Time* XXXIV, No. 11 (September 11, 1939). However, his own texts with images started to appear in October 1939: Julien Bryan, "Documentary Record of the Last Days of Once Proud Warsaw," *Life* magazine (23 October 1939), 73–77 (with sixteen photographs); "Can Hitler's Lightning War Do This To England?" *Look* magazine (5 December 1939), 10–16 (with twenty-six photographs). In 1940, his articles and photographs continued to appear in other illustrated outlets: "Cameraman at the Front, Part I," *Popular Mechanics*, v. 73, No. 3 (March 1940), 328–332, 155A, 157A (with fifteen photographs); "Cameraman at the Front, Part II," *Popular Mechanics* 73, No. 4 (April 1940), 552–557, 139A (with thirteen photographs). Bryan also wrote about his experience in Warsaw without added illustrations; "War Is, Was, and Always Will Be, Hell," *U.S. Camera* 1, No. 8 (February–March 1940), and "Last Days of Warsaw," *Reader's Digest* 36 (April 1940), 27–32. Furthermore, he traveled extensively throughout the country giving lectures with colored slides.

20. Julien Bryan, with introduction by Maurice Hindus, *Siege* (New York: Doubleday/Doran, 1940). Documentary film *Siege* (1940) was produced and edited by Frederick Ullman, Jr. and Frank Donovan, who added sound effects and a score, and recorded Bryan delivering a dramatic narration (nine minutes and forty-eight seconds).

21. Bryan's photographs were published in the United Kingdom by *The War Illustrated*: "Child Victims of Hitler's War of Frightfulness," 231 (two photographs); and Vol. 1, No. 14 (December 16, 1939), 424 (two photographs) as illustrations to a text, "Warsaw is Now a 'City of Dreadful Night'," written by a French woman of her firsthand experience in Warsaw in September 1939 (reprinted from a French newspaper, *Le Petit Parisien*). Bryan's photographs were also published in a French magazine, *L'Illustration* No. 5044 (November 4, 1939), with four photographs illustrating a text "Varsovie après le passage des bombardiers et des mitrailleurs Allemands."

22. Walter Benjamin, "The Work of Art in the Age of Mechanical Reproducibility (Second Version)," in Michael W. Jennings el. (eds.) *The Work of Art in the Age of Its Technological Reproducibility, and Other Writings on Media*, trans. Edmund Jephcott et al. (Cambridge/London: Harvard University Press, 2008), 27.

23. On the uses of Bryan's photographs taken in Warsaw, often with incorrect captions, see Janina Struk, *Photographing the Holocaust: Interpretations of the Evidence* (London/New York: I. B. Tauris, 2004), 34–39.

24. Julien Bryan, *Warsaw: 1939 Siege. 1959 Warsaw Revisited* (Warsaw: Polonia Publishing House, 1959).

25. Errol Morris, *Believing Is Seeing: Observations on the Mysteries of Photography* (New York: Penguin Press, 2011), 32.

26. One cropped photograph from this series was published in the United Kingdom on the cover of *The War Illustrated* with the headline "A Permanent Picture Record of the Second Great War," *The War Illustrated* 1, No. 8 (November 4, 1939), 225. For analysis of the iconic status of this image, see Isabel Wollaston, "The Absent, the Partial and the Iconic in Archival Photographs of the Holocaust," *Jewish Culture and History* 12, No. 3 (2010), 439–462. On "iconic photographs," see Robert Hariman and John Louis Lucaites, *No Caption Needed: Iconic Photographs, Public Culture, and Liberal Democracy* (Chicago/London: University of Chicago Press, 2007).

27. Édouard Herriot, "Introduction," in *L'Invasion Allemande en Pologne – Documents, Temoignages Authentifies et Photographies, Recueillis par le Centre d'Information et de Documentation du Gouvernement Polonais* (Paris: Flammarion, 1940). It is a 126-page publication of documents, maps, reports, and photographs, all describing the German atrocities during the Polish campaign of September 1939. This book was also published in English as *The German Invasion of Poland. Polish Black Book Containing Documents, Authenticated Reports and Photographs* (London: Hutchinson & Co. Ltd., 1940) with a different photograph on its cover.

28. Staying in Montreal, Żarnower produced two photomontages: *For the Polish Army* (after December 15, 1941), and *The Canadian Army* (after August 19, 1942); see Idzior, "Fighting for the Same Cause."

29. Polish Ministry of Information, *The Black Book of Poland* (New York: G. P. Putnam's Sons, 1942) contains two maps and 185 photographs and authentic documents.

30. Georges Didi-Huberman, *Images in Spite of All: Four Photographs from Auschwitz,* trans. Shane B. Lillis (Chicago: University of Chicago Press, 2008), 125, original emphasis.

31. Zygmunt Bauman, *Modernity and the Holocaust* (Ithaca: Cornell University Press, 1989).

32. Irena Piotrowska, "Warsaw's Fight for Freedom and Independence (1794–1944) in Polish Painting," *Bulletin of the Polish Institute of Arts and Sciences in America* 3, No. 1 (October 1944), 47.

33. John Tagg, *The Burden of Representation: Essays on Photographies and Histories* (Minneapolis: University of Minnesota Press, 1993), 20.

34. Iwona Drąg Korga, "The Information Policy of the Polish Government-in-Exile toward the American Public during World War II," *Polish American Studies,* Vol. 64, No.1 (Spring 2007), 28.

35. Sharon Sliwinski, "A Painful Labour: Responsibility and Photography," *Visual Studies* 19, No. 2 (October 2004), 151.

36. I am alluding here to the designation "artistic document of Holocaust" used by Katarzyna Bojarska in reference to Władysław Strzemiński's ten collages in the series *Moim przyjaciolom Żydom* [To my friends, the Jews] of 1945. Katarzyna Bojarska, "Władysław Strzemiński i jego artystyczny dokument Zagłady," in Tomasz Majewski and Anna Zeidler-Janiszewska (eds.), *Pamięć Shoah. Kulturowe reprezentacje i praktyki upamiętnienia* (Łódź: Officyna, 2011), 705–717.

37. *Freie Arbeiter Stimme* (or *Fraye Arbayter Shtimme*) [The Free Voice of Labor] was the lead-ing and longest-running anarchist newspaper in the Yiddish language in the United States (1890–1977).

38. Michael Rothberg, *Traumatic Realism: The Demands of Holocaust Representation* (Minne-apolis/London: University of Minnesota Press, 2000), 103.

39. Between April 23 and May 11, 1946, Żarnower had a solo exhibition at the Art of This Century Gallery run by Peggy Guggenheim in New York. This show was accom-panied by a catalogue containing a text by Barnett Newman.

40. Joseph Brodsky, "The Condition We Call Exile," *The New York Review of Books* XXXIV, 21 and 22 (January 21, 1988), 16, 18.

41. Hannah Arendt, "We Refugee" (1943), in Marc Robinson (ed.), *Altogether Elsewhere: Writers on Exile* (Boston/London: Faber and Faber, 1994), 114.

42. Henryk Grynberg writes that people who commit suicide are also refugees, maybe even more so. Henryk Grynberg *Uchodźcy* [Refugees] (Warszawa: Świat Książki, 2004), 245.

43. On the phenomenon of people taking their own lives during World War II, see David Lester, *Suicide and the Holocaust* (New York: Nova Science Publishers, 2006).

44. Madelaine Hron, *Translating Pain: Immigrant Suffering in Literature and Culture* (Toronto: University of Toronto Press, 2009), 4.

45. Stanley Cohen, *States of Denial: Knowing about Atrocities and Suffering* (Cambridge/Malden: Polity Press/Blackwell Publishers, 2001), 194.

Far from Home

Winston Vargas in Washington Heights

Leslie Ureña

In 1962, a young woman boarded a Pan American flight in Santo Domingo, Dominican Republic, and arrived at John F. Kennedy Airport, in New York.[1] This was the first time she had left her home country. This woman, my mother, was one of thousands of Dominicans who would eventually settle in New York City, which would become the center of the Caribbean country's diaspora. Her story of immigration, as well as that of her compatriots and our family, is marked by the life-altering effects of displacement. This story also unwittingly laid the groundwork for my interest in the imagery and history of people leaving one home for another. When I learned about the work of the Dominican American photographer Winston Vargas (born 1943), I was immediately drawn to its subject matter—the people and streets that comprised the neighborhood I too had come to know throughout my life.[2] His photographs of the northern Manhattan neighborhoods of Washington Heights and Inwood, taken from the 1960s to the 1990s, are evocative portraits of people far from home, caught "between two islands"—the Dominican Republic and Manhattan.[3]

Vargas, himself an immigrant, moved to New York City from Santiago, Dominican Republic, in 1952, as a child. He came of age in Washington Heights, which has served as home to hundreds of thousands of Dominicans who began arriving in greater numbers starting in the 1960s, and is a neighborhood that has played a key role in Dominican cultural consciousness.[4] His photographs depict multiple generations of newcomers becoming part of an already heterogeneous area, which throughout its history, has been populated by New Yorkers hailing from Cuba, Germany, Greece, Puerto Rico, and elsewhere. Their lives unfold as they get married, have children, shop for food, or merely walk down the street (Figs. 1–6). At first glance, the photographs may appear to be documentation of quotidian activities in an urban space, marked by multistory brick buildings, fire escapes, and storefronts. Within these photographs, however, we find hints of the complicated nature of establishing a new home in a foreign land. In undergoing dramatic shifts of assimilating to a new environment, the newcomers in Vargas's

photographs also alter their new homes. Vargas therefore photographed the neighborhood as it changed and also as it left its imprint on those who settled there. As
such, this examination of Vargas's work expands the discussion of how the photographic medium depicts newcomers as both affected by and themselves affecting
their new environments. Vargas's photographs also speak to how photography
mediates the experience of migration, especially in the United States, and as this
volume explores, how "migrant communities […] meliorate cultural dislocation."[5]

When considered against the story of the mutual impact of people and place,
Vargas's oeuvre also provides an opportunity to further explore the concept of *home*
for a diasporic community, marked by pervasive transnationalism.[6] Even when
there was a return home to the Dominican Republic, Washington Heights and
Inwood still served as the other home to which Dominicans often returned once
in the United States. This back and forth between the two was made possible by
a number of factors, including the proximity by air between New York and the
Dominican Republic, as well as that, unlike with many other diasporic communities, the majority of Dominicans *could* return to their home country usually without
fear of political reprisals.[7] There is, as James Clifford explores, no "constitutive
taboo on return."[8]

Within this easy mobility between two "homes," New York City, specifically,
came to hold a special place for the Dominican diaspora. As the historian Jesse
Hoffnung-Garskof has noted, "[t]he distant Empire City, the universal standard
against which Dominican identity could be measured, grew over four decades into
the second-largest Dominican city."[9] Therefore, when Dominicans think of the
United States, it is New York, not Chicago, Boston, or Miami, that comes to mind.
And in the city, Washington Heights and Inwood loom large within the Dominican
imagination and day-to-day reality. The neighborhoods, as explored here, become
what Arjun Appadurai has defined as an "ethnoscape," a "landscape of persons
who constitute the shifting world in which we live."[10] With each visit between the
two islands, parts of Washington Heights and its people have been carried to the
Dominican Republic, and vice versa, inevitably affecting both places.

Likewise, for Vargas, upper Manhattan has had a magnetic draw, akin to an
almost diasporic sentiment toward the neighborhood.[11] As he explains, you "can't
get away from where you grew up."[12] Vargas's sustained engagement with the area
and its residents, even when he no longer lived there, brings to the fore his own
particular experience of the Dominican diaspora. For Vargas, I argue, Washington
Heights and Inwood, with their increasingly Dominican population, businesses,
and customs, were interchangeable with the Dominican Republic.

Photography, displacement, and geography intersect in Vargas's work, which
becomes an example of a "diasporic geographical imagination."[13] He is simultaneously a variably defined diasporic subject, Dominican immigrant, and former

and return resident of Washington Heights and Inwood, who, with his migrant gaze, develops versions of the neighborhood through his photographs. As Joan M. Schwartz and James R. Ryan have discussed, photography has had a significant role in disseminating images of place, and more pressingly for this discussion, in its envisioning. Photographs, they argue, are how "we see, we remember, we imagine: we 'picture place'."[14] Schwartz and Ryan expand on David Harvey's notion of the "geographical imagination," whereby photography becomes a "mechanism by which people come to know the world and situate themselves in space and time."[15] For Vargas, I argue, the photographs that he took of Washington Heights and Inwood served a similar purpose. As he walked the streets he came to know as a child, he positioned himself in relation to his "ethnoscape," the ever-shifting city, and its always changing population.

To elucidate these points, in what follows, I first discuss the histories of Washington Heights and Inwood. Then, I will explore the history of Dominican-United States relations, and, in particular, its effects on Dominican migration to the United States. I position Vargas within a narrative of the photography of immigration that focuses on newcomers once they have arrived and have started settling into their new homes. The challenges that the Dominican community confronted when arriving in Washington Heights, as New York City's and the country's demographics and society changed, also play a significant role. The city could adjust to newcomers, and vice versa, to a certain extent. The intention is not to present an idealized view of New York as an easy place for newcomers. Yet, New York's importance within the patterns of Dominican migration cannot be underestimated. In the end, Vargas's photographs emerge as an understudied visual document of the formation of diasporic identities and the persistent yearning for home of New York's Dominican American community.

At the core of Vargas's work also rests the concept of contact between photographer, place, and subject. In his case, he turns the camera toward a population that is familiar to him, residents of the neighborhood in which he came of age. Vargas's position as a diasporic subject is crucial to his approach to the neighborhood and to its people. The earlier photographs depict an area not too different from what he had experienced on a day-to-day basis during his youth. Yet, just as he had moved away from the Dominican Republic, he also left Washington Heights and Inwood, which had come to supplant his original home. As he continually returned to the same places, he eventually started to document their changes. Vargas's documentation of place, therefore, becomes another sort of contact-zone in which shifting populations of Dominicans in Washington Heights and Inwood brush up against one another, at different phases of their diasporic lives. Their "diasporic identities," such as those discussed by Stuart Hall, "are constantly producing and reproducing themselves anew, through transformation and difference."[16] In Vargas's photographs,

Dominican migratory experiences are multigenerational and multilayered. While some embrace their new or old surroundings, others reject them, and the neighborhood and its people are in a continual process of adjustment.

Well before Washington Heights became the inspiration for *In the Heights* (2007), the Tony Award–winning musical by Inwood-raised Lin-Manuel Miranda, the area roughly bound by Dyckman Street on the north, 155th Street on the south, and the Harlem and Hudson Rivers on the east and west, was a rural outpost that served as the site of military campaigns during the American Revolutionary War (1775–1783). Inwood, initially home to the Lenape people, is bordered by Dyckman Street on the south and the northern tip of Manhattan island on the north. By the mid to late nineteenth century, real-estate development had changed the landscape, with wealthy New Yorkers building estates overlooking the Hudson.[17] By the early twentieth century, with the arrival of the subway and elevated train, new buildings catered to people of more moderate income who wished to avoid the increasingly crowded areas of lower Manhattan.[18]

As housing and transportation changed, so did the population. German and Irish newcomers started moving further uptown in the mid to late nineteenth century. Italians followed at the turn of the century. German Jews arrived in the 1930s and 1940s, and Greeks and Puerto Ricans in the 1950s and 1960s. With each new group, the neighborhood changed. New businesses, religious observations, and favorite pastimes began to alter the urban fabric. This multicultural enclave has not been devoid of frictions among some. As early as the 1920s, segregationist real-estate policies were often used to keep some out, particularly African Americans. These tactics later expanded to exclude others, as building owners tried to maintain middle-class standards, which, within this context, meant White.[19] By the time Dominicans started to settle there in greater numbers in the 1960s and 1970s, the neighborhood's racial divides had coalesced along Black, Latinx, and White lines.[20]

Dominican presence in the New York City area can be traced as far back as 1613, when the merchant Juan Rodríguez arrived in what would become New York. Rodríguez arrived from Hispaniola (the island shared by Haiti and the Dominican Republic) aboard a Dutch ship, and is believed to be the first non-Native person to settle in Manhattan for an extended period of time.[21] Yet the more intermingled histories between the United States and the Dominican Republic gained steam in the nineteenth century. By the early 1870s, the debt-ridden Dominican government had almost sold the country to the United States. Although the US President Ulysses S. Grant could not find the needed support for the measure, this would not be the last time that the government of the United States would be invested, economically, politically, and militarily, in the Dominican Republic.[22] After seizing control of Dominican customs revenue in 1905, with all the economic clout which that entailed, the US military occupied the country between 1916 and 1924.[23] Democratic elections in 1924 led to Dominican self-government, by a US-approved president, and eventually to the lessening of American involvement during the early years of the dictatorship of Rafael Leónidas Trujillo.[24]

Trujillo's dictatorship (1930–1961), which began with his military takeover of the Dominican government, was a defining moment for Dominican migration to the United States. Before then, as the historian Francisco Rodríguez de León has noted, the Dominican Republic itself was a draw for others, and few Dominicans emigrated at all.[25] Trujillo, or *El Jefe* ("the Boss"), continued tightening his grip on Dominican society and the country's economy. Some who feared persecution began to leave in the 1950s before Trujillo's government started imposing immigration restrictions. Many of those who were able to leave were from the Dominican middle class, including professionals, intellectuals, artists, and businesspeople with the means to make the journey given the relative expense of obtaining a passport.[26] Those who settled in New York chose to do so mostly in Manhattan, in the areas of Spanish Harlem (between 96th and 140th Streets, on the east side), Hamilton Place (between 133rd and 155th Streets), and close to what is now Lincoln Center (around West 65th Street).[27] As time went on, many moved to the Lower East Side and the outer boroughs, including Queens.

After 1961, however, with Trujillo's assassination, the floodgates opened. By 1962, it is estimated that there were ten to fifteen thousand Dominicans in the United States.[28] As political upheaval ensued in the Dominican Republic, with elections and coups, the American military intervened again in 1965. That same year, the US Immigration and Nationality Act, that had seemed expansive in its welcoming of newcomers to the United States, imposed limits on Latin American immigrants, including Dominicans.[29] Nevertheless, their numbers continued to increase;[30] by 2000 there were over one million people who identified as Dominican living in the United States.[31] The majority lived in New York, which, as noted earlier, has served as the center of the diaspora, and for many has become a stand-in for the Dominican Republic.

Dominicans' persistent transnationalism, one in which first- and second-generation immigrants often travel between the United States and the Dominican Republic multiple times throughout their lifetimes, has meant that many in New York live "con un pie aquí, y el otro allá"[32] ("one foot here, and the other there"), a refrain that was popularized in one of the merengue hits of the 1980s, by Sandy Reyes. The United States may serve as a temporary home, while returning to the Dominican Republic often occupies the minds of many, even if only for extended temporary stays.[33] Living in one place with the intention of returning "home" has led to a dual existence for Dominicans, and an embrace of transnational practices beyond that of any other immigrant group.[34] Airplanes fly multiple times a day to and from several Dominican cities, remittances are high, children are sent back "home" to study; or entire families, some with US-born children, move "home." As such, *home* is a transnational concept.[35] While this transnationalism may be a form of instability, I argue that it in fact provides a flexible model of what home is. After all, there is still a foot in each place, with a network, even if tenuous, in both.[36]

Winston Vargas's life story, however, does not fit neatly within the model of transnationalism that scholars of Dominican migration have identified. Although he lived in Washington Heights from the time he arrived in 1952 until he joined the US Army in 1962, his trips to the Dominican Republic as a child were somewhat limited. In 1966, one year after the aforementioned US invasion of the Dominican Republic, he returned and took several photographs during a two-week trip. His parents moved back to the Dominican Republic in 1975, and so did he in 1979 to take a job at an advertising company. All the while, Vargas continued photographing in the United States and wherever his travels took him. He did not engage in the *vaivén*, coming and going, that many of his compatriots did. Yet, as I posited earlier, Washington Heights was the place he traveled to and from. As Vargas recently explained about the neighborhood, "In one way, it's always there, and I found it interesting to capture that."[37] And the "that" that he photographed was a neighborhood and a people in continual transition.

When Vargas arrived in Washington Heights, as he recalls, very few residents spoke Spanish, except for several neighbors down the block and a Cuban family in his building. At school, he depended on a Puerto Rican classmate for basic translations, including for words such as "tie" and "shirt". He learned English at his primary school and while there befriended the kids of the neighborhood, whose families were mostly Irish, Italian, Jewish, and Puerto Rican. Despite the neighborhood's documented tensions, Vargas does not recall such moments affecting him directly. In his memory, they "were just kids."[38]

His interest in photography emerged after a school trip to the Bronx Zoo, where his teacher brought along a camera. Vargas's father, who worked as a longshoreman, then gave him a camera of his own. He became an avid snap shooter and read about photography at his local branch library. In essence, Vargas was hooked. Photography was a hobby that became a career and followed him everywhere he went, including around the neighborhood, at his secondary school, George Washington High School, and throughout the city. Outside of school, he focused on the blocks between 164th and 166th streets on Amsterdam Avenue, within two streets from where he lived. Local businesses asked him to photograph their shops, as with the case of Isaac Montes and his Spanish & American barbershop at 2100 Amsterdam Avenue, which appears in the 1961 photograph *Barbershop, Washington Heights, New York* (Fig. 1).

Montes, who lived a few buildings over from Vargas, appears on the barbershop's stoop. He looks to his left, away from the camera, in his crisp light-colored

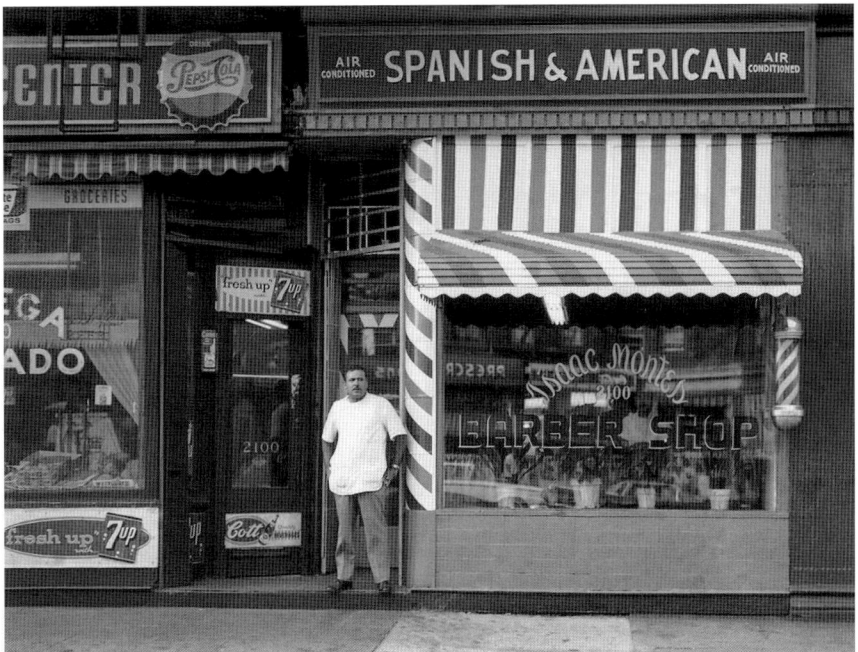

Figure 1: Winston Vargas, *Barbershop, Washington Heights, New York*, 1961, printed 2016, gelatin silver print. Smithsonian American Art Museum, Museum purchase through the Smithsonian Latino Initiatives Pool, administered by the Smithsonian Latino Center, and through the Frank K. Ribelin Endowment, 2017.9.1, © 1961, Winston Vargas.

short-sleeved shirt. Through the barbershop's window, between the words *Barber* and *Shop*, we see another member of the business's staff, staring intently at Vargas's camera. The last three letters of the words *bodega* ("convenience store") and *mercado* ("market") are just visible at the left of the photograph, in the store window of an adjacent business. As a neighborhood kid photographing his environs, in this case at the barbershop owner's request, possibly for a permit, Vargas unwittingly provided a glimpse of how Spanish was becoming part of the area's landscape. Businesses mixed both languages, English and Spanish, thus catering to more than one potential set of customers. Although doing work for hire, Vargas, a relative newcomer to the city with an increasing command of the English language, casts his camera eye on what may have been more welcome—words in Spanish. His dual role as documentarian and diasporic subject, therefore, meant that he had a different approach to how he photographed the neighborhood. In this instance, he is not an outsider looking in,[39] but rather a resident of the area, photographing from within. This positionality, however, would change soon enough.

Vargas joined the Army in January of 1962, and when he returned to New York in the mid 1960s, he moved into an apartment on MacDougal Street in Greenwich

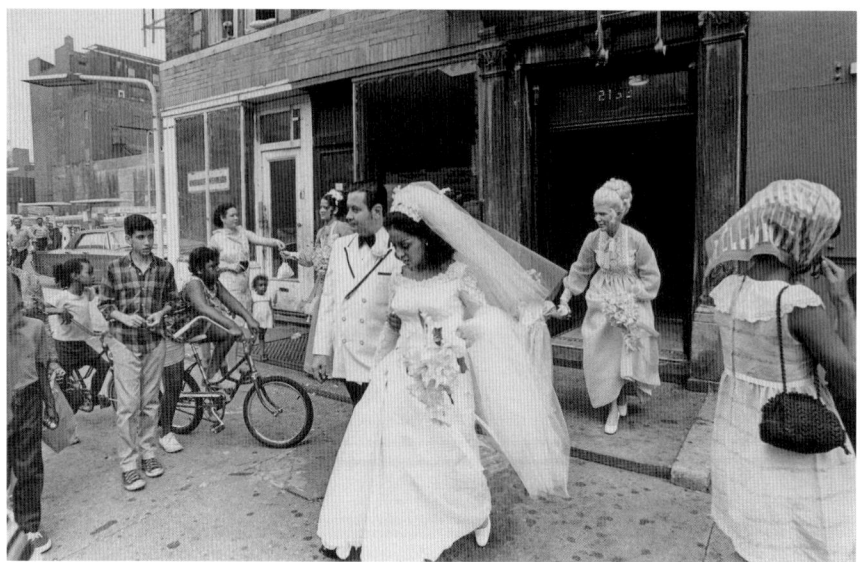

Figure 2: Winston Vargas, *Wedding Day, Washington Heights, New York*, 1970, printed 2016, gelatin
silver print. Smithsonian American Art Museum, Museum purchase through the Smithsonian
Latino Initiatives Pool, administered by the Smithsonian Latino Center, and through the Frank K.
Ribelin Endowment, 2017.9.8, © 1970, Winston Vargas.

Village, in lower Manhattan. Like many at the time, he was drawn to the neighborhood's status as the epicenter of New York's artistic and creative community. While
not at his advertising job, he took photographs at Washington Square Park and
throughout the city. On many weekends, he would return to Washington Heights to
visit his family, and bring along his camera. During these trips, he captured favorite
pastimes and brides on their way to their weddings (Figs. 2–4)—in sum, life being
lived. Although he did not set out to chronicle northern Manhattan in a systematic
manner, the combination of his interests in the neighborhood and its people, as well
as the flexibility of the photographic medium, led him to repeatedly photograph
his home. Now, however, he brought with him another layer of lived experience,
having not only left the United States and been stationed in Europe, but also having
chosen to live outside of Washington Heights upon his return. Vargas's view of the
neighborhood that he had known so well was not quite that of an outsider, but was
nevertheless imbued with, to borrow a phrase from Salman Rushdie, "fractured
perceptions."[40]

In 1971, Vargas took a photograph of two young women whom he remembers
as being of Dominican origin, just up the street from the barbershop he had photographed a decade earlier (Fig. 1). The background of *Sisters, Washington Heights,
New York* (Fig. 3) functions almost as a theatrical backdrop, which depicts the rest

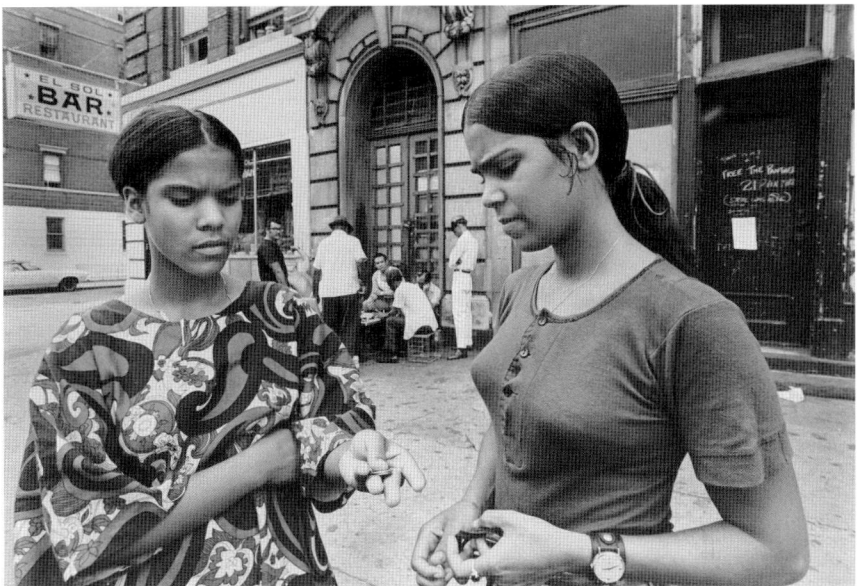

Figure 3: Winston Vargas, *Sisters, Washington Heights, New York*, 1970, printed 2016, gelatin silver print (Plate 14, p. 340). Smithsonian American Art Museum, Museum purchase through the Smithsonian Latino Initiatives Pool, administered by the Smithsonian Latino Center, and through the Frank K. Ribelin Endowment, 2017.9.11, © 1970, Winston Vargas.

of the world in which they lived. At left there is a restaurant and bar named *El Sol* ("The Sun"). At the center of the photograph is a delivery entrance, closed with large padlocks. An intergenerational group of men hovers over a makeshift game of dominos. At right is a doorway with peeling paint and graffiti that reads "Free the Panther" and "21 Panther." The photograph's four sections provide hints of the changes in the neighborhood: from the group of men in the background, to the younger well-coiffed women in the foreground, and back to the signage and graffiti. These last two, in particular, offer an arc to the story of the neighborhood, from what was likely an establishment catering to Latinos to the hints of societal conflicts affecting the city and country at the time.

Throughout the 1950s and 1960s, African American and Puerto Rican residents continued moving into the area, many of them seeking affordable rent in what was considered a good residential neighborhood. Some unwelcoming White residents considered them "invaders."[41] By the early 1970s, Washington Heights had been racked by decades of ethnic and racial tension. Turf battles ensued on the streets and at schools as African American, Irish, and Puerto Rican gangs fought for control. The violence sometimes escalated to bombings, as with that of an apartment building mostly inhabited by Puerto Ricans.[42]

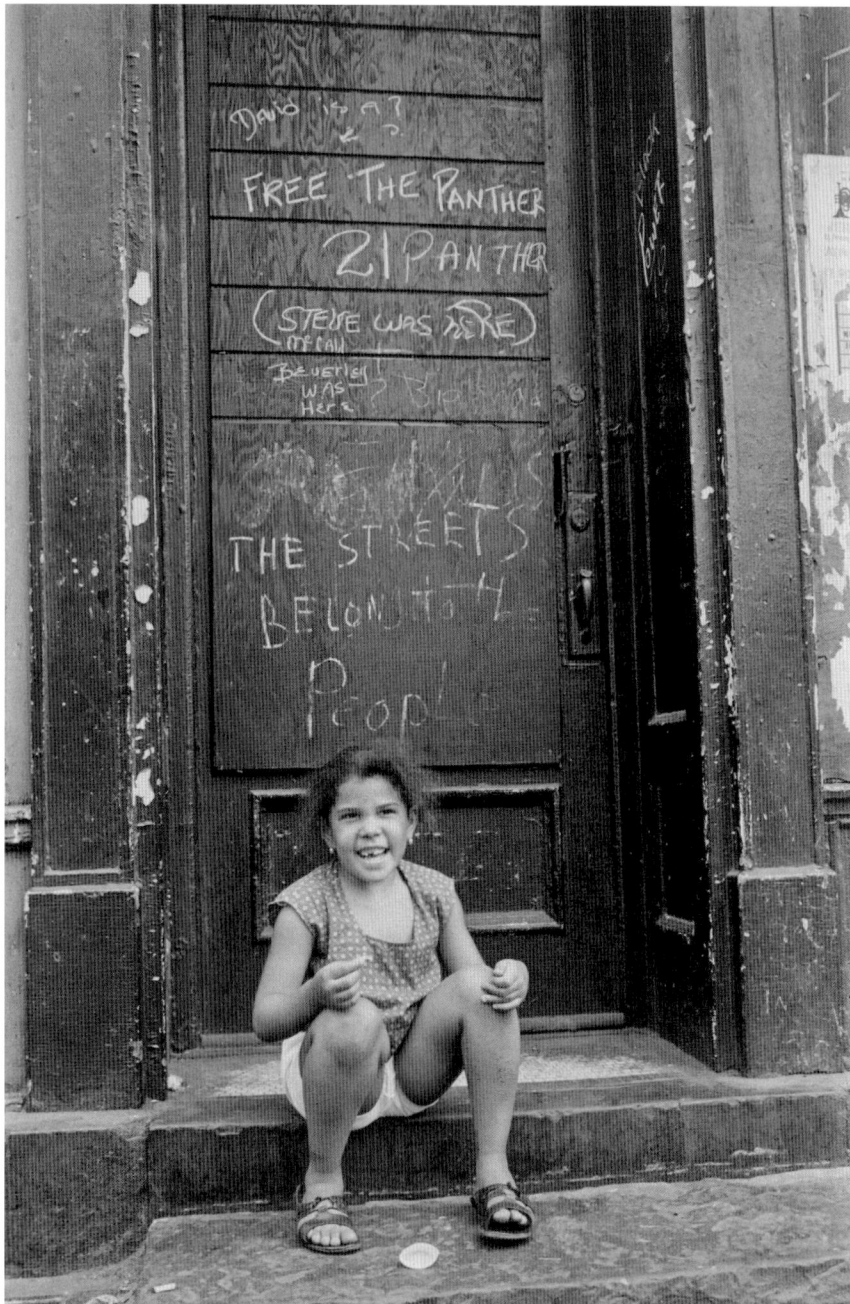

Figure 4: Winston Vargas, *Child Playing, Washington Heights, New York*, 1970, printed 2016, gelatin silver print (Plate 15, p. 341). Smithsonian American Art Museum, Museum purchase through the Smithsonian Latino Initiatives Pool, administered by the Smithsonian Latino Center, and through the Frank K. Ribelin Endowment, 2017.9.7, © 1970, Winston Vargas.

The graffiti in the doorway of *Sisters* comes into better view in *Child Playing, Washington Heights, New York* (1971) (Fig. 4). From top to bottom, it reads: "David is a […]," "Free the Panther," "21 Panther," "Steve [McCaw] was here," "Beverly was Here," "Black Power," and "The Streets Belong to the People." "21 Panther," in particular, references the eight-month Panther 21 Trial, during which twenty-one, later dropped to thirteen, members of the Harlem Chapter of the Black Panthers were put on trial for allegedly having planned bombings across the city. The graffiti writer's intervention compellingly draws our attention to New York's and the country's broader histories of racial inequity. Dominicans, and other newcomers to the neighborhood, were settling there as the country underwent significant changes in the struggle for civil rights. Additionally, when this photograph was taken, the city was also close to financial insolvency.

Seen as dangerous and decaying during the 1970s, New York was on the brink of bankruptcy. When in 1975 the federal government initially denied the city a loan, the sentiment was that New York should "Drop Dead," as the *Daily News*'s sensationalistic headline read on October 30, 1975.[43] The federal government did, in the end, offer assistance. Nevertheless, neighborhoods including Washington Heights and Inwood, suffered from the city's vilification and overall financial shortcomings, as well as the greater implications they had for the economy and overall population.[44]

Underscoring the area's underlying tensions is the slender doorway in *Child Playing*. Whereas its chipping paint and graffiti draw attention to the city's decay, its last line, "The Streets Belong to the People," and the young girl's partly toothless grin, shift our focus back to the neighborhood's residents. Vargas was likewise engaged in chronicling the neighborhood's people, however unsystematically, since to him, "the whole world was there."[45] Everything, including a *frío frío* ("shaved ice") vendor (Fig. 5), people carrying groceries, or children playing, made Washington Heights a place that Vargas wished to continue photographing even after he had moved out of the neighborhood. It was "interesting to see the difference in the neighborhood […] after being away," he recently explained.[46] Even within the same city, and on the same island, the lives he led in the bohemian Greenwich Village and the increasingly Latino Washington Heights were vastly different. He was simultaneously an insider and an outsider, who photographed the rest of the city, including other neighborhoods, such as Brownsville (in Brooklyn) and Harlem. However, he would always return to Washington Heights.

Dominicans started settling in the area in greater numbers during these years and even more so in the 1980s. Much as when African Americans and Puerto Ricans arrived in the neighborhood, Dominicans were not always welcome. Some considered them "unfamiliar."[47] As the historian and journalist Robert W. Snyder notes, existing residents of Washington Heights sometimes received them

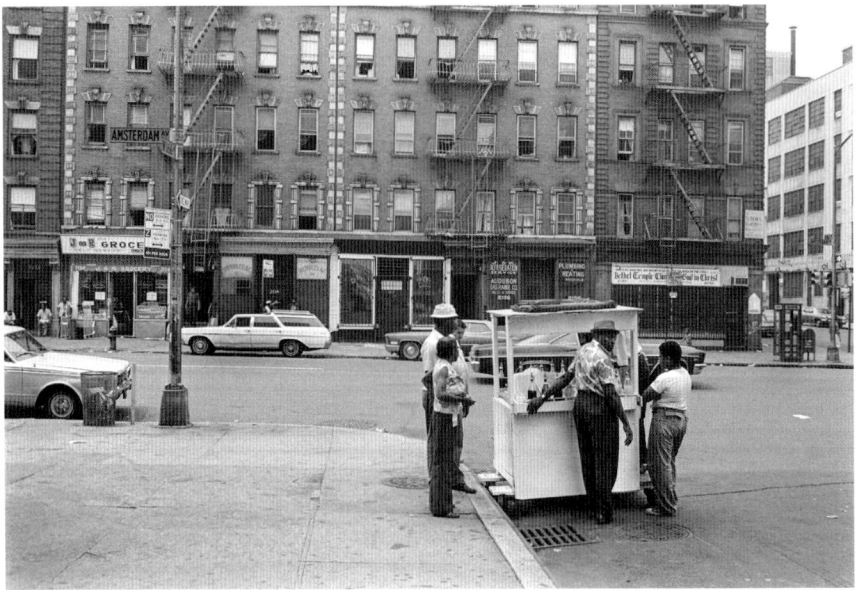

Figure 5: Winston Vargas, *165th & Amsterdam Ave*, New York City, 1970s. © Winston Vargas.

with hostility, even citing the perceived unsettled nature of their transnational existence.[48]

During the 1970s, Vargas worked as staff photographer for Reverend Ike, a charismatic African American evangelist whose base was in Washington Heights, at what had been a Loew's theater at 175th Street and Broadway. As his work with Reverend Ike came to an end, Vargas moved to the Dominican Republic in 1979 to take a job at an advertising firm. He remained there until 1984 and spent some of his free time photographing around the island, including Pope John Paul II's 1979 visit. When Vargas returned to New York in the mid 1980s, he eventually settled in Washington Heights and continued photographing what had become a significantly changed area. In moving to the Dominican Republic, Vargas participated in one of the rituals of the Dominican diasporic experience, returning to the "home" country. Resettling in New York also speaks to another aspect of that experience, whereby Dominican families often went back to the city after having been "home."

Vargas returned to a significantly altered Washington Heights and Inwood, where the Dominican presence was almost inescapable. As Dominicans' clout grew economically, Dominican-owned businesses lined each block. The names of bodegas, hair salons, remittance and travel agencies, taxi services, and more, often referred to Dominican towns or included silhouetted maps of the country. The

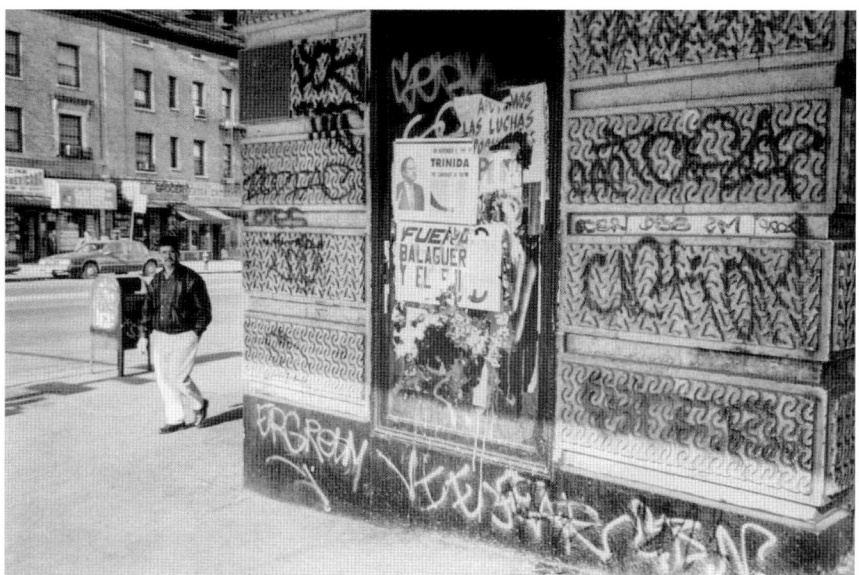

Figure 6: Winston Vargas, *Graffiti, Washington Heights, New York*, 1992, printed 2016, gelatin silver print. Smithsonian American Art Museum, Museum purchase through the Smithsonian Latino Initiatives Pool, administered by the Smithsonian Latino Center, and through the Frank K. Ribelin Endowment, 2017.9.16, © 1992, Winston Vargas.

sounds of merengue emanated from storefronts and moving vehicles. The 1980s and 1990s were also a period during which crime was on the rise in the neighborhood on account of a rampant drug trade.[49]

Yet, despite the increasing crime rates, the area continued to serve as home to many Dominicans. As the neighborhoods changed, some things did not. For instance, the *vaivén*, the coming and going between New York and the Dominican Republic, continued, as did signs of its existence. In Vargas's 1992 photograph *Graffiti, Washington Heights, New York* (Fig. 6), multiple political posters are affixed to a building at the corner of 175th and Broadway. One is for a local election and the other is of the then-president of the Dominican Republic, Joaquín Balaguer.[50] As with the area's inhabitants, politics demonstrated a similar porousness between New York and the Dominican Republic.

The top poster promotes the Dominican-born civil rights activist and "defender of immigrant rights" Apolinar Trinidad, who ran for the New York City Council in November 1991.[51] Trinidad may have lost, yet his example and mentorship inspired other Dominicans to run for office, including the first Dominican American to serve in the US Congress, Adriano Espaillat, who was elected in November 2016. As Snyder and others note, Dominican involvement in New York City's politics, in large part, grew out of locally based concerns. The areas' schools, in particular, were seen as needing attention, as was the increasing crime of the mid 1980s and early 1990s. This period saw the development of local community groups that catered to the interests of Dominicans, as well as a growing involvement in local politics by Trinidad and other politicians.[52]

Despite these inroads, Dominicans were also keenly aware of what was happening back in the Dominican Republic. Dominican political parties established local offices throughout Washington Heights and Inwood, their candidates campaigned in New York, and the details of Dominican local and national elections were often discussed at family gatherings.[53] Just below the Trinidad poster, another one denounces president Balaguer. Dubbed "the blind caudillo" (or strongman) by the *New York Times*,[54] Balaguer had served as vice president and then president during Trujillo's dictatorship. He was then president for twelve years, between 1966 and 1978. In 1986, Balaguer returned to power, yet again, for another ten years. The poster specifically references what many perceived to be Balaguer's "selling" of the country to the International Monetary Fund, as the Dominican Republic's economy spiraled out of control. The Dominican peso lost value, among other national crises, thus affecting many New York-based Dominicans who had returned "home." Years of saving to buy or build homes in neighborhoods geared at the returning diaspora were threatened by the country's unstable economy, and many found themselves with no choice but to return to the United States to try to rebuild their lives yet again, often back in New York. But beyond the specifics of this anti-Balaguer poster, this photograph neatly encapsulates on this one wall that at least two types of Dominican politics—one New York- and the other Dominican Republic-based—could coexist and gain the interest and attention of the same population.

Vargas photographed the continuously shifting natures of the neighborhood and its diaspora, providing views that by no means purport to be complete.[55] His role as a doubly diasporic subject, from both the Dominican Republic and Washington Heights, meant that he too was in persistent transformation, and as such, at the juncture of multiple contact zones, including the changing neighborhoods of Washington Heights and Inwood, the Dominican diaspora, New York City more broadly, and the Dominican Republic. Some of Vargas's photographs confront viewers with the urban decay that befell many parts of New York during the 1970s. Later, his works show how the Dominican Republic had become imbricated in almost every part of the neighborhood.

At their core, therefore, the works taken as a whole depict migratory experiences as processes in which people and place mutually impact one another. They present a community in transition, from new arrivals to active participants in shifting the tenor of an entire neighborhood. In doing so, they also demonstrate the yearning that results from being far from home, particularly as the Dominican diaspora grew in the 1980s. And with this growth came an intensification of the Dominican presence, which for many also meant that Washington Heights and Inwood would become interchangeable with the island country. The yearning that results from being far from home, therefore, could potentially be allayed through the elision of the Dominican Republic with Upper Manhattan. In his images of a Caribbean country to a sliver of a New York island, Vargas captures lives that illustrate the enduring challenge of creating a home far from home. In Vargas's case it was Washington Heights and Inwood from which he could not get away, nor could I. The transnational existence that he photographed has guided much of my research, and specifically, the photographic medium's ability to bear witness to the noisy process of migration.

Notes

1. The airport was then known as Idlewild Airport; its name changed in 1963, in honor of the assassinated president.

2. I wish to thank my colleague E. Carmen Ramos at the Smithsonian American Art Museum for bringing Vargas's work to my attention as she prepared for her exhibition *Down these Mean Streets: Community and Place in Urban America*. Ramos's exhibition, which was on view in Washington in 2017 and then at El Museo del Barrio in New York City in 2018–2019, made abundantly clear the need for a more inclusive reassessment of the photography of urban spaces. Many thanks as well to Justin Carville and Sigrid Lien for organizing the conference "Photography, Migration, and Cultural Encounters in America", in June 2018. The discussions throughout those days and afterwards have all informed my further research and thoughts on the work of Winston Vargas. I am deeply grateful to Winston Vargas for candidly discussing his work and biography, and for trusting me to write about them.

3. See Sherri Grasmuck and Patricia R. Pessar, *Between Two Islands: Dominican International Migration* (Berkeley/Los Angeles/Oxford: University of California Press, 1991). The Dominican Republic and Haiti share the island of Hispaniola.

4. In 1990, there were 332,713 Dominicans in New York City. By 1997, there were 495,000. See "Table 1: The Dominican Population in the U.S. and New York City," in Julissa Reynoso, "Dominican Immigrants and Social Capital in New York City: A Case Study," *Encrucijada/Crossroads: An Online Academic Journal* 1, No. 1 (2003), 59.

5. March 2018 Call for Papers for the Conference "Photography at the Contact Zones: Photography, Migration, and Cultural Encounters in America," June 2018, https://www.photographyascontactzones.com/callforpapers

6. The study of transnationalism in Dominican migration has been discussed by several scholars, including Grasmuck and Pessar; Jorge Duany, "Transnational Migration

from the Dominican Republic: The Cultural Redefinition of Racial Identity," *Caribbean Studies* 29, No. 2 (July–December 1996), 253–282; Jesse Hoffnung-Garskof, *A Tale of Two Cities: Santo Domingo and New York after 1950* (Princeton: Princeton University Press, 2008); and Robert W. Snyder, *Crossing Broadway: Washington Heights and the Promise of New York City* (Ithaca/London: Cornell University Press, 2015), among others.

7. Thanks to my sister, Anyi Hobson, for this reminder. Also see Hoffnung-Garskof, *A Tale of Two Cities*, 97–98.

8. James Clifford, "Diasporas," *Cultural Anthropology* 9, No. 3 (August 1994), 302–338, 304.

9. Hoffnung-Garskof, *A Tale of Two Cities*, 5. For more on the continual exchange, see 6–7.

10. Arjun Appadurai, "Disjuncture and Difference in the Global Cultural Economy," *Theory, Culture & Society* 7, No. 2–3 (June 1990), 295–310, 297.

11. As James Clifford explains, one of William Safran's definitions of diaspora includes "myths/memories of the homeland" as well as a "desire for eventual return." See Clifford, "Diasporas," 304–305.

12. Winston Vargas (artist), in discussion with the author, April 25, 2018.

13. Many thanks to Justin Carville for pinpointing this useful framework for this project.

14. Joan M. Schwartz and James R. Ryan, "Introduction: Photography and the Geographical Imagination," in *Picturing Place: Photography and the Geographical Imagination* (London: I.B. Tauris, 2003), 6.

15. Schwartz and Ryan, "Introduction," *Picturing Place*, 6.

16. Stuart Hall, "Cultural Identity and Diaspora," in Padmini Mongia (ed.), *Contemporary Postcolonial Theory: A Reader* (London: Arnold, 1996), 120.

17. Snyder, *Crossing Broadway*, 13.

18. Snyder, *Crossing Broadway*, 16.

19. For an expanded discussion of demographic shifts and exclusionary policies in real estate in upper Manhattan, see Snyder, *Crossing Broadway*, 6–44.

20. For additional information on the ethnic and racial divides in the neighborhood, and their development in light of world and local politics, see Hoffnung-Garskof, *A Tale of Two Cities*, 99–107.

21. See Anthony Stevens-Acevedo, Tom Weterings, and Leonor Álvarez Francés, "Juan Rodríguez and the Beginnings of New York City," *CUNY Academic Works* (2013), http://academicworks.cuny.edu/dsi_pubs/17. Also see Sam Roberts, "Honoring a Very Early New Yorker," *New York Times*, October 2, 2012, https://cityroom.blogs.nytimes.com/2012/10/02/honoring-a-very-early-new-yorker/.

22. Abraham F. Lowenthal, "The United States and the Dominican Republic to 1965: Background to Intervention," *Caribbean Studies* 10, No. 2 (1970), 30–55, http://www.jstor.org/stable/25612211, for additional details.

23. Hoffnung-Garskof, *A Tale of Two Cities*, 3, and Lowenthal, "The United States and the Dominican Republic," 32. See also "Dominican Republic, 1916–1924," U.S. Department of State, https://2001-2009.state.gov/r/pa/ho/time/wwi/108649.htm.

24. Lowenthal, "The United States and the Dominican Republic," 34.

25. Francisco Rodríguez de León, *El furioso merengue del Norte: una historia de la comunidad dominicana en los Estados Unidos* (New York: [Editorial Sitel], 1998), 43.

26. As Hoffnung-Garskof notes, one hundred plantains cost 1.27 Dominican pesos. A passport and all associated fees cost 125 pesos. See Hoffnung-Garskof, *A Tale of Two Cities*, 70.

27. Rodríguez de León, *El furioso merengue del Norte*, 43, 51.

28. Hoffnung-Garskof, *A Tale of Two Cities*, 4, 70–80.

29. Hoffnung-Garskof, *A Tale of Two Cities*, 69.

30. Hoffnung-Garskof, *A Tale of Two Cities*, 86–96.

31. Ramona Hernández and Francisco L. Rivera-Batiz, *Dominicans in the United States: A Socioeconomic Profile, 2000* (New York: CUNY Dominican Studies Institute, 2003), 2.

32. Snyder, *Crossing Broadway*, 143.

33. See Hoffnung-Garskof, *A Tale of Two Cities*, 164–196 for an expanded account of *home*, including how the concept was wielded by the Dominican Tourism Board in efforts to increase tourism by Dominican-born people to the island country. Furthermore, as Hoffnung-Garskof discusses, the traits of transnationalism had initially been a concern for some, but in the end, "Dominican dreams of home were not deviant […]" (196).

34. Tracy Rodríguez, "Dominicanas Entre La Gran Manzana y Quisqueya: Family, Schooling, and Language Learning in a Transnational Context," *The High School Journal* 92, No. 4, *Special Issue: At the Intersection of Transnationalism, Latina/o Immigrants, and Education* (April–May 2009), 17.

35. Tina Campt's question about what "home" is for an immigrant, at the June 2018 conference, has guided my continuing research on this topic as seen through the work of Winston Vargas.

36. See Reynoso's "Dominican Immigrants," for a discussion of Dominican networks. Also see Hoffnung-Garskof, *A Tale of Two Cities*, 198–199, for a discussion on the difficulties of living in New York and returning to the Dominican Republic.

37. Winston Vargas (artist), in discussion with the author, April 25, 2018.

38. Winston Vargas (artist), in discussion with the author, April 25, 2018.

39. See Joan M. Schwartz, "*The Geography Lesson*: photographs and the construction of imaginative geographies," *Journal of Historical Geography* 22, No. 1 (1996), 16–45, 33.

40. For a description of returning to one's home, and the fractured vision that results from writing from a distance, see Salman Rushdie, "Imaginary Homelands," in *Imaginary Homelands: Essays and Criticism 1981–1991* (London: Granta Books, 1992), 9–21.

41. Snyder, *Crossing Broadway*, 69.

42. Snyder, *Crossing Broadway*, 43.

43. "Ford to City: Drop Dead," *New York Daily News*, October 30, 1975, front page. See Sam Roberts, "Infamous 'Drop Dead' Was Never Said by Ford," *New York Times*, December 28, 2006, https://nyti.ms/2k5wmIg. Also see Snyder, *Crossing Broadway*, 117.

44. Snyder, *Crossing Broadway*, 121–126.

45. Winston Vargas (artist), in discussion with the author, April 25, 2018.

46. Winston Vargas (artist), in discussion with the author, April 25, 2018.

47. Snyder, *Crossing Broadway*, 138–146.

48. Snyder, *Crossing Broadway*, 138–146.

49. See Snyder, *Crossing Broadway*, 158–195, for an in-depth summary.

50. Credit here goes to my father, who became an ad-hoc researcher and asked friends in the neighborhood about the poster when I could not trace its origins.

51. Howard Jordan, "Apolinar Trinidad 1950–2011, Latino Civil Rights Leader dies at sixty," National Institute of Latino Policy (January 23, 2011), https://myemail.con-stantcontact.com/NiLP-FYI--Apolinar-Trinidad--NYC-Latino-Civil-Rights-Leaders--Dies.html?soid=1101040629095&aid=ZkYuFgQB6Ho.

52. Snyder, *Crossing Broadway*, 142–147, 152–156.

53. In the case of the discussions at gatherings, I depend on my own memories of when relatives would often debate Dominican politics, and thank my spouse Justin Miller for this reminder. For more on political dynamics, see Hoffnung-Garskof, *A Tale of Two Cities*, 125–126, 213–221.

54. Mark Kurlansky, "The Dominican Republic: In the Land of the Blind Caudillo," *New York Times*, August 6, 1989, https://nyti.ms/2PMA8L0.

55. Schwartz, "*The Geography Lesson*," 33, for a discussion of how in the case of European photographers in Egypt, for instance, "photographs, of course, could not communicate the experience of a continuous, multi-dimensional, multi-faceted journey."

Exhibiting Migrations

A Box, a Suitcase, a Museum

Photographic Records of Croatian Immigrants to the United States

Sandra Križić Roban

Archives are ambivalent places. Their primary function is to collect the source material that helps in the reconstruction and visualization of historical events. At the same time, archives generate awareness about things that often remain unseen. This is because many written and visual documents that end up in archives were not, in fact, intended for preservation outside of their original context. In Croatia this 'accidental' preservation happened largely due to the changes introduced by the subsequent restructuring of the archives. The significance of these changes for future research is often underestimated. Thus, for example, an insight into the scholarly journalism on Croatian emigration shows that some authors have not even consulted the documents and photographs that once belonged to the emigration museums in Zagreb and Split, which will be discussed in this essay. Although on the margins of interest, these former museum holdings are indispensable aide-mémoire in understanding the complex circumstances of emigrant life and work.

Croats have emigrated to various parts of the world, but for most of them, the United States has been the most desirable destination, a special place—the promised land that, apart from granting them survival as the greatest catalyst for emigration, allowed them to preserve the features of the culture from which they originated. Nevertheless, some documents speak of an ambivalent attitude of emigrants toward the new homeland. Thus, in addition to the promises of economic prosperity and a democratic environment in which the immigrant's origin is not of great importance, these documents also contain warnings about the need for "cultural propaganda to suppress the Americanization of our settlements."[1] Namely, many emigrants nurtured a nostalgic memory of their homeland, insisting on older cultural elements that had meanwhile disappeared in their country of origin. They tried to transfer this image to their new environment, retaining—on a symbolic level—elements of the culture they identified with.

Discussed in the context of the chronology of Croatian emigration, the documents discussed in this essay are today preserved at the Croatian National Archives as two separate collections of photographs and written documents. However, the former Emigration Museum functioned as an intermediary place for exchanging intimate, at times even poetic messages between the emigrants and those whom they had left behind. It is thus to be presumed that some of these materials were not collected with the aim of archiving them.

The Emigration Museum in Zagreb was founded on July 19, 1933 by a decision of the Ministry of Social Policy and Public Health of the Kingdom of Yugoslavia but was not opened to the public as a formal museum collection until 1936. The branch in Split was established a year later. Both museums ceased to operate at the beginning of World War II, when their holdings were handed over to various authorities. The former structure of the institution can be reconstructed based on the ordinance on its operation and the photographs of its exhibitions, but when its holdings were stored in the Croatian State Archives in 1998 and archivally organized in 2005, the photographs were separated from other documents. Therefore, it is now difficult to reconstruct the former links between visual and written documentation. Today, these materials are approached by using various aids of photography—examining, from a distance of several decades, the enlarged images made possible by digitization to discover what Benjamin called the *optical unconscious.*[2] The *instinctive unconscious* is revealed by careful research not only of the visual content of the photographs but also of the letters in which they are described or merely mentioned. Although some of the photographs have meanwhile been lost, presumably due to passing through various institutions that managed the holdings after World War II, the preserved ones are particularly important in identifying the individual destinies decades after they were taken, leading to changes in the standard emigration narratives. Some of them are now interpreted in the light of cognitive processes and mediation of human relations that were not in the focus of research before. However, based on this collection as well as the archival documents and photographs from several exhibitions focusing on Croatian immigration to the United States, which this paper also discusses, the aim has been to identify the features of the world in which the immigrants lived.

Photography offers a unique insight into a more private and intimate realm. The experiences of strangers, the "prey to the camera"[3] recorded in various scenes and eras, allows for a better understanding of the production and use of images about emigration, the as-yet-unstudied motives behind their creation and their movement over time. Although the number of emigrants was significant, and their issues were commented upon in the public media, the discourse within which this topic has been discussed so far has often been politically motivated and modified in relation to the governing regime. The awareness of histories of migration in

Croatia has so far not been associated with photography nor has there been any public discourse of iconic images that specifically shaped public consciousness of migration to the United States. In this essay, therefore, I start from those places that photographs configure memories and histories of Croatian migration —museums, archives, and selected exhibition projects—allowing for the continuity of time. The Emigration Museum as a sort of contact zone no longer exists in Croatia, although the importance of establishing such an institution at the national level has often been acknowledged. Therefore, the question arises as to who manages the history and culture of emigrants, who decides which of the preserved sources will be highlighted, especially when it comes to objects that are not artistic in nature, but mostly belong to what we call "records," according to James Clifford.[4] Although museums of this type often invoke elements of trauma and repression, their aim is not only to present the collected objects, but also to represent those who have participated in the preservation of historical narratives. The loss of contact zones leads to the disappearance of connections and continuity, the knowledge of other histories, while complex relationships are simplified and often transformed into commodified models of entertainment.[5]

Throughout history, Croatia has been part of various geopolitical entities—the Austro-Hungarian Empire, the Kingdom of Italy, the Kingdom of Yugoslavia, socialist Yugoslavia, and currently the Republic of Croatia. The political and economic uncertainties of the past 150 years have played a particularly significant role in the migration of Croats. Despite emigrating in significant numbers, they have always retained elements of their cultural identity. In the so-called modern colonization—from the 1880s onwards—they were drawn to countries characterized by intensive industrial development, particularly to the United States, where it was possible to find work quickly.[6] For the Croatian immigrants in the United States during this period, photography became an important medium for communicating their cultural identity within the American diaspora and to their communities and families back home. Today, Croats are once again emigrating in large numbers, for the most part due to the economic situation in Croatia, and to some extent due to contemporary politics. At first glance, the earlier waves of emigration do not differ greatly from the current wave, while the contemporary questions related to identity have yet to be studied, and potentially connected to the emigrant experiences of the earlier generations.

As many as one-third of all Croats left their homeland at the end of the nineteenth century, largely due to the economic factors. The economic boom in the United States played a major role in their decisions, although visual evidence of the faith that these immigrants put in modernization is meager. A fresh workforce arrived in the United States from underdeveloped countries thanks to immigration agents, who extolled the possibilities to find work and promised to provide positive

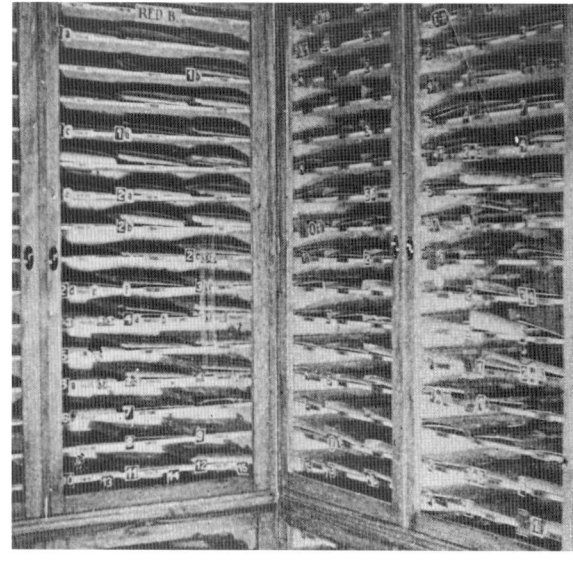

Figure 1: Archive in the Emigration Museum, Split. On the back: "Arhiv u Splitu" [Archive in Split], from the undated album (late 1930s). Croatian State Archives, Zagreb. Fond No. HR-HDA-1610-41-13-480.

change to people's lives.[7] Many people left their homes via Rijeka and Trieste (and to a lesser extent, via Antwerp and other ports of Europe), traveling to the New World beguiled with the promises that the agents had made. In contrast to the rosy future, however, the photographs preserved in the Croatian State Archives reveal the kinds of jobs that really awaited the immigrants—work in mines, construction work on skyscrapers, and, in particular, agricultural work, including fishing. These jobs were very different from the marvels of modernization that the immigrants no doubt expected when they left their homes.

The Croatian diaspora has largely been considered through the prism of politics in a range of social and humanities studies, undertaken largely in a national context. These studies are marked by the shades of history and the stifled memories of migrant narratives. After World War II, the Croatian diaspora was often discussed in Yugoslavia in the context of what has been identified as the "dominant narrative [...] of hostile emigration."[8] Thus, many of the emigrants were considered nationalists, Ustashas, fascists, and terrorists, although the truth is far more complex than the politicized and one-sided leveling to which the emigrants were subjected. To be sure, there were some Nazi-prone emigrants especially in South America, Canada, and Australia, and with Croatia's independence in 1991, their extreme views were reactivated by becoming part of the new political narrative. Nevertheless, the emigrant issue is heterogeneous and requires detailed research and analysis free from ideological exclusivity. The complex issues related to the emigration during the communist and socialist era tend to be brought into what is eventually a simplified binary relationship. This position also includes the discourse on the intellectually inferior position of immigrants in their new homes, largely due to the fact that they mostly belonged to the lower strata of society.[9]

In an attempt to move away from such approaches, I have researched the manner in which the question of emigration is presented to Croatian society in the Emigration Museum, which today forms part of the Croatian State Archives in Zagreb. The numerous photographs that have been preserved as a collection of the former Emigration Museum bear witness not only to the conditions in which the Croatian immigrants had lived prior to their emigration but also to their travel experiences and their new homes. I am specifically interested in the photographs that remain from the earlier periods of Croatian emigration, and what those photographs depict (Fig. 1).

What identities do the migrants strive to preserve when they leave their homes for a new country? Which images do they take with them and which images do they send back to their homelands after they have arrived, as proof of their success in the new country? What kind of identities do the migrants perform in the images that are sent back to their home country? How do they present their environment—their houses, barns, livestock, fields, vineyards, or some other evidence of their new surroundings? Furthermore, what kind of clues to the meaning of the image can be found in the accompanying text; for example, the words written on the back of the photographs?

In addition to focusing on the documentation and photographs of the former Emigrant Museum, I am interested in what was done in this field in terms of museology. Therefore, I have also examined several exhibitions dedicated to the issue of Croatian migration in the United States. In researching several historical waves of Croatian emigration, I have approached the topic from two different perspectives: on the one hand, from the traditional archival-museological perspective; on the other, from a perspective framed by the contemporary artistic practices and participation of a group of female emigrants who took part in the art project entitled *Amerika*, discussed later in the essay. This exhibition and research project differed considerably from the more standard approaches to emigration, such as those presented at the Municipal Museum of Rijeka (*Merika: Emigration from Central Europe to America 1880–1914*) or the Ethnographic Museum of Istria in Pazin (*Suitcases and Destinies: Istria out of Istria*, 2009). Photographic material dominates both exhibitions, allowing for an initial insight into the human relationships and changes that took place after the immigrants took up their new positions in American society. The Emigration Museum's collection, in addition to the documents on emigration to America, also contains visual materials and information about emigration to other overseas and European countries. However, the sources related to the United States are the most numerous: among other reasons, faith in the future, the size of the country, and what the American form of modernization promised had the greatest impact on a large number of people.

Musealizing migration: the Emigration Museum's photography collection

The Emigration Museum was established by a decision of the Kingdom of Yugoslavia's Ministry for Social Affairs and Public Health in Zagreb in 1933. The protocols governing the museum's work were adopted in 1936, and one year later a subsidiary branch was founded in Split. The Split museum took over the majority of the materials organized in the Archive of the Yugoslav People's Defense from South America.[10] The majority of this archival material was dedicated to the organization founded by the Croatian emigrants in Antofagasta, Chile, in 1916. The documentation was temporarily located in the Municipal Library of Split, where it remained until the library's closure in 1941.[11] Then it was sent to Zagreb, where the holdings of both Zagreb's and Split's museums were handed over to the Emigration Office, where they remained until the Centre for Migration and Ethnic Studies was founded in 1965 with the goal of carrying out systematic scholarly research on migration.[12] Finally, in 1998, the materials were handed over to the Croatian State Archives in Zagreb. The visuals were kept in the photography collection, while the documentation related to the organization and operation of the museum, as well as to the diaspora, was archived separately.[13]

The visual archive related to emigration to the United States comprises some 500-odd images. It is part of the photography collection in the Croatian State Archives, collected from various parts of the world with Croatian immigration, but its potential connections with other preserved documents from the Emigration Museum are very difficult to reconstruct. The inscriptions on the backs of the images are particularly interesting. Besides the appeal of these visual materials from past eras, which depict the circumstances of immigrants in various situations, it is this additional information found in inscriptions on the backs of the photographs that helps identify the fates of individuals. Most of these images are of average quality; they were taken by amateurs, mostly for private purposes. The Emigration Museum, and later the Institute for Migration, was primarily interested in statistics when describing the fates of emigrants, as well as the "negative effects that emigration had on individual nations."[14] This collection is thus a kind of construct with little information as to its origins and political intentions.

Archives have been gaining ever more importance in the past few years in the study of migration.[15] Considering the Emigration Museum's photography archive, a number of questions arise about how artists and researchers have utilized photographs in the exploration of Croatian migration to North America. The majority of these images document a new country and society without offering any information about assimilation, the meeting of cultures, or how the immigrants dealt with new ways of life, apart from those elementary details that reveal the lives and struggles of common people in general. Many of the photographs are studio portraits, while photographs that depict the conditions under which the emigrants worked are rare. The photographs in the archive's focus are the farms on which the migrants lived and worked, and the social events in which they participated. Some images depict traces of customs from their homeland, such as traditional tools and costumes, which can be interpreted as identity-markers. Economic prosperity is frequently depicted through new cars or through the formal clothing in which the immigrants posed. The portraits and studio scenes in the archive show the faces of people whose histories remain a mystery; in the same way, it is impossible to determine how they adapted their knowledge, beliefs, and skills to the new society that many of them would remain a part of for many years.

Recent procedures of archival processing and the impossibility to view it within the original thematic units have made it difficult to comprehensively consider the emigration museums in Zagreb and Split. Only a small number of photographs show what the exhibitions looked like, and for a number of items sent or brought by the emigrants, there is no information on where they were stored. The physical, historical, and ontological principles of collecting have been subjected to various new principles of ordering over time, influencing our right to interpret, in addition to archival documentation, the changes we observe or assume.

In the archives of the Emigration Museum, written records bear witness to the way in which photography was acquired for the museum's collection, as well as the archival and display policies. Individual donations of photographs were made through letters. For many immigrants, it was not easy to organize or finance professional photographs to send back home from America. Thus, for instance, two photographs were sent to the museum from the village of Smiljan near Gospić, as records of the childhood of Nikola Tesla in the Lika region.[16] There are no traces of these photographs in the collection, while another photograph is mentioned in a donation made by Josip Nejak, who gave the museum "a lovely large photograph of our famous scholar and physicist from New York."[17] Letters like this, in which a photograph sent for the museum collection is explicitly mentioned although it can no longer be found in the now separate photography collection, speak of the aforementioned changes to the previously established archival order.

The announcement of 1933 setting out the goals and purpose of the museum contains a specific request for images from the lives of scientists and cultural workers, the places where they worked, and their meetings with other Croatian migrants. Among other things, the museum requested photographs of new neighborhoods, homes, celebrations, churches, enterprises, and lands, which reflected the "pioneering undertakings" of the emigrants and their participation in the public life of the countries to which they migrated.[18] Many of the photographs in the archive seem staged. This is especially evident in the early studio photographs, in which people are ceremoniously dressed. Their shirt collars are too tall and stiff, their shoes often too tight. They are evidently tense, and the scenes are too cramped, without a single smiling face. They are isolated subjects—posing for the photograph—and their positions are precarious. By reading the comments on the margins and backs of the photographs, the viewer is invited to imagine the narrative of Croatian experiences of migration to America. The emigrants walk along the unpaved roads in recently founded towns, which had to be built from the ground up. It is rare to come across a proud owner of a new house; it is much more common to encounter group photos showing the construction of a church for the immigrant community.

In the photography archives of the museum, there are very few images of the intercultural encounters that were a feature of the Croatian immigrant experience in America. With the closing of the museum and the subsequent archiving procedures, a place that probably functioned as a contact zone was lost, where social knowledge and ideologies were also mediated through photographs. Accepting the meaning of this term as introduced by Mary Louise Pratt, today we assume that the museums in Zagreb and Split were more than places of consultation and conversation: they were also places of colonial encounters, where people who were geographically and historically distant came into contact and established relationships.[19] Our present knowledge of emigration is not associated with any iconic image. Some of the photographs from the collection at the Croatian State Archives map America through the roads built, among others, by Croatian emigrants, who wanted to send back home some visual evidence of their achievements and their living conditions. The communication has become one-way: without a contact zone, we have lost the context in which subjects are constituted and the historical, political, and moral relations are established. Today, photographs and other documents only present certain historical moments, not allowing for the more complex processes of representing subjects and their ideas, hopes, stories, and testimonies.

The photograph showing a Mexican nanny posing with her charges—the children of Croatian immigrants—is one of the rare examples found in the archive that offers some information about multicultural relations.[20] In a photograph, Nikola Ledinić's young family poses with three children, appearing relaxed and happy. Behind them is a house that reflects certain material security, as well as a car and a small truck—signs of economic prosperity. The nanny is treated like a family member in this scene, while the most interesting character is a young woman in the center, wearing a dark dress. Her relaxed hands gently hold a boy dressed in a white suit like his father, and her gaze is directed at the photographer. The postures and relaxation are in contrast to the majority of photographs in this collection, in which the unknown photographers often approached the Croatian immigrants as if they had never left their homeland, perhaps without even asking questions about the differences, similarities, and social or aesthetic transformations that could be

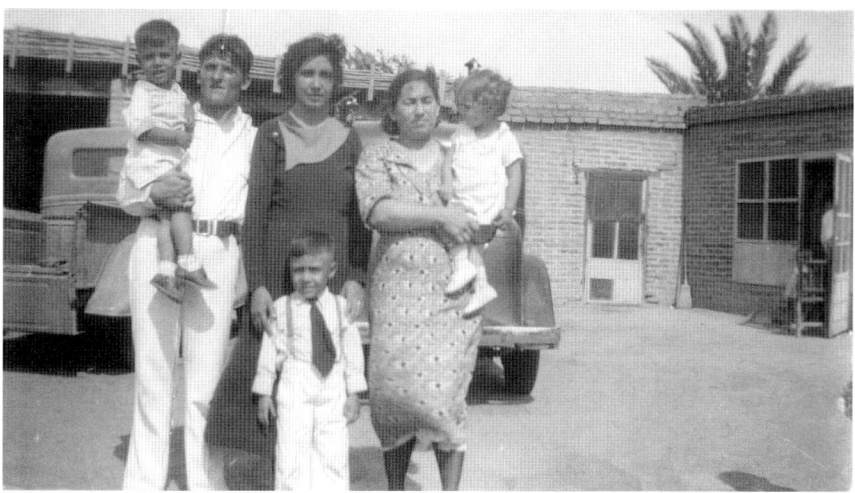

Figure 2: Nikola Ledinić with his family in Obregón, Sonora, New Mexico, July 16, 1936. On the back: "Mr. Nikola Ledinich with family – during celebration 7/16/36 at family Vlašić." Donated by N. Kuraica, Croatian State Archives, Zagreb, HR-HDA-1610-23-13.

traced given the medium in question. In the 1930s, a portrait was taken of a young couple, the Kuraicas, who had moved to Obregon in northern Mexico. The young woman's carefully chosen clothing suggests discomfort, and her pose and communication with the photographer show a certain stiffness. A photograph of the same woman taken outside the photographer's studio has a completely different character; she is wearing everyday clothes and gazing thoughtfully at something outside the frame. She is sitting on a three-legged wooden stool in a room with clumsily painted walls, clearly happier in this space in contrast to the artificial ambience of the staged studio environment. Taken out of its context, this photograph can be interpreted in various ways. Only the visual facts can be explored, while the remaining elements of the context can only be guessed. In this case, the archive is "a form of production surrounding the medium of photography," its content filtered based on the categorization and organization of the collection itself.[21] Today, this photograph can only be considered in the context of the archive in which it is located and alongside the remaining materials, from which it cannot be separated. In keeping with this, the archive is "not only a place of storage, but also a place of production" of knowledge about the past, as well as what the present records for the future (Fig. 2).[22]

The first migrants to the United States largely went to Texas, California, and the areas around the Gulf of Mexico. This information is confirmed by the best organized records of the Croatian immigrant community, kept at the Emigrants' Club in San Francisco.[23] Numerous migrants also went to Pittsburgh, which would become the headquarters of the Croatian Fraternal Union, the strongest national immigrant organization, which is still active today, while Chicago had the largest number of Croatian immigrant educational organizations and newspapers published in America.

Specific topics relevant for the immigrant community were discussed in the museum's journal *Iseljenički muzej* [Emigration Museum]. The journal was published as a supplement to the emigrant newspapers *Novi iseljenik* and *Hrvatski iseljenik* in Zagreb from 1936 to 1940, with six issues. The journal's front pages occasionally showed images of museum displays located in private flats in Zagreb and Split. The Zagreb Museum originally used the premises of the Emigration Commissariat in the Upper Town, and after 1933, moved to a larger building in the Lower Town. Although some documents mention the construction of a separate building, this never happened. The Split branch used the premises of the Municipal Library for a while, and then moved to the premises of the Emigrants' Club. The walls of the rooms and the hallways featured charters, title pages of various publications, graphs with various statistical information, and photographs, and there were also display cases with various items. Photographs of the displays are kept in several albums within the museum's collection. They are of varying sizes, from small, more or less pocket-sized formats, to large ones. From these albums we can learn more about the displays themselves. One photograph stands out in particular: that of the Split museum's neat, organized archive, which offers us the basic information about its structure and the classification of the materials received, labeled in several parallel groups. The museum was founded with the idea of collecting as many sources as possible that illustrated the life of emigrants, divided into twelve segments: in addition to an extensive collection of printed matter (newspapers, books, calendars, leaflets, proclamations, etc.), there was data on the foundation and operation of emigrant societies and institutions (churches, schools, clubs) as well as the economic organizations and enterprises that the emigrants owned or in which they were employed. The museum sought to document the activity of cultural workers, scientists, and other public figures; focused on the historical sources about the origin of emigrant settlements and emigrants' personal achievements, preferably documented photographically; and collected documents on the ways in which emigrants supported their homeland and the customs they retained, noting that photographs of high-ranking personalities in important services were especially sought after. In addition to the above, the museum also collected materials on the return of emigrants to their homeland.[24]

Written sources in the museum collection contributed to the understanding of the archive's structure and the role of Croatian immigrants in donating money to finance the taking and printing of photographs. One such letter, sent in 1934, specifies the value of what the photographs depicted, alongside an exhaustive list of the amounts spent. Similar to the above-mentioned example of the lost photograph of Nikola Tesla is another case of only a letter in which the photograph is mentioned, while the picture cannot be identified today within the photography collection. We seem to be facing two parallel streams of evidence: the visual, which is in some cases unavailable, and the written, which supplements the visual with additional detail. The traces that remain are always to be approached with an awareness of the epistemic uncertainties at the heart of the archival structure. Research makes us aware of the encounters between various types of sources that have been subjected to classification procedures. It is in the impossibility to reconstruct them all that one becomes aware of the inconsistent and uncertain period of the archive, as they "are not simply accounts of actions or records of what people thought happened. They are records of uncertainty and doubt in how people imagined they could and might make the rubrics of rule correspond to a changing imperial world."[25] Although her theses primarily refer to colonial ontology, Ann Laura Stoler writes about the reactivation of archives that are often "aligned" with the new strategies of political rule. The coordinates of her text rely on the positions of the unwritten, hidden message, as well as on general knowledge ("everyone knew it"), all of which are subject to change managed by those in charge of archival heritage. I notice similar "traces of insecurity" in the documentation on Croatian emigrants, which has been subjected to various regimes over time.

An interest in the documentary materials that speak of the "countries and regions in which our settlements exist," as well as the information drawn "from the lives and customs of countries to which our people have emigrated" is highlighted in the very structure of the Emigration Museum.[26] In the context of these materials, photography is used as evidence; it testifies to the success of individuals or shows people who contributed to another's success.[27] A photograph from the Zagreb museum shows a massive boa constrictor skin hanging above a door; to the left, is a textile piece created by indigenous Americans, on the origins of which there is no information. These examples reflect the migrants' need to send in "curiosities" that belonged to other cultures, in search of discoveries such as those undertaken by the Seljan brothers, explorers whose adventures were occasionally written about in immigrant newspapers.[28] Considered from a contemporary cultural-anthropological approach, the artifacts recorded in the photographs reflect an interest in other cultures, and the way they were perceived, both from a passive-observational position and with the inevitably colonial gaze. The Emigration Museum was experienced as a place that existed in a civil context, where various schematic supplements, graphs, and photographs of immigrants were, in the displays, placed on equal footing with items that came from other cultures, however rare these may be. This, at least, is what the photograph of the displays suggests, which is why it does not offer additional evidence that would either deny or confirm what

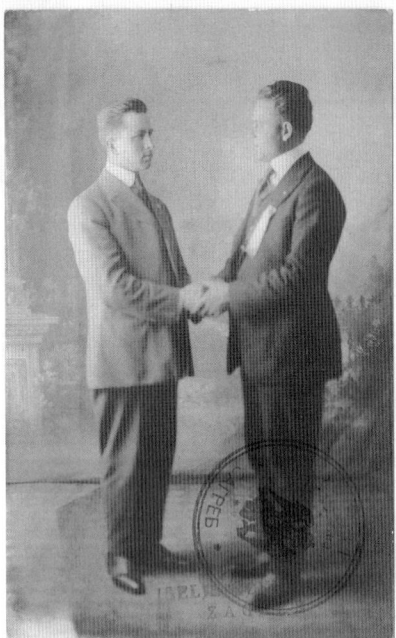

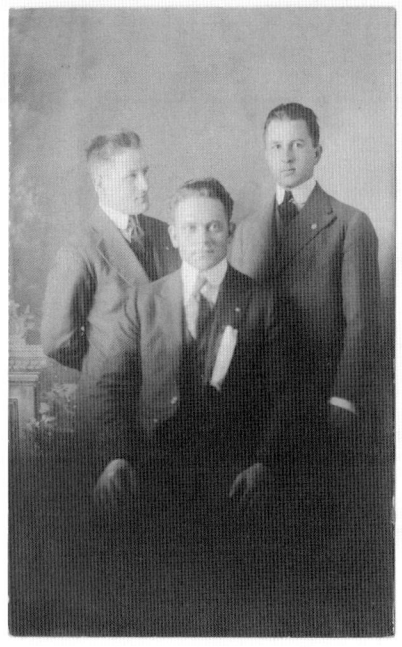

Figure 3: Unknown photographer, "Two
volunteers from America" (Plate 16, p. 342).
Croatian State Archives, Zagreb, Fond
No. HR-HDA-1610-32-166.

Figure 4: Unknown Photographer, "The group
of volunteers, 1916" (Plate 17, p. 343).
Croatian State Archives, Zagreb, Fond
No. HR-HDA-1610-32-167.

is seen. In the remaining photographs of the two museums' displays, there are no
similar cultural encounters, or more precisely, the encounters take place in a tightly
knit culturological environment where there is not a significant difference between
details and their meanings.

In the Emigration Museum's archives, portraits of eminent members of the
immigrant community in the United States show that the assimilated immigrants
largely belonged to wealthier families. The circles in which certain individuals
moved (or aspired to move) come to light in a letter by one Dominio sent from
New York:

> Our meeting was the most interesting and the most important, because the
> presenters and speakers were undoubtedly the most well-known and popular in
> the academic and literary world, such as Thomas Mann, the notable German
> writer, or Mr. Butler, president of Columbia University and the Carnegie
> Endowment.[29]

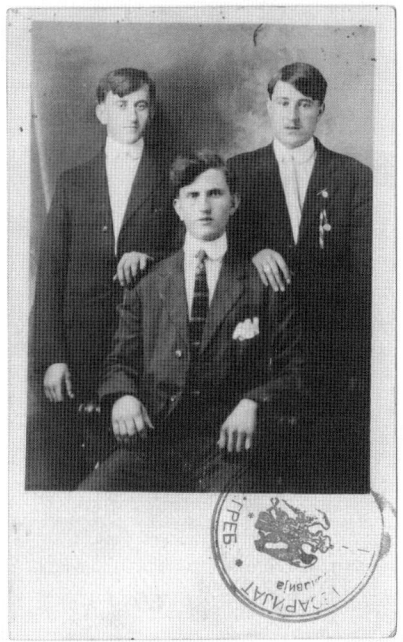

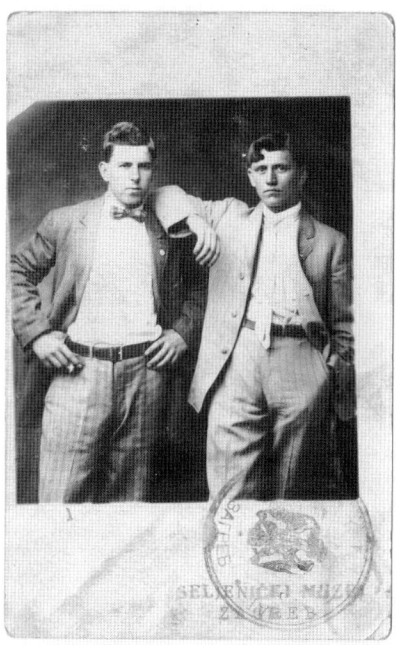

Figure 5: Unknown Photographer, "Volunteers 1916" (Plate 18, p. 344). Croatian State Archives, Zagreb, Fond No. HR-HDA-1610-32-168.

Figure 6: Unknown Photographer, "Two volunteers from America 1916" (Plate 19, p. 345). Croatian State Archives, Zagreb, Fond No. HR-HDA-1610-32-169.

The remaining sources establish a specific view of the conditions under which the immigrants lived, whereby the existence of several photographic sequences helps create the potential narratives. It is therefore worth mentioning several group portraits of young men taken in 1916: volunteers in World War I. Their body language, friendly touches, and a sort of intimacy indicates that they had a common origin. In addition, their connectedness implies an intention to protect each other in battle, aware of the danger they were facing. Judging by their clothing, they are already assimilated members of American society. Their photographs are far from soldier stereotypes, revealing them to be vulnerable and emotional (Figs. 3–6). Such familial and friendly relationships can be noticed in many photographs; for instance, in Joe Tomšić's family portrait made in Wisconsin. A wooden, one-story house stands above the ground on massive logs, and there eleven people are lined up in a row in front of the whitewashed house. A dog is also posing, coyly resting his paws on a bench, while a cat has turned its back on the photographer. Positioning the subjects in a kind of chorus line testifies to a synchronous routine that is not significantly different from the one that they left behind (Fig. 7).

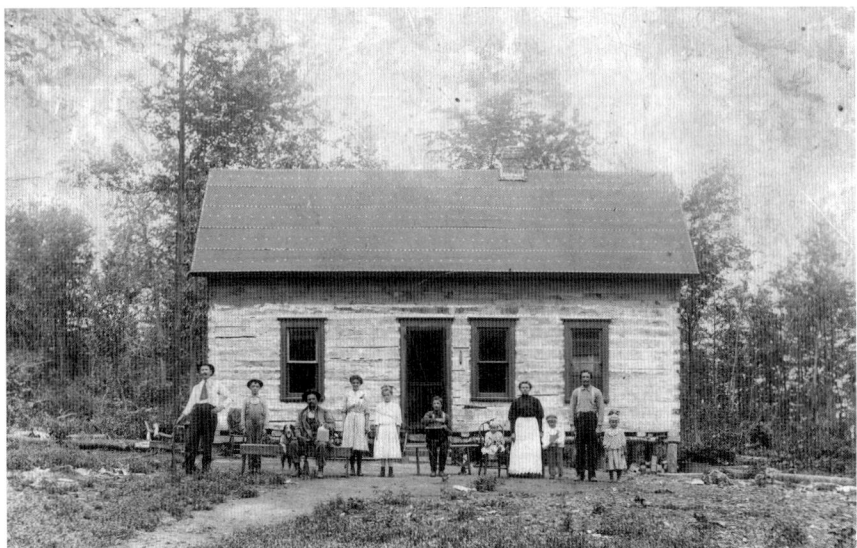

Figure 7: Unknown photographer, *Joe Tomšič i njegova družina* [Joe Tomšič and his family].
On the back of the photo it is indicated they are among first immigrants on the farm in Willard,
Wisconsin, n.d. Croatian State Archives, Zagreb. Fond No. HR-HDA-1610-32-187.

At that time, the Croats in the United States were building workers' club centers for the working people, depicted in a photograph from 1914. The relatively large crowd in this image speaks of several parallel goings-on. In the background, a man is standing and giving a speech, while the political beliefs of the group of people can be read from the partly visible slogans: they speak of the freedom and brotherhood of all people, and help is also called for, although it is not known for precisely what purpose. Most of the image is filled with men in black suits and hats, while in the lower-left corner, musicians are waiting to begin with the merrier part of the event. A small sequence from the same period documents workouts done by the members of Hrvatski Sokol, a sports organization founded in 1874 with the aim of furthering the physical, moral, and intellectual development of the people, with three branches operating among the Croatian immigrants to the United States.

Most of the remaining US photographs taken before WWII are images of agricultural work and livestock breeding. Immigrants also used to have their photographs taken in front of the wooden boxes that they would send back home, full of presents and necessary items. One photograph shows the women and children of the Yugoslav volunteers, "who came to America with their husbands and fathers"; not much is known about their activities.[30] Their low social status is shown by their clothing as well as their acceptance of a donation in a public bathroom. Portraits such as that of Mila Gazvoda from 1906, who has an urban and self-assured air, are extremely rare. On the back of her portrait, there is a message saying: "Remember our acquaintance in the free country" (Fig. 8).

Some of those that chose to stay in America used photographs to prove to themselves and their families back home that they had made the right decision by moving away, visualizing those objects that bore witness to their material improvement, as well as the changes in their appearances and ways of dressing. According to some individual accounts, they cured their homesickness by celebrating their prosperity and recalling the poverty of their homeland.[31] In a way, it is possible to relate these scenes with the leaflets advertising the so-called Emigrants' Congress, first held in Zagreb in 1931. The intention of the congress was to gather the Croatian emigrants to the United States, who were to meet at home for the first time in the history of emigration. On that occasion, flyers were printed with a map of Yugoslavia and a series of photographs of famous sights, which were part of the pilgrimage to the land of "air and sun […], in which they first saw the light of day." Besides showing the itinerary, the leaflet was used to promote the shipping companies that organized the trips, stating all the additional costs that the participants were expected to pay. Photographs in the brochures depicted the natural beauty and cultural values of their ancestors' homeland: Zagreb's parks, a view of Dubrovnik, and the Plitvice Lakes. These images were far from those of the poor regions and difficult conditions that the immigrants had left behind. Due to their newly achieved financial status, however, some of them could afford to travel back to their homeland on "luxurious express ocean steamships," as the advertising leaflet stated, in significantly different conditions from those of the cheap below-deck cabins in which most of them had first traveled to America. This collective "grand tour of the motherland," which awaited its children with open arms, occurred at a time of economic prosperity, intensive modern urbanization; the goal of the tour, as advertised to Croatian emigrants, was to become familiar with everything that defines the identity of a population.[32]

After World War II, there was a change in the perception of archival documents related to immigrants, whose economic aid was expected in the difficult postwar period. At this time, emigrations were no longer as common as they had been in the preceding decades. Emigration had become a sensitive political issue, viewed through the prism of the emigration of members and sympathizers of the Independent State of Croatia (a fascist puppet state of Germany and Italy, 1941–1945) and opponents of the new, communist Yugoslav state. Back then, a political emigration had developed that aimed to "free [the Croatian people] from Communism and from any kind of Yugoslavia, and to help the people in the homeland to establish a democratic and independent Croatian state."[33] During the war, the museums in Split and Zagreb were closed, and the postwar archival materials from the Emigration Museum's collection, which was now controlled by the

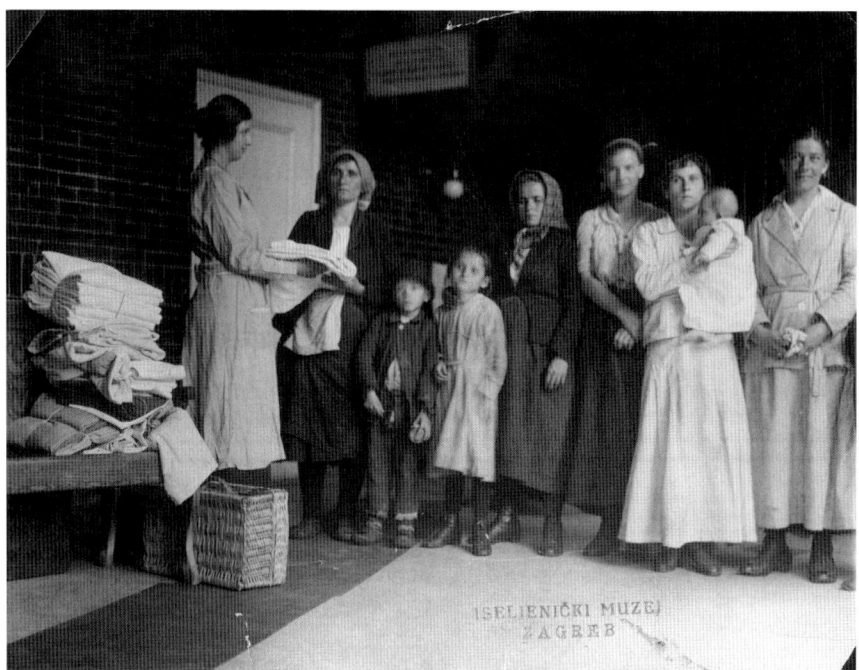

Figure 8: Unknown photographer. Front "Women and children of the volunteers ... from the American Red Cross in the bathroom." Verso "Women and children of Yugoslav volunteers arrived with their husbands and fathers in America.", n.d. Gift of Ivan Mladineo from New York. Museum of Immigration, Zagreb, 1936. Croatian State Archives, Zagreb. Fond No. HR-HDA-1610-32-276.

Ministry of Labor, were most likely collected by Matica hrvatskih iseljenika (the Croatian Heritage Foundation), which continued to communicate intensively with the immigrants. Matica was founded in 1951 as a social organization that established, maintained, and promoted links with the emigrants and their descendants, and it was particularly active in organizing cultural, artistic, and sports events. Among other things, the institution provided emigrants with information on their pension rights, repatriation, customs privileges, and other legal issues.

In the period after World War II, some of the preserved photographs reveal a change in the social paradigm; images celebrating the achievements of prominent Croatian immigrants in America began to proliferate in the postwar period. A fine example is the photograph testifying to the acknowledgment and application of the scientific discoveries of Petar Guberina at the Western Pennsylvania School for the Deaf in Pittsburgh. He had developed his methods in Zagreb during the 1950s, particularly his verbotonal method for working with children who had hearing disabilities and speech disorders. Among the photographs, there are portraits of Anna P. Krasna, editor of *Glas naroda* and *Novi list* in New York, taken while working on

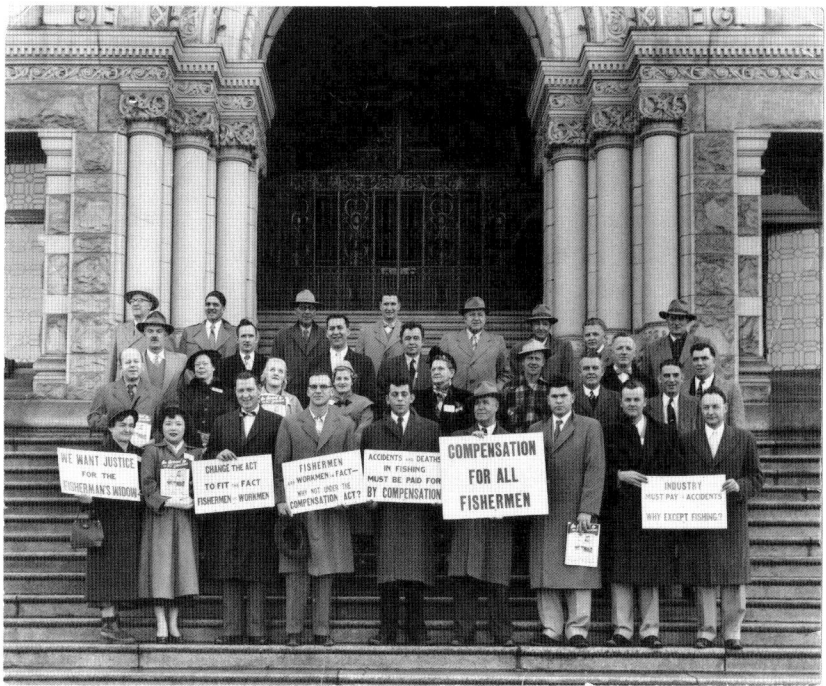

Figure 9: Ken, Appeal of the fishermen union delegates, 1955. On the back: "These are the dele-gates of the fishermen's union in Victoria Parliament for social security, which we got"; Victoria, Canada No. 2-11217 / 1955. Croatian State Archives, Zagreb. Fond No. HR-HDA-1610-19-57

the layout of the new issues, as well as a documentary showing Eleonore Roosevelt awarding the Association of American Magazines Award to Lenka Franulić, a top Chilean journalist of Croatian descent. One of the rare photographs that depicts the impact of the poor working conditions was taken at the end of the 1950s, when the representatives of the Fishing Union visited the Parliament for Social Insurance demanding protection for the wives of fishermen should their husbands have an accident or die (Fig. 9).

It is impossible to consider the photographic material created after the end of World War II outside the context of the Cold War and the specific position of Croatian immigrants in that period. Not much information survives on the rare exhibitions dedicated to immigrant culture, such as those held in 1956 in Zagreb, Rijeka, and Split, but interesting historical materials nevertheless stand out.[34] Although an interest in folklore as a significant marker of the identity of immigrants continued to dominate, featured on the front pages of the calendars that circulated in the immigrant community, the photography collection contains many examples with different content. This particularly concerns those photographs that depict the relations between the nations, the awareness of workers' rights, and the ideological changes that were introduced at the time in Yugoslavia. The Commission for Cultural Relations with Foreign Countries organized Croatian and Serbian language lessons, the students of which can be seen in one of the photographs.[35] Immigrants took part in May Day parades, driving their long worn-out trucks decorated with the appropriate slogans: "Boy o Boy I'm Tired But I Have to Start Over Again." The owner of one such vehicle, Andy Milosevic, documented the old ways of collecting rainwater and other traditional customs in a small photographic sequence taken in a rural community in Trinidad, Colorado. Photographs documenting various get-togethers accompanied by alcohol, as well as the visual proof of a drive in a Rambler from Sarajevo to Slavonski Brod in 1959, which attracted significant attention in the rural Slavonian community, tell interesting details about the social lives of immigrants. By looking at these images, it is possible to come across visual records of the forms of cultural representation used, among other things, in a pedagogical context. We do not know who took most of the photos; their authors are mentioned only in the case of studio photographs in advertising cardboard frames. For many of them, I assume that they were taken by someone close to the people depicted, and some of them are documentary photographs that may have been commissioned by the emigrant club from local professional photographers. Some shots seem uninteresting or unimportant; however, thanks to new theoretical approaches, we now single them out with the aim of acquiring new knowledge about complex emigration issues (Figs. 10–14).

Emigrants as the subjects and producers of exhibition narratives

The displays of an exhibition, *Merika*, dedicated to emigration to the United States in the late nineteenth and early twentieth centuries, were largely based on available written evidence, in particular on letters and articles published in immigrant newspapers, but the displays also contained archival photographs.[36] The exhibition area was designed to look like a boat, where the fates of twenty-six unrelated immigrants were presented. The immigrants discussed in this exhibition were those about whom some information could be uncovered. For the most part linear and two-dimensional, the exhibition did not facilitate interaction in the way that the Red Star Line Museum in Antwerp, for instance, did. The project mostly highlighted the significance of Rijeka as a large port from which many people left their homeland to start a new life, as well as the organizational structure intended especially for emigrants, which many European ports, shipping companies, railways,

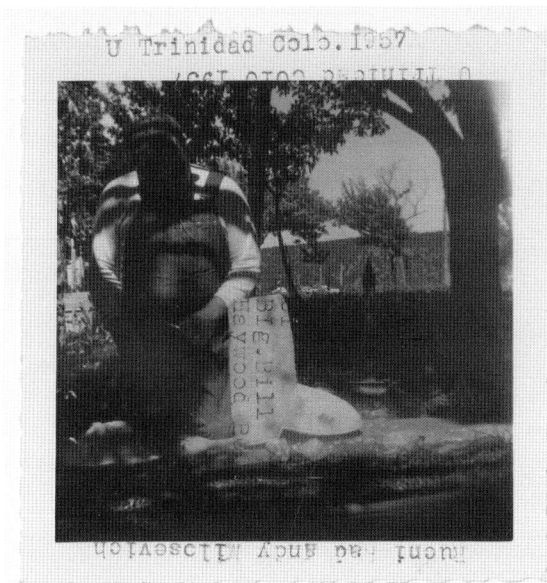

Figure 10: Unknown photographer, "In Trinidad Colo. 1957 / Craft work Andy Milosevic". Croatian State Archives, Zagreb, Fond No. HR-HDA-1610-32-62.

emigration agencies, banks, and postal services participated in. This entire system was put in place so that Europe could deliver a massive new workforce to America and Canada in the shortest time possible. And while the advertising materials regularly displayed the might and power of transatlantic ships, as well as the new technologies that the freshly arrived population could use in their new homes, the reality was very different.

The split opinions on emigration—for and against it—have their historical origins, particularly in the politics of the Habsburg Monarchy, which the visual materials in the catalog indicate as well. Photography, for the most part, reflects historical information, but the content of certain photographs published in the catalog of the Rijeka exhibition differs considerably from those preserved at the Croatian State Archives. For instance, emigration from the Kvarner Islands and the northern littoral led to a change in the traditional gendered separation of tasks: an unusual scene shows women in a boat on a choppy sea, performing the demanding job of fishing because the men had emigrated to America.[37] The photo was taken by Branko Kojić, member of the Photo Club Zagreb, a journalist who later established himself as a scholar in the field of maritime history and aimed at giving his photographs a documentary character and to visualize changes in the social order (Fig. 15).

Cultural encounters are documented in photographs showing various customs and medical inspections, as well as in images that depict the conditions under which the immigrants worked in construction, on the railways, in quarries, and in mines. Immigrants adapted at different paces, depending on the ability of the individuals to focus on the new conditions and only infrequently look back at pictures from their homeland, preserved on color postcards.

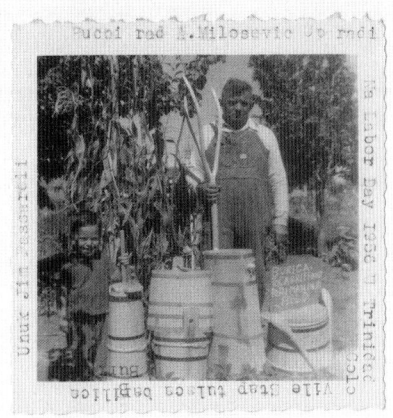

Figure 11: Unknown photographer, "Craft work A. Milosevic works on Labor Day 1956 in Trinidad Colo. / Hay-fork stick 'tulaca' 'babilica' / Grandson Jim Passareli". Croatian State Archives, Zagreb, Fond No. HR-HDA-1610-32-63.

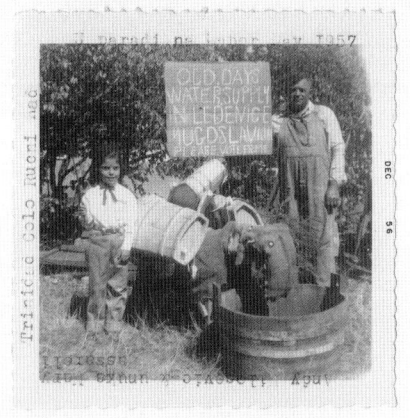

Figure 12: Unknown photographer, "In the Mayday Parade 1957 / Andy Milosevic & grand-daughter Mary Passareli / Trinidad Colo craft work". Croatian State Archives, Zagreb, Fond No. HR-HDA-1610-32-64.

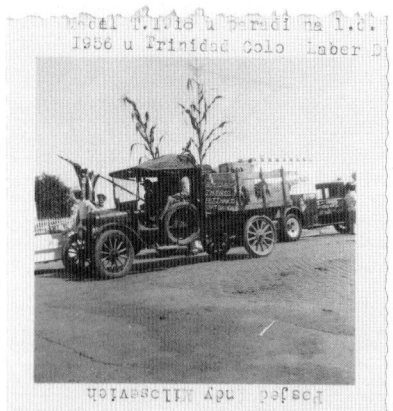

Figure 13: Unknown photographer, "In the L. D. (Labour Day) Parade 1956 in Trinidad Colo / Real Property Andy Milosevic". Croatian State Archives, Zagreb, Fond No. HR-HDA-1610-32-65.

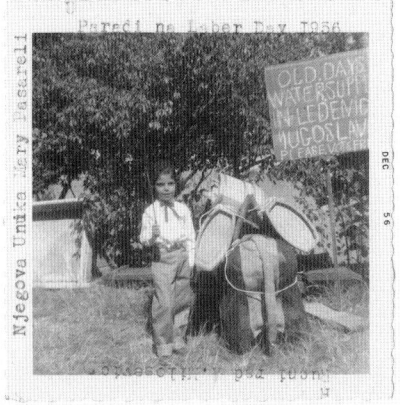

Figure 14: Unknown photographer, "In the Laber Parade 1956 in Trinidad Colo / His granddaughter Mary Pasareli". Croatian State Archives, Zagreb, Fond No. HR-HDA-1610-32-66.

The concept behind the exhibition *Suitcases and Destinies*, which was dedicated to the emigrants from the Croatian region of Istria, was similar to that of the exhibition in Rijeka.[38] Because of the complex historical circumstances (like the rest of Croatia, Istria used to belong to several political entities), Istrian national identity had been frequently overshadowed by other ethnic layers, most prominently that

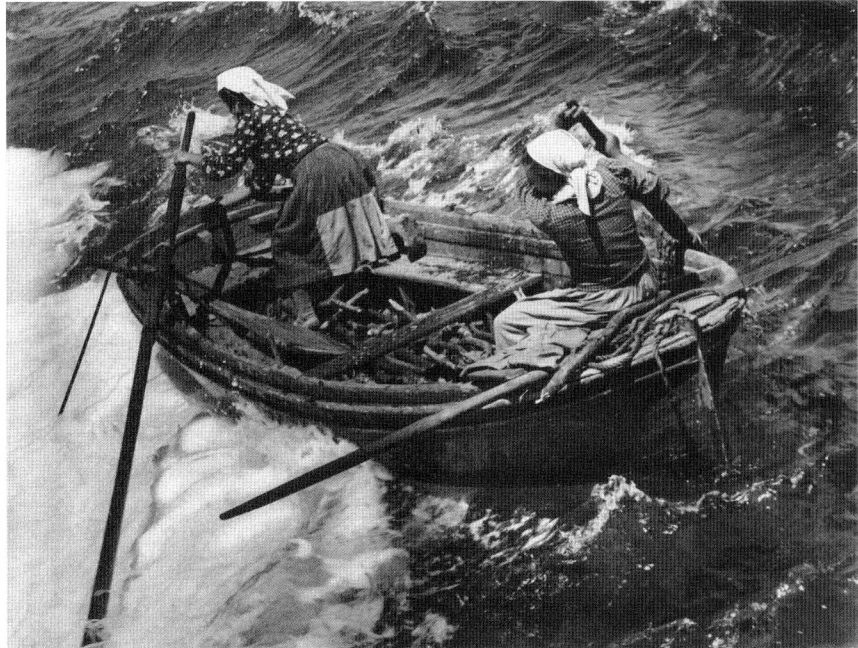

Figure 15: Branko Kojić, *Struggle with the waves*, before 1939. On the back is a seal of the Photo Club Zagreb, 1939. MUO – Museum of Arts and Crafts, Zagreb, MUO-015741.

of northern Italy. The exhibition focused on several individual emigrant stories. Photographs were its visual part, displaying that which is not visible; the photographs are like microscopic images whose true meaning can only begin to be deciphered today, bringing into the discussion new knowledge and understandings. Among other things, on a methodological and theoretical level, the exhibition encouraged a discussion on the notion of time, which according to anthropologists, is not only a natural fact but also an ideologically constructed instrument of power. The interpretation based on the hypothesis of the "ethnographic present," used for the purpose of othering, initiated shifts with regard to the established thinking about emigrants from Istria, whose identity was mostly based on ancient cultural elements of a rural community.[39]

A very different project was created by Kristina Leko in collaboration with five Croatian immigrants after several years of research.[40] Leko approached the immigrant community from an inclusive, socially aware perspective based on the notions of consistency, responsibility, reliability, and ethics. In contrast to the museological and archival formats discussed above, Leko strategically used anthropological methods to develop a unique socio-critical project. In it, the intimate recollections and "small stories" of female immigrants were tied together into a new identity—a collective one. Here, too, there were numerous photographs of everyday people, borrowed from the women's photo albums. Leko chose to work with immigrants from the New York City area, more precisely from Hoboken, the former industrial port of New Jersey, where many of these women's husbands had found work (Fig. 16).

The story of Croatian migration to America, told by the five women, was different because they worked as a group in this project, creating a common narrative within which each of them nevertheless retained her own identity. Kristina Leko took on responsibility for the project along with her cocreators—the "artist-ethnographers" whose photographs of the "old country" were interwoven with documentary images of life in America. These were no longer the stories of anonymous travelers on transatlantic ships, whose identities were created by the exhibition context they all shared. The realistic nature of the exhibition was based on the powerful decisions made by its creators, and film and photography played the most important roles therein.

Freedom, hunger, war, money, family, democracy, capitalism, belief, the American dream, and the old country defined a field of interest struggling to make the ideas that shaped it visible to a wider audience.[41] Leko's open archive, with the exhibition accompanied by workshops, meetings, and other events that addressed the issue of emigration in broader terms, was developed through a combination of narrative, autobiographical, ethnographical, aesthetic, and documentary approaches. To paraphrase Lenin's groundbreaking 1901 text "What Is To Be Done?," Leko started to formulate a kind of response of her own, asking in return, what she should do to make the marginalized groups and their way of life visible and their problems heard, yet without using the stories for political purposes. The photos selected for the exhibition were diverse and did not correspond to any predetermined pattern. Some of them were nostalgic memories of childhood, while others showed a group of young, self-confident women in modern clothing as they embarked on their first visit to their homeland. The images were selected by the participants themselves and did not pass through various institutional or other filters. Thus, they were not based on other people's expectations, but consciously chosen and experienced. The exhibition was a cultural encounter that fulfilled a social function—making decisions about the social and political roles it played, the actors in these stories being neither fragile nor in danger. A shift in understanding the topic of emigration was made possible in this project through a series of meetings, workshops, and talks addressing a wider audience rather than just the emigrant community, their families, and their descendants. There was no insistence on local or national identities or symbols, but on ways of overcoming fear of the other. The intimate testimonies of these "little women," whose emigrant destinies were largely defined by other people's decisions (motivated by familial, economic,

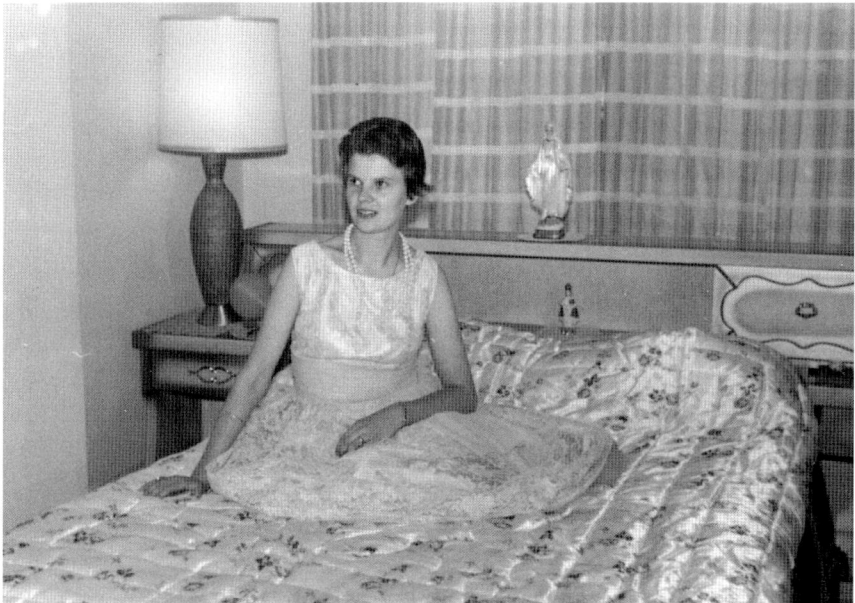

Figure 16: Image from the family album of Ljubica Zic, Astoria, Queens, New York, 1962 (Plate 20, p. 346). Kristina Leko, *AMERIKA*, 2003–2005. In collaboration with Marcella Bonich, Nori Boni-Zorovich, Miriam Busanic, Margaret Zgombic, Ljubica Zic.

political, or other reasons) thus became part of a complex narrative that spoke not only of emigration but also of a broad social commentary through an emotional prism. In this way, it came close to Benjamin's thinking about the encounters whose visibility is not ensured by the development of photographs, but by the later processes of their analysis.

Conclusion

The collections, exhibitions, and the corresponding catalogs of the former Emigration Museum are an archive removed from a stable geographic, institutional, social, or political context. The museum's collection, and the exhibition formats that temporarily archived the source materials associated with emigration, mediated knowledge by using photographs as crucial evidence. Textual documentation has a shaky, but nevertheless unbreakable relationship with photography. Over the years, the archive has been reorganized and its holdings subjected to a kind of negotiation to which new modes of structuring and, finally, understanding are subjected. Among the studied sources, answers to the question about encounters between two different cultures have offered a range of visual confirmations about what can potentially be adopted as general knowledge. Particular stories that arrive via contemporary channels may not provide a particularly serious challenge to the existing frames but will allow for a change in the viewers' way of seeing. The discussed fragments form a representational frame within which the social environment changes the context of the archive, museum, and exhibition. This representational frame is thus opened to the practices of the ephemeral and the everyday, in which, with the help of photography, it is possible to recognize numerous previously untold emigrant narratives.

Notes

*   This work has been supported in part by Croatian Science Foundation under the project IP-2019-04-1772.
1.   It is a document of the Emigration Commissariat of the Kingdom of Serbs, Croats, and Slovenes, dated August 11, 1926, that intones the needs of a singing society in the United States in this way. "Our settlements" refer to the immigrant neighborhoods, which they partly built by themselves. Otherwise, singing societies along with the churches and schools were crucial to preserving national identity. Croatian State Archives, HR-HAD-1619, M 104-11-C2.
2.   Walter Benjamin, "A Short History of Photography" (1931), in Alan Trachtenberg (ed.), *Classic Essays on Photography* (New Haven: Leete's Island Books, 1980), 202–203.
3.   Benjamin, "A Short History of Photography", 212.
4.   James Clifford, *Routes: Travel and Translation in the Late Twentieth Century* (Cambridge: Harvard University Press, 1997), 191.
5.   Clifford, *Routes: Travel and Translation in the Late Twentieth Century*, 197.
6.   Ivan Čižmić et al. (eds.), *Iseljena Hrvatska* (Zagreb: Golden marketing-Tehnička knjiga, 2005), 14.
7.   Čižmić et al., *Iseljena Hrvatska*, 14.
8.   It may be important to note here that after WWII, as well as in the period following the collapse of Yugoslavia in the 1990s, a part of the Croatian immigrant community had a significant impact on the development of nationalistic discourse, a process in which the Catholic Church also played a significant role. Cf. Jasna Čapo, Caroline Hornstein Tomić, and Katica Jurčević (eds.), *Didov san. Transgranična iskustva hrvatskih iseljenika* (Zagreb: Institut za etnologiju i folkloristiku/Institut društvenih znanosti Ivo Pilar, 2014), 10–11.
9.   Čižmić et al., *Iseljena Hrvatska*, 10–11.
10. Both museums were closed during World War II.
11. Yugoslav People's Defense was a Croatian immigrant organization whose political goal was to overthrow the Austro-Hungarian monarchy and create a Yugoslav state,

and they maintained close ties with the homeland. They supported the establishment of economic organizations and immigrant banks that would make life easier for the immigrants. For additional details, see http://arhinet.arhiv.hr/details.aspx-?ItemId=3_8394.

12. The Centre closed in 1987, when along with the Centre for Migration Research, it was integrated into the Institute for Migration and Ethnic Studies, which still exists today. Vlatka Lemić (ed.), *Iseljeništvo. Vodič kroz fondove i zbirke Hrvatskog državnog arhiva* (Zagreb: Hrvatski državni arhiv, 2015), 495.

13. The reference code for the Emigration Museum's collection is HR-HDA-1619. The digitized photography collection is available at http://arhinet.arhiv.hr/digitalobjects.aspx?ItemId=1_32169. Only the photographs have been scanned, without the inscriptions and other information found on the back of the images.

14. Ervin Dubrović, "Iseljavanje u Ameriku od 1880. do 1914. Uz izložbu *Merika* u Muzeju grada Rijeke – prekomorska emigracija iz Srednje Europe i Rijeka kao emigrantska luka 1903.–1914.," *Informatica Muzeologica*, no. 40 (3–4) (2009), 6.

15. Čapo, Hornstein Tomić, and Jurčević (eds.), *Didov san*; Ervin Dubrović (ed.), *Veliki val. Iseljavanje iz srednje Europe u Ameriku 1880.–1914.* (Rijeka: Muzej grada Rijeke, 2012); Branka Bezić Filipović, *Tragom Hrvata u svijetu* (Split: Naklada Bošković, 2016); Rajka Bućin, "Iseljenički muzej u Zagrebu (1933.–1940.)," *Časopis za suvremenu povijest* 50, no. 2 (2018). For further information, see: https://matis.hr/knjige-i-katalozi/.

16. Croatian State Archives, M 104-11-C2, Box 1.

17. *Novi iseljenik* (June 1, 1934). Croatian State Archives.

18. "Iseljenički muzej. Poziv na organizovanje muzeja cjelokupnom našem iseljeništvu" (place of publication unknown). Croatian State Archives, M 104-11-C2, Box 1.

19. Clifford, *Routes*, 192.

20. HR-HDA-1610.1.23.13. I have come to this conclusion about the nanny's background based purely on her appearance; I have not found any written evidence concerning her identity.

21. Ines Schaber, *Obtuse, Flitting by, and in Spite of all – Image Archives in Practice. Notes on Archives 1* (Berlin/Graz: Archive Books/Camera Austria, 2018), 7.

22. Schaber, *Obtuse, Flitting by, and in Spite of all*, 8.

23. Croatian State Archives, M 104-11-C2, Box 9. Guestbooks, books of accounts, meeting minutes, telegrams, letters, and other source materials have been preserved.

24. Ana Holjevac Tuković, *Iseljenički muzej 1933–1941: Sumarni inventar* (Zagreb: Croatian State Archives, 2005), 6–8.

25. Ann Laura Stoler, *Along the Archival Grain: Epistemic Anxieties and Colonial Common Sense* (Princeton/Oxford: Princeton University Press, 2009), 21.

26. Milostislav Bartulica, "O važnosti iseljeničkog muzeja" (1936), typewritten, Croatian State Archives, M104-11-C2.

27. Letter from Ilija Mandić to the director of the Emigration Museum (1934), Croatian State Archives, M104-11-C2. The photograph has not been found.

28. The Seljan brothers traveled in the period between 1899 and 1913, exploring, among other places, some regions in Africa and South America. Their collection is kept in the Ethnography Museum in Zagreb.

29. Private correspondence, Croatian State Archives, M 104-11-C2.

30. An inscription on the back states that the volunteers returned in 1920 in five transports. There were 2500 people in total, who were subsequently transported by the American Red Cross to their homes. The photograph was gifted to the Zagreb museum in 1936 by Ivan Mladineo from New York and was probably taken in the late 1920s.

31. Ervin Dubrović, *Merika. Iseljavanje iz srednje Europe u Ameriku 1880.–1914.* (Rijeka: Muzej grada Rijeke, 2008), 218.

32. Statements from the preserved propaganda leaflets, Croatian State Archives.

33. Ivan Čižmić et al., *Iseljena Hrvatska*, 353.

34. Anonymous, untitled, *Vjesnik* (August 2, 1956).

35. The photograph comes from Chile, but similar courses were also run in America. HR-HDA-1610.

36. The exhibition *Merika. Emigration from Central Europe to America 1880–1914* was held at the City Museum of Rijeka in 2008. The catalog was published by the same institution in 2008.

37. From the Photo Collection of the Museum of Arts and Crafts, Zagreb, inv. no. MUO 15741.

38. The exhibition *Valiže i deštini. Istria out of Istria* was organized by the Ethnographic Museum of Istria, Pazin in 2009, followed by the publication in 2011.

39. Lidija Nikočević, "Istarsko iseljeništvo kao muzejska tema: dileme etnološke reprezentacije," *Zbornik javnih predavanja* 1 (Pazin: Državni arhiv u Pazinu, 2011), 217–226.

40. The exhibition *Amerika* was curated by Kristina Leko in collaboration with Marcella Bonich, Nori Boni Zorovich, Miriam Busanic, Ljubica Zic, and Margaret Zgombic—all immigrants to America. Museum of Contemporary Art, Zagreb, 2005.

41. Barbara Steiner, "Public Matter," in *Amerika* (Zagreb: Museum of Contemporary Art, 2005), exhibition leaflet, n.p.

What Moves You?

Georges Didi-Huberman's Arts of Passage and Pittsburgh Stories of Migration

Alexandra Irimia

"What moves as a body, returns as the movement of thought."
Erin Manning, *Relationscapes*

I migrated from Europe to North America for my studies in 2017. This voluntary relocation has not only "moved" my body and belongings across a continent and an ocean but has also increased my awareness of matters associated with human displacement and the multiple perspectives from which it can be acknowledged. This chapter will focus on two works that have contributed to this awareness and that, although dissimilar in form and content, are connected by a common thread that engages with the coordinates of this volume: photography, migration, and the United States. The following pages bring together and set in productive dialogue a photography exhibition about migration and a book about a documentary on the same topic. Both have caught my eye, in a quite literal sense, in the same year I became a migrant myself—and perhaps for that very reason.

The exhibition was called *Out of Many: Stories of Migration* and was on display between April 5 and April 27, 2018. It was part of a joint curatorial initiative of the Carnegie Nexus Museums in Pittsburgh, Pennsylvania, titled *Becoming Migrant… What Moves You?* Within the framework of this larger project, the exhibition consisted of a selection of works signed by five Pittsburgh-based photographers. In 2017 they undertook a common project to photograph a variety of stories linked to the experiences of migrants that have settled or are in the process of settling in the city of Pittsburgh. Shot from different physical and symbolic angles, the photographs in this exhibition function as local illustrations of the more general landscape of contemporary migration to the United States, a particularly controversial subject after the 2016 presidential election.

Figure 1: Maria Kourkouta and Niki Giannari, *Des spectres hantent l'Europe*, film poster, 2016. © Survivance. Courtesy of Survivance.

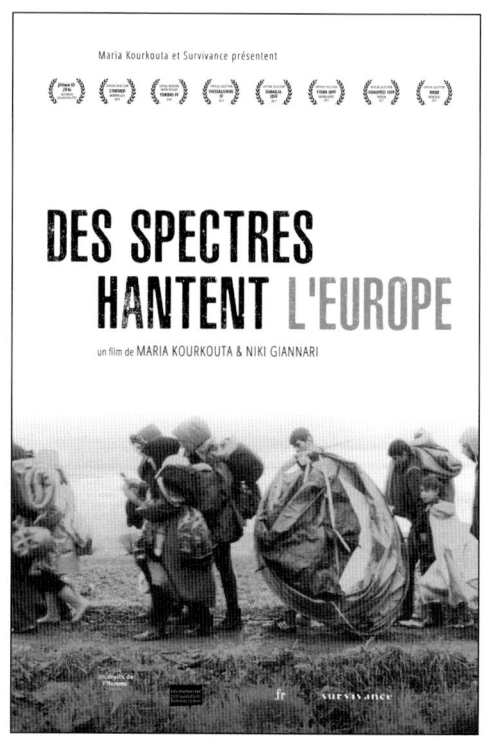

The other pole of my discussion is the volume *Passer, quoi qu'il en coûte* (2017) written by the French art historian Georges Didi-Huberman. This book-length essay is largely the author's response to a documentary film titled *Spectres Are Haunting Europe* and directed by the Greek poet Niki Giannari in 2016 (Fig. 1). The film focuses on the arrested passage of migrants in the camp of Idomeni, Greece (near the border with North Macedonia) during the Mediterranean refugee crisis that started that year.

In drawing a connection between these two works, my argument begins from the rather obvious observation that the book was published in the same year the Pittsburgh photographic project was shot. Far from implying an intended influence or a causal determination at work in this case, I consider this simultaneity to be symptomatic of a broader, ongoing global discussion. In addition, it is evidence of a revived artistic and critical interest in migration as a major subject brought to the ethical, political, and aesthetic scrutiny of both American and European public eye. Discussing the two works in parallel is therefore prone to create a conceptual contact zone where these works illuminate one another, unwillingly and unknowingly, in their invitation to visually engage with several veins of contemporary reflection on migration.[1] Moreover, and perhaps more importantly, their circumstantial juxtaposition is likely to become a ferment for new reflections on photography as a medium, emphasizing its ability to accommodate polymorphous discourses and perspectives on this particular type of cultural encounters. The rather implausible encounter of the documentary work of a group of Pittsburgh photographers with Georges Didi-Huberman's image theory articulates and at the same time performs new strategies for the visual production of meaning. Confirming James Clifford's insights from his "Museums as Contact Zones," these new strategies imply that the photograph is no longer conceived as a static, self-contained unit, but it is instead understood as the expression of a relation, of an asymmetrical and "power-charged set of exchanges," unavoidably accompanied by historical, political, and ethical implications.[2] Erin Manning's concept of "relationscape," cited at the beginning of the chapter, which I will explain later into more detail, resonates strongly with this idea. It must be pointed out that the mediation and exchange facilitated by my comparison as a zone of conceptual contact turn the very images it discusses into migrants. The images assembled in each of the two works, one European and one American, enter an intercontinental dialogue and thus migrate toward new audiences, both ways across the Atlantic. The discussion that follows will only add more mileage to this journey.

In this light, the Pittsburgh photographic project and Didi-Huberman's book may be credited with having set the ground for a comparison of contemporary regimes of photographic visuality, looking at multifaceted experiences of migration. The comparison is motivated by a belief that specificities of American migration stories may transpire with clearer outlines when discussed in contrast with counterparts from a different geopolitical context—in this case, from Europe. For coherence and consistency, the methodology of this study concerned with the imagery of migration adopts, in its turn, a transnational dimension. This essay also compares and contrasts the visual strategies at work in these cultural artifacts, from the perspective of their shared choice to explore the potentialities of a medium that, as Aby Warburg suggested, is one that migrates too.

Out of Many: five photo-narratives of migration in Pittsburgh

As outlined in my introduction, the argument of this essay is set in motion by a collection of images that moved in 2017 from the streets, homes, and courthouses of Pittsburgh, Pennsylvania, to settle on photographic paper and later on gallery walls. The result of this immaterial displacement is an itinerant exhibition that is also readily available online thanks to the generosity of its authors, a group of five Pittsburgh-based photographers working together under the label The Documentary Works.[3]

As I encountered it, the showing of this photographic corpus was part of a joint initiative taken by four museums in Pittsburgh, namely the Carnegie Museum of Art, the Carnegie Science Center, the Carnegie Museum of Natural History, and the Andy Warhol Museum. This large-scale curatorial event unfolded throughout April 2018 and focused on the visual dimension of migration, on the nomadic character of various objects, and on their ability to capture contemporary, human, or nonhuman experiences of displacement. What caught my attention as a visitor was the fact that the entire project, *Becoming Migrant... What Moves you? Nine Compelling Events Traversing the Art and Science of Passage*,[4] problematizes the ways of seeing through which photography is instrumentalized as an appropriate medium for documenting transnational movements. Simultaneously, it foregrounds photography's literal mobility, in the sense of its capacity to be carried across a variety of real and symbolic borders. Last but not least, the project renders explicit the ways in which photography can trigger, portray, summarize, or conclude a wide range of displacements that are not only physical and geographical but also related to human affects. In other words, what is highlighted in the *Becoming Migrant* exhibition is, among other things, photography's ability to "move" its authors, its subjects, and its viewers.

The four museums participating in this initiative had selected from their collections only one object each, to illustrate an aspect of migration in its materiality. The choices they made are rather unusual. The audience is presented with new perspectives on migration in America. The four selected conversation starters were a migratory bird, the naturalization certificate of Andy Warhol's mother after her arrival to the United States, a meteorite fragment that had landed on the American continent, and a Romantic painting of a shipwreck. Their seemingly incongruous juxtaposition extends the understanding of "migration" beyond the human realm and overtly challenges ready-made stereotypes about migration. The simple association of these objects kindles surprise due to their unexpected conceptual proximity, which enables the creation of new contact zones for the discourses that study and interpret them: biology, anthropology, history and art history, and astrophysics. As such, the *Becoming Migrant* series is remarkable for having proposed an original, non-anthropocentric approach to migration. The initiative of these Pittsburgh museums has not only established contacts across the borders of species and even across the organic-inorganic divide; it has also transgressed disciplines and brought together academics, artists, and performers in an intermedial and transdisciplinary journey through the intricate aspects of migration in America. This shows that migration is, in itself, a dynamic concept, requiring its imagery to do some migrating of its own among the rarely overlapping territories of scientific photography, administrative documents, and fine arts.

The space of this chapter does not allow me to discuss all nine events concerned with migration in America that punctuated the audience's itinerary in the larger *Becoming Migrant* exhibit. Instead, my study focuses on a single exhibition, which enters most tellingly in relation with a subsequent discussion of Didi-Huberman's *Passer, quoi qu'il en coûte*. This particular collection of photographs (which happens to be itinerant and therefore migrant in itself) gathers a corpus of seventy-two documentary images under the title *Out of Many: Stories of Migration*.[5] The project has been carried out through the collaboration of a group of five Pittsburgh-based photographers: Brian Cohen, Lynn Johnson, Annie O'Neill, Scott Goldsmith, and

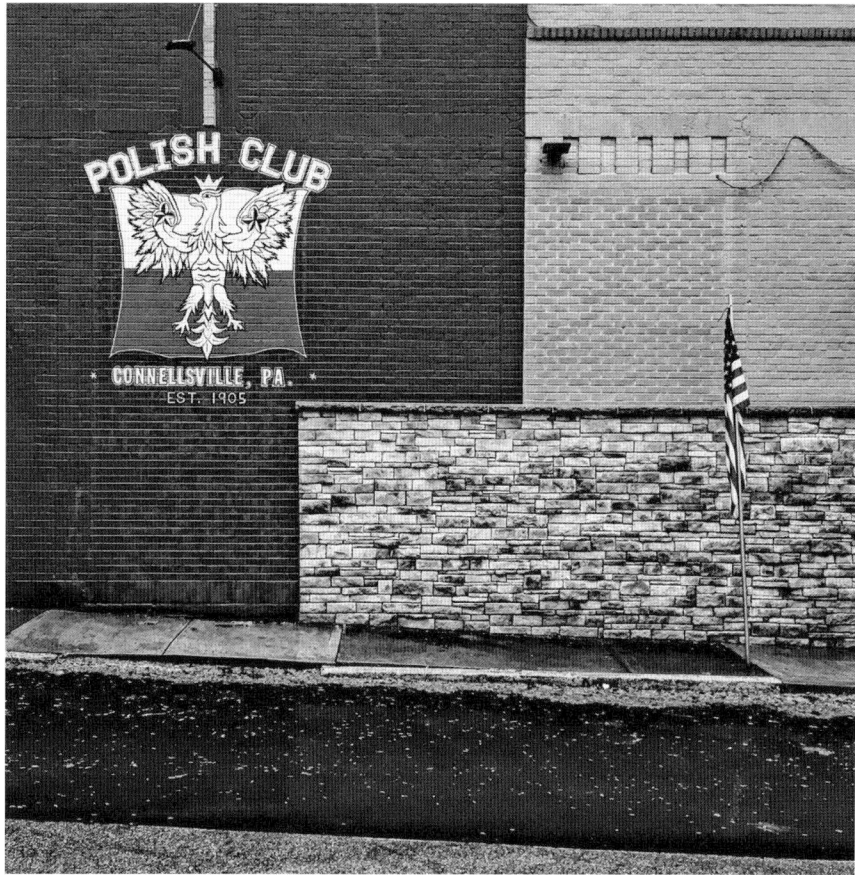

Figure 2: Brian Cohen, *Polish Club Connellsville*, 2017 (Plate 21, p. 347). © Brian Cohen/The Documentary Works, 2017. Courtesy of the author.

Nate Guidry. They captured migration stories in their city roughly at the same time, as part of a yearlong documentation effort. The result of their work is entirely available on the project's website, but it is also open to travel to other American museums and galleries. As the exhibition journeys on, it constantly enriches its corpus by integrating local stories of migration encountered along the way. I will briefly describe the exhibition in the form I encountered it as a visitor in 2018.

Brian Cohen's series of twenty-three photographs documents architectural traces of past waves of migration in contemporary Pittsburgh. The photographer, who is also the coordinator of the project, is interested in capturing the ways in which transnational displacement is figured in contemporary urbanscapes. Cohen's visual argument seems to imply that American cities can be read as palimpsests in which one can decipher layers of metonymic imagery of migration from a variety of countries, including Italy, Poland, Ukraine, Hungary, Croatia, Ireland, and Vietnam, to the United States (Fig. 2).

Cohen's series captures images of migration without making any explicit reference to the migrants themselves. Instead, he chooses to bring to the fore the site-specific traces of the migrants' presence in the urban tissue of an American community. Photos of ethnic restaurants, community centers, national clubs, ceremony halls, and religious landmarks sketch a network of colorful diasporic nuclei superimposed on the map of contemporary Pittsburgh and its surroundings. The photographs show that immigrants do not travel alone, but are rather accompanied by an architectural vision and a sense of spatial organization shaped by their culture of origin and their previous experiences. The buildings that translate these features into material forms point to the migrants' more or less explicit longing and desire to create a home away from home. Sometimes, as the photographer shows, the actualization of this longing can be achieved by "transplanting" fragments of familiar landscape or urban texture into the spatial configurations of the adoptive environment. This movement of figurative translation may also function as a reminder that, just like the buildings in question, the photographic image itself "comes into being only as a consequence of reproduction, displacement, and itinerancy."[6] Pronounced architectural and period differences mark these edifices and speak of their heterogeneity, as if trying to visually destabilize the illusion that migration is a single, unified phenomenon which can be essentialized, regardless of social, historical, and cultural circumstances. Given the diversity of the buildings portrayed and brought together in this series, Brian Cohen's photographs produce a contact zone effect not only through the encounter of the American space with foreignized buildings but also through the encounter of migrant communities with one another. This effect is comparable to what Didi-Huberman does when he creates a symbolic space where visual details of past migrations connect with contemporary visual micro-phenomena.

Lynn Johnson, another member of The Documentary Works and contributor to *Out of Many: Stories of Migration*, chooses a different approach. Her photographs capture scenes from Pittsburgh courthouses, documenting the legal, bureaucratic, and almost sacramental aspects of migration that mark the formal end of the migrants' journey. In her series framing real naturalization ceremonies that took place in these courts throughout 2017, Johnson crowds the photographic space with figures of migrants, focusing on their facial expressions and on the way in which they carry the entire emotional charge of a milestone moment in their passage from immigrant status to American citizenship (Fig. 3).

However, what she seems most interested in is not so much the individual affect, but the black-and-white (mimicking institutional neutral sobriety) recording of the ritualized stages of the naturalization ceremonies as they happened, in the age

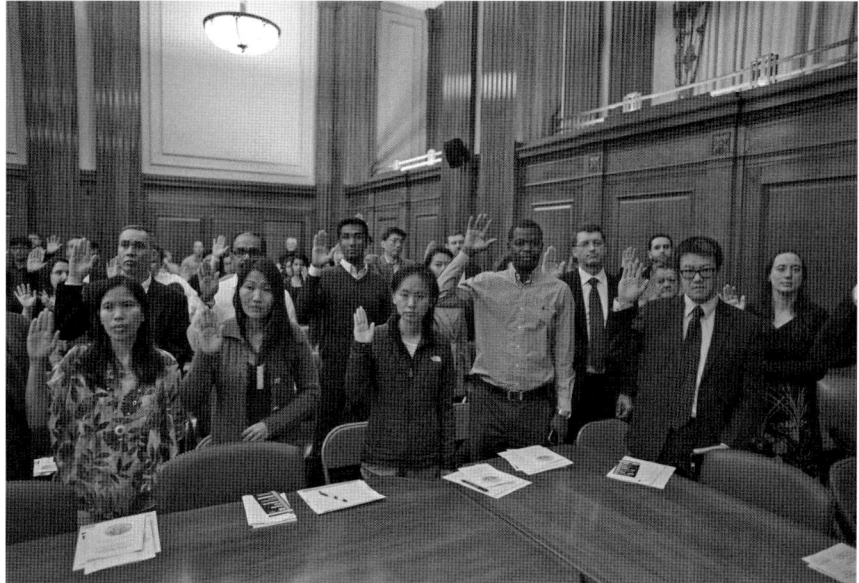

Figure 3: Lynn Johnson, *11/17/17 Federal Courthouse*, Pittsburgh, 2017. © Lynn Johnson/The Documentary Works, 2017. Courtesy of the author.

of Donald Trump's highly disputed migration policies. In one of the photos, the viewer can see the presidential figure in the welcoming video that the candidates are required to watch prior to officially becoming citizens of the United States. In his prerecorded speech, the president addresses the luckiest of American migrants and speaks about America as a land of love, opportunity, and hope (Fig. 4). The informed viewer will not miss the bitter irony at work in this image.

In another photograph, the viewer is presented with the frowning facial expression of a young, newly proclaimed American citizen, contrasted with the sincerely content smile of her mother (Fig. 5). This contrast probably hints at deeper and more cruel implications of the presidential rhetoric, especially regarding the treatment of immigrants' children. With the United States steadily moving toward the model of a "walled democracy," to use a term coined a decade ago by political scientist Wendy Brown,[7] the immigration courts of the United States have become, after 2016, an interesting setting to observe the relief experienced by the immigrants that find themselves at the fortunate end of a both physical and bureaucratic journey marked by uncertainty, frequent setbacks, and merciless biopolitics. The portraits shot here (in black and white, indicating that justice is, at times, if not completely blind, at least colorblind) eerily arrest both the subject of the photograph and its viewer in a silent exchange shaped by the intense affective charge of the ceremony.

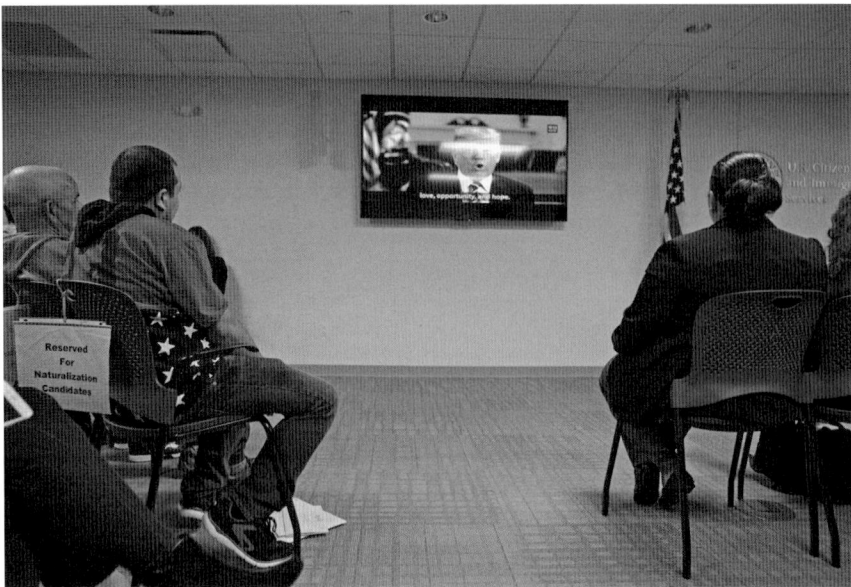

Figure 4: Lynn Johnson, Naturalization Ceremony at the Monroeville Office, 2017. © Lynn Johnson/ The Documentary Works, 2017. Courtesy of the author.

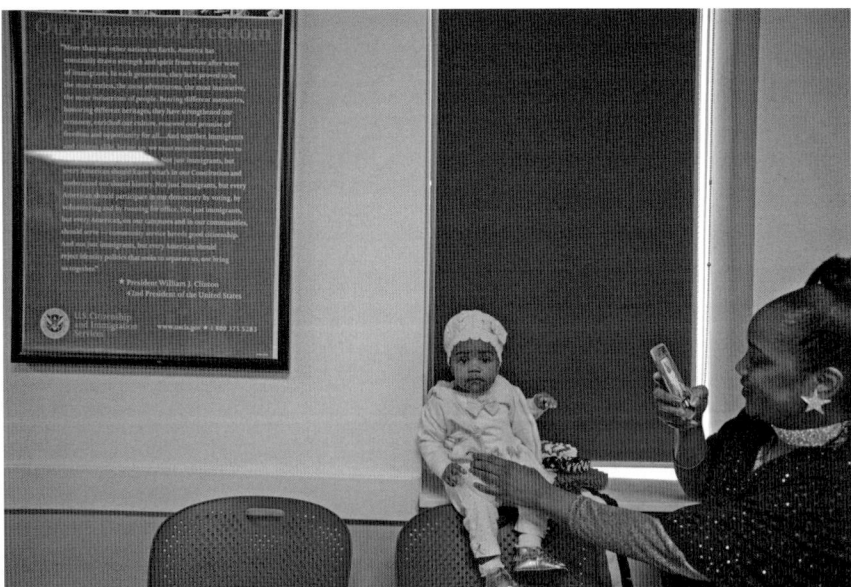

Figure 5: Lynn Johnson, Naturalization Ceremony at the Monroeville Office, 2017. © Lynn Johnson/ The Documentary Works, 2017. Courtesy of the author.

The choice of colors (or the lack thereof) and the use of achromatic contrasts in the depiction of a threshold moment in the passage from noncitizen status to citizenship may be an indication of the ways in which the two legal identities define, imply, and shape one another. In Tim Cresswell's words, "the definition of citizen carries around the noncitizen or the shadow citizen as part of its constitution."[8] A British geographer, Cresswell reflects (not unlike Johnson in her series) on the ways in which "mobilities are produced in the courtroom,"[9] through the workings of laws that regulate the attribution of rights and citizenship. In addition, he notes that mobility, a right associated with citizenship, is a good "indicator for freedom" and a concrete example of how legal systems throughout the world act "on the basis of presumed geographies and produce geographies in the process," including "geographies of mobility."[10] Johnson's crowds are racially and ethnically heterogeneous, and this diversity speaks of unequal limitations of mobility, according to the country of origin (Fig. 3). The different national and ethnic profiles of the immigrants in her photos imply a broad spectrum of legally enforced mobilities, unevenly distributed all over the globe. The interactions between the law and its territorial jurisdiction are, as a result, reciprocal (when they are not downright circular):

> The law […] is an influential site for the production of meanings for mobility, as well as the practices of mobility that such meanings authorize or prohibit. Legal documents, legislation, and courts of law themselves are all entangled in the production of mobilities. Mobilities are produced both in the sense that meanings are ascribed to mobility through the construction of categories, such as *citizen* or *fugitive*, and in the sense that the actual ability to move is legislated and backed up by the threat of force.[11]

Didi-Huberman's remarks, detailed in *Passer, quoi qu'il en coûte* and in the documentary images they refer to, likewise bring up the subject of the law in relation to the Idomeni migrants. They had been denied the right to an accessible application for asylum and, at the same time, the right to move to another country to avoid lingering in territories where their stay is deemed illegal. As Didi-Huberman rightfully notices, the fact that they are not allowed to cross the border, for legal reasons, makes them violate another set of laws, which forbid their staying.[12] In a sense, this legal double bind forces the migrants to become outlaws and to have their mobility reduced to the impossibility of either advancement or return. Regardless of whether they have been forced or have chosen to move, these people find themselves prisoners caught in a juridical and civic limbo as marginal others, who are denied access to fundamental rights granted by international law because of their unlawful status.[13] While strongly attached to the legal dimension of migration in the United States, Johnson's photography does not capture this juridical conundrum.

She focuses exclusively on the best possible outcome of a migrant's confrontation with the immigration laws of the destination country, namely their becoming citizens with full rights (Fig. 3).

Another approach to American experiences of migration through the lens of a Pittsburgh-based photographer is the one adopted by Annie O'Neill in her biographical portraiture project. Her series consists of a set of large-scale double portraits and combines text and image to identify and showcase resemblances and differences across a constellation of personal experiences of migration to the United States. O'Neill pairs in each photograph a long-standing immigrant with one who has recently arrived in Pittsburgh. The texts on display below the pictures preserve the same structure throughout the series. The viewer of each double portrait is first invited to read a brief profile of each of the two migrant figures, including their name, age, profession, and date of arrival in the United States. This is followed by biographical details for each of the migrants and a direct quotation from their testimonies on how they personally experienced migration. The double portraits are shot against a white, neutral background, with great clarity and sharpness. The neatly arranged photographic surface becomes in this way a neutral contact zone for the two individuals who came to the United States from different cultures, at different times in history, and often for different reasons. Their previously separated biographical narratives enter into dialogue, while the diversity of the faces, bodies, and individual stories challenges the essentialized illusion of a uniform portrait of "the immigrant," all too often portrayed in political speeches and domestic media. The subjects are either smiling or striking a professional pose, which also contributes to creating a lighter, more optimistic visual rhetoric for the entire series. This nondramatic tone acts as a counterweight to the sometimes overwhelmingly difficult migration stories that are transparent in Johnson's shots, or implied in Cohen's. The documentary photographer has found a way to balance with optimism, light, and clarity, the "compassion fatigue" frequently experienced by the general audience when confronted with visual or textual reports on the hardships of migration.[14] In addition, by connecting recent stories of migration to past ones, the series highlights yet another set of variables, this time historical ones, traversing O'Neill's photographic contact zones. The interpersonal, transcultural, and transhistorical exchange takes place straightforwardly on the photographic surface, between the two portraits in each shot and also at the points of productive semiotic contact established between the columns of text and the image. This technique of montage is successful in alluding to the multiple reiterations of such experiences in the history of America, while also testifying to the importance of community involvement in accommodating the newcomers.

The other two photographers active in The Documentary Works, Scott Goldsmith and Nate Guidry, similarly depict immigrants in their new American homes, with a special focus on the adaptation process through which the newly arrived begin to domesticate surroundings foreign to them. The point of view in Goldsmith's and Guidry's photographs shifts from the one used by Brian Cohen in his project, which showed attempts to foreignize, with architectural inserts, the landscape of American urban domesticity. Goldsmith's photographs document the arrival and the first days in the United States, as experienced by a family of Bhutanese refugees landed in Pittsburgh. The images capture the cultural shock lived by the family members when exposed to the novelty of their environment. The new house, the television set, and the trips with local public transport show that all kinds of everyday places, objects, and routines can acquire a different aura when seen through the eyes of the newly landed immigrants. This shift in the apprehension of familiar, everyday objects and surroundings has, in a bizarre ricochet, the potential to transfer some of the effect of surprise and novelty on the local viewers as well. It also questions the locals' relationships to the utilities and facilities that shape their lifestyle and which cannot be taken for granted in other places in the world.

Nate Guidry, on the other hand, portrays the daily life of an already adjusted family of Mexican immigrants, composed of José Luis Ibarra and his two young daughters, Emma and Brianna. The family of three is shown cooking, vacuuming, playing in the backyard, eating cheesecake for birthdays, and chatting on the living-room couch, in apparently relaxed poses that show them fully adjusted to the American lifestyle. However, somewhere in the background of the happy family snapshots, lurks the grim possibility of their lives being radically impacted by the tough policies against Mexican immigrants that had already been announced at the beginning of Donald Trump's term.

Guidry and Goldsmith play with the dynamic relations between the domestic and the foreign, the familiar and the utterly new. On a similar note, Didi-Huberman recalls an observation initially formulated by Gérard Bensussan in his article *Difficile hospitalité* [Difficult Hospitality]. According to Bensussan, in Hebrew, "I inhabit" (*ani gar*) is written in the exact same way as "I am foreign" (*ani guer*).[15] Two vowels make the difference between homeliness and estrangement, and even that minor difference may be easily elided in writing, as Hebrew script notes only the consonants. The distinction that separates feeling at home from feeling like a stranger is, in some cases, so fragile that it can be completely silenced by writing. Photography, too, has this power, as Guidry and Goldsmith demonstrate in their shots. This observation confirms Paolo Boccagni's intuitions about the elusive and unstable nature of what seems to be a familiar notion: the home. The author of *Migration and the Search for Home: Mapping Domestic Space in Migrants' Everyday Lives*[16] shows that, in fact, home is not so much a space as it is a process determined by a meaningful (and moveable) relationship with place:

Home, in the eyes of recently settled migrants and asylum seekers, is often conspicuous by its absence. International migration is tantamount to an extended detachment from what used to be home. In practice, it denaturalizes it, as it reveals that the sense of obviousness and familiarity attached to the previous domestic place was ultimately artificial and reversible. Migrants' everyday life, therefore, is a privileged terrain to make sense of home by default. It brings to the fore a range of emotions, practices and living arrangements that mirror the need to recreate home anew, dynamically, rather than a static and a full-fledged identification with one particular dwelling place. This is a still more critical and ambiguous effort for asylum seekers and refugees. At the same time, migrants' life experience can be investigated to assess how far the home experience relies on a specific place, is potentially transferrable elsewhere, and draws on interpersonal relationships as much as material settings.[17]

Therefore, "home" can be conceived as "a situated and interactive endeavour, rather than a physical structure."[18] Moreover, this endeavor is experienced and negotiated differently by social actors and, despite the apparent site-specificity of the concept, what we usually call home can be "transferred and reproduced in multiple settings over time."[19] A redefinition of their home space is what José and his daughters managed to acquire in their Pittsburgh household, and what the Bhutanese family is beginning to acquire as well. On the other side of the spectrum of migration experiences, the prospects of familiarity, security, and control that determine a sense of homeliness are still beyond reach for the migrants sleeping in tents in the Idomeni camp under the heavy rain. Their drenched silhouettes can be seen in the screenshots from *Spectres Are Haunting Europe* that Didi-Huberman comments upon. In looking at these photographs and film stills, the viewer is once again persuaded of the migrants' ability to mediate the infinite diversity of migration experiences and obstacles encountered on the way.

The still that moves: photography as Warburgian migrant

Photography related to migration often exerts a peculiar fascination kindled by the way in which it transgresses the static character of the medium, through its depiction of a subject matter inextricably linked to movement and displacement. This transgressive quality enhances the potential use of photographs as powerful tools for raising social and aesthetic awareness, but also for articulating social and aesthetic critique: "photographs are objects made to have social biographies. Their efficacy is premised specifically on their shifting roles and meanings as they are projected into different spaces to do different things."[20] For example, the efficacy of

Annie O'Neill's set of double portraits is highly dependent on the accompanying textual content, which is in fact the only visible proof of the connection between the images on display and the theme of migration in America. Except for some rather inconclusive cultural, racial, and ethnic traits, her images contain no visual stories of migration; the photographic narrative is inseparable from its textual complement. In the works of the other four photographers, in which visible cues figuring a story of displacement are present with higher intensity, photography lends itself to the exploration of the active interaction between sensation and thought that characterizes what Erin Manning has termed "relationscape"—namely, the spatial arrangement of the relations that occur between individual or collective human and nonhuman entities.[21] All five contributors to *Out of Many: Stories of Migration* frame singular, intriguing relationscapes that have very little in common, aside from their shared location in Pittsburgh and their relevance to the analysis of contemporary aspects of American migration.

The other work that inspired this chapter comments upon photographic images in the form of film stills that accommodate relationscapes. The result of Georges Didi-Huberman's collaboration with the Greek poet and director Niki Giannari, the book is a collective work whose authorship is in itself relational. Its text and illustration create a zone of contact at the convergence of a plurality of discourses (art history and art criticism, poetry, history, sociology), but also a space for the productive encounter of two different sensibilities and subjectivities: Didi-Huberman and Giannari, the art historian and the poet-documentarist. My tentative English translation of the title of this book, *Passer, quoi qu'il en coûte*, would be something along the lines of "Making it across, no matter what" or, more literally, "To pass at all costs."[22] The short volume delves poetically and critically into the visual dynamics of passages, passengers, and passageways, against the background of contemporary migration flows; more precisely, in the context of the 2016 migration crisis in the Mediterranean region. On a literal level, Georges Didi-Huberman sketches an iconological commentary on several frames captured from Maria Kourkouta and Niki Giannari's 2016 documentary *Spectres Are Haunting Europe*. The film is a visual record of the blocked passage of refugees in Idomeni, an improvised camp at the border between Greece and Macedonia. This chapter is not the place to discuss the political and social circumstances of this particular migration crisis. What will be discussed instead are some of the ideas that Didi-Huberman develops from these film stills, which he places alongside a poem by Paul Celan (himself a poet who lived in exile) and Niki Giannari's poem "Spectres Are Haunting Europe (Letter from Idomeni)" read as a voice-over in the film.[23]

Under the easily identifiable influence of Aby Warburg's thought on the "survival" of images, Georges Didi-Huberman sees pictures (be them still, in photography, or moving, in film) not as static objects, but rather as movements, passages, and gestures of memory and/or desire.[24] Contesting the static nature of images is a counterintuitive proposal. As I understand it, this theory stems from the idea that photography captures a sort of affective displacement, something that moves the photographer and, in turn, is equally able to move the viewer. One could therefore read photography as a symbolic space that allows for the migration and the encounter of affects. Moreover, despite its seemingly static character, photography is a highly flexible and easily reproducible medium, hence one that is able to circulate through both space and time. This idea is not new and, as hinted earlier, retracing its genealogy implies a return to Warburg and to his concept of *Nachleben* ("afterlife"). In the Warburgian vocabulary, the term *afterlife* refers to the transhistorical continuity and metamorphosis of visual forms, which are likely to survive, under different guises, the historical event of their apparent extinction. In Warburg's view, images have the capacity to outlive their material determinations and to navigate through discontinuous temporalities from one representation to another, resurging every now and then in larger, overarching structures, such as the collective memory of a community. This principle of transhistorical circulation of images grounds Warburg's essays on Antiquity's legacy in Renaissance art, as well as his famous 1923 lecture on the snake ritual in the Hopi tribe culture in Arizona and, perhaps most famously, his *Mnemosyne Atlas*.[25] Didi-Huberman described the latter as "a tool for sampling, by means of juxtaposed images, the chaos of history" and "finding new ways of thinking about social and cultural temporality."[26] When understood in terms of palimpsests, in which layers of various temporalities and geographies are inscribed onto recurrent visual forms, Cohen's photographic series on urban traces of migration in America more transparently becomes an effort to document migrant-made contact zones embedded in the American urban texture (Fig. 6). Finally, in light of Warburg's image theory, the visual form that survives its demise through cycles of transformation and resurgence can be said to function simultaneously as both a "symptom" and a "phantom" of the past, leaving indelible marks in collective memory and imagery:

> For Warburg, *Nachleben* meant making historical time more complex, recognising specific, non-natural temporalities in the cultural world. Basing a history of art on "natural selection" – through the successive elimination of the weakest styles, thus providing evolution with its perfectibility and history with its teleology – is in opposition to his fundamental project and his temporal models. For Warburg, the surviving form does not triumphantly outlive the death of its competitors. On the contrary, it symptomatically and phantomatically survives its own death: disappearing from a point in history, reappearing much later at a moment when it is perhaps no longer expected, and consequently having survived in the still poorly defined reaches of a "collective memory."[27]

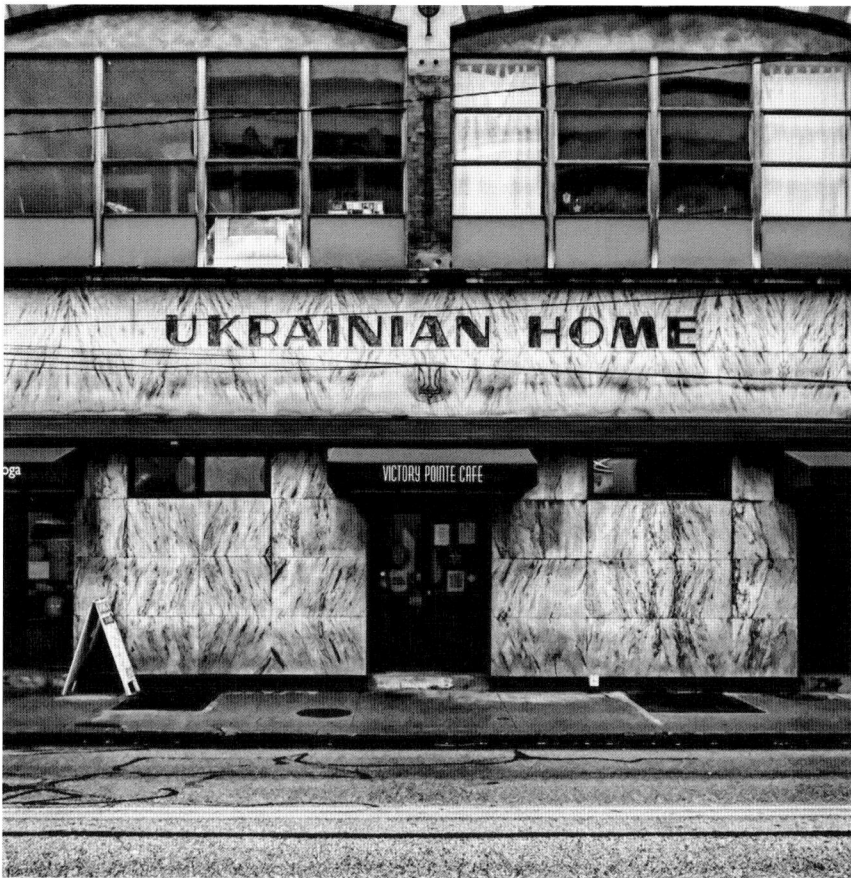

Figure 6: Brian Cohen, *Ukrainian Home*, Pittsburgh, 2017 (Plate 22, p. 348). © Brian Cohen/The Documentary Works, 2017. Courtesy of the author.

As the French art historian rightfully notices, Warburg is the first to formulate the intimate ties between artistic composition and dislocation. In doing so, he inaugurates the conceptual contact zone that frames our discussion of photography and migration. Articulating the relation between representation and displacement has led to a necessary encounter of the two, a contact able "to make a transverse- or cross-section in chaos, which is to say, using Warburg's own term – a *thought-space* (*Denkraum*)."[28] Like other visual arts, photography creates this "space for thought" through a tense relation with a world in crisis:

> The dislocation of the world: that is the subject of art. It is impossible to affirm that, without disorder, there would be no art, nor that there could be one: we know of no world that is not disorder. No matter what the universities whisper

to us regarding Greek harmony, the world of Aeschylus was full of combat and terror, and so were those of Shakespeare and of Homer, of Dante and of Cervantes, of Voltaire and of Goethe. However pacifistic [art] has been said to be, it speaks of wars, and whenever art makes [a peace treaty] with the world, it is always signed with a world at war.[29]

In her book *Frames of War*, Judith Butler argues that, if photography is to be conceived as a field marked by conflicting forces, it is prone to generate a pathos that sets in motion not only affects, but interpretations as well: "It is not only or exclusively at an affective register that the photograph operates, but through instituting a certain mode of acknowledgment. It 'argues' for the grievability of life: its pathos is at once affective and interpretive."[30] Johnson tries to purge this pathos in her photographs by adopting the neutrality of the institutional gaze, yet every time her focus lands on a human figure, the cold, impersonal gaze is shattered by a powerful, albeit quiet, explosion of affects (Fig. 5).

In his own interpretation of the still frames that document the halted passage of refugees during the Mediterranean migration crisis, Didi-Huberman reactualizes Warburg's view on artistic forms that arise more frequently and more intensely in a world in conflict. The French art historian aims to demonstrate the subtle migration of certain visual motifs able to travel across geographical spaces and historical chronology. As an example, he likens the filmed images of endless lines of migrants waiting next to a railway and a barbed wire fence at Idomeni with photographs taken during the Holocaust. Controversial as it may be, the comparison is not implausible in strictly visual terms. Among the photographs taken during the Holocaust, there are some that articulate the same motifs—crowds in a precarious state, the camps, rail tracks, barbed wire, human faces against a grim, hostile landscape—even though they do so in a significantly different historical context generating massive human displacements. While keeping in mind the important distinctions that separate the forced displacement of the Jewish European population in the 1940s from the migrant waves of 2016, Didi-Huberman maintains that these images share, to a certain degree, a figural content that has returned to haunt contemporary imagery. By crossing temporal and spatial limitations and by transgressing their particular circumstances, the return of these visual configurations is meaningful in its ability to reflect and shape resemblances and differences between two historical repositories of grim images that haunt European collective memory. This movement of figural return strengthens the affective force of the surviving images:

D'où vient cette force des images? De là même, peut-être, d'où les « damnés de la terre » tirent la leur : de leur puissance à passer malgré tout. Les images sont fatales, certes, en ce sens qu'elles portent une mémoire tenace. Du moindre souffle elles font un fossile en mouvement. Aby Warburg, on le sait, comprenait l'histoire des images comme une « histoire de fantômes pour grandes personnes » : une histoire où les images se montrent capables de « revenir » depuis des temps tout à fait hétérogènes, de traverser les murs de la périodisation historienne, de flotter antiques dans les espaces mêmes de notre modernité. Et cette puissance-là, Warburg avait choisi de la nommer survivance : un « après-vivre » ou la capacité, extraordinaire si l'on y pense, de traverser les temps, de signifier dans plusieurs temps hétérogènes à la fois, de passer à travers temps. […] elles sont aussi spectrales, donc mobiles, nomades : on persiste mieux quand on sait changer de place. À la survivance des images, qui désignait leur capacité à passer au travers de temps différents, Warburg ajouta donc la migration, qui nommait précisément, selon lui, leur capacité fondamentale à passer au travers d'espaces distincts, voire très éloignés les uns des autres.[31]

This "repetition of the different" is of particular instrumental value in defining categories such as self and other, us and them, domestic and foreign, by stimulating the community to question and problematize binary sets of identities. Photography becomes, in this way, intimately linked to the creation of alterity. In other words, photographing is a witnessing *of* the other, *for* the use of others: "l'image témoigne depuis un lointain, et c'est pourquoi nous voyons Idomeni à travers les images-témoins, grises et quelquefois tremblantes."[32] The image becomes in itself a witness and, in this newly discovered condition, it frames and confides this framing to the eyes of the other, who is absent from the scene. Photography contributes to a new ethical regime that rules over one's relations and contacts with alterity. This argument explains why looking at the photographs shot by Goldsmith and Guidry for the *Out of Many* exhibition is, in a way, an act of voyeurism that intrudes into the domesticated—yet still to some degree, foreign—homeliness of the migrant families that have recently arrived in America. In addition, applying Didi-Huberman's insight to Johnson's courtroom scenes, it becomes apparent how her choice of location enhances the weight and the responsibility of "witnessing" that is subtly imposed upon the viewer. Faced with Johnson's photographs, viewers suddenly find themselves taking part in the naturalization ceremony, together with the eclectic gathering of migrants.

As Mette Sandbye puts it in her study of migration, war, and cultural differences in contemporary art-documentary photography, "the whole spectrum of agency and emotion related to various photographic forms and materialities" can be perceived as an "ethical investment of responsiveness."[33] Even in the absence of human figures, as is the case in Cohen's urbanscapes, one feels compelled to engage with, or at least acknowledge the presence of local migrant communities. The latter are portrayed, even though *in absentia*, as actively asserting their identities by means of the visual insignia they inscribe in various corners of Pittsburgh and, by force of metonymy, in all of North America. Cohen's photographs and Niki Giannari's film both demonstrate the way in which photography refers to itself as a placemaking activity, able to reconfigure the geographical landmarks of America and Europe in light of the ever-new migratory fluxes (Figs. 2 & 6). Like the previously anonymous Idomeni, the photographed locations gain in symbolic charge and significance, particularly through the contrast between the imposed stillness of the migrants and the ease with which the documentarists, their cameras, and the images they produce circulate. This striking contrast in the mobility of the photographic subject and that of the photographic object has been noted, among others, by Tanya Sheehan in her introduction to *Photography and Migration*.[34] She notes that images "are never simply local" and their circulation is embedded in their deceivingly static materiality. Similarly, for the French "historian of passing images," as Didi-Huberman has been called,

> all images are migrants. Images are migrations. Migrations in space and in time. Migrations in time through their survival, as postulated by Warburg, and in space – Warburg used this very word, migration – *Bilderwanderung* – in the sense that […] the images are never simply local. Never.[35]

Elizabeth Edwards expands on the same idea in her study of photography as an object marked by an affect that operates beyond the level of pure imagery. According to her, photographs lend themselves to material translations within processes of remediation and repurposing, which situates them in a "constant state of flux" that endows them with active "social biographies."[36]

The observation strongly echoes the short biographical notes added by Annie O'Neill to her double portraits that thematize (across media, with both image and text) the resemblances and differences between two waves of migration to America. It is important to mention that the two waves vary with each photograph: there is always one older and one more recent, but the actual arrival dates differ as one moves from one photo to the next. The relatively long columns of text below the double portraits seem to drip from the photographs they complement, as if the narrative of these social biographies flows uninterruptedly from the images, as they become verbalized. The placing of these photographs is not inconsequential either:

> They are reframed, replaced, rearranged; negatives become prints, prints become lantern slides or postcards, ID photographs become family treasures, private photographs become archives, analog objects become electronic digital code, private images become public property, and photographs of scientific

production are reclaimed as cultural heritage. […] The placing of photographs as objects in an assemblage of other objects and spaces is integral to the work asked of photographs and human relations with them. Placing is defined as a sense of appropriateness of particular material forms to particular sets of social expectation and desire within space and time.[37]

The main difference between the paradigm advanced by Didi-Huberman and the one shared by the five Pittsburgh-based documentarists can arguably be reduced to the difference between images of migrants on the move (at the Greek-Macedonian border, for example) and images of settled migrants (in their various stages of settlement, integration, and adjustment in Pennsylvania, in particular, and the United States, in general). This distinction could then be rephrased in terms of arts of passage and arts of resettlement. Unavoidably, the difference is maintained in the visual documentation of the two experiences of migration, and in the rhetoric deployed in creating these images.

In more abstract terms, the photographs and film stills that attempt to capture, document, interpret, and disseminate these consecutive, yet distinct realities of migration are part of a split "metaphysics of fixity and flow."[38] The anthropology scholar Liisa Malkki coined the term "sedentarist metaphysics," which valorizes rootedness and belonging and is haunted by threats of mobility, in opposition to what Creswell called a "nomadic metaphysics," which obviously valorizes mobility.[39] While Didi-Huberman and Giannari write and frame the desire for obstacle-free itinerance and easy mobility for global migratory flows, the *Out of Many* project is a kaleidoscopic photo-narrative of a sedentarist metaphysics, applied to migrant individuals or communities. A sedentarist logic accounts for the existence of "walled democracies," as well as for the arrested movement of immigrants, which turns them into outlaws:

> Thinking of the world as rooted and bounded is reflected in language and social practice. Such thoughts actively territorialize identities in property, in region, in nation – in place. They simultaneously produce discourse and practice that treats mobility and displacement as pathological.[40]

This complex assemblage of power relations is materialized not only at the level of discourse but also in practices of unaccountable repression, and it contributes to the highly arbitrary and sometimes inhuman treatment of the displaced. It should be mentioned, however, that migrants are not fully inscribed within the nomadic model either. The radical valorization of mobility renders impossible the dream of settling down (which the migrants obviously hold) and the very idea of destination, which gives a purpose to the migrants' journey, often by being idealized. The nomadic subject is the radical figure of a migrant always on the move, one that, much like Odysseus, is driven only by the fascination of perpetual journey and its lines of flight, rather than by the dream of settling at the destination, no matter how idealized that destination may be:

> The nomad is never reterritorialized, unlike the migrant who slips back into the ordered space of arrival. [...] The state, on the other hand, is the metaphori-cal enemy of the nomad, attempting to take the tactile space and enclose and bound it. It is not that the state opposes mobility, but that it wishes to control flows – to make them run through conduits. It wants to create fixed and well-di-rected paths for movement to flow through.[41]

With this in mind, it becomes clearer why the visual representation of a nomadic subject on a still surface is not as innocent as it may seem. Cresswell is mindful of the intricacies at work in this paradox when he notes that "often, mobility is said to be nonrepresentational or even against representation."[42] The pervasive blur in the images showing endless queues of silhouettes in raincoats at Idomeni is part of this visual rhetoric of resistance to representation. Like the makers of the documen-tary film, Didi-Huberman understands that, for reasons of accuracy, photography cannot stabilize the contours of a community held together precisely by its being in motion (Fig. 1). Optical precision, it seems, is a luxury that only those who stand still can afford. However, since the migrants on the move are neither entirely nomadic, nor is their flow of movement uninterrupted, an approximate representa-tion of their mobility is, after all, possible. By this token, it is not incidental that Giannari's film is entitled *Spectres Are Haunting Europe*. Didi-Huberman elaborates at length on the spectral quality of the migrants' silhouettes, which remain anon-ymous and outside the law. It is also significant to recall Warburg's reference to images as "ghost stories for grown ups" to infer that photographs of migration are marked by some degree of spectrality. For the refugees, as well as for the images depicting them, circulation is a matter of survival.[43] Having fled their homelands, these figures are already situated in some kind of "afterlife" (Warburg's *Nachleben*), in the civil and juridical limbo that, up to a point, effaces all sense of certainty regarding their future.

Unlike the *Out of Many* photographs, the contours in the film stills are fuzzy and destabilized. On a literal level, certainly, it is only due to the torrential rain falling over the unsheltered and to the loose, translucid raincoats the migrants are wearing. On a deeper hermeneutic level, though, the blur testifies to these people's spectral consistency, halfway between the solidity of a legal subject and the abstractness of a pure line of flight. This lack of visual clarity and precision is also a figural marking of the distance that separates the photographer from the subject—a distance that is, nevertheless, essential to photography's existence and functioning as a testifying witness. In Cohen's photographs, the migrants are not even present in the frame, but their presence is implied in and around the buildings that speak of their displacement. In Goldsmith's series, the newly attained feeling of stability and certainty associated with a new home slowly adds more solidity to the profiles of migrants. On the contrary, José's problematic immigrant status in Nate Guidry's series generates a specter of uncertainty that threatens the tranquility of family moments. Johnson's courthouse shots capture the very moments in which instability and uncertainty are replaced by a solid legal status that grants freedom, rights, and a new level of mobility to the newly declared citizens.

Conclusion

To sum up, my argument begins with a collection of recent photographs related to migration in Pittsburgh as a case study for the more general topic of migration in America. The five photographic series that constitute the *Out of Many* project adopt five different angles in approaching this vast theme: the urban, the legal, the biographical, the familial, and the domestic. All of them allow and even encourage the discussion of visual representations of migration in America in terms of contact zones, or sites in which a variety of asymmetrical power relations are revealed in the process of negotiating the terms of their encounter. When dissected in detail, these photographs cease to be isolated and self-contained objects and reveal themselves as spaces of relationality, with profound, intricate ethical and political implications. They become even more significant when discussed in light of Didi-Huberman's critical insights from *Passer, quoi qu'il en coûte*, his commentary on a filmed documentary presenting contemporary migration crisis Europe. These works illuminate one another, while simultaneously echoing Warburg's reflections on the migrant qualities of the image. With his writing about the fundamental role of displacement in the production of images, Warburg has informed Didi-Huberman's thought to the extent that, for the French art historian, photography, just like the migrant, "nous regarde et nous traverse."[44] The ambiguities hidden in this concise French sentence point to the fact that photographs and migrants alike concern us and return our gaze, moved by a desire to pass into, or at least through the space of our awareness. This desire shapes spectral trajectories and keeps the silhouettes of migrants moving across historical epochs, walls, fences, and borders.

The work of the five Pittsburgh-based photographers, Georges Didi-Huberman's book, and the documentary film it comments upon are three different mediations of the theme of contemporary migration that combine several types of discourse, ranging from photography to poetry, art history, and documentary cinema. In themselves, these works are semiotic spaces defined by intermediality, dialogue, and flow. Building on their discursive and formal relationality, this chapter has been my attempt to open a conceptual space in which they resonate or are in tension with one another, by force of a comparison that travels back and forth across the Atlantic, between Europe and America. This comparative, transcontinental approach can also be read as a homecoming for the idea of a "migrating image," formulated by Aby Warburg during a visit to America occasioned by his research on indigenous visual culture at the end of the nineteenth century. Reflecting on the intrinsically nomadic character of images in general, and of photography in particular, the Warburgian tradition informing Didi-Huberman's thought proved particularly useful in deconstructing the visual rhetoric of five contemporary photographic representations of migration in America.

Notes

1. In the sense described by Justin Carville and Sigrid Lien in their Introduction to this volume.
2. James Clifford, "Museums as Contact Zones," *Routes: Travel and Translation in the Late Twentieth Century* (Cambridge: Harvard University Press, 1997), 192.
3. The Documentary Works, http://www.thedocumentaryworks.org/read-me.
4. Carnegie Nexus, "Becoming Migrant… What Moves You? Nine Compelling Events Traversing the Art and Science of Passage," https://nexus.carnegiemuseums.org/event/migration/.
5. The Documentary Works, "Out of Many: Stories of Migration," http://www.thedocumentaryworks.org/future-work/.
6. Publisher's description of the exhibition catalog, Eduardo Cadava and Gabriela Nouzeilles (eds.), *The Itinerant Languages of Photography* (Princeton: Princeton University Art Museum, 2013), https://english.princeton.edu/research/itinerant-languages-photography.
7. Wendy Brown, "Porous Sovereignty, Walled Democracy," lecture delivered at the Walter Chaplin Simpson Center for the Humanities, University of Washington. April 22, 2008, https://arcade.stanford.edu/content/porous-sovereignty-walled-democracy.
8. Tim Cresswell, *On the Move: Mobility in the Modern Western World* (New York: Routledge, 2006), 161.
9. Cresswell, *On the Move,* 147.
10. Cresswell, *On the Move,* 151, 158.
11. Cresswell, *On the Move,* 150–151, original emphasis.
12. Didi-Huberman, *Passer, quoi qu'il en coûte* (Paris: Minuit, 2007), 45–46.

13. Celeste Ianniciello, *Migration, Arts, and Postcoloniality in the Mediterranean* (New York: Routledge, 2018), 8.

14. Mette Sandbye, "New Mixtures: Migration, War, and Cultural Differences in Contemporary Art-Documentary Photography," *Photographies* 11, no. 203 (2018), 280.

15. Gérard Bensussan, "Difficile hospitalité. Entre éthique, droit et politique," *Cités* 68, no. 4 (2016), 18.

16. Paolo Boccagni, *Migration and the Search for Home: Mapping Domestic Space in Migrants' Everyday Lives* (New York: Palgrave Macmillan, 2017).

17. Boccagni, *Migration*, 2.

18. Boccagni, *Migration*, 2.

19. Boccagni, *Migration*, 5.

20. Elizabeth Edwards, "Objects of Affect: Photography Beyond the Image," *Annual Review of Anthropology* 41 (2012), 222.

21. Erin Manning, *Relationscapes: Movement, Art, Philosophy* (Cambridge: The MIT Press, 2009).

22. As of March 2021, an English translation has not yet been published.

23. Niki Giannari, "Des spectres hantent l'Europe (Lettre de Idomeni)" in *Passer, quoi qu'il en coûte*, 10-21, originally in French and Greek. The English title is my translation.

24. Georges Didi-Huberman, *The Surviving Image. Phantoms of Time and Time of Phantoms: Aby Warburg's History of Art*, trans. Harvey Mendelsohn (University Park: Pennsylvania State University Press, 2016).

25. Aby Warburg, *Essais florentins* (Paris: Editions Hazan, 2015); Aby Warburg and W. F. Mainland, "A Lecture on Serpent Ritual," *Journal of the Warburg Institute* 2, no. 4 (1939), 277–292, doi:10.2307/750040; Aby Warburg, *L'Atlas Mnémosyne*, trans. Sacha Zilberfarb (Paris: L'Ecarquillé, 2013).

26. Georges Didi-Huberman, "Warburg's Haunted House," *Common Knowledge* 18, no. 1 (2018), 50.

27. Georges Didi-Huberman, "The Surviving Image: Aby Warburg and Tylorian Anthropology," *Oxford Art Journal* 25, no. 1 (2002), 68.

28. Georges Didi-Huberman, "Warburg's Haunted House," 55, original emphasis.

29. Aby Warburg quoted Didi-Huberman, "Warburg's Haunted House," 55.

30. Judith Butler, *Frames of War: When Is Life Grievable?* (New York/London: Verso, 2010), 98.

31. "Where does this force of the images spring from? Perhaps from the very source from which 'the wretched of the Earth' draw their own force: from their ability to pass, no matter what. The images are fatal, of course, in the sense that they are the bearers of a tenacious memory. They turn the faintest breath into a moving fossil. Aby Warburg, as we know, understood the history of images as a 'ghost story for adults': a narrative in which the images show themselves capable of 'returning' from heterogenous temporalities, of passing through the walls of our historical periodizations, of making antiquities

float in the very spaces of our modernity. It is this power that Warburg chose to name 'survival': an 'after-life' or the capacity – extraordinary, if we think of it – to run across historical ages, to be significant in multiple temporalities at a time, to pass through time. […] they are also spectral, and therefore mobile, nomadic: the one who knows how to move has better chances of survival. To the survival of the images, which designated their capacity to pass through different temporalities, Warburg adds thus their migration, which names precisely, according to him, their fundamental capacity to pass through different spaces, at times very remote from one another." Didi-Huberman, *Passer, quoi qu'il en coûte*, 60–61, my translation.

32. Didi-Huberman, *Passer, quoi qu'il en coûte*, 58.

33. Mette Sandbye, "New Mixtures: Migration, War, and Cultural Differences in Contemporary Art-Documentary Photography," *Photographies* 11, no. 203 (2018), 269, 283.

34. Tanya Sheehan (ed.), *Photography and Migration* (New York: Routledge, 2018), 6.

35. Georges Didi-Huberman. Interview by Frédéric Worms. "Sous nos yeux ils demandent à passer," *Matières à penser avec Frédéric Worms*, France Culture. November 13, 2017, https://www.franceculture.fr/emissions/matieres-a-penser-avec-frederic-worms/sous-nos-yeux-ils-demandent-a-passer.

36. Edwards, "Objects of Affect", 225, 222.

37. Edwards, "Objects of Affect," 225–226.

38. Liisa Malkki, "National Geographic: The Rooting of Peoples and the Territorialization of National Identity among Scholars and Refugees," *Cultural Anthropology* 7, no. 1 (1992), 31; Cresswell, *On the Move*, 25.

39. Cresswell, *On the Move*, 26; Malkki, "National Geographic: The Rooting of Peoples and the Territorialization of National Identity among Scholars and Refugees," 31.

40. Cresswell, *On the Move*, 27.

41. Gilles Deleuze and Félix Guattari, *Nomadology: The War Machine* (New York: Semiotext(e), 1986), 50–51.

42. Cresswell, *On the Move*, 47.

43. Didi-Huberman, *Passer, quoi qu'il en coûte*, 67–84.

44. Didi-Huberman, *Passer, quoi qu'il en coûte*, 67.

Documenting Migrations

Searching for Oleana

Contemporary Photographic Negotiations of Migration and Settler-Colonial Tropes

Sigrid Lien

A series of photographs takes us to a damp, luxuriant forest, where the vegetation is wild and abundant in numerous shades of green. The densely wooded area is devoid of any sign of human presence (Fig. 1), except for a superhighway that, in some of the images, sharply cuts through the landscape. Most of the photographs are taken from a distance. Yet, one image invites the viewer to gaze into the wilderness at closer range: warmed by a streak of sunshine, a rattlesnake curls its way through stones and withered leaves on the forest floor (Fig. 2)—like a reminder of how biological life unfolds when undisturbed by human interruption.

This photograph series was produced by the Italian documentary photographer, Giulia Mangione (b. 1987), who visited the Susquehannock forest in the Allegheny mountains during the summer of 2019. The forest area that she captured through her camera forms part of the Appalachian mountain range that stretches all the way from Newfoundland in the north, to Alabama in the south. Mangione was there to search for traces of Norwegian migration to this part of North America. Having lived in Scandinavia for many years, she was intrigued by how many people, perhaps especially in Sweden and Norway, hold such a strong fascination for American culture. Prior to her journey, she carried out a project in Sweden, where she photographically addressed the peculiarity of this Nordic *Americana*, manifested mainly through playful, sometimes bordering on burlesque, appropriations of American lifestyle, clothing, and cars. By traveling to the United States, Mangione wanted to add a historical dimension to her explorations of these Scandinavian American cultural affiliations, and chose to focus particularly on the history of the Norwegian immigration to the United States.

This grand-scale migration is a particularly important dimension of Norwegian history and identity. Between 1836 and 1915, no less than 750,000 Norwegians migrated to North America. Until 1890, only Ireland had a greater migration rate (in relation to the total population) than Norway.[1] In the Norwegian and Norwegian

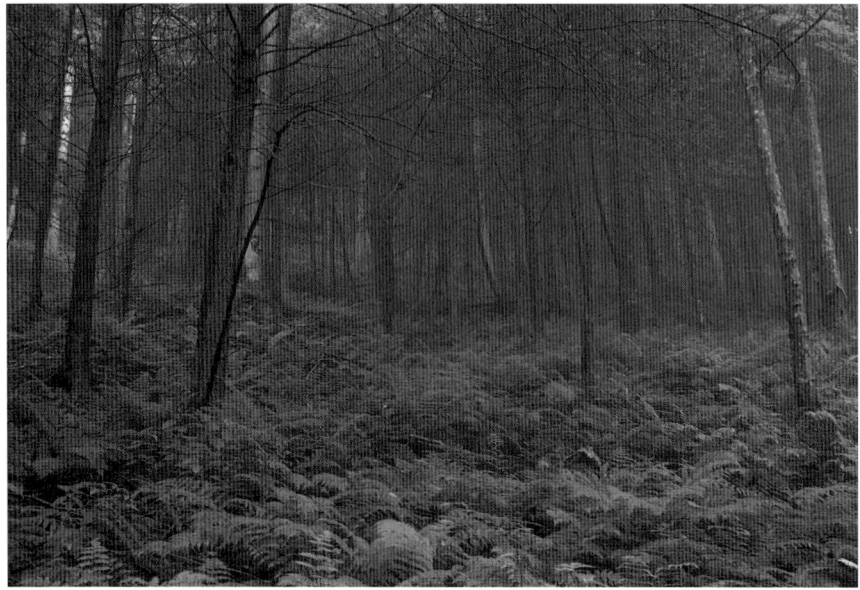

Figure 1: Giulia Mangione. The Susquehannock forest in the Allegheny mountains, where, in 1852, Ole Bull tried to materialize his utopian dream of a New Norway, 2019. Courtesy of Giulia Mangione.

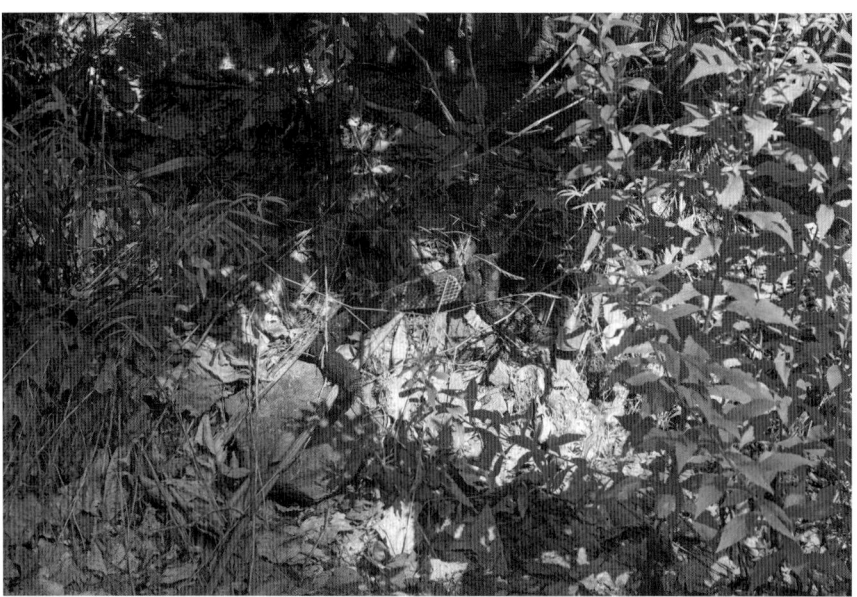

Figure 2: Giulia Mangione. Rattlesnake in the sunshine, Allegheny mountains, 2019 (Plate 23, p. 349). Courtesy of Giulia Mangione.

American migration historiography, it has been customary to regard this process as part of the larger frontier history, a line of thought that may be traced back to the American historian Jackson Turner's frontier thesis of 1893. This kind of historical understanding centers on the frontier, and the westbound movement in search of free land, as a movement also toward freedom, democracy, and egalitarianism. Today, however, the frontier paradigm has been subjected to heavy criticism. Many historians have argued that it fails to grasp not only how this kind of expansionism also entailed grimmer stories about dependencies, exploitation, and violence but also that the colonialism of the American West undertaken by Europeans is no different from other European modes of empire and colonialism elsewhere in the world—and should be conceptualized as such.[2] Norway's settler colonialism is no exception. As part of this colonial expansion, Norwegian immigration followed the overall settler-colonial movement westward from the American continent's east coast. But Norwegian Americans nevertheless made their distinctive mark as the most rural of all the newly arrived groups of migrants, and most of them settled in the Midwest.[3]

However, rather than turning her attention to this dominant pattern of Norwegian migration history and the many heroic stories about successful settlements on the prairie, Mangione followed another path. She found herself drawn to a legendary history of failure that took place further east. In 1852, the internationally renowned Norwegian violinist virtuoso Ole Bull (1810–1880) attempted to establish a Norwegian colony in the forest area of Potter County, Pennsylvania. Fueled by a mixture of national romanticist ideas and socialist visions of personal freedom, the artist named his colony Oleana.[4] Bull's utopian enterprise did not last long. Not only was he was the victim of fraud (this will be explained later), the land he bought was hilly and difficult to clear, and totally unsuitable for farming.[5] Soon, the Norwegian immigrants who had settled in his colony, mostly poor Norwegian farmers, left to settle anew further west.

But why does this story about a brief and failed nineteenth-century settler-colonial utopian venture still attract artistic attention? Why did the Susquehannock forest, the now desolate site of Ole Bull's former colony, become the major destination of Mangione's exploratory journey? And to what extent is the Oleana story of relevance today? In Giulia Mangione's own words, she wanted to use this story "as an allegory to describe the will, the vision, the hopes and the dreams that have united the Scandinavian emigrants to America throughout a century – from the 1840s to the 1960s."[6] However, as I will argue in this chapter, Mangione's project also has the capacity to initiate broader discussions, related not only to migration and settler colonialism but also, importantly, to the significant role of photographs in these historical and highly political processes.

The utopian drive in settler colonialism, the will, visions, hopes, and dreams that Mangione refers to, is clearly something that contrasts to what is now considered the dystopian counter-stories of settler colonialism. First, as demonstrated by Patrick Wolfe, settler colonialism is integrally linked to a logic of elimination. The process of erecting a new colonial society on an expropriated land base ultimately entails the invasion and dissolution of Native societies.[7] Second, as recently argued by Eileen Crist, the expansion of Western culture, of which settler colonialism formed an intrinsic part, and its inherent understanding of human supremacy over nature, has also caused a colonization of the Earth in a way that now seriously threatens biodiversity. It is not just Native societies that are eliminated, humanity's expansionism has created an ecological crisis in which biological abundance and wilderness are destroyed.[8]

In this chapter, I will adapt Mary Louise Pratt's concept of contact zone to explore what I conceive to be a tension in Giulia Mangione's series of photographs between settler-colonial utopia and its bleak, dystopian counterpart. As remarked in the introductory chapter of this volume, Pratt developed her notion of contact zone to describe places of colonial encounter through which cultural exchange and transformation take place.[9] Mangione has photographed places, faces, and bodies marked by processes of migration and colonial expansion. I will explore how her photographs also become contact zones. Notably, she not only records traces of neglected or forgotten histories, or draws attention to the apparent lack thereof, in culture and landscapes; through juxtapositions of her own work with archival images. She also negotiates the settler-colonial past and the political and ecological dystopias of the present, while simultaneously challenging the conventions of settler colonialism's celebratory aesthetics. Thus, as I will assert in the following, her images may bring alternative and more unsettling visual manifestations of settler colonialism to the fore. I will start this journey of exploration by taking a closer look at the photographic work she has produced and found in the archives while searching for Oleana.

Giulia Mangione's documentary storytelling

Giulia Mangione describes herself as a documentary photographer. But she is also constantly pushing and expanding the boundaries of this genre through experimentation. In this sense, she forms part of a new direction within documentary photography that has developed over the last ten years. Describing this tendency, Mette Sandbye remarks how it takes the form of "a fusion, or a welcome blurring, of the borders separating the classical genres of documentary and art photography, and politics and aesthetics."[10] Similarly, Mangione states that she likes "to work at the crossing between journalism and fiction, to create a more compelling piece of storytelling, where facts are mixed and reinterpreted in the contemporary time."[11]

This is exactly what she does in her Oleana project; she has set herself the task of exploring a story about an event that took place more than one and a half centuries ago, through the medium of photography. To enhance her storytelling, she has searched for images in historical archives, and placed them beside her own contemporary photographs:

> I thought that incorporating some archive images into my own work would provide the viewer with a sense of the time when this story took place. Some of the images also look quite unusual to us today, so I thought they would add a certain surreal, almost oneiric flavour.[12]

However, photography was still in its early days when Bull set up his colony in 1852. During the 1850s, it was the daguerreotype (a polished copperplate upon which an image was directly exposed) that was the most popular form of photographic image production. It was predominantly used for portraiture—both in Norway and in the United States. It was not until the 1860s, and the introduction of the wet collodion process, that photographers started to explore the American landscapes and environments where European migrants had settled.[13] Thus, original photographic documentation of the establishment and development of Bull's early settler-colonial enterprises does not exist.

But there are masses of photographs produced later, largely during the late nineteenth and early twentieth century, that bear witness to the broader history of Norwegian American migration. Thousands of letters and photographs were sent back and forth across the Atlantic Ocean. Now kept in private and public museums and archives, these photographs materialize local Norwegian and American communities' own stories about migration: emotional goodbyes, dramatic ocean crossings, and encounters with and assimilation to an alien lifestyle and culture. Importantly, they also contribute to the creation of continuity between the past and the present; they accentuate family values such as closeness and loyalty; and they work as testaments to the newcomers' sense of ethnic belonging.[14]

As part of her efforts to create a historical visual backdrop to the Oleana story, Mangione has appropriated images from the rich reservoirs of these Norwegian American archives. Even if they are produced many decades (some even almost a century) after the rise and fall of Oleana, they generate reflections about how it must have been to leave everything behind to start a new life in a distant country. In this way, the photographs invite the viewer to participate in the journey across the sea, surrounded only by tall waves and a seemingly endless open sea (Fig. 3). Other images, such as those of men cutting enormous pine trees, allude to the processes

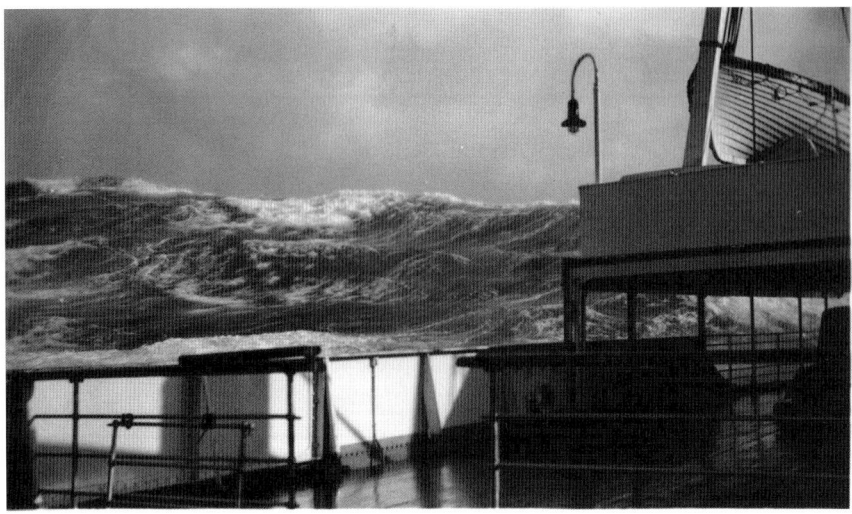

Figure 3: Unknown photographer. Photograph taken on the deck of a ship heading for the United States, 1920s. Courtesy Setesdalsmuseet, Norway.

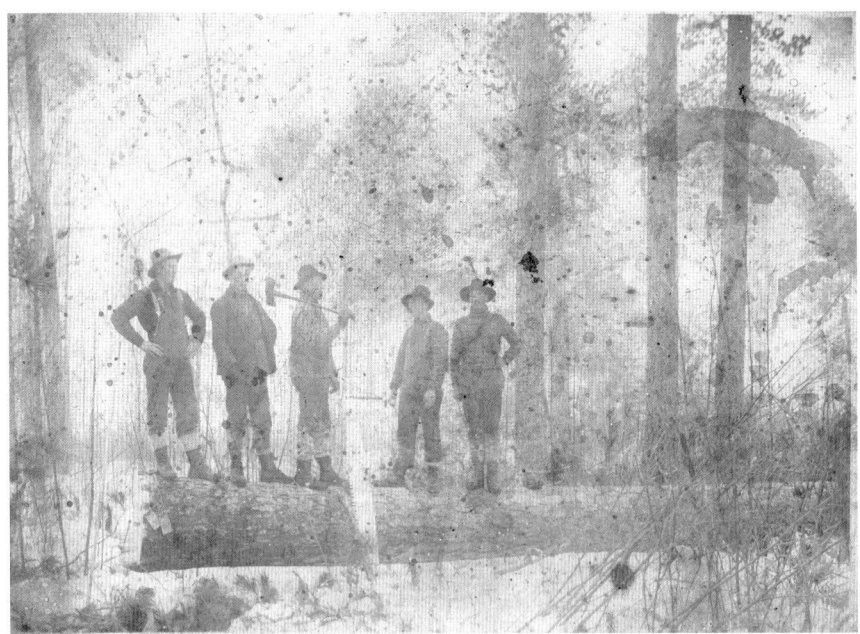

Figure 4: Unknown photographer. Immigrants from Setesdal, Norway, cutting trees, probably 1910–1920 (Plate 24, p. 349). Courtesy Setesdalsmuseet, Norway

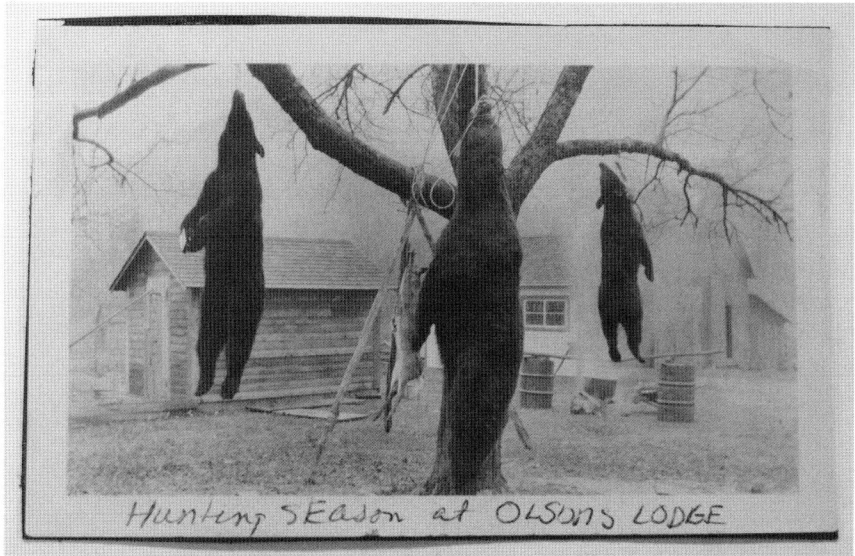

Figure 5: Unknown photographer, "Hunting Season at Olson's Lodge." Archive image from Potter County Historical Society, Pennsylvania, United States.

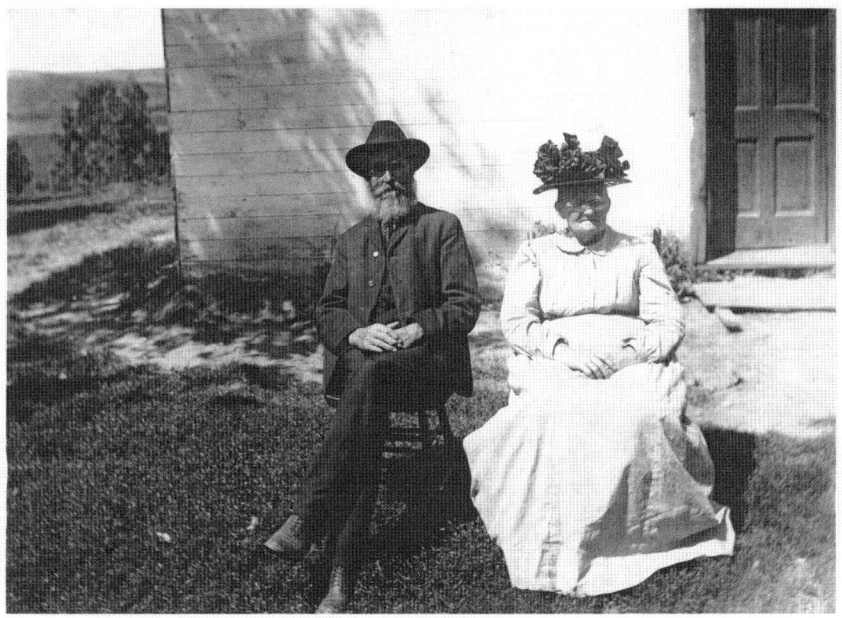

Figure 6: Unknown photographer. Portrait of Paul and Serene Tappen Strom in front of their Wisconsin home, probably around 1900. From Terry Everson's family album.

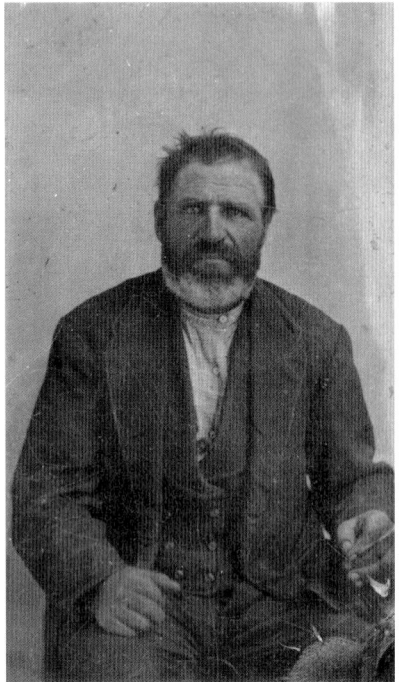

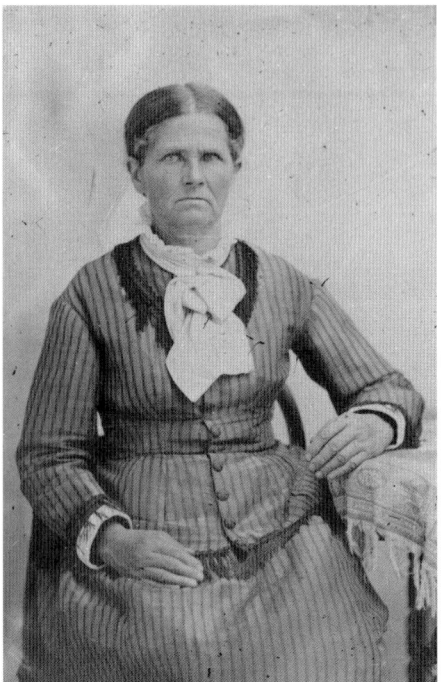

Figure 7: Unknown photographer. Portrait of Syver Everson (1832–1911). From Terry Everson's family album.

Figure 8: Unknown photographer. Helene Pedersdatter Everson (1828–1920). From Terry Everson's family album.

of settling, as, for example, the shooting of wild animals (Fig. 4), or the strenuous efforts of clearing the land that took place in Ole Bull's colony (Fig. 5). Such photographs bear witness to how the settlers strived to domesticate and claim control over the land they had colonized.[15] They are in this sense part of a well-known register of settler-colonial visual tropes. Notably, the most dominant trope in Norwegian settle-colonial culture by far is the image of the migrant family posing, often surrounded by their most precious belongs, in front of their modern and relatively spacious American home on the prairie. In the newly civilized prairie landscape, they are surrounded by seemingly endless fields, stretching toward the horizon.[16]

Mangione has also included a photograph of this kind in her selection of archival photographs. It is an image appropriated from a family album, a double portrait of a Norwegian couple, Paul and Serene Tappen Strom (Fig. 6). Paul, a Civil War veteran, came to Oleana with his parents in 1852, and stayed there for a while. The portrait shows him and his wife in their old age. They are photographed on a summer's day while sitting in their best clothes in front of their Wisconsin home with far-reaching hills and acres of land in the background. It is obviously an important

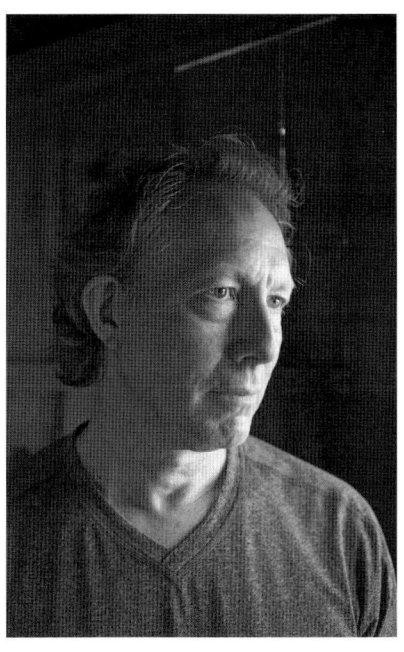

Figure 9: Giulia Mangione. Portrait of Terry Everson, descendant of Syver Everson and Helene Pedersdatter Everson, 2019. Courtesy of Giulia Mangione

moment. They are displaying their presence at the place where they finally managed to realize their ambitions to settle for good as farmers in America.

In the same album, Mangione found the portraits of another couple, Syver Everson and Helene Pedersdatter Everson, who met on the boat to America, and married in Ole Bull's Oleana (Figs. 7–8). In the photographs taken many decades later, their bodies are worn, but their postures are still strong and proud. Clearing land was not an easy task in the Pennsylvania wilderness. When the young couple arrived, the area was just as wild as Giulia Mangione has recorded it in her photographs. Many of the trees were so large, it took three men to reach around a single tree. Syver, his father, and one of his brothers spent a whole year clearing just one acre of land. Syver and Helene stayed in Oleana after it failed in 1853. However, six years later, in 1858, they left and traveled thirty-four miles on foot to Wisconsin.[17]

As mentioned above, Mangione has composed a visual account that brings the past into dialogue with the present. She juxtaposes the historical images of the former Oleana residents with her own close-up portraits of some of their living descendants (who still make a living as farmers in Wisconsin) (Fig. 9); she lets images of past processes of cutting trees for clearing the land (Fig. 4), or of

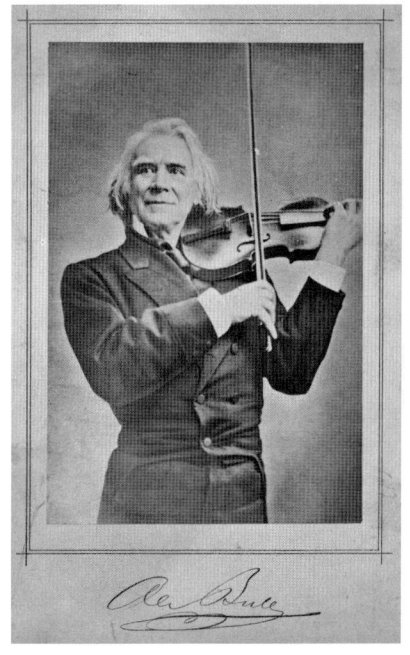

Figure 10: Unknown photographer, carte-de-visit-portrait of Ole Bull, with Bull's signature probably 1860s. National Library, Oslo.

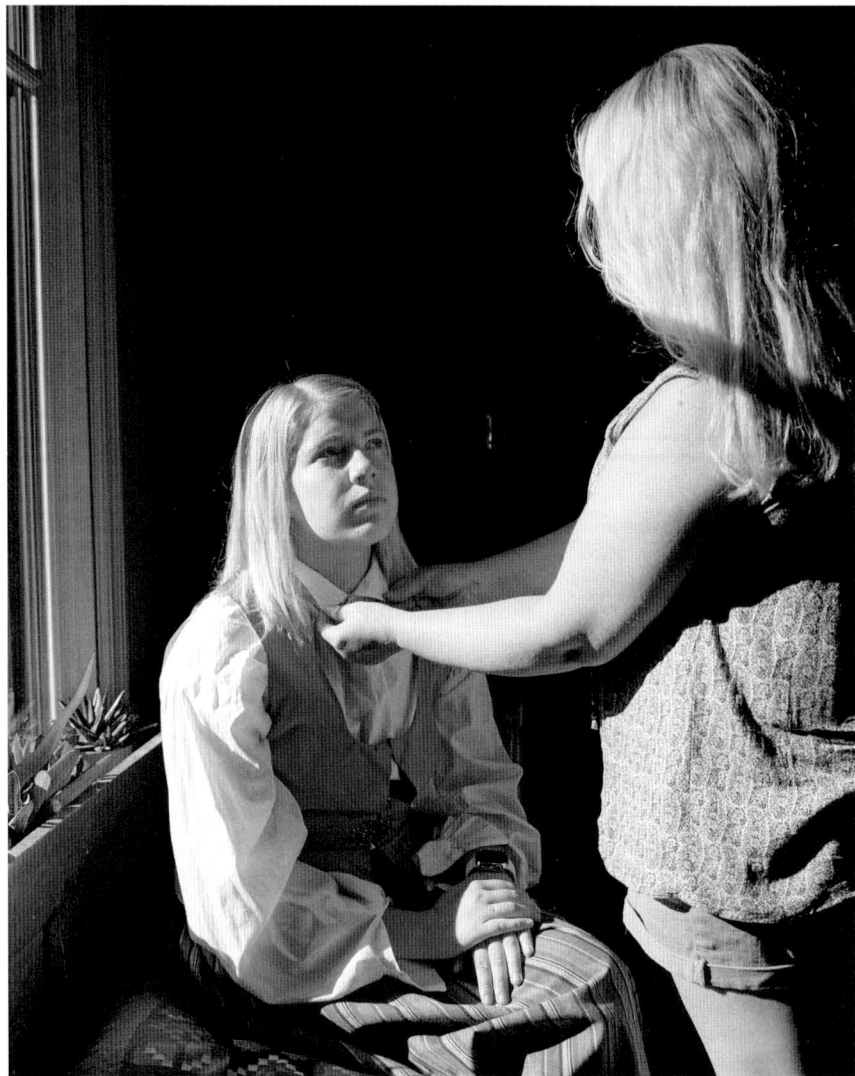

Figure 11: Giulia Mangione, 2019. Hilda Everson, daughter of Terry Everson, with her mother Charlotte, who is fixing the collar of the shirt of her *bunad* (national costume). The family is very interested in knowing and connecting with old Norwegian traditions. (27 on Giulia's list.) (Plate 25, p. 350). Courtesy of Giulia Mangione.

hunting bears (Fig. 5) encounter her own photographic documentation of the present wilderness in the former Oleana area (Figs. 1–2); and she places an historical image of the colony's founder, the violinist virtuoso and fervent nationalist Ole Bull (Fig. 10), adjacent to her own documentations of the still existing affective bonds to Norway and to the Ole Bull legend. She records the Eversons' family

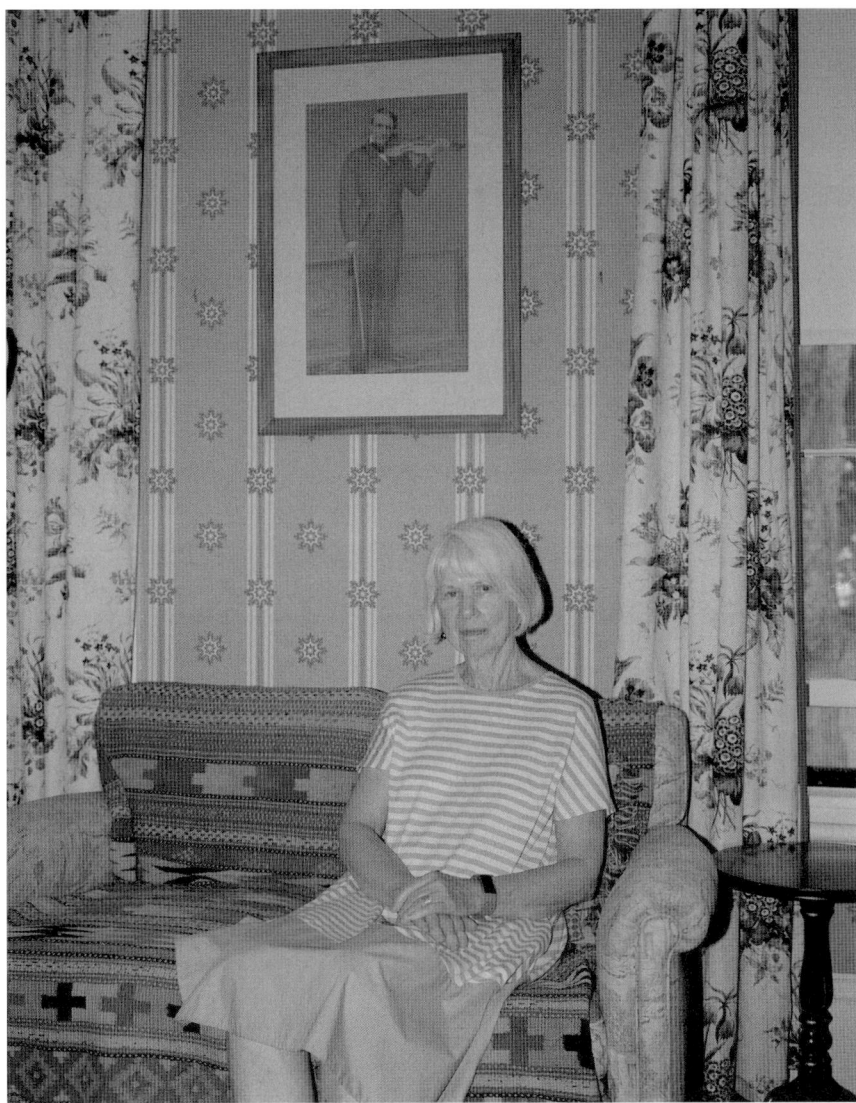

Figure 12: Giulia Mangione, 2019. Portrait of Olea Kaland Smith, great granddaughter of Ole Bull, from his second marriage. Olea is portrayed in the house where Ole and Sara Bull lived in Maine, United States, after the collapse of the colony (Plate 26, p. 351). Courtesy of Giulia Mangione.

members in the Midwest, even today, proudly display their Norwegian heritage by, for example, dressing up in Norwegian national costumes (Fig. 11). She also portrays one of Ole Bull's descendants, Olea Kaland Smith, posing under his portrait, in the home that he established in Maine after the collapse of his colony (Fig. 12).

In this way, Mangione's experimental documentary comes across as an assemblage of photographic fragments loaded with narrative potential. Nevertheless, to bring out this potential, it is necessary to weave the visual fragments into a larger discursive framework, which will be done in the following. This entails critical engagement, not only with the tales of the mythical figure, Ole Bull and his Oleana utopia, but also by confronting these stories as part of a larger process of European colonialism—as well as of the continued coloniality of the present.

A portrait of Ole Bull, the romantic visionary

The portrait of the famous violin player that Mangione has appropriated for her documentary storytelling is a signed carte de visit portrait (Fig. 10). Bull is photographed in his usual celebrity-musician pose, en-face, with the violin steadily placed under his chin. His burning gaze, square face, strong physical appearance, and long and unruly, almost white, hair immediately catches the eye. All of these were features that, at the time, evoked Romantic notions of the wild and exotic nature in human terms—in short, a virile virtuosity.[18] The portrait is undated, but based on comparisons to other, similar portraits of him, it appears to have been shot sometime in the 1860s, when he was in his fifties, when his failed Oleana adventure had long since become something of the past. Throughout his life, Ole Bull posed for a huge number of such portraits, first graphic prints and later photographs, that were widely dispersed to his many admirers.[19]

This part of his visual legacy therefore comes across as an invitation to ponder on the charisma and persuasive power of this legendary personality—and how these capacities ultimately drove many Norwegians, among them the families of Syver and Helene Everson, to cross the Atlantic Ocean to start a new life in Bull's American colony. The portraits formed part of the intense cult of celebrity that revolved around the virtuoso. Ole Bull both presented himself, and was perceived by the public, as the ultimate Romantic artist hero. As early as 1843, at the age of 33, he paid Norway's romanticist poet, Henrik Wergeland (1808–1845) to write the first of many biographies about him.[20] Wergeland portrays his artist friend as a genius, an autodidact, who already as a twelve-year-old boy, was capable of performing Paganini's Caprices. He describes in detail—based on Bull's own stories—how the young violinist worked his way from poverty, illness, and not least the "unbearable insensitivity of the French public," to rising fame in Paris—the very capital of nineteenth-century virtuosity. He accounts, with great pathos, how the despairing artist "many a night wandered penniless […], through the empty streets of Paris, through the cholera-infected night air, [while] listening the sights of the dying in nearby houses."[21]

Notably, he also explains how it turned out to be Bull's Norwegian-ness, and the way he was conceived as an exotic outsider, that paradoxically paved the way for his success and acknowledgment in Paris: "That Bull is born there, in the old Thule [the farthest North], not so far from where the North Pole rises up like the top of an umbrella, has also increased interest in him."[22] The biographer further dwells on how Bull was heralded as the barbarian, the young wild one from the north, and adored by the Parisian audience due to "his natural, unforced expressivity," which was seen as a refreshing contrast to the overly emotional artifice of the great Italian artist Paganini.[23]

The purity and expressive innocence ascribed to his Norwegian background was similarly valued by his American audiences. In one of his poems, Henry Wadsworth Longfellow (1807–1882), also a close friend of Bull, typically portrayed him in a highly emotional style as no less than a northern angel:

> His figure tall and straight and lithe/ And every feature of his face/ Revealing his Norwegian race: / A radiance streaming from within, / Around his face and forehead beamed. /The Angel with the violin, / Painted by Raphael he seemed. / He lived in that ideal world. / Whose language is not speech, but song […][24]

However, while hugely popular, Bull was also a highly controversial character—and his portrait is embedded in a patchwork consisting not only of passionate celebrity tales, but also of equally heated, critical counter-narratives. The complexity of this audience response was by no means unique to Ole Bull. In a study of the nineteenth-century reception of musical virtuosos, Zarko Cvejić holds that Bull lived in an era that "was at once fascinated with virtuosity and profoundly suspicious of it."[25] Virtuous musical performers were simultaneously admired, due to their unrestrained performance or individuality, and subjected to harsh criticism, for at the same time, compromising the autonomous musical work of art.[26] This criticism was most typically expressed by the German philosopher Hegel, who saw virtuosos as people who, while stealing the limelight, put themselves at the center, at the expense of everyone else.[27]

Cvejić points to how Bull, on the one hand, was a veritable sensation through-out Europe and much of the United States, well known for his idiosyncratic way of playing. Bull modified his violin to make it sound like a traditional Norwegian fiddle. This enabled him to play polyphonically, something "which invariably put his audiences into hysterics wherever he went."[28] But on the other hand, he was seen as too individual and original: "a virtuoso that most critics loved to hate," someone who was said to be a "supreme charlatan," and who let "the autocracy of feeling generate into sentimentalism."[29]

Such a polarity is similarly brought to the forefront in the most recent Bull biography, written by Harald Herresthal. On the positive side, the biographer continuously refers to the way the Norwegian violinist never ceased improving his technical skills in the process of exploring the potentiality of his instrument.[30] But he also draws a contrasting image of him, one that is far less pleasant than the one that Bull created himself. What he reveals is a personality that matches Hegel's negative understanding of the virtuoso as ruthlessly self-absorbed:

> [...] a neurotically offended, whiny, moody person with a definite bipolar psyche and strongly paranoid features, and a totally inconsiderate relationship both to the truth and to other people, including his wife and children. He overslept, lost valuable objects, forgot his violins when on tour, staked fortunes at the gambling table, borrowed money without paying it back, duelled and drank. The money rolled out of his hands at the same pace as the tones from his violin.[31]

Herresthal also sees Bull's ill-fated establishment of his own Norwegian colony in the United States as one of the most typical, perhaps also the wildest, example of his outsized personality. Even so, his discussion of the colonial enterprise points to the necessity of understanding it in the context of the liberal and nationalistic waves that swept through Europe in the 1840s.[32]

At the time, Norway was a young nation searching for identity, and Bull wholeheartedly took part in the efforts of the Norwegian cultural elite to establish the country's cultural identity by rediscovering and promoting unacknowledged cultural treasures. He included folk musicians in his concerts and he worked to establish a Norwegian Language Theatre in his hometown, Bergen.[33] While advancing an awareness of Norwegian national identity both at home and abroad, Bull made a great effort to present himself not only as a patriot, but also as a friend of the people—who showed solidarity with sailors and artisans.[34] When the February Revolution broke out in France in 1848, he traveled to Paris to form part of the people's revolution. He played for the wounded and bereaved and fronted a delegation who greeted the French Republic on behalf of Norway.[35]

But on his return to Norway, he encountered huge disappointments. The establishment of his National Theatre was not, as he saw it, properly appreciated by the Norwegian authorities. Deeply frustrated, Ole Bull warned his brother against the dangers of "drowning in patriotism."[36] Soon after, he left his beloved Norway, invigorated by the idea of establishing a "New Norway dedicated to freedom, baptized in independence, and protected by the Union's mighty flag"[37] in the United States.

Oleana and the thin line between utopia and dystopia

The story about the rise and fall of Oleana, Ole Bull's settler-colonial utopia, is thus an important part of the mythical universe in which the portraits of both Bull and of Syver and Helene Everson are embedded. This tale, which has been told and retold,[38] and which also inspired Mangione's photographic project on Oleana, can in short be summed up in the following.

In April 1852, Bull was offered and purchased the land in Potter County, Pennsylvania. He had not even set eyes on the property when he agreed to the deal. In the same year, a book, published anonymously in Norway, titled *Amerika, Ole Bull og det nye Norge* [America, Ole Bull and the New Norway], built enthusiasm for Bull's colony through an elaborate and passionate description of his enterprise. The Norwegian labor press also hailed Bull's colony, while emphasizing its potential for creating a better life for people of the working classes. As noted by historian Ingrid Semmingsen, "Oleana had become a dreamland for masses of people [Norwegian migrants] – almost as appealing as the Gold Country, California."[39] The first colonist arrived in September, and as many as 250 Norwegians had arrived by the end of 1852. A schoolhouse and a hotel were built, and Bull made plans for three villages, to be named New Bergen, New Norway, and Valhalla. The colony founder also provided for a stately home for himself on a high slope, called the Castle.

However, the area soon proved difficult for farming. It was a hilly region covered by large pine trees, and the soil was meager. Oleana was also without the railway connections necessary for a farming community to prosper. Furthermore, it became impossible for Bull to provide the Norwegian settlers with the conditions that he had initially promised them. Most of the colonists were extremely poor and dependent on his generosity and financial support, while he was not only impractical and unreliable, but also lacked business acumen. This situation caused large conflicts, and the difficulties accelerated as it became clear that Bull had fallen victim to fraud. He had bought land from swindlers who did not actually own most of the area that they had sold to him.

Oleana, Bull's utopia, only lasted for a year. In September 1853, Bull sold off the section of land that he rightfully owned and withdrew from the board of the colony. By then most of the settlers had moved from the colony. Nevertheless, his colony lived on in the popular imagination. In Norway, it was long remembered through a satirical ballad, written by Ditmar Meidell, that ridiculed naïve expectations about America:

In Oleana, that's where I'd like to be,
And not drag the chains of slavery in
Norway
Ole- Ole – Ole- oh! Oleana
Aye, got to Oleana where you will begin to live!
The poorest wretch in Norway is a count
over there
Ole- Ole – Ole- oh! Oleana[40]

This ballad was most likely also the source of inspiration for a scene in *Peer Gynt* (1867), the most renowned work of Norway's great playwright, Henrik Ibsen. With great irony, Ibsen's protagonist, Peer (a charming, gifted, but also totally undependable narcissist with many similarities to Ole Bull), fantasizes about colonizing the Sahara Desert, naming his new colony Gyntiana.[41] In more recent times, the Oleana song was reintroduced by the American songwriter, folk singer, and peace activist Peter Seeger, as a renewed statement of the contrast between the American dream and the realities that met poor newcomers in the United States.

To Giulia Mangione, the Oleana story primarily signifies what she sees as the thin line between utopia and dystopia, heroes and antiheroes, migration and colonization.[42] It is therefore pertinent to compare her work to Pratt's decolonial analysis of European travel books from the colonial period, the work in which Pratt first introduces the concept of *contact zones*. While Pratt analyzes literature to understand how Europeans came to feel so "naturally" entitled to the non-European places in the world that they explored and invaded,[43] Mangione uses photography in an effort to grasp a specific part of this larger pattern—the Norwegian settlers' sense of entitlement to certain areas in the United States. The settler-colonial tropes that she reveals in the photography archives, such as the images of clearing and domesticating land, of new houses and of wide acres of land, were perhaps just as instrumental as the travel writing discussed by Pratt. On a personal level, photographs were crucial in the processes of making people, such as, for example, the Eversons, feel at home, and to justify individual choices to migrate. But, on a broader ideological level, these images also served to legitimate the European expansion in America.

Indigenous absences

There are, however, other striking parallels between Pratt's analysis and Mangione's Oleana project. In her analysis, Pratt draws attention to the contact zones of the colonial encounter as such, what she terms the "social spaces where disparate cultures meet, clash, and grapple with each other, often in highly asymmetrical relations of domination and subordination."[44] But importantly, she also describes her experience of discovering absences, huge gaps in the archive, in the process of exploring such encounters. What she missed while working on this material were the voices she "wasn't hearing" and the evidence of how colonialism impacted "those whose lives it intervened."[45]

Mangione's archival photographs similarly accentuate a sense of absence. At first glance, the historical images do not appear to bear witness to any kind of past asymmetrical relations or conflicts. Nevertheless, they testify to how the visual legacy of Norwegian settler colonialism that she encounters in museums and archives appears to be devoid of any traces of the Indigenous Americans that were driven away for settler colonialism to take place. This absence is in itself an indication of the way settler colonialism, as argued by Wolfe, is integrally linked to processes of invasion and dissolution of Indigenous societies.[46] In Norwegian American archives, the voices that cannot be heard are the voices of Indigenous North Americans, people who, in the words of Wolfe, were "killed, driven away, romanticized, assimilated, fenced in, bred White, and otherwise eliminated as the original owners of the land,"[47] simply because they were in the way of the European settler-colonialists' access to territory.

These are the untold accounts that are not immediately available in the Norwegian and Norwegian American settler migration archives that Mangione has drawn her material from. Rather, the visual rhetoric of settler colonialism that she appropriates in her project is dominated by what Anthony Moran has termed ideas of "newness."[48] The migrant settlers are clearing new land or are posing in front of new houses, dressed in new modern clothes, in newly cultivated landscapes, while their entitlement is ideologically based on the Western myth of emptiness. As noted by Andrew Sluyter, this myth encapsulates the colonizer's model of the world by privileging diffusion from the West into the supposed vacuum of the non-West.[49]

The myth of emptiness is also poignantly expressed in the early historiography of Norwegian American migration, in, for example, Ingrid Semmingsen's influential work *Veien mot Vest: Utvandringen fra Norge til Amerika 1825–1965* [The Road to the West: Immigration from Norway to America, 1825–1965]. Semmingsen rarely mentions the Indigenous population that lived for centuries in the areas where the Norwegian settlers arrived. When she does, she merely states that their land was underdeveloped, and thus, in a sense, was empty and vacant. Their way of life was also one that could not survive. It was doomed in the face of progress and modernity.[50]

It was also this widespread understanding that made it possible for settlers to build utopias, such as Ole Bull's Oleana, without hindrances, while the Indigenous American population was "safely" categorized as something of the past. Bull definitely saw himself as a man destined to bring freedom and equality to the frontier, but the Bull historiography typically only provides a small glimpse of indigenous existence in Potter County, Pennsylvania. His biographer, Herresthal, gives a short account of how Ole Bull visited the neighboring Seneca tribe a few times; after having lost much of their land to the United States, the Seneca tribe had received a grant of land in Warren County, Pennsylvania. This community was named after their renowned chief Cornplanter. According to this account, Bull was appointed chief of honor during one of his visits at the Cornplanter reservation by the Allegheny river, and he was given the name *Aquas Hau Nioh Tirorech Aogarraine*, which is said to mean "he who creates divine music on the violin." Bull did of course play for them, in addition to vividly explaining how elk were hunted in Norway.[51] The short anecdote indicates how the local Indigenous American population, even if almost invisible, was paternalistically romanticized, and treated as some kind of stowed-away local heritage that had originally formed part of the environment, like exotic plants. Or, as Sleyter contends, "Noble savages blend into a primordial wilderness that [...] formed a blank page on which an egalitarian nation of rugged individualists could inscribe a homegrown progression of land-scape morphologies [...]."[52]

Ole Bull's kind of individualism was, as mentioned above, based on his art-ist-hero identity, but also on egalitarian ideas and Norwegian nationalism, and the popular understanding, even today, of Norway as exceptional in the larger history of European colonialism: as a small and innocent country, itself the victim of many hundreds of years of Danish and Swedish colonialism.[53] Ironically, the formerly colonized Norwegian citizen, invigorated by nationalism, became a for-merly colonized colonizer in the United States. Thus, Bull was only one of many Norwegian settlers in the United States that held on to Norwegian ethnicity no matter what, while at the same time suppressing or romanticizing local Indigenous ethnic identities.

The colonial aftermath and a utopia for the future

Like Pratt, Mangione also engages with the aftermath of colonialism in her work. Her contemporary photographs address the social as well as the environmental legacy of settler colonialism. She traveled to Wisconsin and photographed the descendants of families that started their new life in America in Ole Bull's col-ony. She portrays them and their communities in a way that emphasizes not only their persistent emotional attachment to Norway (Fig. 11) but also their continued investment in the cultivation of land and the taming of the American wilderness. She tellingly records them in their homes, surrounded by walls ornately decorated with hunting and fishing trophies (Fig. 13). As such, these images do not directly confront colonialism as a historical legacy. Rather, her portraits allude to the way the subjects in front of her camera are still situated in what has been termed as ongoing structures of coloniality. Furthermore, they bring to the fore a sense of absence that points back to the archival element of her project. What they seem to confront is the normalization of the past processes of dispossession. The indi-viduals that Mangione encounters through her camera, whether she travels in the now desolate former Oleana in Potter County, Pennsylvania, or in the farming areas in Wisconsin, are, with no exceptions, descendants of white settler families. She records the present white "normality" in a way that makes the absence of the

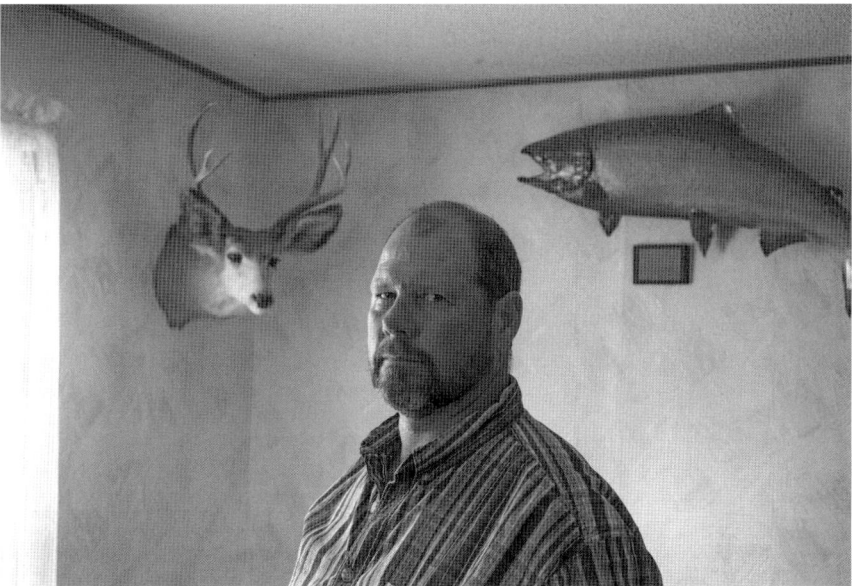

Figure 13: Giulia Mangione, 2019. Portrait of Jay Everson, cousin of Terry Everson, in his father Truman Everson's house in Blair, Wisconsin. Courtesy of Giulia Mangione.

Indigenous American people, whose land these Norwegian settlers took over, perhaps even more striking than in her archival images.

Structures of coloniality also encompass the landscapes that are inhabited by her portrait subjects. Even though Mangione has refrained from literally documenting these Midwestern landscapes, the environmental impact of settler colonialism seems to form the intellectual backdrop of her project. Recent research points to how such impacts are starkly visible in the landscapes they produce. According to Tracey Banivanua Mar and Penelope Edmonds, land and the organized spaces on it, also narrate the stories of colonization. These land changes are wide ranging and include:

> […] symmetrically surveyed divisions of land; fences, roads, power lines, dams and mines; the vast monocultural expanses of single-cropped fields; carved and preserved national forest, and marine and wilderness parks; the expansive and gridded cities; and the socially coded areas of human habitation and trespass that are bordered, policed, and defended.[54]

The land changes that took place in the Midwest, where the majority of Mangione's portrait subjects are currently situated, figure predominantly on Mar and Edmond's list. Some of the consequences of the settler-colonial introduction of monocultural agriculture in this region, such as erosion and dust storms, were already photographically recorded in the 1930s in the now canonical Farm Security Administration (FSA) documentary project. Back then, the dystopian FSA photographs of the environmental disaster were rhetorically inscribed in positivist notions of a scientific management of nature, and were framed accordingly to demonstrate how this disaster was caused by the destructive forces of nature, and could be controlled by modern technology in the future.[55]

Today, however, there is a more acute awareness of how the monocultural cultivation of the North American prairie landscape represents a serious threat to the biological diversity that is essential for the survival of humanity. In her analysis of the present demolition of life's biological variety, Eileen Crist states that North America's largest biome, the prairie, is now almost gone. The mono-agricultural takeover of the prairie land exterminated not only the bison migrations but also annihilated the grassland and put numerous forms of prairie life on the endangered list.[56]

Crist's observations of the dystopian land changes in the Midwest relate to the broader issue of colonization, not only in terms of the West's position as a dominant socioeconomic civilization, but also in reference to what she sees as the human takeover of the Earth and the current global ecological crisis. Western culture, "the expansionism of growing economies, escalating global trade, climbing population numbers, sprawling infrastructures and spreading destructive technologies" are all drivers in the current development that is leading the biosphere toward mass extinction.[57] Crist's argument is therefore also a call for the recognition of how ceding human dominance is the only resolution for preserving and restoring life's richness, and a defense for wilderness, "nature's original blueprint."[58]

According to Crist, the settler migration to the United States was one of the most totalizing ways to bring wilderness under the governance of a monoculture of rational control. While she holds that most of the immigrant settlers remained complaisant about their entitlement to the earth, she stresses that there were also other voices, who were jolted into an awakening. Intellectuals such as Henry David Thoreau, Ralph Emerson, Walt Whitman, and Emily Dickenson started to reconceptualize wilderness while agitating for the value of protecting wild nature.[59]

Even among the settler families in the Midwest, these kinds of ideas were expressed, as, for example, in the poems and writings of the Minnesota farmer, second-generation Norwegian American, cartoonist, poet, and photographer Peter Julius Rosendahl (1878–1942). For Rosendahl, the uncultivated landscape had its own value, a place where the simple elements stand in meaningful relationship to each other and the larger space. In the poem "A Cabin in the Woods" (1925), he writes suggestively of the small cabin he is going to build in a quiet wood of hazel trees, as a retreat from the world, and in intimate proximity to "Nature and Nature's God":

I'm going to build the cabin of pounded earth and stone
I'm going to build it simple and build it all alone
And the door shall face the sunset – and I'll let it stand ajar,
So, I can see what's going on where the forest creatures are:
And, at dusk, I'll hear the crickets and watch the bat's erratic flight,
While the owl shall call off the hours through the stillness of the night,
And the winds of night shall lull me as I sit and dream'ly nod.
For I'll be close to Nature and close to Nature's God.[60]

Rosendahl's photographs seem to reflect the same attitude to nature that is expressed in his poems. He photographs when he is walking through the wilderness of the woods, while for example directing his attention to the sun's flickering play along the thick fern undergrowth (Fig. 14), in a way that bears a strong resemblance to Mangione's way of documenting the wilderness in the landscape that used to

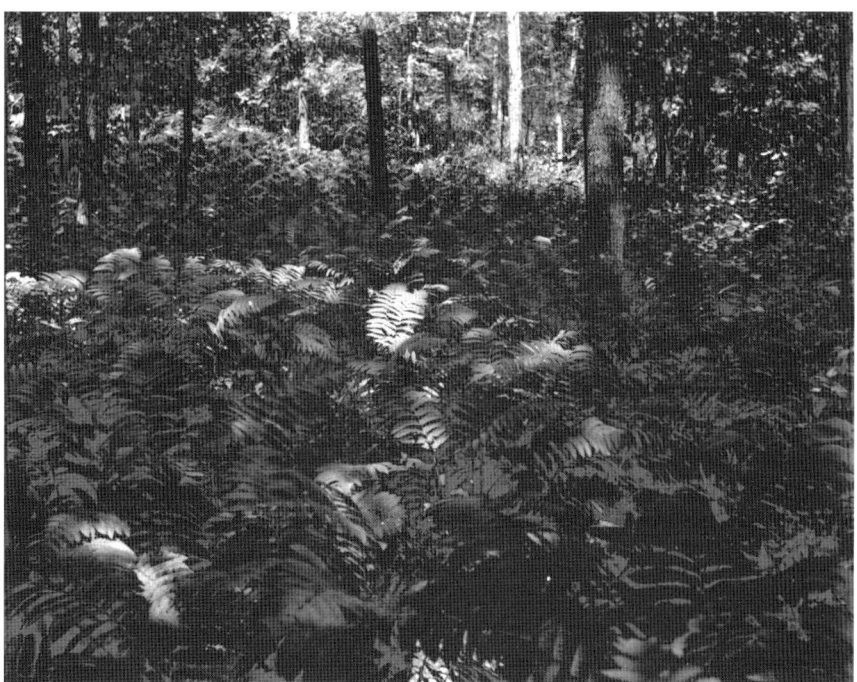

Figure 14: Peter Julius Rosendahl (ca. 1913–1914). The forest path in summer, Spring Grove, Minnesota. Courtesy Vesterheim Norwegian-American Museum, Decorah, Iowa.

be the home of Ole Bull's Oleana. This brings us back to the starting point of the chapter and Mangione's images of the Susquehannock forest in the Allegheny mountains (Figs. 1–2). Mangione talks about her photographs of this wilderness as a way of imagining how this landscape must have looked, before it was invaded by Ole Bull's settler colonists, and later by modern large-scale forestry: "It used to an untouched virgin forest, but then the timber industry and development of it began. Everything was cut down."[61] She documents the wilderness of the area that has been turned into a national state park named after Ole Bull, aware of how its history changed due to colonialism. She points to how it, at present, is carved and preserved as a result of the same processes; safeguarded, but still penetrated by the motorway. But her photographs are also intended to attest to the current preservation and defense of nature's autonomy—and the way the settler utopia turned into an industrial dystopia, and ultimately, now, in this particular case, is emerging as a possible utopia for the future: "[…] it finally was regulated. Now you cannot cut trees there. Everything is protected by law. And the trees are growing again."[62]

Mangione's work thus demonstrates how photography may work as a contact zone between past processes of migration and colonialism on the one hand, and the present coloniality, on the other. Her experimental documentary dismantles the structures that settler colonialism seeks to preserve, while opening up for new ways of understanding the relationship between humans and the land in a time when, in the words of Eileen Crist, "nature's freedom is screaming for defense."[63]

Notes

1. Nils Olav Østrem, *Norsk utvandringshistorie* (Oslo: Det Norske Samlaget, 2014), 33.
2. Janne Lahti, *The American West and the World. Transnational and Comparative Perspectives* (New York/Abingdon: Routledge, 2019), 4–5.
3. Østrem, *Norsk utvandringshistorie*, 62.
4. Bull quoted in Odd Lovoll, *The Promise of America: A History of the Norwegian American People* (Minneapolis: University of Minnesota Press, 1991), 61.
5. Lovoll, *The Promise of America*, 61.
6. From Giulia Mangone's own account of her project. Unpublished text. 2 pages.
7. Patrick Wolfe, "Settler colonialism and the elimination of the native," *Journal of Genocide Research* 8, no. 4 (2006), 387–388, DOI: 10.1080/14623520601056240
8. Eileen Crist, *Abundant Earth: Toward an Ecological Civilization* (Chicago/London: University of Chicago Press, 2019), 11–46.
9. Mary Louise Pratt, *Imperial Eyes: Travel Writing and Transculturation*, 2nd edition (London: Routledge, 2008), 3.

10. Mette Sandbye, "New Mixtures. Migration, war and cultural differences in contemporary art-documentary photography," *Photographies* 11, Nos. 2–3 (2018), 267–287, https://doi.org/10.1080/17540763.2018.1445017

11. E-mail correspondence between Mangione and the author, June 14, 2020.

12. E-mail correspondence between Mangione and the author, June 14, 2020.

13. See Peter Larsen and Sigrid Lien, *Norsk fotohistorie: fra daguerreotypi til digitalisering* [Norwegian History of Photography: From Daguerreotypes to Digitization] (Oslo: Det Norske Samlaget, 2007), and Miles Orvell, *American Photography* (Oxford/New York: Oxford University Press, 2003).

14. Sigrid Lien, *Pictures of Longing. Photography and the Norwegian-American Migration* (Minneapolis/London: University of Minnesota Press, 2018).

15. For a discussion about such processes, see Lahti, *The American West,* 122–129.

16. For a discussion about this genre, see Sigrid Lien, "Ragnhild's images: Migration, Settler Colonialism and Photography," *International Journal for History, Culture and Modernity* Volume 8, Issue 1 (2020), 1–22.

17. A short account of the lives of Syver and Helene Pedersdatter can be found at the website: Wisconsin Scandinavian Obituaries, https://sites.rootsweb.com/~wisobits/name/er_ez.html#EversonSyver

18. See, for example, Ivan Raykoff, *Dreams of Love. Playing the Romantic Pianist* (Oxford/New York: Oxford University Press, 2014), 211, and Alessandra Comini, *The Changing Image of Beethoven: A Study in Mythmaking* (Santa Fe: Sunstone Press, 2008), 31.

19. For a digital collection of these images, see: https://www.flickr.com/photos/bergen_public_library/sets/72157617212205314/

20. Henrik Wergeland, *Ole Bull. Efter Opgivelser af ham selv biografisk skildret* [Ole Bull. After biographical accounts provided by himself] (Kristiania: Guldberg & Dzwonkowski 1843; Bergen: John Grieg, 1974).

21. Wergeland, *Ole Bull,* 11, my translation.

22. Wergeland, *Ole Bull,* 19, my translation.

23. Wergeland, *Ole Bull,* 25, my translation.

24. Longfellow quoted in Rasmus B. Anderson, "Ole Bull, Norwegian Violinist Appeared in Madison In 1868," *The Wisconsin State Journal,* February 3, 1924.

25. Zarko Cvejić, *The Virtuoso as Subject: The Reception of Instrumental Virtuosity, c. 1815–c.1850* (Newcastle upon Tyne: Cambridge Scholars Publishing, 2016), 14.

26. Cvejić, *The Virtuoso,* 13.

27. Cvejić, *The Virtuoso,* 15.

28. Cvejić, *The Virtuoso,* 122.

29. Cvejić, *The Virtuoso,* 121.

30. Harald Herresthal, *Ole Bull. Vidunderbarnet erobrer verden 1810–1837* [Ole Bull. The Prodigy Child conquers the World 1810–1837] (Oslo: Unipub, 2006).

31. Mona Levin, "Ole Bull i gåtefull helfigur" [Ole Bull in enigmatic full figure], review article, *Aftenposten,* July 30, 2006, my translation.

32. In 1814, Norway was separated from Denmark and got its own constitution. It entered a new union with Sweden. In this situation, Norway, due to its democratic constitution, started to consider itself a modern nation-state. See Gudleiv Bø, "The History of a Norwegian National Identity," https://www.tsu.ge/data/file_db/scandinavian-studies/Nation-building-the-Norwegian-way.pdf.

33. See also Einar Haugen and Camilla Cai, *Ole Bull: Norway's Romantic Musician and Cosmopolitan Patriot* (Madison: University of Wisconsin Press, 1993), 102–114.

34. Harald Herresthal, *Ole Bull. Teaterdirektør, koloniherre og norskdomsmann* [Ole Bull. Theatre Director, Colonial Master and Nationalist 1848–1862] (Oslo: Unipub, 2009), 55.

35. Harald Herresthal, *Ole Bull. Teaterdirektør*, 369.

36. Harald Herresthal, *Ole Bull. Teaterdirektør*, 132.

37. Lovoll, *The Promise of America*, 61.

38. This summary is based on Lovoll, *The Promise of America*; Ingrid Semmingsen, *Veien mot vest. Utvandringen fra Norge til Amerika 1825–1865* [The Road to the West. Immigration from Norway to America] (Oslo: Aschehoug), 392–415; Harald Herresthal, *Ole Bull. Teaterdirektør*, 130–198, Haugen and Cai, *Ole Bull: Norway's Romantic Musician*, 115–136.

39. Semmingsen, *Veien mot vest*, 405.

40. Quoted from Lovoll, *The Promise of America*, 61–62.

41. Semmingsen, *Veien mot vest*, 415.

42. Giulia Mangione in conversation with Sigrid Lien, April 2020.

43. Pratt, *Imperial Eyes*, 15.

44. Pratt, *Imperial Eyes*, 18

45. Pratt, *Imperial Eyes*, 16.

46. Wolfe, "Settler colonialism," 388–489.

47. Wolfe, "Settler colonialism," 388.

48. Anthony Moran, "As Australia Decolonizes: Indigenizing Settler Nationalism and the Challenges of Settler / Indigenous Relations," *Ethnic and Racial Studies* 25, no. 6 (2002), 1016.

49. Andrew Sluyter, "Colonialism and Landscape in the Americas: Material/Conceptual Transformations and Continuing Consequences," *Annals of the American Association of Geographers* 91 (2001), 410–428, 412.

50. Semmingsen, *Veien mot vest*, 226. See also Lien, "Ragnhild's images" for further discussion of this historiography.

51. Harald Herresthal, *Ole Bull. Teaterdirektør*, 188.

52. Sluyter, "Colonialism and Landscape," 417.

53. Kirsten Alsaker Kjerland and Knut Rio (eds.), *Kolonitid, Nordmenn på eventyr og big business i Afrika og Stillehavet* [Colonial Times, Norwegians on adventure and in big

business in Africa and in the Pacific] (Oslo: Scandinavian Academic Press/Spartacus Forlag, 2009), 6, 8.

54. Tracey Banivanua Mar and Penelope Edmonds, "Introduction: Making Space in Settler Colonies," in Tracey Banivanua Mar and Penelope Edmonds (eds.), *Making Settler Colonial Space: Perspectives on Race, Place and Identity* (New York: Palgrave Macmillan, 2010), 2.

55. Gisela Parak, *Photographs of Environmental Phenomena* (Bielefeld: Transcript Verlag, 2015), 97.

56. Crist, *Abundant Earth*, 23.

57. Crist, *Abundant Earth*, 2.

58. Crist, *Abundant Earth*, 5.

59. Crist, *Abundant Earth*, 133.

60. For a discussion about Peter Rosendahl's aesthetic productions, poems, cartoons, and particularly his photographs, see Sigrid Lien, *Pictures of Longing*, Chapter 4, 121–147.

61. Giulia Mangione in conversation with Sigrid Lien, April 2020.

62. Giulia Mangione in conversation with Sigrid Lien, April 2020.

63. Crist, *Abundant Earth*, 5.

The Photographer as Advocate

Representing Migrant Communities in San Francisco and Tijuana

Bridget Gilman

Amidst the current tide of political jingoism and xenophobia rising across the West, to speak of post-border regions or hybrid cultures that efface national boundaries may seem unduly optimistic.[1] And yet, the present moment is undeniably defined by migration. The United Nations reports that 70.8 million people were forcibly displaced in 2018, sixty percent more than were displaced in 2009.[2] This global rise in the number of refugees, asylum seekers, and displaced persons will undoubtedly yield further cross-cultural contact, but, as anthropologist Néstor García Canclini has noted, the hybridization produced by migration does not reconcile what is different or unequal. Though migration fuses together distinct cultures, economies, and social networks, such movements are simultaneously defined by exclusion, contradiction, and conflict.[3]

Canclini's notion of hybridity without equivalence is key to the two photographic case studies considered in this essay. In San Francisco's South of Market or SoMa neighborhood, Janet Delaney documents the social and spatial pressures of gentrification.[4] A former working-class neighborhood rooted in the industrial waterfront, throughout the nineteenth and early twentieth centuries, SoMa was largely comprised of manual laborers and recent immigrants, most often single men.[5] By the time Delaney arrived in the late 1970s, the area was home to a mix of Black, Asian, queer, and artist residents—migrants were drawn to the neighborhood's affordable rents and social inclusivity, but struggled to fend off redevelopment interests. In Tijuana's Nueva Esperanza ("New Hope") neighborhood, Ingrid Hernández records the details of improvised communities forged from found materials along the US-Mexico border. Nueva Esperanza's residents are primarily women working in local *maquiladoras*, assembly factories owned by foreign companies that rely on comparatively low-cost Mexican labor and duty-free trade agreements. Hernández photographed the area in the early 2000s, when the US economy's contraction and increased global competition from China and Central America triggered precipitous decline for these manufacturers.[6]

Though working in socioeconomically distinct neighborhoods and nations defined by vastly different immigration policies, Delaney and Hernández are both dedicated to documenting urban regions defined by the movement of people, goods, and capital; in short, these are the contact zones of migration. The contact zone, a concept developed by Mary Louise Pratt in her study of travel and exploration literature, offers a framework to study intercultural exchange—where "disparate cultures meet, clash, and grapple with each other"—in the context of asymmetrical power relations.[7] As Pratt notes, these colonial encounters are not simply ones of conquest and domination, but rather are defined by interaction, emphasizing how "subjects are constituted in and by their relations to each other."[8] The migrations Delaney and Hernández document are likewise sites of transcultural negotiation. Such migrations occur across and within national borders: they include not only the traditional pattern of singular, generational immigration, but also the flow of labor back and forth between Mexico and the United States, and the multinational populations that establish diverse urban communities. These movements forge new cultural intimacies, yet also reveal the repressive influences of transnational corporations, free-trade agreements, and political bodies that exercise power over local populations. Delaney and Hernández aim to make these complex connections more transparent, using the particulars of each urban contact zone to illuminate the personal costs of global migratory forces.

In addition to reflecting on the extensive struggle between the local and the global experienced by migratory populations, this essay examines the evolving role of the photographer as social documentarian. Delaney and Hernández work as image-makers "embedded" in their communities: they commit to years of interviews and research on-site in order to build long-term relationships with their subjects and a more nuanced understanding of the environments they seek to represent. Both women staunchly resist what Martha Rosler calls "slumming spectacle"; they are cognizant that images of poverty or disempowered subjects are all too easily exploited, even if made in the spirit of reform.[9] As photographers conscious of the practical and ideological risks of documenting migration, Delaney and Hernández draw attention to the practice of documentation itself. They continually assess how to make photographs that are not just aesthetically or emotionally compelling, but are also socially productive. Each stage of their photographic process—from research to exhibition—is developed in concert with their subjects and is attentive to the politics of representation.

The shared activism of Delaney and Hernández raises a perennial, but, in the case of migration, particularly urgent question of photographic ethics: How are photographers responsible to the community they represent? By this I mean to ask not simply whether image-makers can avoid touristic pity or fetishization of suffer-ing, but to ascertain how they can successfully speak for or with others, to engage what Ariella Azoula calls the "civil contract of photography."[10] In Azoula's formu-lation, photography is the expression of citizenship beyond nationalism, a partner-ship between photographer and subject that transcends ownership of the image and actualizes a sense of mutual responsibility and resistance to governmental power.[11] For migratory subjects, this question is especially pressing, as photographers seek to represent those who are not only at risk of abuse due to class, race, gender, sexual identity, or national origin, but also vulnerable to the fickle tides of international immigration politics, national trade policies, and local housing markets.

Though the conditions migrant communities face in San Francisco and Tijuana are by no means identical, both are directly tied to the larger forces of the United States' economic and immigration policies. Delaney and Hernández are acutely aware of the power these macro forces exert on their subjects, and are committed to making and displaying photographs in ways that shed light on such power relations. Both photographers seek out spaces in the transformational process of migration, and make images that function as visual contact zones; their works serve as active sites of community formation and spatial negotiation. Each photograph constitutes an exchange not simply between photographer and subject but also between local resident and city government, between individual and corporation, and between migrant and nation-state. Tijuana and San Francisco are key to understanding the defining debates of contemporary American politics: at the border and in the center of the tech industry, shortages of affordable housing and governments beholden to corporate interests have resulted in a civic calamity—residents in both cities tena-ciously cling to the neighborhoods they helped build, and are often evicted or live pre-cariously off-grid. Ultimately, the stakes are difficult to overstate: by laying bare the two cities' spatial relations and power dynamics, Delaney's and Hernández's projects illuminate the roots of the two cities' housing, homelessness, and migration crises.

South of Market: *Five Alarm Neighborhood*

When Janet Delaney moved to the South of Market neighborhood in 1978, she began photographing construction sites such as the Moscone Convention Center, alongside fellow photographer Catherine Wagner. These sites were not simply banal locations of architectural expansion, but rather flashpoints for the area's protracted urban renewal battles and long-standing debates over who belonged in the city. SoMa's redevelopment was conceived in the 1950s but dragged on for several decades, delayed by lawsuits brought by local residents—mostly retired, former union men living in inexpensive residential hotels known as single-room

occupancies (SROs).[12] By the time Delaney arrived, demolition of SROs and evictions of longtime residents were well underway; over four thousand residents and
seven hundred small businesses had been displaced. Backlash against the city's
incipient "Manhattanization" had gained support among the local populace, and
residents' legal resistance to redevelopment in the neighborhood's center brought
many building projects to a halt.[13] Looking out at SoMa's shifting landscape from
her vantage point at the Moscone construction site, Delaney wondered about the
fate of the area's homes and businesses. Ultimately, she resolved to move away from
the formalist architectural images she was then making to instead photograph those
who lived and worked in the neighborhood.[14] These images would come to define
the power struggle between SoMa's residents—migrants of all stripes—and a city
that hoped to remake its immigrant, low-income, and industrial neighborhoods
into centers of tourist appeal and corporate wealth.

This shift in subject matter also marked the beginning of Delaney's collaborations
with photographer Connie Hatch and filmmaker Laura Graham. Working under
the moniker D.Art (short for Documentary Art), Hatch and Delaney made images
of South of Market's redevelopment meant to challenge the norms of documentary
practice in distinct ways. Hatch's black-and-white photographs were superimposed
with text aimed at undercutting the pro-growth narrative promoted by local news
outlets and city officials, while Delaney created an unusual hybrid of color images
and oral-history documentation, a mixture she has described as "Stephen Shore
meets Stud Terkel."[15] To realize this project, Delaney also worked with Graham,
who was then her roommate on Langton Street, shooting Kodachrome slides and
recording interviews with their neighbors. This suite of works was exhibited under
the title *Form Follows Finance: A Survey of the South of Market*; the exhibition urged
San Franciscans to recognize the magnitude of its loss, as "truly human elements of
our community are replaced by fabricated surrogates imported to fill the void once
occupied by tradition and genuine cultural diversity."[16] The D.Art collective hoped
their novel forms of documentation and aesthetic activism would yield support for
practical solutions such as rent control, increased affordable housing, local control
of development processes, guaranteed city services, and anti-speculative legislation.[17] Their art would not only offer a reflection of a changing neighborhood but
also a point of contact for residents and city power brokers—an interface to actively
engage urgent issues of community livelihood.

Delaney's work on SoMa's socioeconomic transformation was made within a
community of artists devoted to the neighborhood. Delaney was first drawn to
make images of the area's redevelopment through her journeys to construction
sites with Wagner, and her choice of subject and location built on an earlier photographic series by Ira Nowinksi. Nowinski's *No Vacancy* photographs, published in
1979, document the men who staunchly resisted the city's efforts to clear SoMa's

SROs with quiet poignancy.[18] Yet, while Delaney aligned with other local artists in social purpose, her aesthetic and self-positioning ultimately produced a much different kind of project. Wagner's elegantly formulated architectural studies of the Moscone development reveal the social and physical strata of the building process—what the artist describes as "archeology in reverse"—while Nowinski's portraits of the neighborhood's elderly residents are intimately elegiac.[19] Taken together, Nowinski's and Wagner's work could imply SoMa exists only in the past, as a lost working-class haven for single men, or in the future, as burgeoning locale for corporate development.

By comparison, Delaney's images are insistently of the present. Her photographs stand apart not only for their vivid use of color but also for their sense of the natural diversity and social complexity of street life. Though she frequently shot interiors and portraits, the street was the primary space where the personal and political met head-on—the site of intersection between those migrating into and out of the neighborhood. Thus, in *Eviction, 158–160 Langton Street* (Fig. 1) we are privy to both cause and effect. Several construction workers remodel apartments while a freshly evicted father and his young son stand curbside with a shopping cart full of their belongings bundled into garbage bags. Although Mayor Diane Feinstein had just signed San Francisco's first rent-control law in June of 1979, the ordinance exempted owner-occupied buildings with four or less units.[20] Moreover, Proposition R, a stronger housing-reform measure that included the establishment of a publicly elected rent-control board with the power to regulate rents and finance new construction through revenue bonds, failed by a wide margin in the subsequent November election.[21] This clash over San Francisco's rental market echoes throughout Delaney's photograph, as father and son rely on makeshift materials to move their possessions, apparently forced from their apartment with little notice and few resources at hand. The young boy looks to his father for guidance, but the elder man does not return his gaze; with his back turned toward a quintessential symbol of the city's hippie liberalism—a faded Volkswagen van with a rainbow decal in the rear window—he can seemingly offer little reassurance of what lies ahead.

Other images, such as *Langton Park, Langton and Howard Streets* (Fig. 2), forego such obvious evidence of redevelopment to plum strange, yet equally revealing zones of migratory contact. Here, the playground initially appears to be an oasis for neighborhood families, but further inspection reveals two fully supine men—as Delaney recalls, a frequent occurrence due to a nearby drug and alcohol rehabilitation center's midday closure.[22] The broken record, empty liquor bottle, and partially completed palm tree mural seem aptly symbolic of the Golden State's failed promises. In reality, the painting is a sign of another community laying claim to this space: Filipino American residents recently banded together to create a Filipino American Friendship Mural and remake what locals referred to as "needle park."

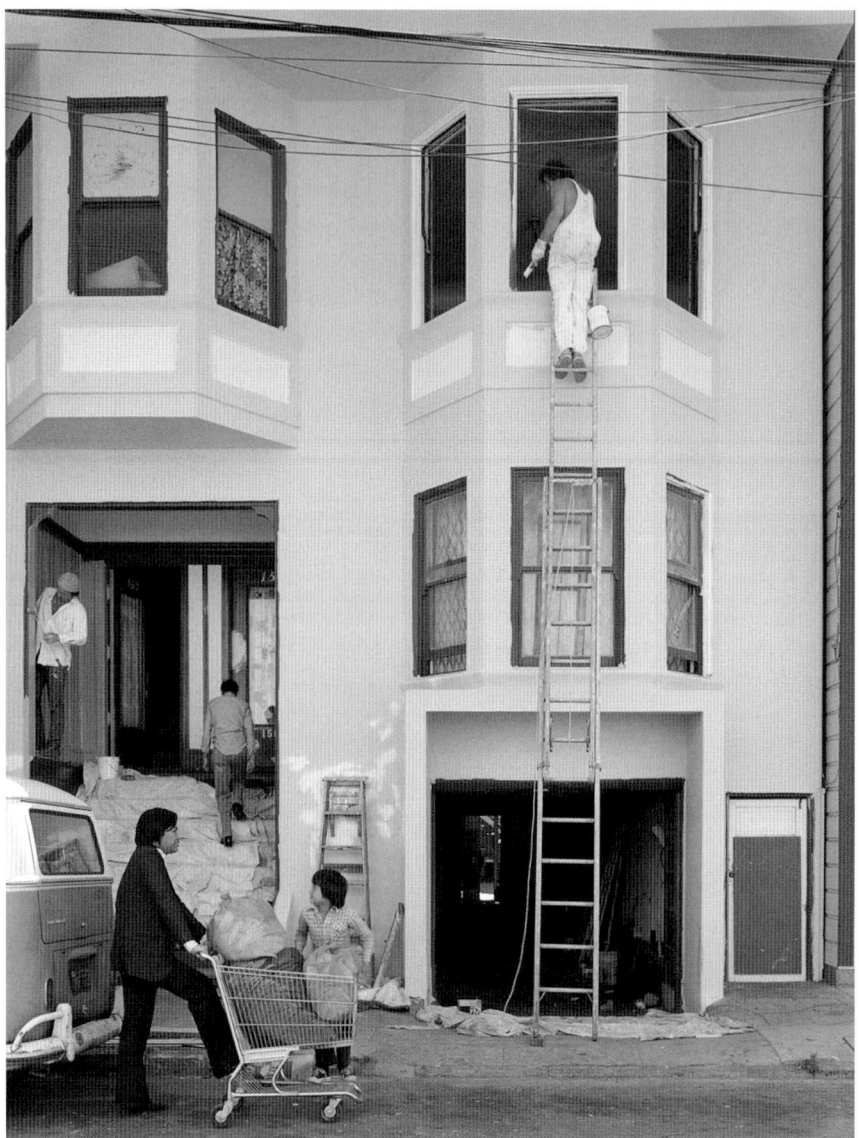

Figure 1: Janet Delaney, *Eviction, 158-160 Langton Street*, 1980. Chromogenic print. Dimensions variable (Plate 27, p. 352). Courtesy of the artist.

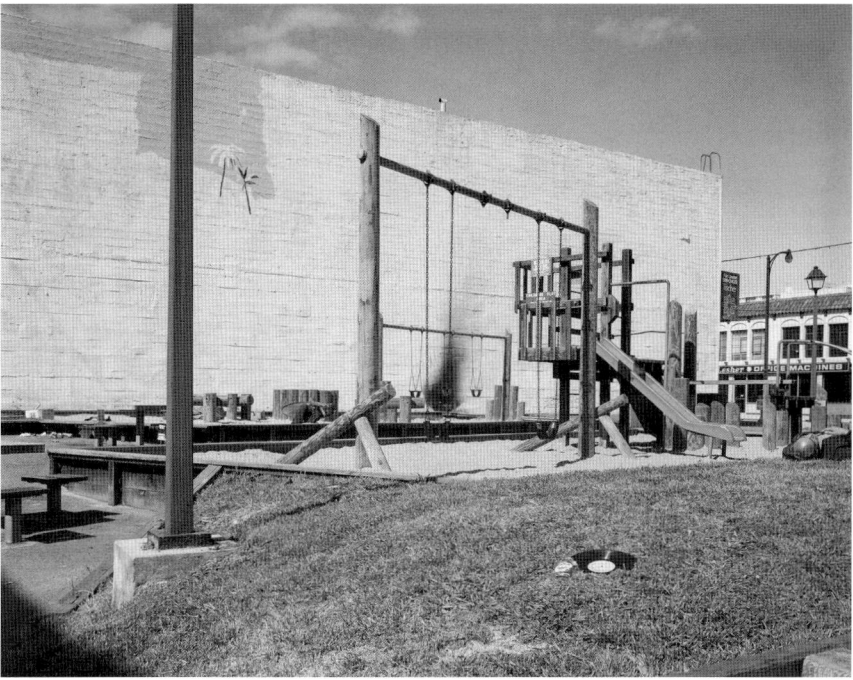

Figure 2: Janet Delaney, *Langton Park, Langton and Howard Streets*, 1981. Chromogenic print. Dimensions variable. Courtesy of the artist.

San Francisco's primary Filipino community, Manilatown, was originally located about a mile north of SoMa, adjacent to the city's famed Chinatown, but as urban renewal took hold in the 1950s, many in the neighborhood were forced to relocate. Filipino Americans—the city's second-largest population of Asian Americans in the 1970s and 1980s—played an integral role in the fight to maintain historic spaces, most notably in the dramatic International Hotel protests in August 1977.[23] The I-Hotel's residents were primarily first-generation *manongs*, or male migrant workers; the hotel was ultimately demolished and its elderly residents evicted after nine years of tenants' resistance, but the associated protests marked an integral moment of Asian American alliance.[24] Though not a registration of protest, *Langton Park* is also a record of the Filipino community's tenacious efforts to improve the urban fabric through the creation and preservation of shared spaces. This record of community formation is echoed in Delaney's many photographs of her Filipino neighbors, and their consistent presence in her interviews. As Lalett Fernandez observed, SoMa was a pivotal landing ground for Filipinos. But the burgeoning community often struggled to gain a permanent footing: while the United States offered greater job opportunities and some were fortunate enough to buy their own homes in San Francisco's suburbs, many others were priced out of SoMa and forced to relocate, as Delaney documented in *Eviction, 158–160 Langton Street*. Three years after immigrating, Fernandez concluded that "it's better to live in your own country, there you can do everything you want."[25]

Against the competing interests of the city's dispossessed and immigrant populations, a third demand on the space emerges in *Langton Park*: in the background, a bright blue "For Lease" sign hangs across the street from a light industrial storefront, subtly evoking the area's disputes over gentrification. Ultimately, the photograph avoids predictive sentiment; it is difficult to ascertain which party will emerge as the owner of this space. This instability is echoed in the center of the image, just behind the swing set, where a dark brown mark mars the white brick building adjacent to the park. The trace seems unrelated to the mural; its splash form, covering nearly illegible bits of graffiti, connotes a messy or violent incident, and calls further attention to the conspicuous absence of children. The locale is clearly a refuge for those in need, but Delaney's layered image, which contains competing aspects of sunny bliss and substantial deprivation, never settles clearly as a sign of hope or despair.

This push and pull between the city's dispossessed, its migrant communities, and real-estate capital continued for decades; the competing forces Delaney identified over thirty years ago persist today. Langton Park became a community garden in 1996, after a long battle with the city over conversion labor costs.[26] Bits of the completed mural, which depicts a Filipino festival, now peek through a densely foliated urban refuge, while across the street, a shop called Artitud peddles high-end custom furniture. Homeless San Franciscans still congregate outside the garden's locked gates, though now without an open space to call their own.

Though Delaney's images are undoubtedly powerful as visual documents, they were not created as stand-alone works of art. Working with Laura Graham, the photographer compiled many hours of interviews with a cross section of local residents, to be displayed as text alongside her photographs or as an audiovisual piece at local community meetings.[27] These interviews express anxiety over rising rents, evictions, and loss of diversity, but also evidence prejudice against new migrants and suggest potential complicities among both the artists and their subjects. For instance, interviewees Philip Kiely and Ted Haack proclaimed outrage over city governance's support of redevelopment; Kiely referred to former Mayor George Christopher's prioritization of business interests as "criminal," while Haack lamented the neighborhood's apparent transformation into another "tourist trap."[28] Notably, though, both men were landlords who stood to profit from gentrification. Haack and his partner Tom Whiting were, in fact, Delaney and Graham's landlords, and the artists' rent, though comparatively affordable in a citywide context, was double that of the former tenants.[29]

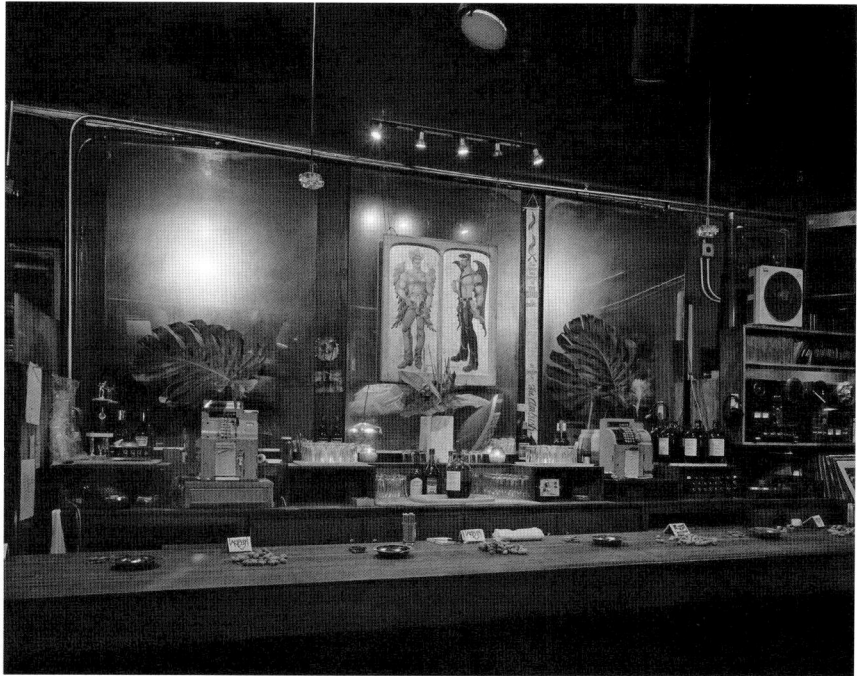

Figure 3: Janet Delaney, *Ambush Bar, 1051 Harrison Street*, 1981. Chromogenic print. Dimensions variable (Plate 28, p. 353). Courtesy of the artist.

Delaney was open about the ethical quandaries her status as a recently arrived artist could imply. These compromises are illustrated in her connections to a local gay bar, the Ambush, where her landlord Tom Whiting worked. Delaney photographed the Ambush (Fig. 3) and showed her photographs there; as an exhibition venue, the locale formed an essential component of her desire to engage the neighborhood's diverse populace. South of Market's gay leather bars had been an integral part of the area since the mid 1960s, and by the late 1970s the queer community formed a key constituency of the area's diverse migratory populations. The community was drawn to the area's relative solitude as a refuge for stigmatized lifestyles, though it did face significant discrimination, as with the city fire chief's unfounded accusation that "gay sex dens" were responsible for a large neighborhood fire in 1981, and the forced closure of many leather clubs during the AIDS crisis in the mid 1980s.[30]

In her recollections of the Ambush exhibition, Delaney notes that the bar's patrons thanked her for providing a community-focused break from its typically sexually explicit décor—much like the cheeky angel-devil diptych featured in the photographer's image of the bar.[31] But Delaney also recalls that, as she readied for the show at a new neighborhood frame shop owned by Jeffrey Krieger, she encountered two Filipino men in the same building being evicted. Krieger owned the entire property and was in the process of remodeling in order to increase rents by three hundred percent.[32] Delaney photographed this process of displacement, making images of Krieger, the recently cleared apartments that were formerly home to ninety Filipino tenants, and Krieger's chicly refurbished frame shop.

Unlike *Eviction, 158–160 Langton Street*, these images do not picture the evicted residents, but Delaney makes clear the cycle of forced removal and gentrification in the titles of her photographs: *Jeffrey Krieger, new landlord, 152 Russ Street*; *Front parlor of one of six apartments from which 90 Filipinos were recently evicted, Russ Street*; and *Jeffrey Krieger's frame shop, 152 Russ Street*. Indeed, the photographs were originally exhibited with a caption that plainly singled out the landlord's culpability: "With renovation the rents will increase from $125 to $450 a month. 'I told them they could move back in after I finished the work, but of course I didn't mean it,' [said] the new owner." This forthright censure produced some backlash: *ArtWeek* critic Donna Lee Philips accused Delaney of misquoting Krieger and, in an attempt to create a local villain, obscuring "the real question of just who *is* 'community' South of Market."[33] In fact, Delaney was precisely attuned to the question of who constituted the SoMa community; the question of who belongs recurs frequently in her published interviews. For instance, another SoMa landlord, Philip Kiely, openly mocked the streets renamed in honor of the Filipino community:

> There were never Filipinos over on Clara Street where I grew up. Why, if Clara Street was there for 100 years […] why is it now renamed Flip-on Flip-on or Lapa-Lapa or whatever name it is? What about our families who have lived here? We're third generation and now our street doesn't even exist anymore.[34]

Kiely was likely referring to Lapu Lapu Street, renamed for a Filipino hero who resisted Spanish colonization; for Kiely, recognition of the Filipino community could only be seen as an erasure of his Irish American family.[35] Though Delaney's rich color images, made with a large-format camera, visually honor the diversity of her neighborhood, the project does not omit the ugly bias immigrant residents experienced.[36] Her focus on migrants subject to eviction and her interviews with white landlords make obvious the nativist sentiments that denigrated and forcefully excluded recent arrivals.

Again, it is worth noting that Delaney herself was a patron of the frame shop featured in the series of images that document a mass eviction. In her photograph of the space, the new shop appears bright and freshly painted, scrubbed free of the recently cast out Filipino residents. These admissions of ethical compromise not only reveal the photographer's honest assessment of her own potential impact in priming the neighborhood for gentrification, but also indicate her awareness that documentation itself often affects the documented. Delaney consistently presented her series as a multidimensional record of migration and redevelopment in progress, feeding the images back into the community they represent and propelling a self-reflective conversation about the costs and concessions of urban renewal.

Delaney's desire to foment dialogue is again illustrated by her work devoted to the July 10, 1981 fire, the incident the fire chief falsely attributed to the neighborhood's gay leather clubs. Her photographs, which include images of the conflagration, its aftermath, and the media coverage, were shown only a month later at New Langton Arts—just down the street from the site of the fire. The exhibition was titled *Five Alarm Neighborhood*; Delaney and several other neighborhood artists displayed photographs, maps, text, and written and audio narratives to illuminate what they viewed as the "relationships between civic-sanctioned disinvestment, arson, and redevelopment."[37] Their assessment of success was likewise forthright: *Five Alarm Neighborhood* managed to engage even the neighborhood firefighters, but a later exhibition at SF Camerawork was deemed a "neutralizing" middle ground between "non-artist residents and photographic connoisseurs" and thus a less powerful community intervention.[38] Ultimately, the act of resistance was itself under constant revision; just as SoMa was constituted by a diverse populace, accumulated in layered waves of migration that redefined the neighborhood, artistic practice itself would need to respond to a continually evolving social and economic environment.

Nueva Esperanza: New Hope?

As with Delaney's photograph *Front parlor of one of six apartments from which 90 Filipinos were recently evicted, Russ Street*, wherein the enumerated bodies are strikingly absent, Ingrid Hernández's images do not picture the residents of the communities she documents. Hernández explains that she wishes to avoid the specificity implied in portraiture; without faces and bodies, her images are less foreclosed, and the viewer is encouraged construct what is not present.[39] Hernández's work in Nueva Esperanza, like Delaney's SoMa photographs, is defined by her sensitivity to the social layers of the built environment. The series is titled *Tijuana Comprimida* [Compressed Tijuana], a name that registers the spatial and economic pressures exerted on her subjects. Though by 2004 Nueva Esperanza was over two decades old and thus one of Tijuana's longest-standing illegal settlements, Hernández anticipated it would likely disappear. Just as Delaney foresaw SoMa's radical remaking into a corporate hub, Hernández's premonition proved right when the neighborhood was dismantled several years later. Hoping to stave off historical erasure and counter xenophobic stereotypes that painted Nueva Esperanza as a zone of

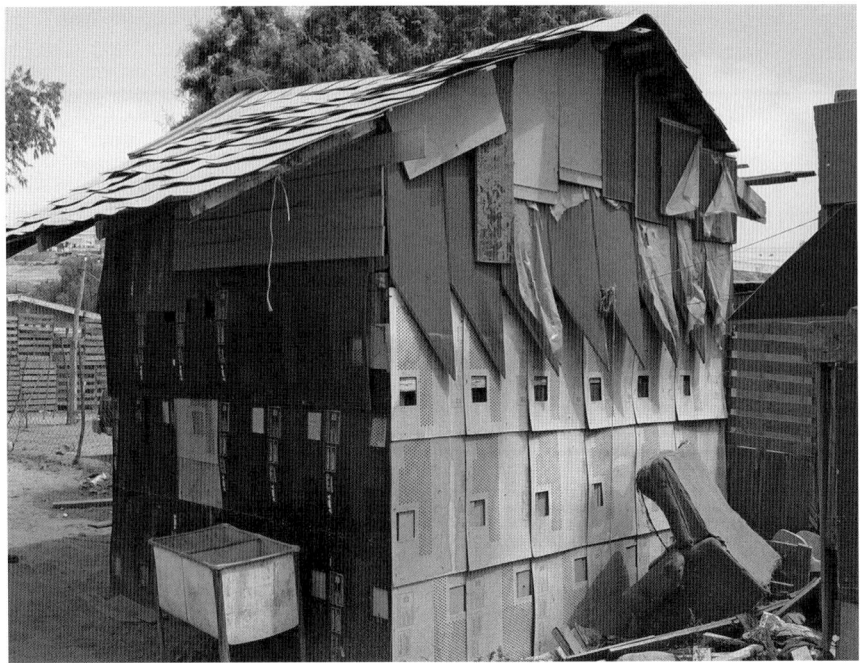

Figure 4: Ingrid Hernández, *Casa hecha con respaldos de televisión, Tijuana* [House made of television backings, Tijuana], 2004. From the series *Tijuana Comprimida* [Compressed Tijuana]. Digital print (Plate 29, p. 354). Courtesy of the artist.

invasion, the artist set out to make images that accessed the inhabitants' own perceptions of the spaces they designed.[40]

Nueva Esperanza was situated just below Ciudad Industrial in Mesa de Otay; waste from the maquiladoras located in this manufacturing zone was frequently used to construct homes here. The dwellings in Hernández's photographs were often fabricated with castoffs from the American economy, as depicted in *Casa hecha con respaldos de televisión, Tijuana* [House made of television backings, Tijuana] (Fig. 4), which features a house made of pressed cardboard from the backs of old television sets that were discarded by a local maquiladora.[41] Though the small home appears almost monumental in the photograph, nearly filling the entire frame, the images are not meant to tell an uplifting story of ingenious reuse. Hernández explains:

> I don't want to say that in Tijuana we like to live off of what the United States throws out, or that this is something positive. What I want to say is that it's a particular reality of a city that is on the border of the richest state in the United States.[42]

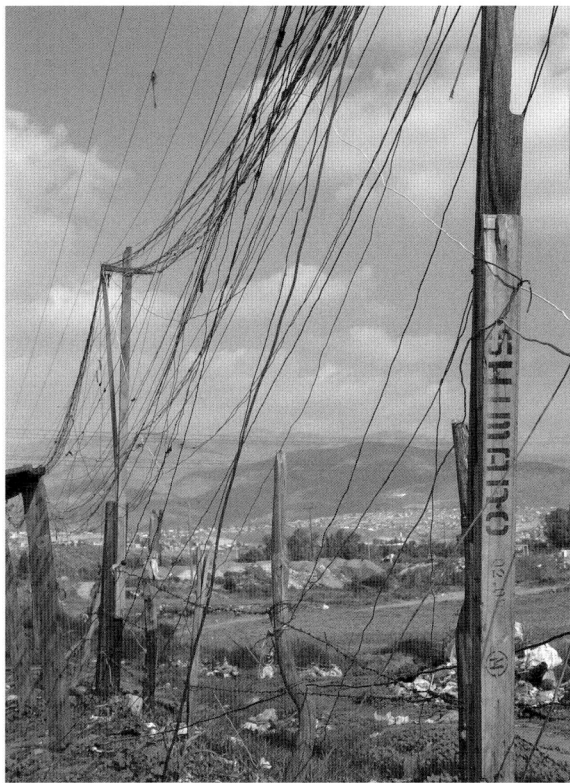

Figure 5: Ingrid Hernández, *Diablitos 2, Tijuana* [Illegal electricity connections, Tijuana], 2004. From the series *Tijuana Comprimida* [Compressed Tijuana]. Digital print. Courtesy of the artist.

Casa hecha con respaldos de televisión is likewise a product of life lived and worked across the border: the house was built by a man who had been employed in roofing construction in the United States and applied these skills to the fabrication of his own home.[43]

These structures also record Tijuana as a community of migrants from within Mexico; houses may be constructed with American castoffs or with skills garnered across the border, but they often reflect the architectural style of the occupants' homeland, echoing far-flung states like Veracruz or Chiapas.[44] As many flock from these regions to the border for work, the city struggles to provide adequate housing. When Hernández began to document Tijuana, over half of its population was born outside the state, and rapid growth created significant deficits in basic services such as electricity, water, and sewer lines.[45] Evidence of these shortages is found in improvised infrastructure such as the *diablitos*, or illegal electrical connections, that dot such neighborhoods. Sometimes, these connections hang precariously from Comisión Federal de Electricidad streetlight poles, or reflect extra-governmental agreements between neighbors, as in *Diablitos 2, Tijuana* (Fig. 5), in which a ranch owner granted use of a large transformer to the residents of Nueva Esperanza.[46] Hernández's photograph of these power lines initially appears chaotic, a hazardous tangle of wires draped diagonally over the landscape. But, upon closer examination, this impression gives way to a sense of inhabitants' persistent initiative: softly framing the nearby hillsides on the horizon are the neat markers of the official electrical grid—a distinct contrast to the dense cluster of wires in the foreground

assembled on irregular posts, one imprinted with the logo of the Japanese corporation Shimano.[47] The jumbled *diablitos* and surrounding settlements are self-built
networks of support, established organically and without the city's assistance; these
environments draw together people and materials from within and far beyond the
Mexican border, forging a contact zone of formerly disparate cultures and geographies. As the photographer writes, her images are meant to encourage us to look
beyond poverty and vulnerability, to see migration as a vehicle of transformation
and recognize these claims to the city space as assertions of agency.[48]

For Hernández, a native of Tijuana, the city is a place of both circulatory cur-
rents and barriers, flows and impediments that result in a heterogeneous space
of constant renewal.[49] This perspective is markedly different from that offered by
many US photographers making border images. These image-makers often concentrate on the physical act of crossing, journeys presented as singular, harrowing
events made by migrants seeking to escape Central America.[50] Hernández has
documented immigration to the United States, though within the well-established
domestic scenes of her series *Dentro, Nueva York* [Inside, New York]. Here she
focuses on migrants' striking ability to transport their way of living to an entirely
new locale; as the photographer remarks, "[…] when you look at the photos, you
would think that you are in a *pueblo*; you would never believe that you were looking
at New York."[51] The basement converted into living quarters featured in *Habitación
de la casa de Angélica Hernández* [Room in Angélica Hernández's Home] (Fig. 6) is
dense with ordered accumulations of personal belongings and utilitarian items—
markers of a life transposed and established anew. Hernández explains that these
accumulations are indications of the habit of stockpiling common among immigrants new to the United States' consumption-focused culture.[52] But the *Dentro*
images also contain distinct ties to Mexican culture, as with the carefully arranged
altars that recur throughout the twenty homes Hernández documented, regardless
of the occupants' economic status. These ties are pursued outside of the home as
well: Hernández found her subjects through adult education classes, but, contrary
to her expectations, the students were learning to read and write in Spanish, not
in English.[53] This decision to focus on the language of their native country attests
to the fact that migration is not an act of cultural or social severance, and that
maintaining connections to one's homeland is a conscious investment often equal
to the efforts of assimilation.

Hernández's photographs also resist the common strategy of removing or tax-
onomizing artifacts from these environments, as Tom Kiefer does in his images
of items confiscated from migrants apprehended by the US Customs and Border
Patrol in southern Arizona.[54] Collected en masse and photographed against plain
studio backdrops, Kiefer's photographs are poignant but ultimately elusive documents: they attest to punishingly stringent border policies, but only allude to the

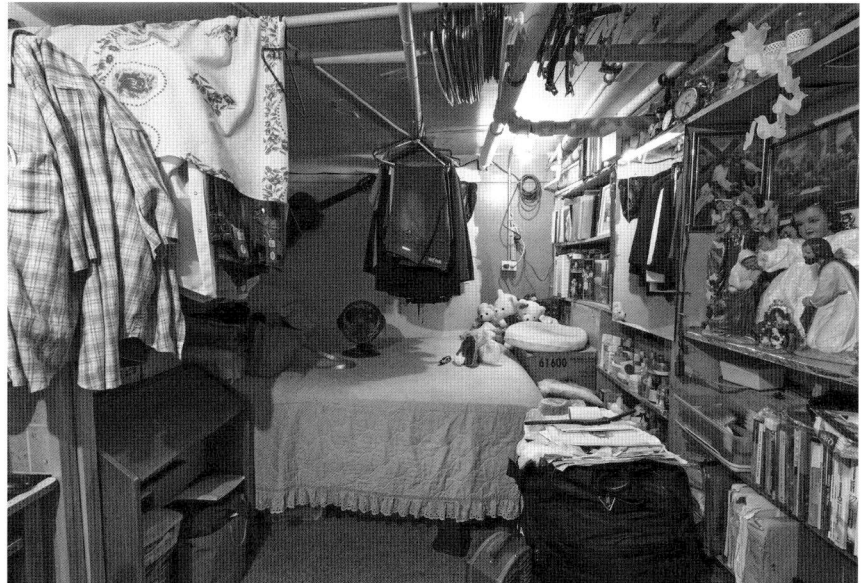

Figure 6: Ingrid Hernández, *Habitación de la casa de Angélica Hernández* [Room in Angélica Hernández's home], 2011. From the series *Dentro, Nueva York* [Inside, New York]. Digital print. Courtesy of the artist.

volume of unheard migrant stories, and cannot render the detailed fabric of these lives. Projects like Kiefer's are not without compassion or social value, but they often imply a discreteness to border relations—even in the act of crossing—that belies the complexity of economic and cultural dependencies. Hernández works in opposition to such abstracted taxonomies, instead seeking to elucidate what she calls the "syntax of objects."[55] Working with a digital camera and making images at eye level, the photographer aims to highlight arrangements and spatial relationships within each home, thus providing a more intimate and less stereotypical representation of impoverished communities.[56]

Perhaps, though, there is a limit to the messaging of Hernández's strict environmental focus. Unless one is well versed in the social and economic consequences of the North American Free Trade Agreement, it may be unclear that the primary inhabitants of Nueva Esperanza were the women employed by maquiladoras in the border zone. For, unlike Delaney's images of SoMa's working women, who made clear imprints on their environments—as with the casket company workers memorably surrounded by pinup posters of John Travolta and Tom Jones in *Bay Casket Company, 1020 Folsom Street*, or the still remarkable women-owned and -operated auto mechanic shop in *Labyris Auto Repair, "Complete Car Care By Women," 240 6th Street*—Hernández's key collaborators are not pictured in her photographs.[57] This is likely in part because maquila labor conditions are far more perilous. As Mara D. Giles demonstrates in her study of women's rights in Central America, such factories exploit lower class women, knowing that their precarious economic position and the legacy of national patriarchy that stigmatizes women's labor result in few options for employment.[58] Indeed, the women's workplaces might vanish altogether, a phenomenon known as *la maquila-golondrina*, or the swallow factory, named for the intentionally mobile industries that take flight in the face of demands for better wages, stricter environmental regulations, or increased taxation.[59]

When Hernández began working in Nueva Esperanza, she sought out the neighborhood's leader, a woman named Vicky, who organizes and advocates for her community of mostly fellow single mothers with the local government. Vicky—and similar women in other neighborhoods—served as Hernández's guide, introducing her to residents, relaying personal histories, and sharing the latest community gossip. The photographer describes this socializing process as one of intense intimacy, one that requires her to be "very sensitive to the space, to everything and everyone inside, to the women who are talking as I am taking the pictures."[60] In *Tijuana Comprimida*, the identities and appearances of these women remain private, but other artists, most notably Krzysztof Wodiczko, have used maquila women as the face of what Wodiczko refers to as the "catastrophe of progress and modern industry."[61] In 2001, Wodiczko staged one of his large-scale projections on the face of El Centro Cultural's domed theater, using prerecorded statements and live testimonies to make the public aware of the women's experiences of sexual harassment, domestic violence, family disintegration, and police brutality. Though his subjects participated in a yearlong development process and he assisted by psychologists in Tijuana during the interviews, a number of critics have wondered whether the women faced reprisals, or whether a consistent focus on the victims of abuse elides the culpability of their abusers.[62] These questions are particularly relevant in the wake of the recent news that the United States will no longer accept asylum requests from those fleeing domestic abuse or gang violence.[63]

Hernández resists this kind of representation, purposefully moving from people to objects and spaces in order to counterbalance what she calls the camera's "power of appearance."[64] But ultimately the women of Nueva Esperanza do figure in other, essential ways. The *Tijuana Comprimida* series was first exhibited in the community it depicts. In the documentation of the exhibition, the neighborhood gazes back on itself, taking pictures of Hernández's pictures, which now adorn the cardboard walls of a local home. These documents may initially appear to be perfunctory records of artistic presentation. In fact, like Delaney's integration of interviews with her neighbors and her insistence on showing in local spaces, the images are essential proof of community activation and collaboration. Hernández's exhibition documents reveal the vital moment when her subjects participate in the citizenry of photography. As Azoulay explains, the citizen of photography, whether photographer, subject, or spectator, can demand a role in the image: "She is someone who speaks on behalf of the photograph itself."[65] Unlike the nation-state, which defines citizenship in exclusionary, territorial terms, photography offers the possibility of partnership and restitution of basic rights—to see and be seen, to move freely, and to share information. Hernández and the residents of Nueva Esperanza act as fellow citizens participating in a dynamic exchange; Hernández records the physical and social structures built by the community, and, in turn, these images are physically reintegrated into the neighborhood's homes and socially absorbed as part of the women's collective stories.

This partnership is likewise echoed in the photographer's community-focused process and ultimate formulation of her *Dentro, Nueva York* images. Hernández initially presented her photographs to her subjects in discussion groups, asking them to speak about what is Mexican in the images. These conversations served as a springboard for wide-ranging reflections on the experience of being a migrant in New York. Finally, Hernández asked each of her subjects to write a letter dedicated to Mexico, missives that were exhibited and published alongside the photographs. These personal testimonies are often hopeful, but also attest to the immense pressures of separation from one's family and native culture. In art-world contexts, the presence of her subjects' handwriting next to images of the domestic spaces they have created forms a striking testimony of self-determination—the quintessence of authoring one's own story.[66]

Hernández's tripartite work process—time in the community, work in the studio, and a period of public display—always includes some form of exhibition in the community space at the end of the first stage.[67] This phase of dialogue directs the more traditional studio and museum or gallery exhibition phases that follow, ensuring that the subjects remain participants in the image, even if they do not physically appear. Delaney likewise joins her work with community activism. As a part of the South of Market Alliance, a consortium of local groups that petitioned to protect local residents' housing and labor rights, her photographs were shown at community centers and media events that included question and answer sessions with local politicians.[68] Attempting to bridge the gap between community advocate and art-world advancement remains a difficult endeavor, one that both Hernández and Delaney address head-on. Neither photographer attempts to evade evaluation of her work in aesthetic terms, instead insisting that the photographs are seen in contexts of both art and activism. Such diverse (and often divergent) presentations are intended to simultaneously empower the migrants they document, and to reach those who already hold considerable power as enfranchised, economically privileged viewers. As Delaney's collaborator Connie Hatch wrote in 1983, such activity assumes no easy conclusions, but nevertheless persists in pursuit of change:

We believe oppositional documentary practice can and does offer serious investigation, revealing the before unseen, and breaking the silence with visual and
verbal resistance. A radical documentary practice demands discipline, rigor
and resilience—not posed against the art world [but] projected toward an active
moment for social change.[69]

Conclusion

In the months leading up to the 2016 US presidential election, Hernández collab-
orated with Peter Wisse, a Dutch artist who had never seen the Mexico-US border.
Their project, titled *Nada Que Déclarar* [Nothing to Declare], solicited photographs
through Facebook and local newscasts from people who cross the border at the San
Ysidro Port of Entry daily. Select images were then printed as Risograph posters,
with advertising slogans also derived from the border zone, and distributed for
free at San Ysidro. Hernández describes the project as attempting to capture "the
absurdity that is *el bordo*."[70] The collaboration is more legibly activist than her
earlier work in Nueva Esparanza; for example, an image of three heavily armed
border patrol agents is imprinted with the insistent question directed at those who
cross: "*¿A donde va?*" ("Where are you going?"). Delaney has likewise moved toward
work that could be viewed as more strident. Returning to photograph SoMa in
the past few years, Delaney's new images make clear that the gentrification many
feared in the early 1980s has now fully arrived: the neighborhood is home to legions
of tech companies, the median rent price in 2018 was $3,500/month, and the city
has recently begun clearing homeless encampments.[71]

Other developments seem more hopeful. In 2008, Nueva Esperanza's residents
negotiated with the government to move to another site and become a legally constituted colony, and in the 2018 midterm elections, Californians passed two statewide propositions aimed at creating more affordable housing, providing housing
loans for veterans, and creating measures to prevent homelessness.[72] But sizable
hurdles remain. To obtain legal status, the entire settlement of Nueva Esperanza
was dismantled; houses in the new location are similarly improvised, and residents
are now required to pay rent on the land they occupy.[73] Likewise, Californian voters
approved some efforts to counteract skyrocketing housing markets, but rejected a
measure allowing local governments to adopt rent control on any kind of rental
housing.[74]

As urban migratory circumstances have shifted, so have the photographers
documenting these phenomena. Delaney, who was herself priced out of SoMa,
moved to the Mission District in the mid 1980s, and currently lives across the
bay in Berkeley. The photographer is an "outsider" to San Francisco now, just as

Hernández distanced herself by choosing a European collaborator with no knowledge of the border to create *Nada Que Déclarar*.[75] Proximity, though, is an insufficient measure for projects that, by their very definition, are about fluid, mutable spaces and persons whose lives are in flux. Both photographers are undeniably enmeshed in their subject matter, and yet neither are native to the neighborhoods they document. The power of their work rests not simply in translating specific hardships to the universal realm of empathy or compassion, but in demonstrating how photography may provide chronically devalued subjects the chance to be recognized outside the traditional power structures of national boundaries and formal economies. More than simple evidence of inequities and injustices, Delaney's and Hernández's photographs offer access points to understand the communities that form contact zones and engage their subjects in collaborative forms of representation. These projects work to remind us that migratory spaces are defined by competing interests and layered identities, and thus serve as visual incitements to our sense of collective accountability.

Notes

1. On "postborder" space, see Michael Dear and Héctor Manual Lecero, "Postborder Cities, Postborder World: The Rise of Bajalta California," *Environmental Planning D: Society and Space* 23 (2005), 317–321.

2. United Nations Refugee Agency, *Global Trends in Forced Displacement in 2018*, June 20, 2019, https://www.unhcr.org/5d08d7ee7.pdf.

3. Fiamma Montezemolo, "Tijuana: Hybridity and Beyond, A Conversation with Néstor García Canclini," *Third Text* 23, no. 6 (November 2009), 740.

4. South of Market's name owes to an old nickname: South of the Slot. The "Slot" was the iron cable-car track that ran through the center of Market Street, marking a pivotal class division. As Jack London wrote in his 1909 short story set in the neighborhood, "North of the Slot were theaters, hotels, and shopping district, the banks and the staid, respectable business houses. South of the slot were the factories, slums, laundries, machine-shops, boiler works, and the abodes of the working class." Jack London, "South of the Slot," in *Jack London: Novels and Stories* (New York: Library of America, 1982), 817. Notably the SoMa, or SOMA, nickname is relatively recent; in the 1970s and 1980s, media often referred to the area as "SoMar." The SoMa moniker seems to have arrived with corporate redevelopment, perhaps to echo the fashionable gentrification of SoHo (South of Houston) in New York.

5. For a detailed history of South of Market's development, see Anne B. Bloomfield, "A History of the California Historical Society's New Mission Street Neighborhood," *California History* 74, no. 4 (Winter 1995–1996), 372–393.

6. United States Government Accountability Office, "Mexico's Mauqiladora Decline Affects U.S.-Mexico Border Communities and Trade; Recovery Depends in Part on Mexico's Actions," July 2003, https://www.gao.gov/products/GAO-03-891.

7. Mary Louise Pratt, "Art of the Contact Zone," *Profession* (1991), 34.

8. Pratt, *Imperial Eyes: Travel Writing and Transculturation* (London: Routledge, 1992), 7.

9. Martha Rosler, "In, Around, and Afterthoughts (On Documentary Photography)," in *Martha Rosler: Decoys and Disruptions, Selected Writings, 1975–2001* (Cambridge: MIT Press, 2004), 175.

10. On the complex issue of speaking for others, see Linda Alcoff, "The Problem of Speaking for Others," *Cultural Critique* 20 (Winter 1991–1992), 5–32.

11. Ariella Azoulay, *The Civil Contract of Photography* (New York: Zone Books, 2008), 104–105.

12. Chester Hartman, *City For Sale: The Transformation of San Francisco* (Berkeley: University of California Press, 1984), 56–75.

13. Erin O'Toole, "South of Market: Zone of Transition," in Janet Delaney, Julian Cox, and Erin O'Toole, *Janet Delaney: South of Market* (San Francisco: Fine Arts Museums of San Francisco, 2015), xii.

14. Janet Delaney, "Interview: Janet Delaney on South of Market," *photo-eye*, May 9, 2014, http://blog.photoeye.com/2014/05/interview-janet-delaney-on-south-of.html.

15. Delaney, "Interview:"

16. D.Art/Janet Delaney and Connie Hatch, *Form Follows Finance: A Survey of the South of Market*, Exhibition at SF Camerawork, 1981, Janet Delaney Archive, Bancroft Library Special Collections, University of California, Berkeley.

17. Delaney and Hatch, *Form Follows*

18. Ira Nowinsky, *No Vacancy: Urban Renewal and the Elderly* (San Francisco: C. Bean Associates, 1979).

19. Catherine Wagner, "Moscone Center," http://www.catherinewagner.org/moscone-center/.

20. Rebecca Diamond, Tim McQuade, and Franklin Qian, "The Effects of Rent Control Expansion on Tenants, Landlords, and Inequality: Evidence from San Francisco," August 24, 2018, https://web.stanford.edu/~diamondr/DMQ.pdf.

21. San Francisco Voter Information Pamphlet, Municipal Election, November 6, 1979, https://sfpl.org/pdf/main/gic/elections/November6_1979.pdf; and San Francisco Department of Elections, Historical Ballot Propositions Data, http://sfelections.sfgov.org/ftp/uploadedfiles/elections/ElectionsArchives/opendata/HistoricalBallotPropositions.txt.

22. Delaney, "Witness to the Destruction of a Working Class Neighborhood," in *Janet Delaney: South of Market*, i.

23. Filipino Americans made up 3.5% of the city's population in 1970 and 5.7% in 1980. Chinese Americans were the most populous Asian American group (8.2% in 1970 and

12.1% in 1980). See Bay Area Census, San Francisco City and County Decennial Census Data, http://www.bayareacensus.ca.gov/counties/SanFranciscoCounty70.htm.

24. Hartman, 337–339.

25. Lalett Fernandez, quoted in *Janet Delaney: South of Market*, vi.

26. Maitland Zane, "Needle Park Renaissance: Once-blighted playground transformed into SoMa Gardens," *San Francisco Chronicle,* April 1, 1996 https://www.sfgate.com/news/article/Needle-Park-Renaissance-Once-blighted-2988268.php.

27. Delaney, *photo-eye*.

28. Philip Kiely and Ted Haack quoted in *Janet Delaney: South of Market*, v, viii.

29. Delaney, interviewed by Nick Kaye, Berkeley, April 30, 2015 http://siteworks.exeter.ac.uk/interviews/janetdelaney.

30. Delaney, *Janet Delaney: South of Market*, ii; and Gayle S. Rubin "The Miracle Mile, South of Market and Gay Male Leather 1962–1997," in *Reclaiming San Francisco: History, Politics, Culture* (San Francisco: City Lights Books, 1998), 255–258, 262.

31. The painting is likely by Chuck Arnett, who designed the Ambush's logo and created other iconic artworks at SoMa leather bars. On the visual culture of these institutions, see Jack Fritscher, *Gay San Francisco: Eyewitness Drummer, Vol. 1* (San Francisco: Palm Drive Publishing, 2007), 355–357.

32. Delaney, *South of Market*, ii.

33. Donna Lee Phillips, "Biased Documents," *ArtWeek,* June 19, 1982, 13, 16. Philips does not provide any evidence for her accusation of libel; no further statements from the landlord (or Delaney) are included in her review. Philips also writes that the former owner was a Filipino slumlord renting out units with inadequate plumbing and safety features but provides no supporting documentation or references to reporting on these infractions. While Philips's contention that these conditions were both legally and ethically intolerable is undoubtedly right, her case is undercut by a lack of evidence and the misleading implication that gentrification is the only solution to such housing crises.

34. Philip Kiely quoted in Delaney, *South of Market*, v.

35. Kiely quoted in Delaney, *South of Market*, v. Lapu Lapu is one of several streets named for significant figures in Filipino history. See Center of Asian American Media, "Filipino Americans Make a New Name for Their San Francisco Neighborhood," October 5, 2016 https://caamedia.org/blog/2016/10/05/filipino-americans-make-a-new-name-for-their-san-francisco-neighborhood/. Unsurprisingly, casually derogatory references to these street names persist. See, for instance, SFist, "Double Your Lapu," August 12, 2008, https://sfist.com/2008/08/12/double_your_lapu/.

36. Delany, *South of Market*, i.

37. Connie Hatch, "Notes from a Photographic Survey: Form Follows Finance," *Obscura* 2, no. 5 (1983), 31.

38. Hatch, "Notes," 32–33.

39. Ingrid Hernández, "Bioethnography of an Artist," in Josh Kun and Fiamma Montezemolo (eds.), *Tijuana Dreaming: Life and Art at the Global Border* (Durham: Duke University Press, 2012), 250.

40. Hernández, "Práctica artística y contexto: representación, metodología y narrativa en mi producción," in *Migración y Creación: Antropologías de Frontera* (Mexico City: UNESCO, 2018), 242.

41. Hernández, "Práctica," 239.

42. Hernández quoted in Caitlin Donohue, "El Bordo: Conversations with Tijuana's Border Artists in the Trump Era," *Open Space*, February 23, 2017, https://openspace.sfmoma.org/2017/02/el-bordo-conversations-with-tijuanas-border-artists-in-the-trump-era/.

43. Hernández, "Práctica artística y context," 239.

44. Michelle Marie Robles Wallace, "Ingrid Hernández Explores the Meaning of Home in the Outskirts of Tijuana," *Women Arts*, February 17, 2017, https://www.womenarts.org/2017/02/09/ingrid-hernandez-explores-the-meaning-of-home-in-the-outskirts-of-tijuana/.

45. Andrew Selee, *Decentralization, Democratization and Informal Power in Mexico* (University Park: Penn State University Press, 2011), 103–104.

46. Hernández, "Bioethnography of an Artist," 251–252.

47. Shimano produces bicycle components, fishing tackle, and rowing equipment. Shimano, Company Profile, https://www.shimano.com/en/company/profile.html.

48. Hernández, "Práctica artística y context," 237.

49. Hernández, "Bioethnography of an Artist," 246.

50. See, for instance, the photographs made by Richard Misrach for his recent project *Border Cantos*. Richard Misrach and Guillermo Galindo, *Border Cantos* (New York: Aperture, 2016).

51. Wallace, "Ingrid Hernández".

52. El Colegio de la Frontera Norte, "Detrás de la cámara con Ingrid Hernández," March 3, 2015 https://www.youtube.com/watch?v=Mb8txTWSOK8.

53. Hernández, "Práctica artística y context," 243.

54. See Tom Kiefer, *El Sueño Americano (2007–)*, http://www.tomkiefer.com/.

55. Hernández, "Bioethnography of an Artist," 245.

56. Hernández, "Bioethnography of an Artist," 245.

57. Labyris Auto Repair was founded in 1978 by Nancy Rupprecht and was run by queer women. Rupprecht closed Labyris and moved to the East Bay to open Grandma's Garage in 1988. Grandma's Garage, http://grandmasgarage.biz/grandmasgarage/About.html.

58. Mara D. Giles, "An Understanding of the Relationship between *Maquiladoras* and Women's Rights in Central America," *Nebraska Anthropologist* 18 (2006), 5–19.

59. Hernández has made photographs of *maquila-golondrinas*. On the function and representation of these spaces, see Amy Sara Carroll, *Remex: Toward an Art History of the NAFTA Era* (Austin: University of Texas, 2017), 312–313.

60. Hernández, "Bioethnography of an Artist," 249.

61. Patricia C. Phillips, "Creating Democracy: A Dialogue with Krzysztof Wodiczko," *Art Journal* 62, no. 4 (Winter 2003), 44–45.

62. Montezemolo, "Tijuana: Hybridity and Beyond," 749.

63. Katie Brenner and Caitlin Dickerson, "Sessions Says Domestic and Gang Violence Are Not Grounds for Asylum," *New York Times,* June 11, 2018, https://www.nytimes.com/2018/06/11/us/politics/sessions-domestic-violence-asylum.html.

64. Hernández, "Bioethnography of an Artist," 250.

65. Azoulay, *The Civil Contract of Photography*, 117.

66. For examples of the letters included in the project see Hernández, "Práctica artística y context," 247.

67. Hernández, "Práctica," 238.

68. Hatch, "Notes from a Photographic Survey," 31–32.

69. Hatch, "Notes, 33.

70. Hernández quoted in Donohue, "El Bordo".

71. US Department of Housing and Urban Development, "Comprehensive Housing Market Analysis: San Francisco-Redwood City-South San Francisco, California," November 1, 2018, https://www.huduser.gov/portal/publications/pdf/SanFranciscoCA-CHMA-19.pdf; and Kevin Fagan, "SF Mayor vows that clearing homeless tents from the Mission just a start," *San Francisco Chronicle,* April 25, 2018, https://www.sfchronicle.com/bayarea/article/SF-mayor-vows-that-clearing-homeless-tents-from-12864999.php.

72. California Secretary of State, General Election – Statement of Vote, November 6, 2018, https://www.sos.ca.gov/elections/prior-elections/statewide-election-results/general-election-november-6-2018/statement-vote/.

73. Hernández, "Práctica artística y context," 242.

74. California Secretary of State, General Election – Statement of Vote, November 6, 2018. Another statewide rent control initiative has qualified for the November 2020 ballot. Hannah Wiley, "Rent control will be on the California ballot again. Here's how it's different this time," *The Sacramento Bee,* February 20, 2020, https://www.sacbee.com/news/politics-government/capitol-alert/article239950073.html.

75. D.F. Young, "Photographer Janet Delaney returns to SoMa for a fresh look," *hoodline*, March 25, 2016, https://hoodline.com/2016/03/photographer-janet-delaney-returns-to-soma.

Witnessing the Trauma of Undocumented Migrants in Mexico

Sarah Bassnett

Between the years 2000 and 2013, approximately 11.7 million people were apprehended trying to cross the southern border of the United States. Although many were Mexicans, millions more were Central Americans, primarily from Honduras, Guatemala, and El Salvador. Migrants from these countries leave their homes because of abject poverty, or because of violence, extortion, and the threat of forced recruitment into international gangs.[1] On the journey north, they face a variety of dangers, particularly once they reach Mexico. Within Central America, the four-visa system allows Hondurans, Salvadorans, Guatemalans, and Nicaraguans to travel between these countries without visas or passports.[2] However, as undocumented migrants in transit through Mexico, they are targeted by criminal networks who are involved in kidnapping and human trafficking. The gang MS-13, for instance, is both a reason people flee the Northern Triangle and an ongoing source of danger for migrants. Rather than protecting the vulnerable, Mexican officials frequently add to the risks by beating, robbing, and apprehending migrants, as well as by colluding with gangs.[3] Human rights organizations and migrant support agencies have collected testimonies documenting these abuses. However, government officials in the United States and Mexico refuse to acknowledge the connection between their immigration policies and practices and the violence perpetrated against migrants.

Instead of raising public awareness and revealing how public policy affects experiences of undocumented migration, the mainstream media currently relies on a series of tropes to represent migration. In this chapter, I first look at how these outdated motifs preserve the status quo and then consider how Mexican photojournalist Moysés Zuñiga Santiago (b. 1979) engages with photography as a contact zone to expose human rights violations. Drawing on Mary Louise Pratt's concept of the contact zone as a realm where subjects from different cultures are present together and impact one another, and Steven Hoelscher's adaptation of the contact zone as it relates to photographic encounters, I consider the interaction between photographer and subject as a contact zone where power relations and agency are negotiated.[4] At the same time, I also take up one of the central preoccupations of photography studies, which has been to examine portrayals of human suffering and to consider the ethics of witnessing. In the late twentieth century, it was common for critics to worry that images of trauma would cause compassion fatigue.[5] Over the last twenty years, however, scholars have shifted away from ideology critique to examine the productive possibilities of photography, including how images of suffering can produce new identities and forms of subjectivity, how photographic subjects can assert agency, and how witnessing can variously influence and foreclose political action.[6] Looking at Zuñiga's work in the context of recent literature on the political potential of photography, I show how his practice engages photography as a site of encounter, mediating experiences of loss and trauma by telling the stories of undocumented migrants. His approach sensitively combines photographs and narrative to bear witness to the traumatic consequences of government policy.[7] These overlooked stories show that migration to the United States is often a complex process involving dangerous journeys through multiple geographical and political territories and does not simply entail moving from one nation-state to another. Zuñiga's photography conveys stories that at once reveal the human cost of indifference toward migrants and the resilience of the people who undertake the difficult process of migration.

Tropes of migration

Visual tropes are used in photography to suggest broad themes that are easily understood by most viewers, but they are also loaded with preconceptions.[8] When mainstream news agencies report on Central American migration, they commonly use a series of tropes to turn complex issues into predictable narratives. Motifs from twentieth-century crises are common. Imagine depression-era breadlines and crowds of displaced people on the move in postwar Europe. Many of these images draw on stereotypes or borrow from portrayals of the displaced in Christian iconography.[9] Editors often select formulaic photographs from subscription news agencies to illustrate stories, even when they have a wide range of images to choose from. Numerous news stories on Central American migrants are illustrated with images depicting groups of people walking, lining up, or resting.[10] A photograph of an orderly lineup may serve to reassure readers that officials have a situation under control. These kinds of images may report on events but gloss over the complex nature of the crisis.

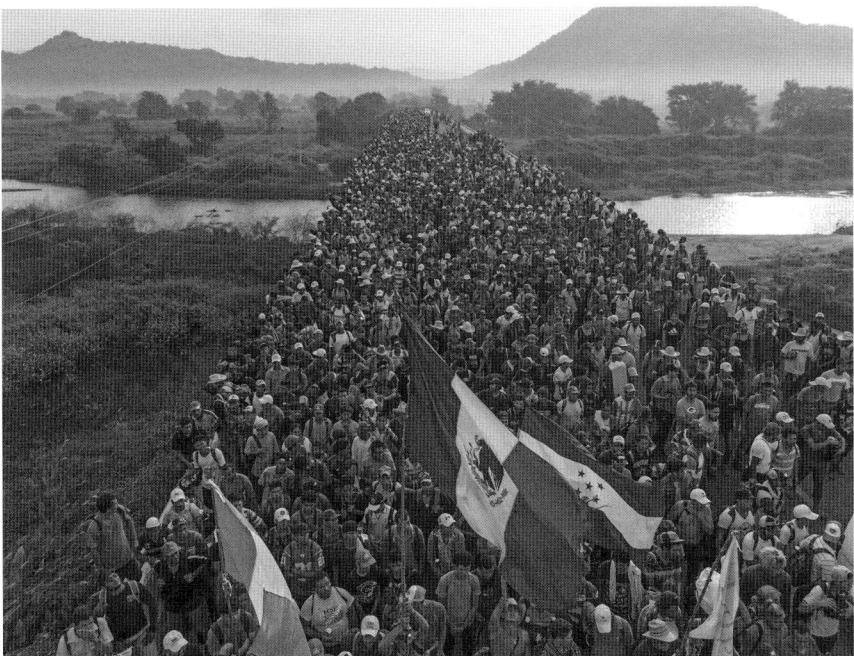

Figure 1: Guillermo Arias/AFP via Getty Images, Aerial view of Honduran migrants heading in a caravan to the US, as they leave Arriaga on their way to San Pedro Tapanatepec, in southern Mexico on October 27, 2018. Guillermo Arias/AFP via Getty Images.

Also popular are crowd motifs. On the one hand, the trope of the disorderly crowd is a common means of representing migrants as a threat, and these images often rely on stereotypes to associate nonwhite men with violence and criminality.[11] Such images can convey what media theorists Lilie Chouliaraki and Tijana Stolic refer to as "biopolitical humanity," or the idea of humans as bodies that need to be managed. The effect is to disconnect migrants from the problems that have caused their displacement and to conceal the political failures that have led to the crisis.[12] Instead of picturing the dangers migrants face on their journey, they are portrayed as a menace. On the other hand, the crowd of people in transit is typically used to convey the scale of migration from Central America to the United States. Sometimes these stories are sympathetic toward migrants, but often the images are used to express or agitate already existing anxiety about waves of foreigners. In a striking photograph by Guillermo Arias (b. 1976), viewers look down on a bridge in southern Mexico packed with bodies stretching as far as the eye can see (Fig. 1). The people are represented as an anonymous mass, making it hard for viewers to identify with their plight. The figures spill off the edge of the frame, suggesting an unceasing flow, an allusion to the exodus. While the image references the biblical

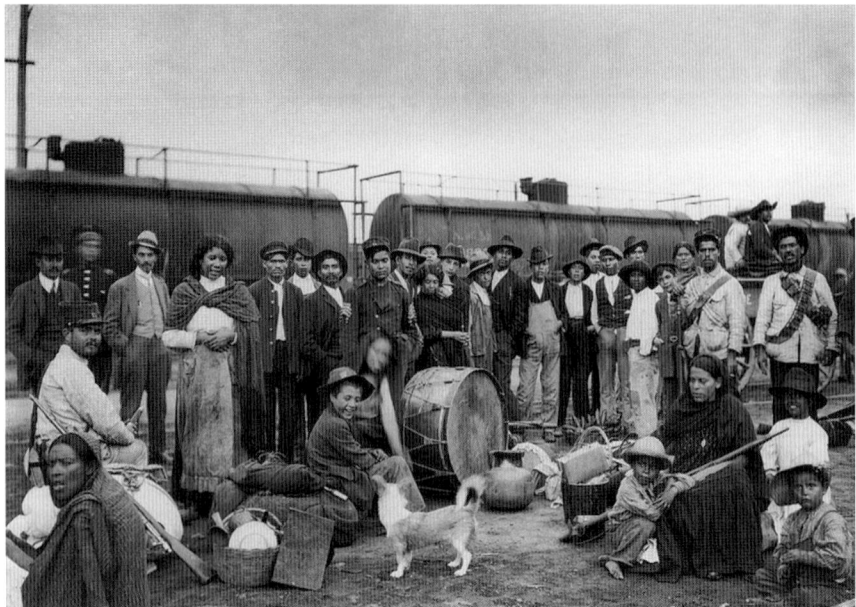

Figure 2: Agustín Víctor Casasola, *Federal Army music band during a break in the courtyards of Buenavista*, Mexico City, ca. 1913–1915. SINAFO, Fototeca Nacional del Instituto Nacional de Antropología e Historia.

story of a people escaping from persecution for a new life, it could be used to sug-gest a foreign invasion. Whether you perceive the "migrant caravan" as deserving of aid or as a threat to national security, this trope elicits polarized viewpoints. Although the same image may be used to support different ideologies (normally in different publications and with modified captions), a visual trope invariably simpli-fies a story by making it familiar. When photographs are used to reinscribe tropes, when they are used to uphold, rather than to challenge, assumptions about an issue, the media is complicit in maintaining the status quo.[13] They situate viewers as mere spectators to formulaic narratives with foregone conclusions.

Tropes may also tap into specific political or national narratives. The freight train, known as *la bestia*, or the beast, became a symbol of the dangers of migration in Mexico in the late twentieth century. However, images of trains have a longer history that stretches back to the Mexican Revolution. A notable photograph by Agustín Víctor Casasola (1874–1938), known as "chronicler of the Mexican Revolution," depicts a deliberately arranged band of musicians and others stand-ing in front of a train (Fig. 2). According to Leonard Folgarait, this image uses the train as a metaphor to suggest the revolution itself as a vehicle of movement and social transformation.[14] He describes the cross section of displaced people coming together in the image to signify a new social order bound together by a shared national culture. But, whereas this historic image of a train represents the unification of Mexico, contemporary depictions of groups of people on or near trains are more likely to be interpreted as a threat to the nation.

Another set of tropes are at play in depictions of the dead. While news reports often describe the dangers migrants face on their journey, violence is rarely pictured, and for most readers, the effects of immigration policies remain distant and abstract. When atrocities are committed, drug cartels are blamed, and images and captions emphasize the brutality of the killers. For instance, news reports of the 2010 massacre of seventy-two Central American migrants by the Zetas cartel in northeastern Mexico were illustrated with images of bodies, although, following convention, mainstream agencies selected photographs that obscured, rather than graphically depicted the corpses of migrants.[15] As media theorist Jessica Fishman explains, editors are inclined to choose images with "a lower volume" when illustrating stories about death. In other words, they select images that suggest death but do not explicitly show a body, thus diminishing the emotional responses of viewers.[16] By maintaining the status quo, the media avoids connecting either US or Mexican immigration policy with the violence perpetrated against migrants. Tropes are used to stand in for, and make recognizable, traumatic events that cannot be represented because, by definition, trauma is a violent disruption of experience.[17]

Investigative journalism

In contrast to mainstream media coverage, investigative projects allow for in-depth research; for a photographer, these investigative projects create opportunities to make images that are neither graphic nor conventional. Other forums for dissemination, such as independent online publications, or venues such as exhibitions, can circumvent the usual editorial protocols. Mexican photojournalist Moysés Zuñiga Santiago transformed his practice as he spent five years investigating Central American migration. During this period, Zuñiga worked freelance for *La Jornada*, an influential daily newspaper in Mexico, as well as for international agencies such as the Associated Press, Agence France-Press, and Reuters. He was also a member of Periodistas de a pie ("Journalists on foot"), a group of investigative journalists who focus on human rights and social justice issues.[18] Although *La Jornada* paid his living expenses and purchased some images, Zuñiga worked on spec, meaning he was not instructed how to undertake the project or what to photograph.

The project began in 2010, when Zuñiga noticed an influx of Central Americans, especially Hondurans, in his home state of Chiapas in southern Mexico. From the mid 1990s until 2014, the main migration routes through Mexico were concentrated along the freight train routes, so Zuñiga began his investigation in

Arriaga, a municipality in southern Chiapas, which is the location of one of the primary rail links to the north. Because a hurricane destroyed the track along the Pacific coast in 2005, most migrants had to walk the 262-kilometer route from the Guatemalan border to Arriaga.[19] Over the course of the project, Zuñiga traveled with migrants on the train to Mexico's northern border with the United States. In the beginning, he said, "I was taking too many photographs, because it […] was having a great impact on me. I was in risky situations to which I never thought I would return […] so I would shoot, and shoot, and shoot."[20] Gradually, he became accustomed to these situations and turned off his camera for longer periods in order to interact more with the migrants.

During this period, there was a network of shelters in towns along the rail line, mainly run either by Catholics or Jesuits. Zuñiga stayed in these hostels and talked to the priests and their assistants. They would tell him about important cases and tell him which people to talk to. They would introduce and vouch for him, explaining to the person, "[Zuñiga] is a good journalist. Talk to him, tell him anything you want."[21] He listened to stories of why people had fled their homes, of where they hoped to go, and of what had happened to them on their journey. He would only take out his camera if they agreed to be photographed. Sometimes, he worked with reporter Ángeles Mariscal or other journalists, but most of the time he was alone, because, he explained, "not many journalists in Mexico want to travel these routes. Not only is it dangerous, but it also wears one down, economically, emotionally […]"[22]

When Zuñiga began photographing migration, he had no idea it would become a long-term project. He explained, "I was going for news photographs, on a week-end, and I thought I would never be back." At first, he shot in JPEG format on his digital single-lens reflex camera. He would go to a cybercafe to upload the photos and then, using a portable version of Photoshop on a memory stick, he added captions, but did not make changes to the images themselves. He sent some of these photographs to *La Jornada* and others to international news agencies.[23] There were times when this kind of "fast journalism" felt satisfying, such as when he reported on incidents of Mexican police persecuting migrants. He said,

> sometimes there would be an operation on the train route, and I would take photos. Then, I would go quickly to the cybercafe and would call the paper to say, "Put it online, right now. This is happening at this very moment."

Because *La Jornada* is a prominent news agency, there was often a quick response. He explained that the story would be seen

> by the governor of Chiapas or the chief of police, and so, very quickly, the police on site were receiving calls on their radios telling them, "Get out of there. Leave

the people in peace." […] the police would then call an end to the operation and stop beating people up […][24]

However, his work generating quick responses to local affairs gradually gave way to documenting personal accounts of trauma.

After several months, Zuñiga's investigative project began to take shape. Although he did not conceive of his process in theoretical terms, his approach was such that photography became a contact zone where he would interact with undocumented migrants as they traveled through Mexico on their way to the United States. Pratt describes contact zones as improvised, chaotic spaces where subjects are constituted in and by their relation to others, even as imbalances of power are negotiated.[25] Zuñiga engaged with migrants by traveling together with them on trains and by staying with them in hostels along the migration routes. His Mexican citizenship and professional status gave him privileges and protections that undocumented migrants lack, yet he relied on his subjects to determine the nature and extent of photographic encounters. He adapted to the unpredictable environment, which meant, in some instances, he did not even make photographs. Zuñiga explained:

> If I was walking along the train tracks, and suddenly I saw someone sleeping there, but couldn't see from a distance if the person was on a drug high, if there was a *pollero* [human trafficker] nearby, if they were asleep or not, I would decide whether to approach or greet them. Later, after I got to know them, is when I would begin to shoot. But when I saw someone asleep, when I saw some-one –I don't know; on the train, in certain postures that drew my attention; sometimes I couldn't just take that photograph. For me […] that would be ideal in photography because it would reflect a bit better that physical spontaneity.[26]

Instead of looking for news photographs, he began to consider a more in-depth approach that would allow him to connect individual stories to broader concerns about the treatment of migrants in Mexico.

As Zuñiga continued the project, he considered how his subjects could assert their agency by telling their stories and by affecting how they were represented. He became increasingly aware that many of the migrants were at risk: "I realized that there were more migrants going into exile—seeking asylum—or trying to escape from very dangerous threats and persecution, for example, because they had already had relatives killed in their own countries."[27] This affected his work, because, he said, "I had to be more careful […] with the ones who had been threatened. I couldn't just arrive, take the photograph, and show it, because I didn't know what the implications would be."[28] In some instances, he avoided showing faces.

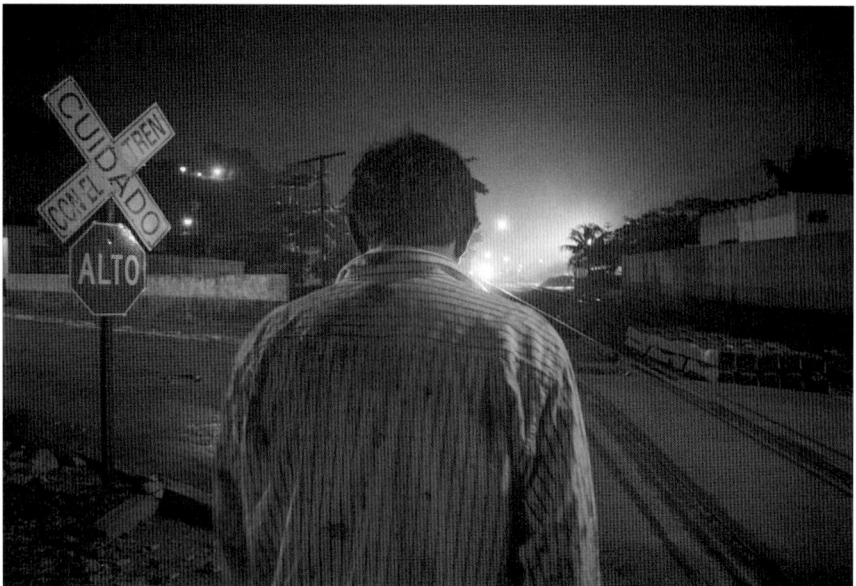

Figure 3: Moysés Zuñiga Santiago, *Manuel*, Coatzacoalcos, Veracruz, Mexico, October 29, 2012
(Plate 30, p. 355). Photograph courtesy of Moysés Zuñiga Santiago.

One such case is the photograph of Manuel, his back turned to the camera. The
caption explains that Manuel walks at night because of his insomnia. In this photograph, he was in a particularly dangerous area along the Gulf of Mexico route,
where the Zetas cartel stops trains and charges migrants one hundred US dollars. If
they cannot pay, they are executed. Ironically, the sign on the left of the photograph
warns: *Alto. Cuidado con el tren* ("Stop. Beware of the train"). Because the threat of
violence is conveyed in words and graphically via the signs, Zuñiga preserves both
the privacy and dignity of his subject. Like many photographs in the series, this one
leaves viewers with an unsettling, fragmented narrative of an individual's struggles.
The body of work as a whole presents a little-known picture of the situation for
migrants in Mexico and raises awareness about the traumatic consequences of
immigration policies. Exhibitions of Zuñiga's photographs at conferences and sym-
posia on migration in New York City, Toronto, and Tucson have offered important
opportunities for the work to reach new international audiences.[29] Working periodically over the course of five years to reveal crucial aspects of the story of Central
American migration in Mexico, Zuñiga's work responds to the changing dynamics
of immigration policy (Fig. 3).

Border security and the persecution of undocumented migrants

The US-Mexico border has been an important frontier in American migration history since the early twentieth century, when Mexicans displaced by the Mexican Revolution (1910–1920) sought asylum in the United States and when, during the First World War, the American government introduced passport controls over concerns that enemies could cross from Mexico into the United States.[30] Throughout the twentieth century, the border became increasingly regulated and subject to new forms of surveillance. The persecution of undocumented migrants in Mexico during the twenty-first century is directly related to today's heightened border security measures. Since 2001, the US-Mexico border has become increasingly militarized. The policies and procedures that characterize this shift began in the 1980s under Ronald Reagan, when the United States used Latin America as a testing ground for military development and proxy wars.[31] Harsh border control measures were sanctioned in 1994, when the United States implemented the Southwest Border Strategy and a policy known as Prevention Through Deterrence (PTD).[32] This policy formalized what decades of experience had taught immigration officers: dangerous environments and the risk of death deters migrants from attempting the journey to the United States.[33] The deterrence approach replaced an ineffective and politically problematic policy of catching people after they had already crossed the border.[34] The new policy increased border patrol agents and technology around centralized entry points, forcing undocumented migrants along more remote routes and into difficult terrain. Anthropologist Jason De León argues that the Immigration and Naturalization Service (INS) intentionally used the inhospitable environment to discourage people from trying to reach the United States, as well as to abdicate responsibility for migrant deaths.[35]

Near the US border, a leading cause of death is the desert itself. Bodies are consumed by animals, and because few traces remain, these deaths are difficult to track. The desert essentially obliterates all evidence of the human cost of the government's immigration policy.[36] However, on the journey through Mexico, the PTD policy magnified a range of other hazards. By pushing people away from established migration routes and into more remote areas, it made them more vulnerable to crime and violence. During this period, it became routine for gangs to demand payment from migrants or their smugglers for each person who crossed their territory.[37] Women and girls were especially at risk of rape and abduction for the purposes of human trafficking.[38] The PTD policy normalized hostility toward undocumented migrants and heightened a variety of conditions that continue to endanger them.

The Department of Homeland Security was formed in 2002 following the Bush administration's expansion of border security after the 9/11 attacks of 2001 and the US government's launch of its War on Terror. It absorbed the INS, and new agencies were created to handle immigration and border security: Immigration and Customs Enforcement (ICE) and Customs and Border Patrol (CBP).[39] In 2005, Homeland Security introduced a formal deportation process to replace the previous system of voluntary departure (known as "catch and release"). The new process channels apprehended migrants into the federal criminal justice system, resulting in jail sentences. But due to the volume of cases and systemic racism, there is a lack of due process.[40] When migrants are not incarcerated, they are dropped off in one of Mexico's border towns, often at night and at a different port of entry than the one where they crossed into the United States. Often disoriented and frightened, these migrants are then at increased risk of violence.[41] These changes, along with increased spending and more detention facilities, rendered US border enforcement even more brutal than before. At the same time, the United States intensified its program of outsourcing deportation with an agreement to pay Mexico for repatriating Central Americans to their home countries, thereby decreasing the likelihood that they would try to reach the United States again.[42]

The situation in Mexico has also changed since the turn of the twenty-first century. For years, the state focused on security along the Mexico-Guatemala border in an attempt to address drug trafficking and human smuggling. A 2005 policy, the Integral Migratory Policy Proposal for the Mexican Southern Border, increased the number of agents and introduced surveillance technology, but with little success.[43] Until the Zetas cartel murdered seventy-two Central Americans in 2010 there was little recognition that migrants were under threat while in Mexico. The following year, Mexico signed a migration law that acknowledged the scale of transit migration and sought to ensure humane conditions for migrants while they were in the country. In spite of this law, Central Americans have continued to experience human rights violations. The main causes remain organized crime and corruption among immigration and law enforcement personnel. And when migrants are apprehended, conditions in Mexican detention facilities are deplorable.[44] The violence and abuse that migrants experience on their journey to the United States is difficult to photograph and, as previously discussed, the mainstream media consistently uses visual tropes to simplify complex issues.

Witnessing trauma

Unlike most representations of migration in the mainstream media, Zuñiga's photographs acknowledge the power differential between photographer and subject, and subject and viewer. Positioning viewers as witnesses, he sensitively combines photographs with narrative to convey how loss and trauma shape the experience of undocumented migrants. As Hoelscher's research on indigenous Americans makes

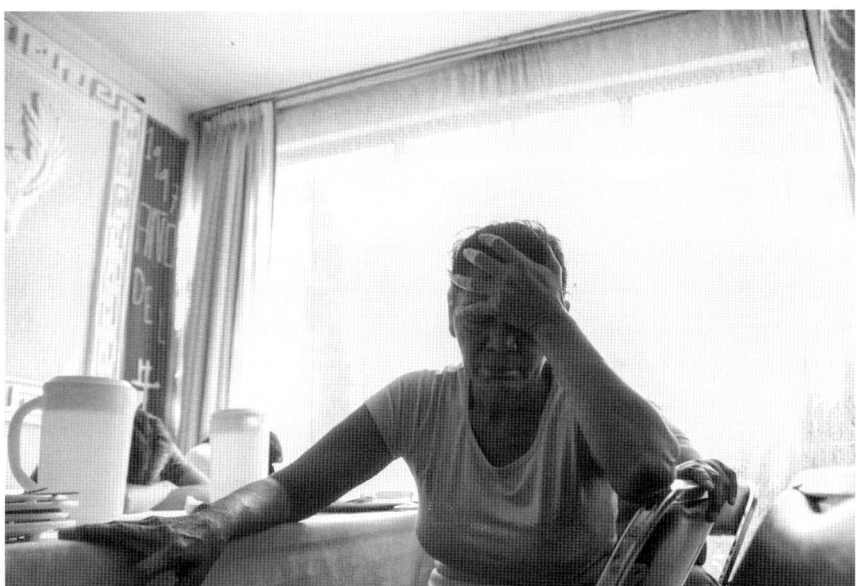

Figure 4: Moysés Zuñiga Santiago, *Narcisa González*, Tequisqulapan, Mexico, October 24, 2012 (Plate 31, p. 355). Photograph courtesy of Moysés Zuñiga Santiago.

clear, marginalized people have long agreed to have their photographs taken to achieve their personal and political goals.[45] As a persecuted minority in Mexico, undocumented migrants have benefited from photographic encounters with Zuñiga in various ways. For some, there was the emotional release of sharing their burden and having their hardships recognized by others. Many of the photographs focus on one or two people and their immediate surroundings. Zuñiga is attentive to how people inhabit space, and his photographs acknowledge his subjects' suffering through their gestures and postures. Their stories, which he includes in captions when he exhibits the work, reveal the challenges they face on their journey to the United States. One photograph depicts a Nicaraguan woman named Narcisa González; the caption accompanying the photograph explains that she is sitting silently in prayer (Fig. 4). Eyes closed, her hand clutches her head in anguish and exhaustion. Diffuse sunlight streams through the window of a hostel, and a few other people are visible in the background, slumped on tables, reflecting her position, although this photograph focuses on her story. Viewers may recognize her unconscious expression of grief, but the explanation accompanying the image is necessary to understand its source. When the photograph was taken, her son had been missing for nine years. As Judith Butler suggests, grief is a constitutive and relational experience through which we recognize another's subjectivity.[46] When we acknowledge Narcisa's suffering, we recognize her humanity.

Photographs have long served as important forms of testimony for survivors of violence, but in this project, Zuñiga was faced with the challenge of visualizing trauma without revictimizing his subjects. After 2006, when Mexican President Felipe Calderón launched a war on drugs, journalism in Mexico was dominated by sensational stories that gradually normalized violence. Zuñiga worked with fellow investigative journalists to develop ways of communicating what was happening without using language that would replicate the violence.[47] Take, for example, a photograph of Esther, a young woman from Honduras who was seven months pregnant, pictured with her arms wrapped protectively around her two-year-old daughter (Fig. 5). Zuñiga has used setting and framing to foreground their affective gestures. Standing in front of a white wall under posters informing migrants about their right to claim asylum in Mexico, Esther's passive gaze could be interpreted as an indication that she has suffered. From the caption, viewers learn that she was assaulted on her journey to Arriaga and was left without clothes. She did not want to get on the train and was staying at a hostel looking for a way to carry on.[48] Zuñiga's pairing of image and caption does not turn the mother and daughter into a spectacle, a tendency Wendy Kozal identifies as a common feature of exposés of human rights violations.[49] Instead, it allows viewers to experience a range of affective responses, while also recognizing Esther's pain. The contrast between the drawings of refugees on the posters and the image of Esther and her daughter reminds us that contact zones are sites where marginalized subjects must negotiate representations that foreground their experiences of subjugation.[50] Looking at this photograph, we might wonder whether Esther identified with the refugees depicted on the wall. Would the caricatured style allow her to see herself as potentially eligible to claim asylum?

At times, the photographs, and Zuñiga's presence as a witness, became a form of protection for migrants. In one case, he met a man who had lost several friends on his journey and was being followed by members of a cartel who were attempting to kidnap him. The man was on the verge of crossing into the United States, but he knew he would not escape their grasp. If he turned back, he feared the Mexican police would hand him over to the cartel that was pursuing him. Neither was it safe to go to the immigration authorities to be deported because corruption is widespread, and they are also linked to organized crime. In this situation, Zuñiga's photographs, along with the photographer's presence at the *Instituto Nacional de Migración* ("National Migration Institute") seemed the most likely way to secure the man's survival. At least it ensured the man's apprehension was witnessed, which increased the likelihood that he would be deported (Fig. 6). And if he did not survive, the photographs meant that someone would know what had happened.[51]

In Mexico, where journalists covering organized crime or political corruption regularly face intimidation and violence from drug cartels and the police, Zuñiga

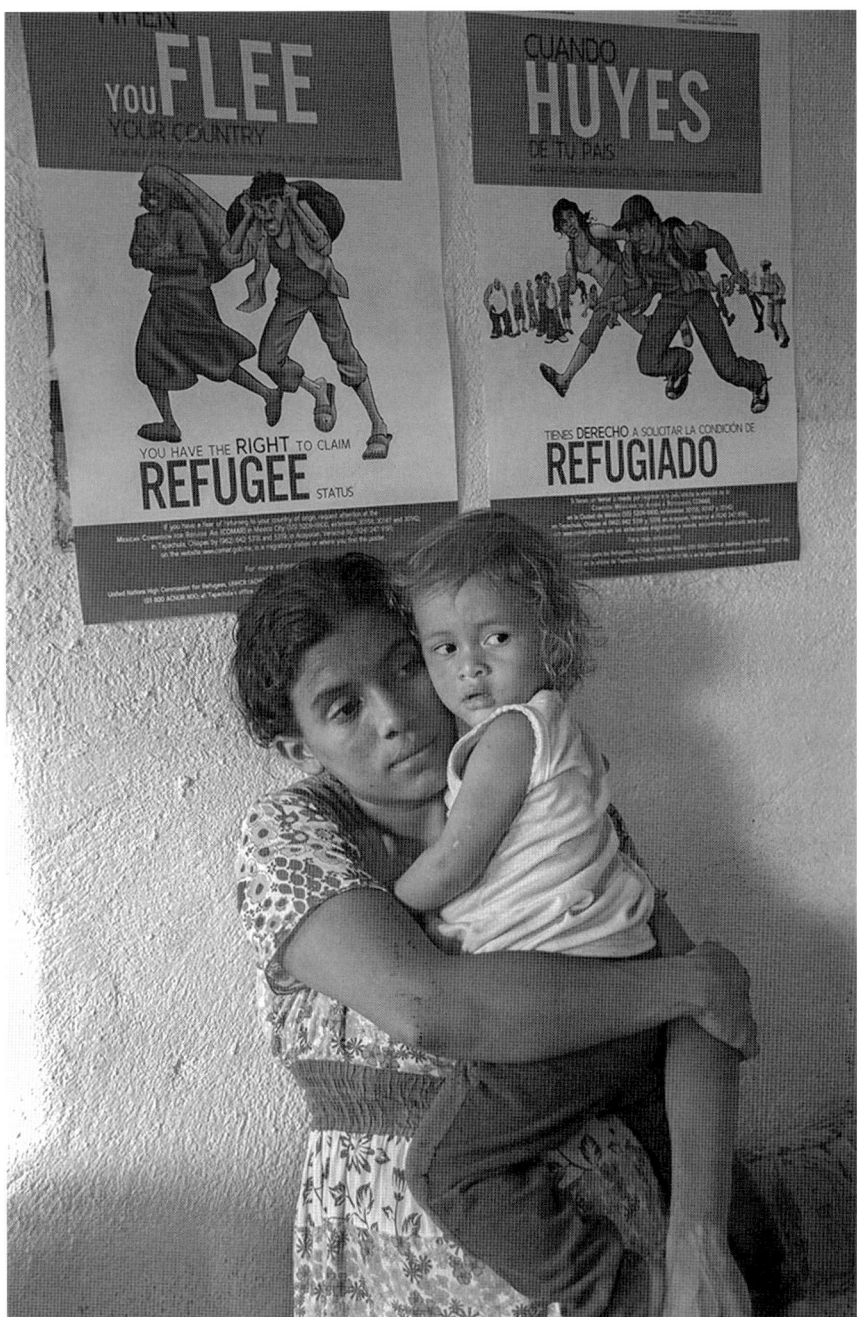

Figure 5: Moysés Zuñiga Santiago, *Esther*, Arriaga, Chiapas, Mexico, May 6, 2014 (Plate 32, p. 356).
Photograph courtesy of Moysés Zuñiga Santiago.

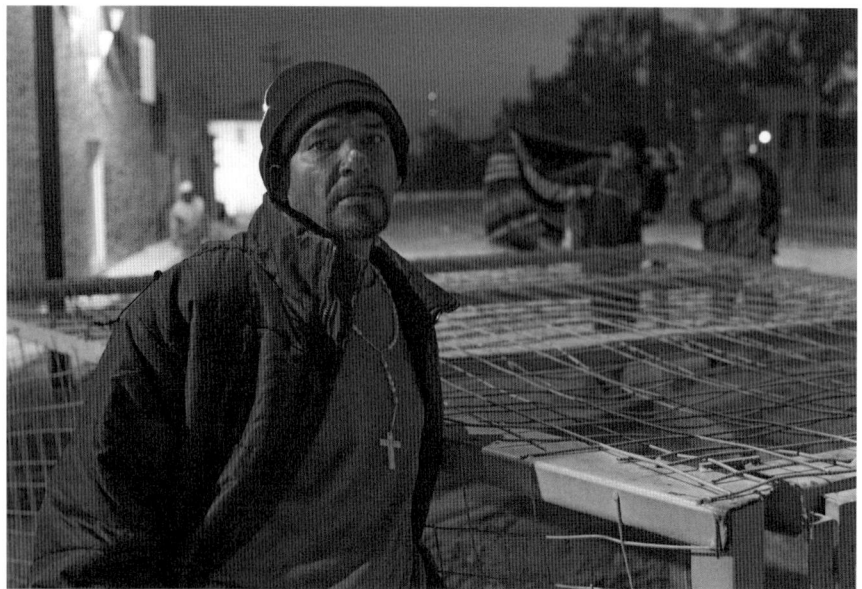

Figure 6: Moysés Zuñiga Santiago, *Caught between two borders*, Saltillo Coahuila, Mexico, October 23, 2012. Photograph courtesy of Moysés Zuñiga Santiago.

also had to consider his own safety.[52] Because he never hid his camera, traffickers, as well as migrants, knew he was a journalist. Cartel informants travel on trains, blending in with migrants. They investigate who has relatives in the United States and kidnap people, sometimes demanding thousands of dollars. Under these conditions, it was dangerous for Zuñiga to travel for long stretches because, as he explained, "people from the cartels identify you at one stage and they look for you at the next."[53] When I asked Zuñiga whether he felt as if he was in danger, he answered no, but laughed and added, "I have already normalized it, and that's why I say no." However, he also explained that he was fortunate not to live near the train route and could go home when he felt threatened.[54] He recognized that he had a measure of protection that was unavailable to undocumented migrants.

While the risks of transit migration are difficult to convey visually, one of Zuñiga's photographs offers a powerful example of the unbearable conditions that immigration policies have produced (Fig. 7). In the foreground, a woman sits with a few belongings, a vacant look on her face, lightly touching her fingers together. In the middle ground, a man lounges in the grass, smoking, with both the woman and the photographer in his sights. In the background, soldiers gaze over from the rear of their truck. When Zuñiga exhibits this photograph, the accompanying caption identifies the woman and explains the scene: Cristina, a Guatemalan woman, is guarded by a *pollero* while a Mexican army patrol drives past the train tracks.

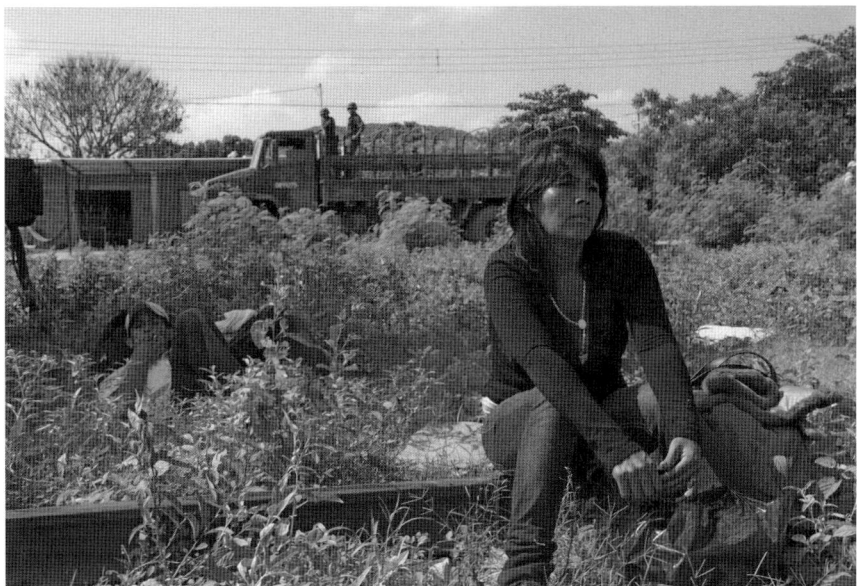

Figure 7: Moysés Zuñiga Santiago, *Cristina*, Arriaga, Chiapas, Mexico, July 21, 2012 (Plate 33, p. 357). Photograph courtesy of Moysés Zuñiga Santiago.

Zuñiga tells us she is a sex worker, and in addition to looking for clients, she waits for the departure of the train. Under the watchful eye of her trafficker, she answered *yes* or *no* to Zuñiga's questions. The information, coupled with the vantage point of the image, offers a deeply uncomfortable experience for viewers. One woman's experience of structural violence is laid bare by the way the photograph emphasizes the surveillance and control of her body. The image signals that the Mexican military is complicit in human trafficking. On the one hand, this photograph connects the media and viewers to these networks of exploitation, and on the other, during the encounter with Zuñiga, photography became a contact zone in which Cristina's distress could be witnessed.

Southern Border Plan

Since Zuñiga began his photographic investigation in 2010, the situation for undocumented migrants traveling through Mexico has deteriorated. Media images of migrants riding atop freight trains and stories about thousands of unaccompanied minors from Central America arriving in Mexico and the United States in late 2013 and early 2014 were likely the impetus for a new border security agreement. However, with the introduction of the Southern Border Plan (*Plan Frontera Sur*) in

July 2014, violence against migrants has only increased. Under the new agreement between the United States and Mexico, enforcement extends as far south as the Mexico-Guatemala border and along the country's migration routes. Christopher Wilson, vice president of the Mexico Institute, a think tank in Washington, explained that the border has been reconceived "as a system rather than as a line in the sand."[55] In an attempt to slow the flow of migrants from Central America, the United States gave Mexico eighty-six million dollars for training and equipment.[56] This "layered approach" to the border includes an increase in highway and railway checkpoints, raids on shelters, and tactics meant to keep migrants off the trains.[57] Specifically, the rail company upgraded the tracks so trains can travel at higher speeds, and it introduced a satellite monitoring system to prevent migrants from boarding.[58] The federal police apprehend undocumented migrants or force them into gang territory, where they are abducted or murdered.[59] Zuñiga described the Southern Border Plan as devastating for migrants because it prevents people from using the trains or the established shelters, so they have to forge new paths through difficult mountainous and forested terrain.[60] In essence, the journey has become even more dangerous, as corruption continues and organized crime is allowed to thrive.

With the introduction of the Southern Border Plan, it has become even more difficult to represent the experiences of undocumented migrants in Mexico. The risks have increased for everyone, and, Zuñiga explained, if journalists travel with the migrants, they face many of the same dangers. They, too, will be assaulted by cartels. As an alternative, he has tried to photograph the authorities, the Mexican army and the police who monitor and carry out surveillance operations. Nevertheless, even though journalists have the right to photograph these activities, in practice, the officials do not allow it unless the photographer obtains a permit. Then, he explained, the authorities act like fools, as if they are performing in a military film. While these images are useful to show the vehicles and equipment, he said, they do not convey the conditions that migrants experience, nor do they show how the police "hunt" migrants in their vehicles and then fail to protect them when they cross into gang territory.[61] The uniforms of the officers are thus a way of making visible the invisible wall created by the restrictions of the Southern Border Plan (Fig. 8).

As Jacques Rancière notes, we cannot assume that political action will result from looking at images of trauma.[62] Tragically, the late twentieth century left us with at least two instances (Rwanda and the former Yugoslavia) in which visual evidence of atrocities had little political effect.[63] However, rather than picturing atrocity, Zuñiga's photographs point to the brutal consequences of government policy. His approach to photography as a contact zone offers his subjects an opportunity to convey their experiences of migration through facial expressions, gestures,

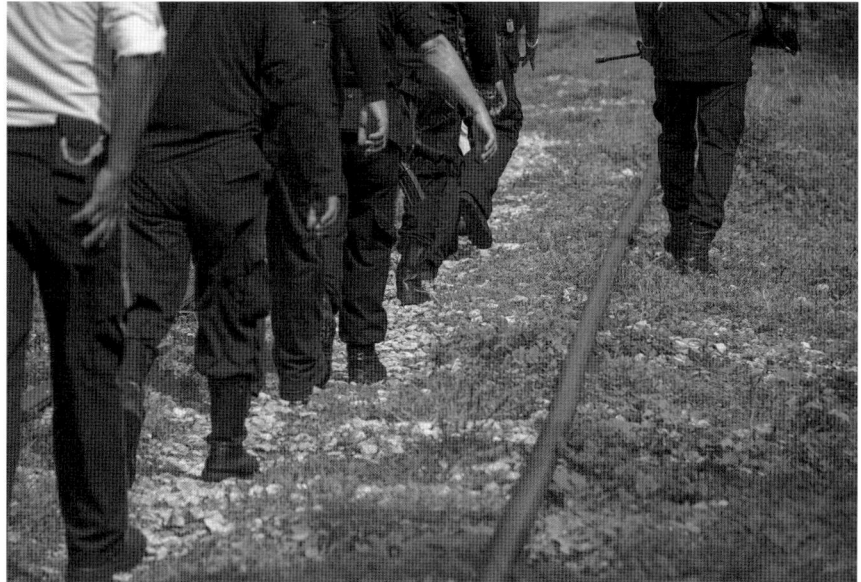

Figure 8: Moysés Zuñiga Santiago, *Southern Border Plan*, Tapachula, Chiapas. Mexico. April 20, 2015. Photograph courtesy of Moysés Zuñiga Santiago.

and stories. This work raises questions of accountability, and public recognition of the United States' and Mexico's culpability in human rights violations is a first step toward holding them responsible. At a time when anti-immigrant sentiment runs high, fewer asylum claims are approved, and neither the United States nor Mexico are complying with international human rights law, Zuñiga's investigation offers a much-needed counterpoint that constitutes viewers as witnesses to state-sanctioned violence.

Acknowledgments

This research is funded by a grant from the Social Science and Humanities Research Council of Canada. Special thanks to Moysés Zuñiga Santiago for sharing his experiences and to Andrés Villar for translation. Also thank you to Madeline Bassnett, Anahí Gonzalez Teran, Laura Levin, Sarah Parsons, and Linda Steer. I am grateful to the editors Justin Carville and Sigrid Lien, as well as to participants of the conference "Photography, Migration, and Cultural Encounters in America," held at IADT, Dún Laoghaire in 2018.

Notes

1. On the history of gangs in Central America and their connection to US immigration policy, see Al Valdez, "The Origin of Southern California Latino Gangs," in Thomas C. Bruneau, Licía Damert, and Elizabeth Skinner (eds.), *Maras: Gang Violence and Security in Central America* (Austin: University of Texas Press, 2011), 23–42.

2. Adam Isacson, Maureen Meyer, and Gabriela Morales, "Mexico's Other Border: Security, Migration, and the Humanitarian Crisis at the Line with Central America," Report from Washington Office on Latin America (2014), 13, https://www.wola.org/files/mxgt/report/. The CA-4 Control Agreement came into effect in June 2006.

3. Isacson, Meyer, and Morales, "Mexico's Other Border," 17. Also see Oscar Martinez, *The Beast: Riding the Rails and Dodging Narcos on the Migrant Trail*, trans. Daniela Maria Ugaz and John Washington (London: Verso, 2013).

4. Mary Louise Pratt, *Imperial Eyes: Travel Writing and Transculturation*, 1st edition (London: Routledge, 1992), 6–7; Steven Hoelscher, *Picturing Indians: Photographic Encounters and Tourist Fantasies in H. H. Bennett's Wisconsin Dells* (Madison: The University of Wisconsin Press, 2008), 12–13.

5. Susan Sontag, *On Photography* (New York: Farrar, Straus and Giroux, 1977) and *Regarding the Pain of Others* (New York: Picador, 2003); Allan Sekula, *Photography Against the Grain: Essays and Photo Works 1973–1983* (Halifax: Nova Scotia College of Art and Design, 1984); Martha Rosler, "In, Around, and Afterthoughts (on documentary photography)," in Richard Bolton (ed.), *The Contest of Meaning: Critical Histories of Photography* (Cambridge: MIT Press, 1989), 303–340.

6. Mark Reinhardt, Holly Edwards, and Erina Duganne (eds.), *Beautiful Suffering: Photography and the Traffic in Pain* (Chicago: University of Chicago Press/Williams College Museum of Art, 2007); Ariella Azoulay, *The Civil Contract of Photography* (New York: Zone Books, 2008) and *Civil Imagination: A Political Ontology of Photography*, trans. Louise Bethlehem (London/New York: Verso, 2012); Sharon Sliwinski, *Human Rights in Camera* (Chicago: University of Chicago Press, 2011); Geoffrey Batchen, M. Gidley, Nancy Miller et al., *Picturing Atrocity: Photography in Crisis* (London: Reaktion Books, 2012); David Campbell, "The Myth of Compassion Fatigue," in Liam Kennedy and Caitlin Patrick (eds.), *The Violence of the Image: Photography and International Conflict* (London: I.B. Tauris, 2014), 97–124; Wendy Kozal, *Distant Wars Visible: The Ambivalence of Witnessing* (Minneapolis: University of Minnesota Press, 2014).

7. A word about terminology: I use the term *migrant* to refer to people from Central America who are attempting to settle in the United States. Terms such as *asylum seeker* and *refugee* convey an intent or status not always attributable to people migrating from countries in the Northern Triangle, particularly during the early twenty-first century. These terms describe those making a formal claim of asylum or someone whose claim has been accepted, and although some Central Americans do apply, the majority do

not, either because they do not have the required evidence and fear their persecution will not be recognized, or because they are not aware of their right to claim asylum. A report by Amnesty International indicated that seventy-five percent of people detained by Mexico's National Institute of Migration were not informed of their right to seek asylum, even though it is mandatory to do so under Mexican law. See "Overlooked, Under-Protected: Mexico's Deadly *Refoulement* of Central Americans Seeking Asylum," Amnesty International, 2018, https://www.amnestyusa.org/reports/overlooked-under-protected-mexicos-deadly-refoulement-of-central-americans-seeking-asylum/.

8. Marta Zarzycka, *Gendered Tropes in War Photography* (New York: Routledge, 2017), xvi–xx; Jessica M. Fishman, *Death Makes the News: How the Media Censor and Display the Dead* (New York: New York University Press, 2017). Also see Barbie Zelizer's analysis of what she calls the "about-to-die" trope in photojournalism, *About to Die: How News Images Move the Public* (Oxford: Oxford University Press, 2010).

9. Terence Wright, "Moving Images: The Media Representation of Refugees," *Visual Studies* 17, no. 1 (2002), 57.

10. See, for example, a photograph by Brett Gundlock in Kirk Semple, "Inside an Immigrant Caravan: Women and Children Fleeing Violence," *New York Times*, 4 April 2018, https://www.nytimes.com/2018/04/04/world/americas/mexico-trump-caravan.html.

11. See Sarah Bassnett, "Visual Tropes of Migration tell Predictable but Misleading Stories," *The Conversation*, November 5, 2018, https://theconversation.com/visual-tropes-of-migration-tell-predictable-but-misleading-stories-106121.

12. Lilie Chouliaraki and Tijana Stolic. "Rethinking Media Responsibility in the Refugee 'Crisis': A Visual Typology of European News," *Media, Culture & Society* 39, no. 8 (November 2017), 1167–1168.

13. Barbie Zelizer, "Death in Wartime: Photographs and the 'Other War' in Afghanistan," *Harvard International Journal of Press / Politics* 10, no. 3 (2005), 34. Judith Butler argues that the media upholds conventions because the media is aligned with corporate interests, and corporations want to maintain control over public perception. See *Precarious Life: The Powers of Mourning and Violence* (New York: Verso, 2004), 147.

14. Leonard Folgarait, *Seeing Mexico Photographed: The Work of Horne, Casasola, Modotti, and Álvarez Bravo* (New Haven: Yale University Press, 2008), 19–29. Thanks to Monica Bravo for this reference and to Anahí Gonzalez Teran for tracking down the title of the photograph.

15. See Jo Tuckman, "Survivor Tells of Escape from Mexican Massacre in which 72 Were Left Dead," *The Guardian*, August 26, 2010, https://www.theguardian.com/world/2010/aug/25/mexico-massacre-central-american-migrants; and "Mexican officials: Gunmen behind massacre of 72 have been killed," CNN, September 7, 2010, http://www.cnn.com/2010/WORLD/americas/09/06/mexico.massacre.suspects/index.html.

16. Jessica M. Fishman, *Death Makes the News: How the Media Censor and Display the Dead* (New York: New York University Press, 2017), 76-77.

17. Ulrich Baer, *Spectral Evidence: The Photography of Trauma* (Cambridge: MIT Press, 2005), 8.

18. Periodistas de a pie was founded in 2007, http://www.periodistasdeapie.org.mx/. For articles, see: https://enelcamino.piedepagina.mx/coautores/?author=moyses-zuni-ga-santiago and the English translation of one article on Mexico as a transit country: http://sites.sandiego.edu/tbi-foe/2015/05/12/how-did-mexico-become-so-hellish-for-mi-grants-by-alberto-najar/.

19. The trip from the border to Arriaga would normally take five to six days, although it could take longer because avoiding authorities and evading cartels makes it consider-ably more complicated. The train track was repaired in 2014. For an account of the dangers on the journey, see Rodrigo Dominguez Villega, "Central American Migrants and 'La Bestia': The Route, Dangers, and Government Responses," Migration Policy Institute, September 10, 2014, https://www.migrationpolicy.org/article/central-amer-ican-migrants-and-%E2%80%9Cla-bestia%E2%80%9D-route-dangers-and-govern-ment-responses.

20. Interview between the author and Zuñiga, October 7, 2017.

21. Interview between the author and Zuñiga, October 7, 2017.

22. Interview between the author and Zuñiga, October 7, 2017.

23. Interview between the author and Zuñiga, October 7, 2017.

24. Interview between the author and Zuñiga, October 7, 2017.

25. Pratt, *Imperial Eyes*, 7.

26. Interview between the author and Zuñiga, October 7, 2017.

27. Interview between the author and Zuñiga, October 7, 2017.

28. Interview between the author and Zuñiga, October 7, 2017.

29. Exhibitions were held at the Hemispheric Institute of Performance and Politics, New York University, November 2013; the Hemispheric Institute Conference, Toronto, October 5–8, 2017; and at The University of Arizona Museum of Art, September 16, 2017 – March 11, 2018. The exhibition *In Transit / En Tránsito: Arts, Migration, Resist-ance* at The University of Arizona Museum of Art was curated by Anita Huizar-Her-nandez and Kailtin Murphy and did not include the narrative captions discussed in this article. See Murphy's article "Against Precarious Abstraction: Bearing Witness to Migration Through Moysés Zuñiga Santiago's *La Bestia* Photographs, *Latin American and Latinx Visual Culture* 1, no. 1 (2019): 7–22.

30. Anna Pegler-Gordon, *In Sight of America: Photography and the Development of US Immigra-tion Policy* (Berkeley: University of California Press, 2009), 174–190.

31. Karma R. Chávez, "Border Interventions: The Need to Shift from a Rhetoric of Secu-rity to a Rhetoric of Militarization," in D. Robert DeChaine (ed.), *Border Rhetorics: Cit-izenship and Identity on the US-Mexico Frontier* (Tuscaloosa: The University of Alabama

Press, 2012), 49; and Greg Grandin, *Empire's Workshop: Latin America, the United States, and the Rise of the New Imperialism* (New York: Holt, 2010), 3–4.

32. United States Border Patrol, *Border Patrol Strategic Plan 1994 and Beyond*, Government Report (1994), 2, 7.

33. Jason De León, *The Land of Open Graves: Living and Dying on the Migrant Trail* (Oakland: University of California Press, 2015), 31–34. The Government Accountability Office Report of 1997 explains: "The overarching goal of the strategy is to make it so difficult and so costly to enter this country illegally that fewer individuals even try."

34. The Immigration and Naturalization Service (INS) recognized that, under the old system, most migrants chose to voluntarily return to their home country once apprehended, and then they tried again.

35. De León, *The Land of Open Graves*, 66–73. From 1940 until 2003, the INS was a US government agency that dealt with immigration, citizenship, and border security. In 2003, three new agencies took over responsibility for its functions: US Customs and Border Patrol (CBP), Immigration and Customs Enforcement (ICE), and US Citizenship and Immigration Services (USCIS).

36. De León, *The Land of Open Graves*, 66–73.

37. Most migrants hire smugglers to guide them on the journey. Although smugglers are often blamed for the violence experienced by migrants crossing Mexico, research shows they are not normally affiliated with gangs. Simón Pedro Izcara Palacios, "Migrant Smuggling on Mexico's Gulf Route: The Actors Involved," *Latin American Perspectives* 44, no. 6 (2017), 16–30.

38. Isacson, Meyer, and Morales, "Mexico's Other Border," 9.

39. Staffing levels and budgets increased, and with the Secure Border Initiative, introduced in 2005 under the guise of counterterror measures, new infrastructure, technology, and communications systems established what became known as a virtual fence along the southern border of the United States. See Karma R. Chávez, "Border Interventions: The Need to Shift from a Rhetoric of Security to a Rhetoric of Militarization," in D. Robert DeChaine (ed.), *Border Rhetorics: Citizenship and Identity on the US-Mexico Frontier* (Tuscaloosa: The University of Alabama Press, 2012), 55–56.

40. De León, 109–110.

41. De León, 115–116.

42. Adam Goodman, "Human Costs of Outsourcing Deportation," *Humanitarian: An International Journal of Human Rights, Humanitarianism, and Development* 8, No. 3 (Winter 2017), 527–528.

43. Roberto Dominguez and Martin Iñiguez Ramos, "South/North Axis of Border Management in Mexico," in Ruben Zaiotti (ed.), *Externalizing Migration Management: Europe, North America and the Spread of 'Remote Control' Practices* (London: Routledge, 2016), 228–229.

44. Dominguez and Iñiguez Ramos, "South/North Axis of Border Management in Mexico," in *Externalizing Migration Management*, 228–229.

45. Hoelscher, *Picturing Indians*, 13.

46. Judith Butler, *Precarious Life: The Powers of Mourning and Violence* (New York: Verso, 2004), 30.

47. Interview between the author and Zuñiga, October 7, 2017.

48. "Fewer Rivers to Cross: Mexico Becomes a Destination for Migrants," *The Economist*, July 27, 2017, https://www.economist.com/the-americas/2017/07/27/mexico-be-comes-a-destination-for-migrants.

49. Wendy Kozal, *Distant Wars Visible*, 187.

50. Pratt, *Imperial Eyes*, 7.

51. Jason De León has also indicated that the migrants he talked to wanted to have their photographs taken. See "The Indecisive Moment: Photoethnography on the Undoc-umented Migrant Trail," in Tanya Sheehan (ed.), *Photography and Migration* (London: Routledge, 2018), 120.

52. Reporters Without Borders ranked Mexico 153 out of 180 on the World Press Free-dom Index in 2013. See https://rsf.org/en/mexico and Human Rights Watch https://www.hrw.org/world-report/2018/country-chapters/mexico.

53. Interview between the author and Zuñiga, October 7, 2017.

54. Interview between the author and Zuñiga, October 7, 2017.

55. Stephanie Nolen, "Southern Exposure: The Costly Border Plan Mexico Won't Dis-cuss," *Globe and Mail*, 10 June 2016.

56. Nolen, "Southern Exposure," *Globe and Mail*, 10 June 2016.

57. Border Patrol Chief Mike Fisher, quoted in Todd Miller, "Mexico: The US Border Patrol's Latest Hire," in *Aljazeera America*, 4 October 2014, http://america.aljazeera.com/opinions/2014/10/mexico-us-borderpatrolsecurityimmigrants.html.

58. Dominguez and Iñiguez Ramos, "South/North Axis of Border Management in Mex-ico," in *Externalizing Migration Management*, 227, 232.

59. Sofia Espenoza Álvarez and Marin Guevara Urbina (eds.), *Immigration and the Law: Race, Citizenship, and Social Control* (Tucson: University of Arizona Press, 2018), 14–17.

60. Interview between the author and Zuñiga, October 7, 2017

61. Email correspondence between the author and Zuñiga, 12 October 2017.

62. Jacques Rancière, *The Emancipated Spectator* (New York: Verso, 2009), 75.

63. Sliwinski, *Human Rights in Camera*, 111–113, 126.

There Was no Record of Her Smile

Muriel Hasbun's *X post facto*

Erina Duganne

In 2009, seventeen years after the Chapultepec Peace Accords brought an end to
El Salvador's twelve-year civil war, and twenty-nine years after she immigrated to
the United States at the age of eighteen, Muriel Hasbun (b. 1961) completed *X post
facto*. This series, like much of her artwork, explores her "multivalent, multilingual,
and multicultural family history."[1] Hasbun and her family are the product of "multiple exiles and diasporas."[2] Her Salvadoran-born father was the son of Palestinian
Christians who moved to El Salvador shortly before World War I. Her mother, a
Polish-French Jew, moved to El Salvador in 1958 to work as a teacher for the children
of the French consul.[3] In her artwork, Hasbun often turns to her family's photographs and documents, especially those of her father Antonio Hasbun Z., who was an
accomplished amateur photographer, to engage with the complexities and contradictions of this "intergenerational, transnational, and transcultural"[4] migratory history.

In her artworks, Hasbun frequently mines these materials to bridge past and
present and to restore bonds separated by time and distance. But whereas images
such as *Family Frames* (Fig. 1) from her series *si je meurs / if I die*, rely on intimate
and personal associations, or referentiality, of her family's photographs and documents, *X post facto* does not depict the intricacies of her family's migratory history.[5]
It is made up, instead, of X-rays—discovered while packing up her father's dental
office and personal belongings in El Salvador after he died in 2004—that record
teeth development and placement as well bone structure and decay (Fig. 2). The
series consists, in other words, of mechanical images, which Hasbun likens, in her
artist statement for this project, to "document[s] signed with an X." Although these
X-rays seem unrelated to her family's migratory history, after laboriously examining
them, these seemingly mechanical images began to take on "an emotional register"
for Hasbun.[6] This affect, moreover, manifested itself not just personally but also collectively. In her father's dental X-rays of teeth, cavities, and dental fixtures, Hasbun
began to feel the collective trauma of her family's migratory history and, most especially, how this experience was irrevocably tied to the Salvadoran Civil War (Fig. 3).

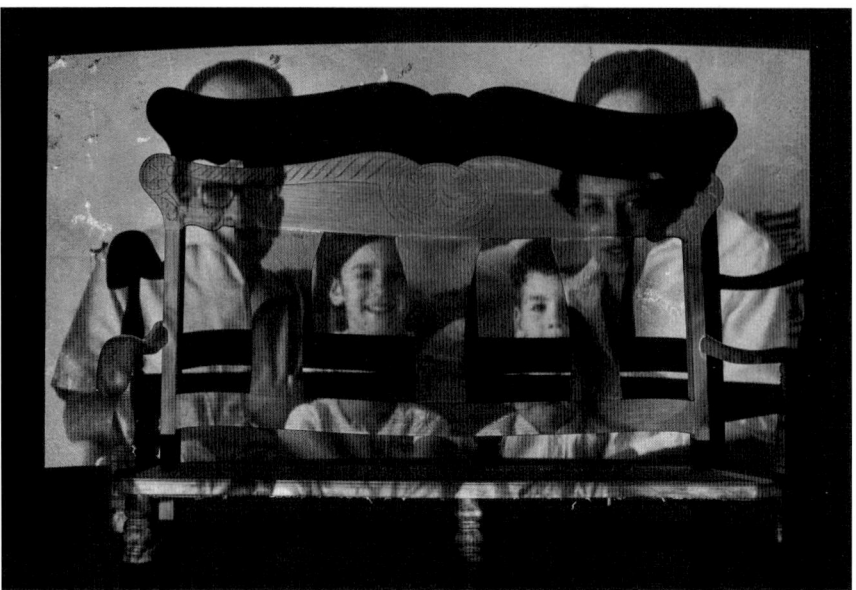

Figure 1: Muriel Hasbun, *Family Frames*, 2016.07.06, ca. 1960s, El Congo, archival pigment print, 2016 (Plate 34, p. 357). Courtesy of the artist.

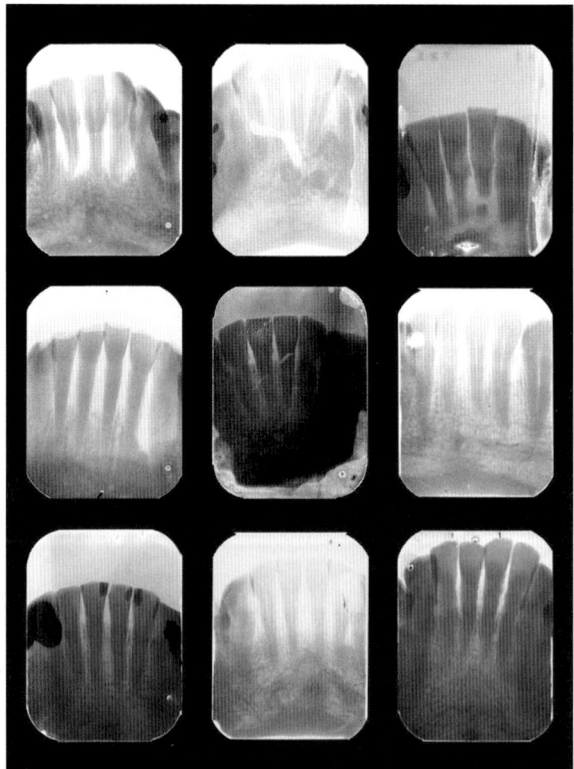

Figure 2: Muriel Hasbun,
Study for *X post facto*
(0.1-0.9), nine archival
pigment prints, 2009
(Plate 35, p. 358). Courtesy of
the artist.

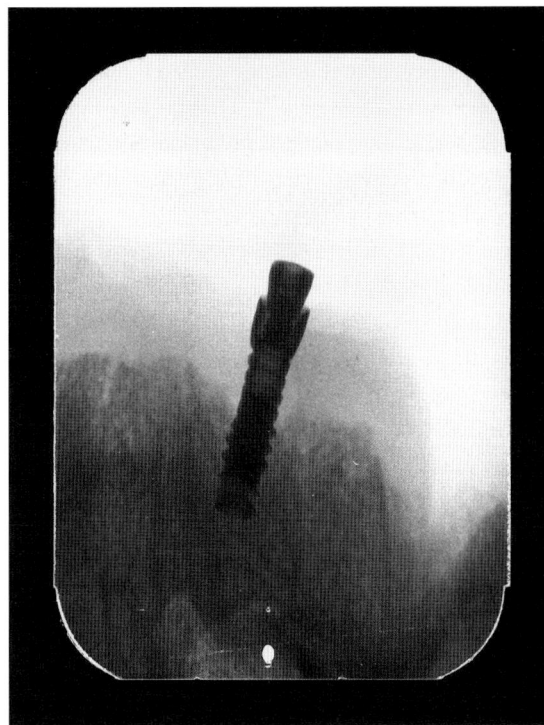

Figure 3: Muriel Hasbun, *X post facto* (6.7), archival pigment print, 2009/2013. Courtesy of the artist.

To "explore the territory of [this] shared history,"[7] Hasbun selected thirty-two X-rays from her father's archive, each of which she enlarged and reprinted from the original negative. What makes this series especially compelling is how it reimagines the testimonial scope of mechanical images and thereby rethinks the political and affective potential of migration photography. Because of photography's ability to render migrants visible, many scholarly accounts situate migration photography within traditions of documentary photography.[8] As part of this genre, these images are generally discussed either in terms of their ability to humanize migrants (Hasbun's *Family Frames* would fit here) or in relation to their regulatory purposes and uses by governmental and other similar institutions. They belong, in other words, to what photographer and critic Allan Sekula calls, in his influential essay "The Body and the Archive," "a double system: a system of representation capable of functioning both *honorifically* and *repressively*."[9] X-rays, though technically documents as well, are not among the images that usually make up such histories of migration photography. This exclusion may be attributed in part to their evidentiary status. As examples of the genre of "applied photography," which serve "to testify to a *present* state of affairs" that can be acted upon, they seem to belong to a different category of documentary photography, one that Sekula, in an essay from 1975, terms as *instrumental*.[10]

Sekula first develops his ideas about instrumental images in relation to Edward Steichen's work in the First World War as the commander of US aerial reconnaissance operations in France. He notes that the reconnaissance photographs produced under Steichen's command came about because of "fundamental *tactical* concerns." Moreover, "These pictures," he continues, "carried an almost wholly denotative significance [...] and seemed to have been devoid of any rhetorical structure."[11] For Sekula, in other words, instrumental images "need no interpretation in order to work; or, rather," as human rights scholar Thomas Keenan more recently has reflected, "they include something like interpretation as part of the image-making process."[12] This evidentiary status renders instrumental images different; unlike photographs usually categorized as documentary, there is nothing to unmask or deconstruct in instrumental images because what they depict and what they mean are one and the same. But, of course, those familiar with Sekula's writings about "the folklore of photographic truth,"[13] know the importance of the qualifier "seemed" in his above statement about the "rhetorical structure" of instrumental images. Though these photographs may "seem" objective and are "apparently free from 'higher meaning',"[14] they are still capable of being used for other ideological purposes including, in the case of the reconnaissance photographs overseen by Steichen, for the art market. Even so, what is key for Sekula is that, while this usage depends on the evidentiary potential of instrumental images, it also transcends this status. This is because an instrumental image's position as evidence is tethered not to its referent, nor to that of which it is a trace, but rather to its conditions, namely how it is used, which in turn is always in flux and indeterminate. In short, "the only 'objective' truth," about instrumental images, Sekula explains, "is the assertion that somebody or something [...] was somewhere and took a picture. Everything else, everything beyond the imprinting of a trace, is up for grabs."[15]

By "up for grabs," Sekula infers that the significance of evidence—"the imprinting of a trace"—lies not in what it depicts but in how it is read. This is because, returning to Keenan, evidence "does not speak for itself," which makes the act of reading of it, "a 'forensic' sensibility." In making this connection, Keenan relies on what seems, at first glance, to be a counterintuitive definition of forensics. Whereas the term *forensics* is most often associated with scientific analysis, especially in relation to a criminal investigation, Keenan turns to its Latin origin: "*forensis*, which refers to the 'forum' and the practice and skill of making an argument before a professional, political, or legal gathering." Using this definition, Keenan proposes that forensics is "not simply about science in the service of law or the police but is, much more broadly, about objects as they become evidence, things submitted for interpretation in an effort to persuade."[16] He calls this practice "counter-forensics," an inversion that he credits to Sekula. This framework of *counter-forensics* provides the basis for my discussion of Hasbun's series *X post facto* and its mediation of the experiences of trauma, migration, and war that are so central to the figure of the migrant and the Central American migrant in particular.

Sekula initially uses the neologism *counter-forensics* in his 1993 essay, "Photography and the Limits of National Identity."[17] This short piece of writing, which Sekula updated in 2006, centers on Magnum photographer Susan

Meiselas's efforts to build a public archive of the history of the Kurdish people, whose struggle to create a homeland was impeded at the end of World War I, when the Middle East was carved into its modern-day nation-states. Today, the Kurds, who number around thirty million people, live on mountainous land that forms parts of eastern Turkey, northern Syria, northern Iraq, and northwestern Iran, thus making them one of the largest ethnic groups of stateless people.[18] Meiselas began this archival project in 1991, after seeing the exhumation of mass graves in northern Iraq caused by Saddam Hussein's genocidal campaign against the Kurds in 1987 and 1988. Moved by her experiences there, Meiselas's six-year project on Kurdistan is a monumental visual history of a people who otherwise have no national archive.[19]

Written in response to this project by Meiselas, Sekula's essay examines how forensic methods, including surveillance and cataloging, have been used against the Kurds in both the modern and premodern periods as a "display of power" and "a tool of oppressive states." But Sekula does not end his discussion there. Instead, somewhat unexpectedly in the middle of his essay, he appends the following statement: "but forensic methods have also become tools of opposition."[20] Here, Sekula shifts his largely Foucauldian argument about the repressive uses of photography to one that takes up the medium's humanistic potential. But not "the bogus humanism," as Sekula calls it in "The Instrumental Image," generally thought of in relation to the efforts of so-called concerned (documentary) photography to depict universal human equality.[21] Rather, this humanism, returning to Keenan, is "a *basic* one." Keenan continues: "Basic precisely to the extent that it refers not to abstract metaphysical foundations but rather to the traces of specific individuals and events, the testimony of the bones and the images."[22] In linking forensics practices to an oppositional politics, Sekula harnesses photography's evidentiary potential to "a process of political resistance and mourning,"[23] or what he calls *counter-forensics*. For Sekula, then, this act of reading "the traces of specific individuals and events"[24] is fundamentally human, because it is part of a political struggle to name those who have disappeared and thereby safeguard, he explains, using the words of Albert Camus, "that something once existed in this place."[25]

The work of forensic anthropologist Clyde Snow, whom Meiselas photographed as part of her Kurdistan project, holding the blindfolded skull of an executed male teenager, exemplifies this approach.[26] In his anthropological work, Sekula explains, Snow adopts the identificatory tactics of forensic science through his

exhumation and identification of the anonymized ("disappeared") bodies of the oppressor state's victims [...] first, in Argentina with survivors of the "dirty war," then in El Salvador at the massacre site of El Mozote, and then again with the remains of the Iraqi campaign of extermination of the Kurds.[27]

But unlike the regime of the state, which has used such evidence to repress and annihilate, Snow's forensic work functions differently. Like Meiselas's archival project on Kurdistan, which likewise evolved from documenting evidence of the genocide and exile of the Kurdish people to gathering a visual history that portrayed their desire for a homeland, Snow's work counters the tactics of forensics as "dismal sciences" by placing this evidence in service of "a humanism of mournful reindividuation." And, in so doing, as Sekula notably elaborates, "[lays] the groundwork for a collective memory of suffering."[28]

Hasbun's series *X post facto* seems to functions in an analogous way. In her artist statement, Hasbun likens the process of selecting the images for her series from the over one thousand X-rays in her father's archive, to the work of a "medical examiner or forensic anthropologist."[29] In making these references to scientific investigation, Hasbun evokes the use of dental records as physical evidence in alleged human rights abuse cases. A relatively recent phenomenon, forensic odontology is often associated with the practices of the Argentine Forensic Anthropology Team (Equipo Argentino de Antropología Forense, EAAF), whose members in the early 1980s sought to recover and identify individuals from the over nine thousand "disappeared ones," or *desaparecidos*, eliminated by government death squads during Argentina's "dirty war," or *guerra sucia*.[30] The forensic methods developed by this team were subsequently applied to human rights cases in countries ranging from Chile, Guatemala, and the Philippines, to Sri Lanka, El Salvador, Ethiopia, Iraqi Kurdistan, and the former Yugoslavia.[31]

Although Hasbun initially likens her encounter with the X-rays in her father's dental archive to forensic work, the instrumentality of the X-rays quickly surpasses this evidentiary function of recovery and identification. Returning to her artist statement, Hasbun explains: "*X post facto* would become an emotional register for my experience during and after the Salvadoran civil war."[32] Here, Hasbun suggests that the *forensic* significance of her father's dental X-rays both lies in as well as exceeds their status as evidence or as traces. This is because, returning to the Latin origin of *forensics*, her father's dental X-rays hold not only scientific value but, more critically, the potential to be used as part of an argument about the Salvadoran Civil War. This means that, as traces, their meanings are "up for grabs."[33] It is precisely this indeterminacy that renders them political and, returning to Sekula, "[lays] the groundwork for a collective memory of suffering."[34] Hasbun also recognizes this political maneuvering. In her artist statement, she extrapolates further that the X-rays in her father's archive resonated not only personally but also collectively:

> The 32 photographs of *X post facto* […] link me to the faces of those who perished or to the phantom limbs of those who suffered violence in my country of origin […] They mediate a site where we might explore the territory of our shared history.[35]

It would seem, then, that Hasbun's series belongs to what Sekula identifies as the practice of *counter-forensics*.

Even as Hasbun seeks to employ her father's X-rays for political as well as collective ends, several crucial differences remain between her series and the counter-forensics that Sekula associates with Meiselas and, by extension, Snow. For Sekula, Meiselas's Kurdistan project, which builds off the Snow's forensic work, is fundamentally a nationalist project. This does not mean that Sekula believes that Meiselas wants to create a coherent or stable image of Kurdish national identity. Rather, as the range and even contradictions within Meiselas's visual archive of the Kurds make clear, the images in the archive are "constructed from discontinuous and even mutually antagonistic sources," which, most significantly, she uses to attach names to the bodies of those who had previously been "anonymized ('disappeared')" so that "the project of building a usable archive of the Kurdish 'nation' begins."[36] It is through this process of re-individuation, which functions directly in opposition to the annihilation of individual subjects by the state, that the nation building in Meiselas's project commences. In her project, however, Hasbun is less interested in how the X-rays in her father's archive might be harnessed for re-individuation purposes to create a national archive in opposition to the state. Instead, Hasbun uses the evidentiary nature of these X-rays to make a different kind of political argument. She uses the *forensic* significance or instrumentality of the dental records not as oppositional tools but as a means to build community and, more specifically, *visual solidarity* across national divides and linear temporalities.[37] To make this visual solidarity possible, the framework of Sekula's counter-forensics must shift from a national context to a transnational one so as to emphasize not only the ways in which evidence circulates across space and over time but also how these systems of circulation and exchange—or contact zones—produce what feminist scholar Sara Ahmed terms "affective economies" that work to "align individuals with communities—or bodily space with social space—through the very intensity of their attachments."[38]

For Ahmed, feelings and emotions do not belong to or "reside in" subjects or objects. Rather, as a result of their circulation between subjects and objects, certain feelings and emotions attach or "stick" to them. Ahmed explains that "emotions work as a form of capital: affect does not reside positive in the sign or commodity, but is produced only as an effect of its circulation."[39] This means that, like monetary value, which in a capitalist economy becomes attached to commodities, certain subjects and objects accumulate affect as these emotions circulate over time and across space. Through the effect or accumulation of this "sticking," subjects and objects are bound together into collectives. But whereas Ahmed theorizes this attachment in her essay "Affective Economies," in reference to how hate and fear work within discourses on asylum and migration to transform otherwise incongruous figures into a "common" threat, I take up how feelings of pain and suffering, or trauma more broadly, bind subjects and objects together in solidarity with one another. In making this argument, my claim is not that the X-rays in Hasbun's series *X post facto* depict pain and suffering. Rather, my focus is how these feelings of trauma have become bound or stuck to them across space and over time. To begin to unravel this attachment process, it is necessary to turn to a photograph of Hasbun's second cousin, Janet (Yanet) Samour Hasbun.[40]

Hasbun first encountered Janet's photograph in 2006, during a visit to Perquín, El Salvador (Fig. 4).[41] Located in the eastern region of El Salvador, in an area known as Morazán, Perquín was a site of intense fighting during the country's brutal and protracted civil war, which killed approximately seventy-five thousand of its citizens, wounded three hundred fifty thousand more, and displaced nearly one million, many of whom, like Hasbun, migrated to the United States. To honor the revolutionaries who died during the conflict, in 1992, at the end of the civil war, a group of guerillas from Morazán founded the Museo de la Revolución Salvadoreña. At this museum, among images of other fallen revolutionary heroes, anti-war posters, and weapons used by the guerrillas to battle the Salvadoran National Guard, Hasbun encountered Janet's photograph.

Prior to viewing this image, the last time that Hasbun recollects seeing Janet was at age ten; Hasbun remembers Janet at that age as "a beauty queen, with long black hair."[42] But in this photograph, as she reminisces in her artist statement, Janet appeared different. She no longer looks particularly feminine but instead wears the de facto uniform—pants, backpack, and camouflage hat—of the People's Revolutionary Army (El Ejército Revolucionario del Pueblo, ERP), one of the five leftist guerrilla organizations that make up the Farabundo Martí National Liberation Front (Frente Farabundo Martí para la Liberación Nacional, FMLN).[43] Moreover, in her right hand, she steadied a M-16 rifle, thereby confirming her status, as the photograph's caption identifies her, as Comandante Filomena.

For Hasbun, seeing Janet as Comandante Filomena was initially disorienting. The photograph, as she explains, depicted "an utterly different reality, unspoken and untold,"[44] from what she remembered about her cousin. But these personal feelings of perplexity and confusion were quickly replaced with ones of pain and suffering. In December 1984, as the photograph's caption continues, Janet was captured in the town of San Miguel. One month later, she was assassinated by Biri Arce, one of the six Rapid Reaction Infantry Battalions (Batallones de Infantería de Reacción Inmediata, BIRIs) formed in the early 1980s, with the training and assistance of the United States.[45] Moreover, as Hasbun remembers while looking at the photograph, when Janet's remains were eventually recovered, her father who sometimes received requests to use his dental archive to assist with the identification of bodies of the disappeared and other victims of El Salvador's civil war had been

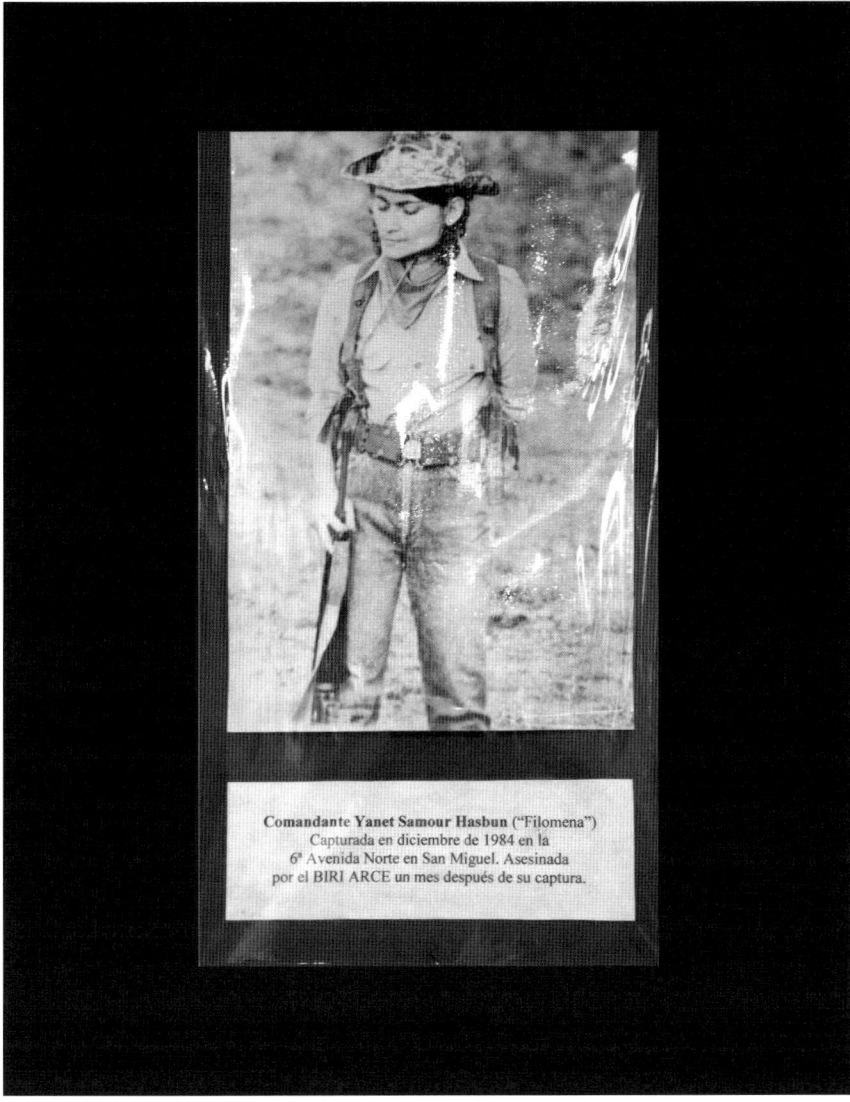

Figure 4: Muriel Hasbun, *Comandante Filomena*, Museo de la Revolución, Perquín, El Salvador, archival pigment print, 2012/2017. Courtesy of the artist.

asked to confirm the identification of Janet's murdered body. "His dental archive," however, "could not produce casts or X-rays of her smile," since, as Hasbun distinctively recalls her father telling her, "She was never his patient."[46] Here, it becomes apparent how the feelings evoked by Janet's photograph shift as Hasbun recognizes, first, that Janet no longer resembles Hasbun's memory of her and, second, that Hasbun's own father had been asked to identify Janet's tortured body.

These traumatic feelings shift yet again when, several years later, Hasbun begins to sort through her father's dental archive after having returned with them to the United States. It is then that the "memory" of both seeing Janet's photograph in the Museo de la Revolución Salvadoreña and of hearing her father's story about Janet's remains, comes into her "consciousness like a lightning bolt."[47] Yet, unlike the pain and suffering that Hasbun initially feels while looking at the photograph of Janet, the emotions, in this instance, are not a result of what or even who her father's dental X-rays depict. These feelings, in other words, do not reside in these images. Rather, they become attached, or "stick" to them, returning to Ahmed, through Hasbun's recognition, or "naming," of them. This is because, as Ahmed explains, "emotions may not have a referent, but naming an emotion has effects that we can describe as referential."[48] Here, it is clear, again, how the forensic significance of her father's dental X-rays both depend on as well as exceed their referential status. Her father's dental X-rays hold not only scientific value; more critically, returning once more to the Latin origin of *forensics*, they have the potential to be used as part of an affective and visual argument about the Salvadoran Civil War.

In her artist statement, Hasbun further address the limitations of her father's X-rays as forensic science. Even though X-rays have historically played a prominent role as evidence in human rights cases, the images in her father's dental archive cannot participate in such a re-individuation process of Janet since, as Hasbun's father explains, "she was never his patient." But for Hasbun, the limitations of these images do not end there. It is not just that they cannot identify Janet but, more pertinently, that they are unable to produce a record of "her smile." In making this affective distinction, Hasbun alludes to the limitations of photography's truth value and, in so doing, calls attention to the uncertainty of photography's, and more pertinently, the X-ray's evidentiary status. Yet, for Hasbun, establishing photography's indeterminacy comes not from an ontological interest in the medium. For her, it remains critical that the X-rays still function as "relics, traces, signposts,"[49] as she calls them. In short, their indexicality, and by extension, their referentiality, matter. But this instrumentality centers not on what or even who they depict but rather on what they cause her to feel and, by extension, remember. Hasbun's title for her series, *X post facto*—a play on *ex post facto*, which is Latin for "from a thing done afterward"—speaks to this distinction. It is not the referentiality of the trace that is noteworthy but what impact it makes *after the fact* or across space and over time. It is here that Hasbun's project differs most significantly from Sekula's theorization of *counter-forensics*. Whereas Sekula develops this term in relation to the prospect of Kurdish nation building and in opposition to the state, for Hasbun, *counter-forensics* provides a way to build affective familial and national relationships, or visual solidarities, across and over spatial and temporal divides.

The collective feelings of trauma referenced by these X-rays depend not only on Hasbun's encounter with Janet's photograph in the Museo de la Revolución Salvadoreña. They are likewise contingent on Janet's position as a symbol. Janet joined the ERP sometime in the mid 1970s, while she was studying philosophy (concurrently with Hasbun's mother) at the Universidad Centroamericana José Simeón Cañas, a private Jesuit university in San Salvador. As part of the ERP, Janet rose in the ranks to become Comandante Filomena, as she is pictured in the photograph that hangs in the Museo de la Revolución Salvadoreña, in her de facto uniform and with her rifle positioned by her side. In the image, in other words, her individual identity as Janet, including her position as a woman, is largely suppressed. Instead, along with her nom de guerre, she is presented as an *icon*, which as historians Thy Phu, Evyn Lê Espiritu, and Donya Ziaee argue elsewhere in relation to images of revolutionary Vietnamese woman, would have been used "to conjure a collective, a sense of solidarity made legible to individuals who position themselves in relation to the ideals associated with this icon."[50]

While this idealized photograph of Janet would have initially been used to arouse feelings of belonging in support of the Salvadoran insurgency, as the photograph moved in and through space and time, its affective potential shifted. Around December 30 or 31, 1984, Janet and her younger ERP colleague, Máximina Reyes Villatoro, were captured in the city of San Miguel. On January 2, 1985, the women were brought to San Salvador, where they were turned over to the Salvadoran National Guard. Because the Salvadoran government denied any involvement in or knowledge of the women's whereabouts and one of San Salvador's newspapers ran a story accusing the FMLN of trying to purge one of their own, three weeks after their capture, Radio Venceremos ("Radio Overcome"), the influential and clandestine radio station associated with the FMLN, sent out a broadcast stating that "both comrades continued to be detained by the intelligence agencies of the high command and to be submitted to strong physical and psychological torture, in addition to not being sent to any court of the regime and processed."[51] In addition to this broadcast, the FMLN also actively lobbied for the release of Janet as well as other Salvadoran revolutionaries detained by the Salvadoran National Guard through the networks associated with the Central American peace and solidarity movement. Made up of both US and Central American citizens, including Central American émigrés who had fled the violence of the region, this 1980s transnational social movement used various tactics, including visual images, to stop US aid to Central American governments and bring international attention to the region's humanitarian crisis, including the disappearances of individuals such as Janet.[52] But, like the X-rays that make up *X post facto*, it was less what or even who these images depicted that contributed to their emotional resonance. Rather, it was how these representations circulated transnationally across space and over time.

The reproduction of Janet's photographs on a poster, produced in 1985, through a partnership between a number of US-based Central American activist organizations, speaks to this transnational circulation (Fig. 5).[53] As part of this poster, Janet's photograph was paired with an image of Nidia Díaz, a high-ranking commander in the FMLN, who wears a camouflage hat and backpack similar to the ones Janet wears.[54] Although both photographs evoke feelings of solidarity and collectivity in terms of the Salvadoran insurgency, these affects are not bound to these figures. Like Janet and her younger colleague, Nidia Díaz was also captured, imprisoned, and tortured by the Salvadoran National Guard. To garner international support against these atrocities, the poster juxtaposes the photographs of these women revolutionaries with the following text addressed to the president of El Salvador, José Napoleón Duarte: 'We Demand That Duarte's Government Respect The Geneva Convention on POWs.' To further situate the women visually as prisoners of war, below the photographs appears an illustration of a blindfolded figure, hunched over, with arms crossed in pain. This figure, whose national identity is difficult to situate, becomes interchangeable with the women and in so doing, "constructs," returning to Ahmed, "a relation of resemblance between the figures."[55] No longer is the emotive potential of these women tied to the specificity of their situation as revolutionaries in the Salvadoran Civil War. Instead, the feelings of solidarity and collectivity initially evoked by Janet's photograph slides from Salvadoran guerilla to prisoner of war, whose human rights have been violated under the terms of international humanitarian law first set forth in the Geneva Convention of 1929. In short, the affective economy of Janet's photograph shifts from serving as an icon of the Salvadoran Civil War to that of an international prisoner of war.

Earlier that same year, Janet's photograph also appeared in publicity materials for an International Women's Day celebration held in March 1985, in Charlotte, North Carolina (Fig. 6). In the booklet *Southern Sisters: Heroines Making History*, produced for this event, the photograph is reproduced alongside a lengthy text, which, similar to the aforementioned poster, situates Janet in terms of human rights violations, represented by her capture and torture by the Salvadoran military. But whereas the poster evoked feelings of solidarity and collectivity in terms of prisoners of war, the reproduction of her photograph in this booklet again slides these emotions onto another set of subjects: the "everyday women […] who have provided," as the introduction to the booklet details, "outstanding leadership in the struggles for freedom, equality, and world peace,"[56] including South African educator Charlotte Maxeke, US labor organizer Ella May Wiggins, and African American activist Moranda Smith, who are each pictured on a separate page of the booklet. Through this visual juxtaposition of Janet with other "everyday women," as part of an International Women's Day celebration in the United States, viewers are encouraged to identify with Janet again in idealized terms. Her iconic power,

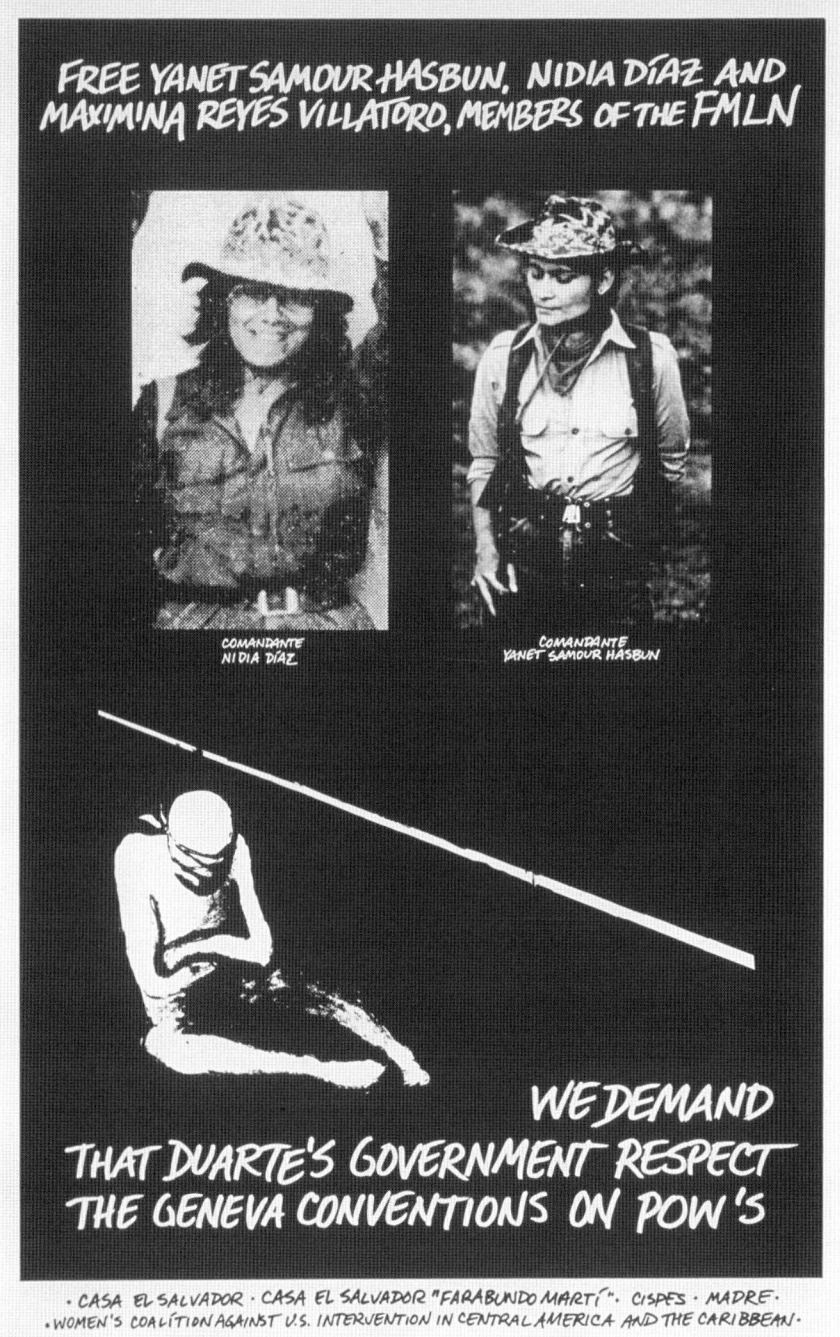

Figure 5: CISPES; Casa El Salvador F.M.; Casa El Salvador; Women's Coalition Against US Intervention in Central America and the Caribbean, *Free Yanet Samour Hasbun, Nidia Diaz And Maximina Reyes Villatoro, Members of the FMLN*, ca. 1985, 50.8 cm × 33 cm; 20 in × 13 in. Courtesy of the Center for the Study of Political Graphics.

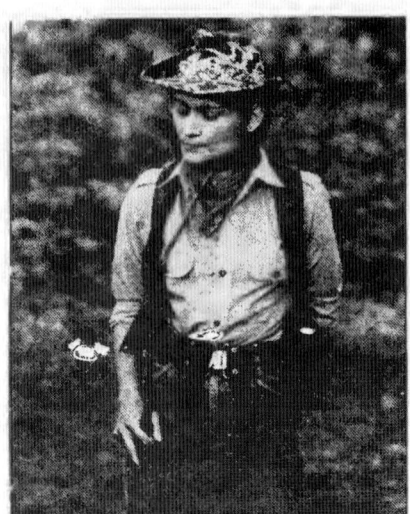

Captured Salvadoran Janet Samour Hasbun.

YANET SAMOUR HASBUN AND MAXIMINA REYES VILLATORO

These two Latin American heroines were captured by the
National Guard of El Salvador on December 30, 1984.
On January 2, 1985, they were placed in the custody of
the Central High Command of the Army, where they were
subjected to heavy physical and psychological torture.
Neither has been brought before a court of law. We
do not know where they are, or if they are still alive.

Companeras Yanet (34) and Maximina (26) joined the
national liberation movement in El Salvador because
they wanted to see a better life for thier people,
who were living in poverty and oppression, while a
few rich families owned everything.

The U.S. government has continued to support the
Salvadorean Army, which has committed many human rigts
violations, such as the torture of these two women.
Even as prisoners, they should have the right to trial.

An international solidarity movement is campaigning to
secure their release. Petitions will be available
at the International Women's Day program through CITCA,
Charolina Interfaith Task Force on Central America.

Figure 6: *Southern Sisters: Heroines Making History* (Charlotte: International Women's Day
Committee, 1985). Photo by Erina Duganne.

however, comes not just from her position as a Salvadoran revolutionary but from her status as a Third World *woman*. In other words, her image works to broker feelings of solidarity, or a commonality of experiences and political objectives, across different women's liberation movements around the globe, even when the figure in the image itself, as Hasbun noted when first seeing it in Perquín, lacks the feminine features that she remembers her cousin as having.

Janet gained further international notoriety when, later that same year, at the peak of the Salvadoran Civil War, she became one of the revolutionaries who were part of the initial negotiations for the release of Inés Guadalupe Duarte, the daughter of El Salvador's President José Napoleón Duarte. On September 10, 1985, FMLN guerillas kidnapped Inés and her friend, Ana Cecilia Villeda, from a private university in the capital of San Salvador. In response to this kidnapping, the Committee of the Mothers of the Disappeared, one of El Salvador's most active human rights groups, bought an advertisement in the local newspaper, *El Diario del Mundo*, in which they expressed hope for the quick return of Duarte's daughter but also implored the president to "open his heart […] free our imprisoned and disappeared relatives [and] stop the arbitrary arrests and tortures."[57] In response, on October 24, 1985, twenty-two left-wing political prisoners, including Nidia Díaz (featured in the poster with Janet) were released from Salvadoran jails as part of an exchange brokered between the FMLN and the Salvadoran government for the release of Duarte's daughter and her friend. Janet, who had most likely already been killed, was dropped from the deal.[58] Janet's photograph does not depict this tragic ending to her story, and neither do the X-rays that make up *X post facto*, since, after all, there was no record of her smile. Still, because the emotions of pain and suffering caused by the capture, torture, and death of Janet do not reside in her image, its affective economy, returning to Ahmed, is likewise not limited to what it depicts but rather depends on the emotions that accumulate as the photograph circulates across space and over time, including its display in the Museo de la Revolución Salvadoreña, where first Hasbun encounters it, and its subsequent elicitation, when Hasbun sorts through her father's dental archive after his death.

For Hasbun, as has already been noted, these affects manifested themselves not just personally but also collectively. In her artist statement, Hasbun writes that through her father's dental X-rays of teeth, cavities, and dental fixtures, she also felt the collective trauma of El Salvador's civil war, which, in turn, "link[ed] [her] to the faces of those who perished or to the phantom limbs of those who suffered violence in [her] country of origin" (Fig. 7).[59] This "align[ing] of individuals with communities," to borrow once more from Ahmed, is most evident in the installation of *X post facto* in the 2013 exhibition, *Inter Vivos: Margaret Adams, Gabriela Bulisova, Muriel Hasbun*. In this exhibition, on view at the Corcoran's Gallery 31 in Washington, DC, viewers engaged with Hasbun's *X post facto* series not just as

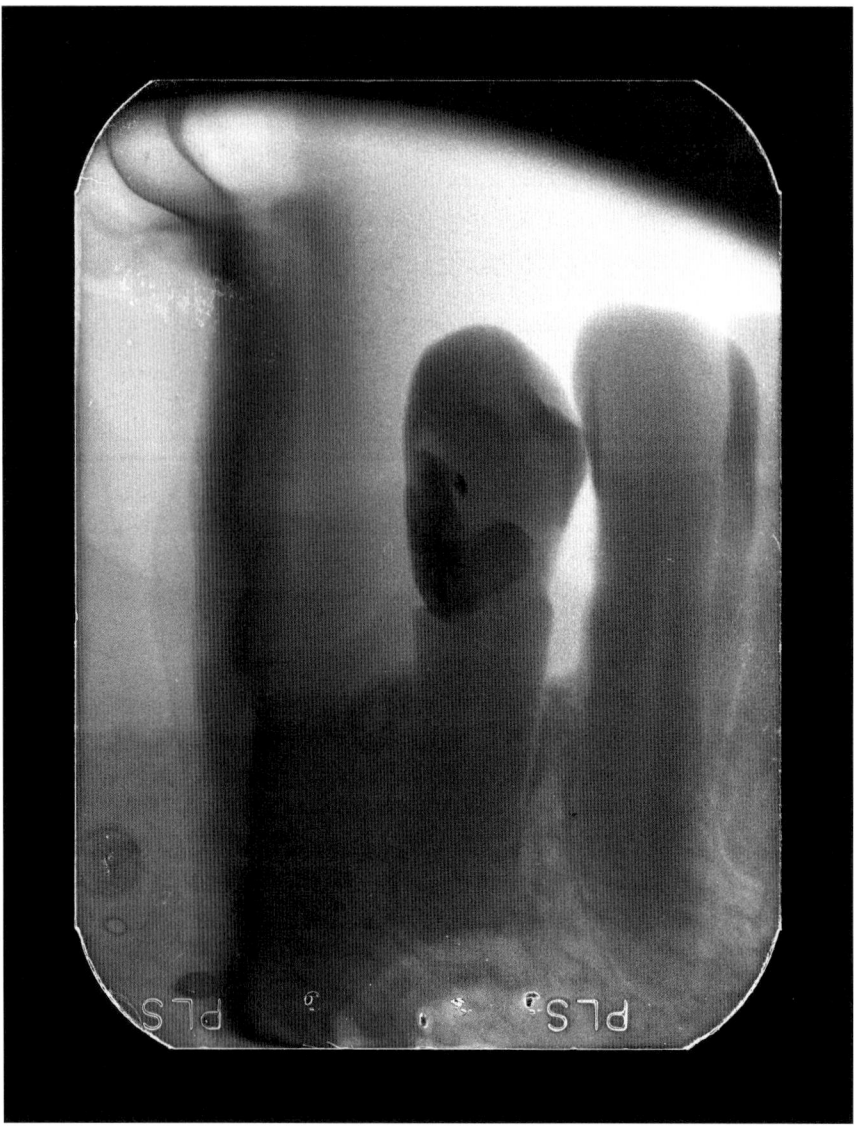

Figure 7: Muriel Hasbun, *X post facto* (12.3), archival pigment print, 2009/2013 (Plate 36, p. 359).
Courtesy of the artist.

images on the wall. In the center of the room, Hasbun assembled a rectangular
table on top of which she placed one of the X-rays from her father's dental archive
(Fig. 8). Over this image, which depicts mostly undefined gum tissue as opposed to
teeth, is a grid structure of interlocking black lines (similar to ones found on maps
to locate a specific region or area) used to measure depth and distance in the gums.

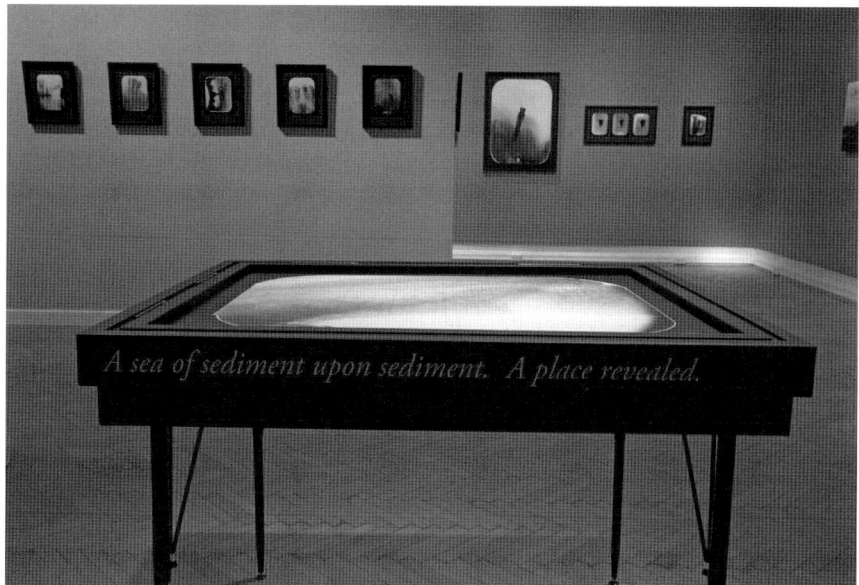

Figure 8: Installation view, *Inter Vivos: Margaret Adams, Gabriela Bulisova, Muriel Hasbun*, Corcoran Gallery of Art, Gallery 31, 2013 (Plate 37, p. 360). Photo by Muriel Hasbun.

Hasbun encouraged viewers to write and draw "their own stories of trauma occasioned by war" on top of this grid, which they did, both within the square shapes and outside of them, with statements and illustrations that both relate explicitly to trauma, migration, and war and, at the same time, have nothing to do with them at all. Together, these individual marks or traces become, as Hasbun writes on the side of the table in italicized letters, "A sea of sediment upon sediment. A place revealed." In so doing, the interactive table compiles, in Hasbun's words, "a collective archive that sheds light on the interconnections and shared experiences that exist between us, regardless of which nation's passport we might happen to carry."[60] It is here, then, returning to Sekula, that Hasbun's series as a framework of counter-forensics, which works not against but in between, crystalizes. More than a way to challenge and resist, *X post facto* uses photography's instrumentality and affective economy to build visual solidarity between migrant communities who become bound together in and through the contact spaces of the present and past, the individual and collective, as well as at home and abroad.

Notes

1. Muriel Hasbun, "Five Questions with Photographer Muriel Hasbun," Smithsonian American Art Museum, December 12, 2013, https://americanart.si.edu/blog/eye-level/2013/12/564/five-questions-photographer-muriel-hasbun.

2. Hasbun, "Five Questions."

3. In 1977, Hasbun's mother, Janine Janowski, became the founder and director of San Salvador's pioneering artist space and cultural center, Galería el laberinto, where she exhibited installations, performances, and conceptual art, in the midst of the violence of El Salvador's civil war. For more about Hasbun's mother as well as the innovative exhibitions that took place at Galería el laberinto, see Muriel Hasbun, "Galería el laberinto: Art in a Time of War," *Diálogo* 20, no. 1 (Spring 2017), 165–172. Today, the experimental nature of the gallery lives on through *laberinto projects*, a cultural memory and contemporary arts initiative that was founded by Hasbun, after her mother's death in 2012, to foster contemporary art practices, social inclusion, and dialogue in El Salvador and its diaspora. See also http://laberintoprojects.com/.

4. Hasbun, "Five Questions."

5. *Family Frames* superimposes a family portrait, taken by Hasbun's father, on top of an image of a bench, the first piece of furniture her parents owned.

6. Muriel Hasbun, "Artist Statement," emisférica: On the Subject of Archives 9, no. 1–2 (Summer 2012), *http://www.hemisphericinstitute.org/hemi/en/e91-hasbun-artist-statement*. For more on this series, see Sareh Afshar, "Tracing the Image, Imagining the Trace: Seeing Through, Looking Between, and Feeling with Muriel Hasbun's X post facto," emisférica: On the Subject of Archives 9, no. 1–2 (Summer 2012), www.hemisphericinstitute.org/hemi/en/e91-hasbun-essay.

7. Hasbun, "Five Questions."

8. While the literature on migration and documentary photography is vast, some recent publications include Sebastião Salgado, *Migrations: Humanity in Transition* (New York: Aperture, 2000); Anna Pegler-Gordon, *In Sight of America: Photography and the Development of U.S. Immigration Policy* (Berkeley: University of California Press, 2009); T.J. Demos, *The Migrant Image: The Art and Politics of Documentary during Global Crisis* (Durham: Duke University Press, 2013); Rebecca M. Schreiber, *The Undocumented Everyday: Migrant Lives and the Politics of Visibility* (Minneapolis: University of Minnesota Press, 2018).

9. Allan Sekula, "The Body and the Archive," *October* 39 (Winter 1986), 5, original emphasis. Pegler-Gordon, in *In Sight of America*, challenges Sekula's oppositional model of the honorific and repressive through the examples of Chinese immigration identity documentation as well as immigration official Augustus Sherman and documentary photographer Lewis Hine. Likewise, in her book, *Picturing Model Citizens: Civility in Asian American Visual Culture* (Philadelphia: Temple University Press, 2012), Thy Phu also complicates these binary terms.

10. Allan Sekula, "The Instrumental Image: Steichen at War," *Artforum* 14, no. 4 (December 1975), 27, original emphasis.

11. Sekula, "The Instrumental Image," 27, 28, original emphasis.

12. Thomas Keenan, "Counter-forensics and Photography," *Grey Room* 55 (Spring 2014), 54.

13. In his, "Dismantling Modernism, Reinventing Documentary (Notes on the Politics of Representation)," *Massachusetts Review* 19, no. 4 (Winter 1978), 862–863, Sekula identifies "the folklore of photographic truth," as the belief that photography "reproduces the visible world: the camera is an engine of fact, the generator of a duplicate world of fetishized appearances, independent of human practice."

14. Sekula, "The Instrumental Image," 28.

15. Sekula, "Dismantling Modernism, Reinventing Documentary," 863.

16. Keenan, "Counter-forensics," 68, original emphasis. Keenan further discusses a forensic approach and how it differs from a document or a witness in Thomas Keenan and Eyal Weizman, *Mengele's Skull: The Advent of a Forensic Aesthetics* (Berlin: Sternberg Press, 2012).

17. Allan Sekula, "Photography and the Limits of National Identity," *Grey Room* 55 (Spring 2014), 30. This essay was originally published in *Culturefront* 2, no. 3 (Fall 1993), 54–55. The *Grey Room* version was revised with an afterword. This revised version was also published as "A Portable National Archive for a Stateless People: Susan Meiselas and the Kurds," in *Camera Austria* 95 (Autumn 2002), 9–11; and in Kristen Lubben, (ed.), *Susan Meiselas: In History* (New York/Göttingen: International Center of Photography/Steidl, 2008), 342–344. For an excellent discussion of Sekula's shift in this essay to embrace photography's testimonial potential, see Keenan, "Counter-forensics."

18. For a general overview of Kurdistan's complicated political history and identity, see Carole O'Leary and Charles G. MacDonald (eds.), *Kurdish Identity: Human Rights and Political Status* (Gainesville: University Press of Florida, 2007).

19. Meiselas's project culminated in the 1997 book *Kurdistan: In the Shadow of History*, a hundred-year photographic history of Kurdistan that integrated her own work as well as images and accounts by colonial administrators, anthropologists, missionaries, soldiers, journalists, and others who travelled to Kurdistan over the previous century, including the Kurds themselves. In addition to the book, in 1998 Meiselas produced an online archive of collective memory and cultural exchange, www.akakurdistan.com, as well as a traveling exhibition. The book is now in its second edition. See Susan Meiselas, *Kurdistan: In the Shadow of History*, 2nd edition (Chicago: University of Chicago Press, 2008).

20. Sekula, "Photography and the Limits of National Identity," 30.

21. Sekula, "The Instrumental Image," 32.

22. Keenan, "Counter-forensics," 72, original emphasis.

23. Sekula, "Photography and the Limits of National Identity," 30.

24. Keenan, "Counter-forensics," 72.

25. Sekula, "Photography and the Limits of National Identity," 30.

26. Meiselas's photograph of Dr. Clyde Snow also appears as a figure illustration in Sekula's "Photography and the Limits of National Identity," 28.

27. Sekula, "Photography and the Limits of National Identity," 30–31.

28. Sekula, "Photography and the Limits of National Identity," 30–31.

29. Hasbun, "Artist Statement."

30. Though the term *dirty war* derives from the French phrase *la sale guerre*, which was used by French leftist intellectuals to describe the First Indochina War, it subsequently came to be associated with state repression, first as part of the Algerian conflict of 1954 to 1962, and then, most notably, in Argentina from 1976 to 1983, during which some ten thousand persons were disappeared by the military junta. For a discussion of the etymology and shifting meanings of *dirty war*, see M.L.R. Smith and Sophie Rogers, "War in Gray: Exploring the Concept of Dirty War," *Studies in Conflict & Terrorism* 31, no. (2008), 377–298.

31. A history of the EAAF can be found at http://eaaf.typepad.com/, and in Luis Fondebrider and Vivian Scheinsohn, "Forensic archaeology: the Argentinian way," in W.J. Mike Groen, Nicholas Márquez-Grant, and Robert C. Janaway (eds.), *Forensic Archaeology: A Global Perspective* (Chichester: Wiley-Blackwell, 2015), 369–378. For a general overview of forensic odontology, see Lowell J. Levine, "The Role of the Forensic Odonatologist in Human Rights Investigations," *The American Journal of Forensic Medicine and Pathology* 5, no. 4 (December 1984), 317–320.

32. Hasbun, "Artist Statement."

33. Sekula, "Dismantling Modernism, Reinventing Documentary," 863.

34. Sekula, "Photography and the Limits of National Identity," 30, 31.

35. Hasbun, "Artist Statement."

36. Sekula, "Photography and the Limits of National Identity," 31.

37. I use the term *visual solidarity* to suggest how photography's ubiquity—or its ability to move across time and space—opens up the possibility for affective, transnational connections to take place between photographers, spectators, and subjects. I explore this concept further in my "Group Material's 'Art for the Future': Visualizing Inter-American Solidarity at the End of the Global Cold War," in Thy Phu, Andrea Noble, and Erina Duganne (eds.), *Cold War Camera* (Durham: Duke University Press, 2022).

38. Sara Ahmed, "Affective Economies," *Social Text* 22, no. 2 (Summer 2004), 119. For a related discussion of how emotional ties allowed the British empire to make and re-make itself across vast spatial distances, see Jane Lydon, *Imperial Emotions: The Politics of Empathy across the British Empire* (Cambridge: Cambridge University Press, 2020).

39. Ahmed, "Affective Economies," 121.

40. In addition to Yanet, Janet is also referenced in some publications as Janeth. See, for instance, Tommie Sue Montgomery, *Revolution in El Salvador: From Civil Strife to Civil*

Peace, 2nd edition (Boulder: Westview Press, 1995), 17. Janet's and Hasbun's fathers were cousins, but not first cousins in the same generation. The relationship extends back to Hasbun's paternal grandfather and Janet's maternal grandfather. There might also be another family relationship through the Samour side as well (Janet's paternal side and Hasbun's father's maternal side), because both these Bethlehem families intermarried over the generations. Janet was younger than Hasbun's father by about twenty years and older than Hasbun by about ten years. Hasbun's father photographed Janet as a young girl and, in Hasbun's artist talks, she often shows a picture of Janet as a toddler made by her father, along with the photograph of Janet from the Museo de la Revolución. See Muriel Hasbun, email conversation with author, March 28, 2018.

41. This trip was Hasbun's first visit to Perquín, and the first time since she was fifteen years old, that she had returned to this part of her home country.

42. Hasbun, "Artist Statement."

43. The FMLN formed in October 1980, out of five revolutionary groups, in opposition to El Salvador's repressive military government The five groups included the Popular Liberation Forces Farabundo Marti (Fuerzas Populares de Liberación Farabundo Marti, FPL), the People's Revolutionary Army (Ejército Revolucionario del Pueblo, ERP); the National Resistance (Resistencia Nacional, RN); the Revolutionary Party of the Central American Workers (Partido Revolucionario de los Trabajadores Centroamericanos, PRTC), and the Salvadoran Communist Party (Partido Comunista de El Salvador, PCS). The formation of the FMLN from these groups is part of a complex trajectory that draws on a long history of social movements and international organizing that took place in both the urban centers and rural countryside. For an overviews of the Salvadoran Civil War, see Montgomery, *Revolution in El Salvador*; Hugh Byrne, *El Salvador's Civil War: A Study of Revolution* (Boulder: Lynne Rienner, 1996); William Stanley, *The Protection Racket State: Elite Politics, Military Extortion and Civil War in El Salvador* (Philadelphia: Temple University Press, 1996); and Elisabeth Jean Wood, *Insurgent Collective Action and Civil War in El Salvador* (Cambridge: Cambridge University Press, 2003).

44. Hasbun, "Artist Statement."

45. Of the six BIRIs, all of them airmobile and each with about one thousand specially trained men, the most notorious was the Atlacatl Battalion, which carried out the El Mozote massacre in December 1981 and the murder of six Jesuit priests, their housekeeper, and her daughter in November 1989. See Human Rights Watch, *El Salvador's Decade of Terror: Human Rights Since the Assassination of Archbishop Romero* (New Haven: Yale University Press, 1991); and Mark Danner, *The Massacre at El Mozote* (New York: Vintage Books, 1994).

46. Hasbun, "Artist Statement."

47. Hasbun, "Artist Statement."

48. Sara Ahmed, *The Cultural Politics of Emotion*, 2nd edition (New York: Routledge, 2012), 14.

49. Hasbun, "Artist Statement."

50. Thy Phu, Evyn Lê Espiritu, and Donya Ziaee, "Icon of Solidarity: The Revolutionary Vietnamese Woman in Vietnam, Palestine, and Iran," in *Cold War Camera*, forthcoming. For more on the overlooked history of political solidarity between Vietnam and Palestine during the Third World Liberation movement, see Evyn Lê Espiritu, "Cold War Entanglements, Third World Solidarities: Vietnam and Palestine, 1967–75," *Canadian Review of American Studies* 48, no. 3 (Winter 2018), 352–386.

51. Radio Venceremos, quoted in Annie Cabrera, "Rebels Say Army Guerrilla Captured Commander and Another Woman," *AP News*, January 22, 1985, https://www.apnews.com/5d1f3b066c7ce71d34f42eb46f1c7548. For more on Radio Venceremos, see Carlos Henríquez Consalvi, *Broadcasting the Civil War in El Salvador* (Austin: The University of Texas Press, 2010).

52. For general information on the Central American solidarity and peace movement, see Van Gosse, "'The North American Front': Central American solidarity in the Reagan Era," in Mike Davis and Michael Sprinker (eds.), *Reshaping the U.S. Left* (New York: Verso, 1988), 11–50; and Christian Smith, *Resisting Reagan* (Chicago: University of Chicago Press, 1996).

53. The partnership included the Committee in Solidarity with the People of El Salvador (or CISPES), Casa El Salvador, and the Women's Coalition Against US Intervention in Central America and the Caribbean.

54. For more on Nidia Díaz, see Nidia Díaz, *I Was Never Alone: A Prison Diary from El Salvador* (New York: Ocean, 1992).

55. Ahmed, "Affective Economies," 119.

56. *Southern Sisters: Heroines Making History* (Charlotte: International Women's Day Committee, 1985), n.p.

57. Quoted in Margaret Jayko, "22 Salvadoran Rebels Freed," *The Militant* 49, no. 43 (November 8, 1985), 8.

58. See Marlise Simons, "Daughter of Duarte is Released by Rebels in a Complex Exchange," *New York Times*, October 25, 1985, 1, 9.

59. Hasbun, "Artist Statement."

60. Hasbun, "Five Questions."

Contributors

Sarah Bassnett is an associate professor of art history at Western University in Canada. Her research focuses on the intersections of photography and social change, especially as it relates to issues of power and resistance. Her award-winning book, *Picturing Toronto: Photography and the Making of a Modern City* (McGill-Queen's University Press, 2016), looks at photography's role in the liberal reform of early twentieth-century Toronto. Her articles have been published in journals such as *Photography & Culture*, *Photographies*, and *History of Photography*. Her current research, funded by the Social Science and Humanities Research Council of Canada, examines the photography of twenty-first–century migration.

David Bate is a professor of photography at the University of Westminster, London, UK. He has published extensively on the history, theory, and practice of photography, including his books, *Photography as Critical Practice: Notes on Otherness* (Intellect 2020); *Photography: Key Concepts*, second edition (Routledge, 2019); *Art Photography* (Tate Publications, 2015); *Zone* (Artworks, 2012); and *Photography and Surrealism* (I.B. Tauris, 2004). Alongside many other publications and exhibitions of his own photographic artworks, he has also been a cofounding editor of the theoretical journal *Photographies* since 2008. He has lectured all over the world. He was a recipient of the Royal Photographic Society Education Award in 2018.

Justin Carville teaches historical and theoretical studies in photography at the Institute of Art, Design & Technology, Dún Laoghaire. A former government of Ireland Senior Research Scholar in the Humanities and Social Sciences and an IRCHSS Research Fellow in the Humanities and Social Sciences, he is the author of *Photography and Ireland* (Reaktion, 2011) and *Visualizing Dublin: Visual Culture, Modernity and the Representation of Urban Space* (Peter Lang, 2013). He is currently working on a book-length study on photography, governmentality, and race.

Erina Duganne is an associate professor of art history at Texas State University. Her research explores intersections between art and politics as well as race and its representation. She is the author of *The Self in Black and White: Race and Subjectivity in Postwar American Photography* (University Press of New England, 2010) and a coeditor of *Beautiful Suffering: Photography and the Traffic in Pain* (University of Chicago Press, 2007). She is currently working on three projects: *Artists Call: Building Visual Solidarity Across the Americas*, a study of transnational visual practices deployed as part of the 1984 ad hoc activist campaign Artists Call Against US Intervention in Central America; *Global Photography: A Critical Introduction,* a collaborative project that links international contemporary photographic practices with their historical pasts; and *Cold War Camera*, a comparative analysis of the visual mediation of the global Cold War.

Orla Fitzpatrick is a librarian, writer, and photographic historian from Dublin, Ireland. She writes a column for *Source* magazine on the photographic market. She is the librarian at the National Museum of Ireland and teaches photographic history in the Continuing Adult Education Department at the National College of Art and Design, Dublin.

Bridget Gilman is an independent scholar specializing in modern and contemporary art. Her research and writing concern the development of photographic media, the visual history of American cities and suburbs, and questions of ethics in image production and reception. Her current book project, *Chromatic Landscapes: The Politics of Color Photography in Postwar America*, focuses on the role of color photography in American struggles over race, class, and gender.

Aleksandra Idzior is an associate professor of art history and visual studies in the School of Creative Arts at the University of the Fraser Valley in Abbotsford, Canada. Educated in Poland (MA from Adam Mickiewicz University in Poznań) and Canada (MA and Ph.D. from the University of Toronto and University of British Columbia in Vancouver, respectively), she has taught art history in both countries. Alongside her teaching work, she has maintained an active contribution to conferences together with her writing for numerous exhibition catalogs and critical anthologies. She has published on a number of topics, ranging from the rendition of national politics and memory in the nineteenth-century history painting in Germany, Poland, and the United States, to the politics and utopian visualization of urban space in Moscow and New York during the late 1920s; and from the war and trauma in photomontages by Teresa Żarnower, to Ericka Walker's prints on colonial and wartime propaganda in North America. Her scholarly research has focused around a few areas related to artistic responses to social and political crisis. One has to do with the convergence of concepts related to frontiers, utopian imagination, and artistic intervention in urban space. The other is particularly involved with visualization of war, migration, exile, and trauma, intersected with memory and memorialization.

Alexandra Irimia is a PhD candidate at Western University in London, Ontario, with a background in comparative literature and political science. With studies completed in Bucharest, Prague, and Montreal, she is currently conducting research on text-image relations, bureaucratic poetics, and empty signifiers in literature and visual arts. Her work experience combines freelance translation projects with teaching and research assistantships in world literature, film studies, and image studies. Alexandra's writing and translations have been published in collective volumes, the most recent of which are *Socializing Art Museums: Rethinking the Public's Experience* (DeGruyter, 2020), *Working Through the Figure: Theory, Practice, Method* (Bucharest University Press, 2019), and *Usages de la figure, régimes de la figuration* (Bucharest University Press, 2017). She contributes to academic journals such as *Ekphrasis, MuseMedusa*, and *The Scattered Pelican*, and works as a peer reviewer for *TBA: Journal of Art, Media, and Visual Culture.*

Sigrid Lien, PhD, is a professor in art history and photography studies at the University of Bergen, Norway. She was project leader for the Norwegian team in the HERA-project PhotoClec: Museums, Colonial Past and Photography (2010–2012) and for Negotiating History: Photography in Sámi Culture (2014–2017). Lien has published extensively on nineteenth-century as well as modern and contemporary photography. Recent publications include *Pictures of Longing. Photography and the History of the Norwegian U.S.-migration,* (University of Minnesota Press, 2018) and, with Elizabeth Edwards, *Uncertain Images: Museums and the Work of Photographs* (Ashgate, 2014).

Sandra Križić Roban, is a critic, curator and senior research advisor at the Institute of Art History in Zagreb; and the lead investigator on the scholarly project Ekspozicija – Themes and Aspects of Croatian Photography from the 19th Century until Today (2020–2024), funded by the Croatian Science Foundation. Her research topics include contemporary art, the history and theory of photography, postwar architecture, and contemporary war memorials in Croatia. As the head of the Office for Photography, established in 2013 as a nonprofit association dedicated to contemporary photography, she is responsible for the program of Gallery Spot, and national and international research projects (Forgotten Heritage, Not Yet Written Stories, Common Photographic Narratives). Her publications include *At Second Glance. The Positions of Contemporary Croatian Photography* (Institute of Art History/UPI-2M, 2010); *Croatian Painting from 1945 until Today: Responsibility of Image at the Time of Impatient Look* (Ljevak, 2013); *Anabel Zanze – Text in Tension*

(HAZU, 2019), *Vlado Martek – Preparing for Photography* (UzF, 2018), and *Hana Miletić – Street Photography* (UzF, 2016).

Helene Roth is a research assistant of art history at the Ludwig-Maximilians-Universität (LMU) in Munich and a member of the Gesellschaft für Exilforschung e.V. (Society for Exile Studies). Since September 2017, she is associated with the ERC Project Global Metropolises, Modern Art and Exile (METROMOD). Her research areas are the art and photography of the twentieth and twenty-first century with a specification focus on exile, migration, urbanity, architecture, and fashion. Her recent publications include "The Bar Sammy's Bowery Follies as Microcosm and Photographic Milieu Study for Emigrated European Photographers in 1930's and 40's New York," in Burcu Dogramaci et al. *Arrival Cities. Migrating Artists and New Metropolitan Topographies in the 20th century* (Leuven University Press, 2020); with Mareike Hetschold et al., "Lebensrouten der Emigration: Abreise, Passage, (Zwischen-)Exil und Ankunft," in Burcu Dogramaci, Berenika Szymanski-Düll, Wolfgang Rathert, *Leave, left, left. Migrationsphänomene in den Künsten in aktueller und historischer Perspektive* (Neofelis Verlag 2020), 105–126; with Burcu Dogramaci, *Nomadic Camera. Fotografie, Exil und Migration*, special issue of the *Zeitschrift für Fotogeschichte. Beiträge zur Geschichte und Ästhetik der Fotografie*, no. 151 (2019); and coedited with Burcu Dogramaci, "Fotografie als Mittler im Exil: Fotojournalismus bei Picture Post in London und Fototheorie und -praxis an der New School for Social Research in New York," in *VermittlerInnen zwischen den Kulturen, Zeitschrift für Museum und Bildung*, 86–87 (2019), 13–44.

Leslie Ureña is the associate curator of photographs at the Smithsonian National Portrait Gallery, Washington, DC. A historian of photography, her research and exhibitions focus on migration, transnational art practices, and photography as an agent of social change. Prior to arriving at the Portrait Gallery, Ureña worked in the Department of Photographs at the National Gallery of Art, in Washington, DC, and the Department of Photography at the Museum of Modern Art (New York), as well as in curatorial departments at the Dallas Museum of Art, the Walters Art Museum, and the Yale University Art Gallery. She has also taught courses on the history of photography and modern art in Washington, DC; Taipei, Taiwan; and New York. Her writing has appeared in exhibition catalogs, on *Artforum.com, caa. reviews*, and *ART iT*, and in the *International Journal for History, Culture and Modernity*. Ureña received a BA in art history from Yale University and an MA and PhD in art history from Northwestern University.

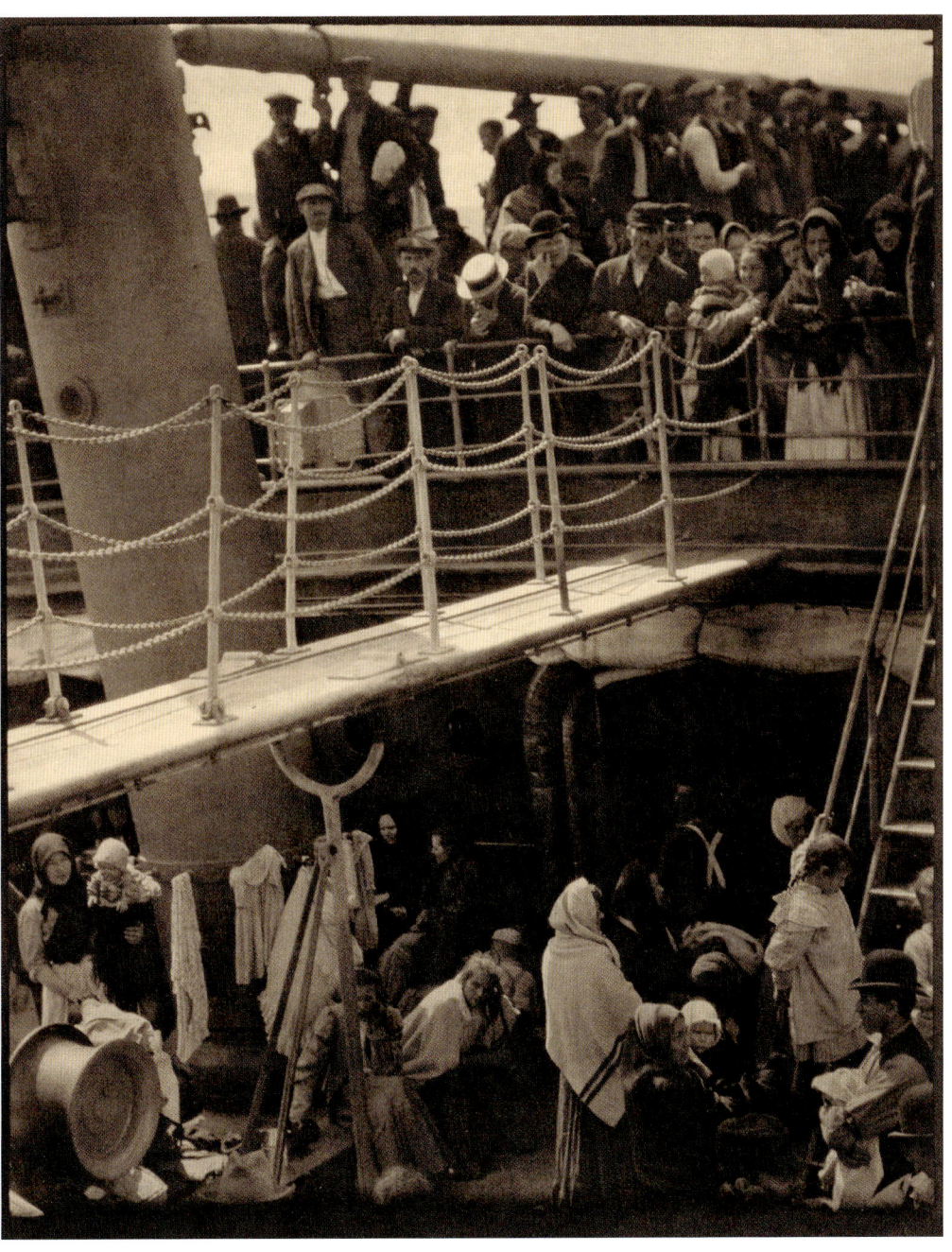

Plate 1: Alfred Stieglitz, *The Steerage*, 1907 (Fig. 4, p. 38). National Gallery of Scotland, presented by Mrs. Elizabeth Uldall in memory of her sister, Ruth Anderson, 1998.

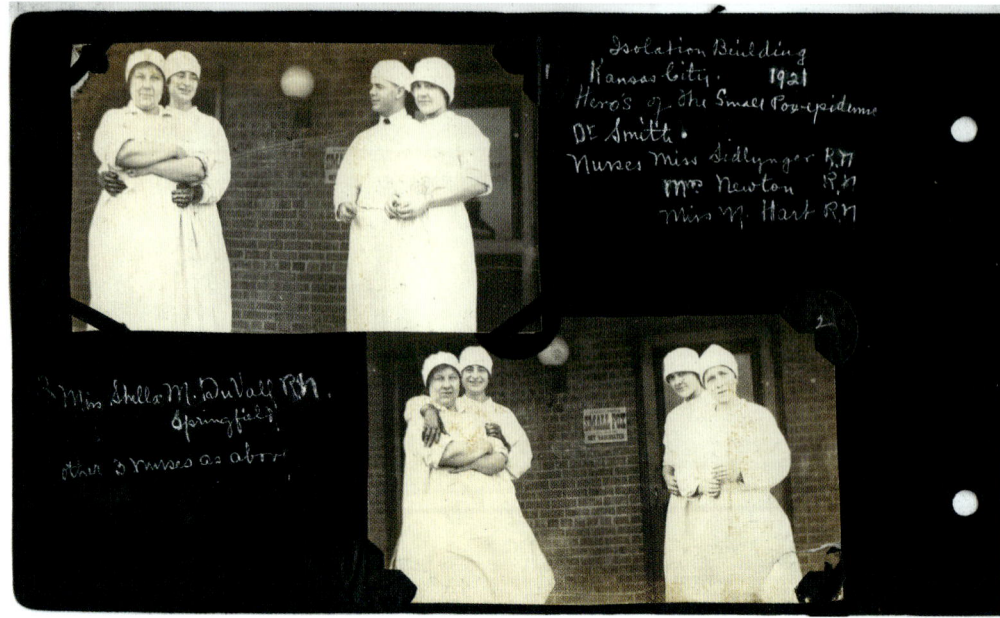

Plate 2: Kansas City Hospital, Smallpox epidemic, 1921 (Fig. 1, p. 62). Page from Whitfield album, snapshots on craft paper, ink captions. Source: Author's collection.

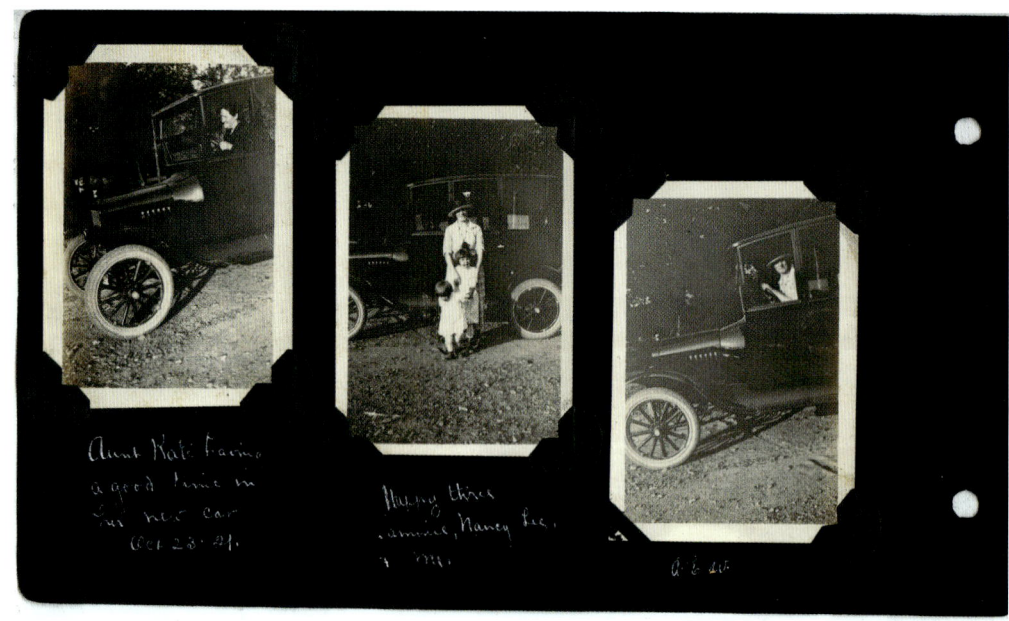

Plate 3: Aunt Kate and her new car, 1922 (Fig. 5, p. 67). Page from Whitfield family album, snapshots on craft paper, ink captions. Source: Author's collection.

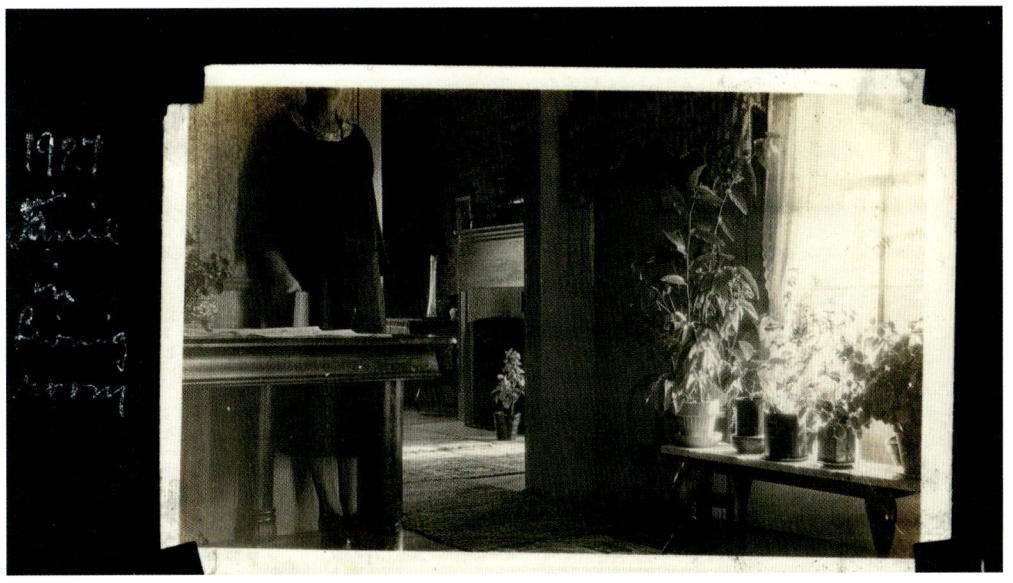

Plate 4: Interior of Whitfield/Bradbury farmhouse, Jasper, Missouri, 1927 (Fig. 6, p. 69). Page from Whitfield family album, snapshots on craft paper, ink captions. Source: Author's collection.

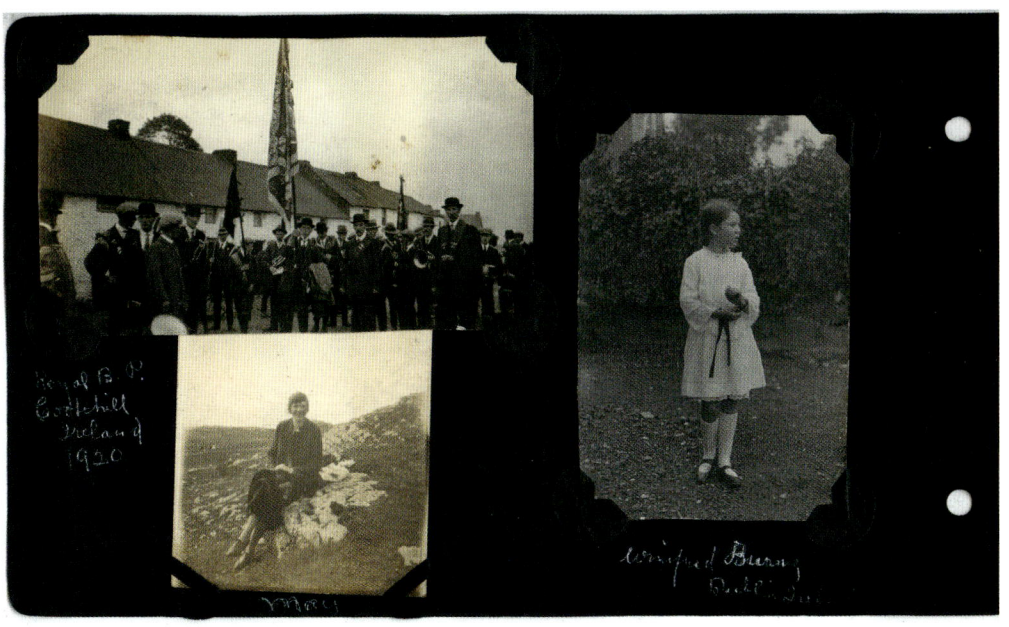

Plate 5: Scenes from Ireland, including Royal Black Preceptory March, n.d. (Fig. 8, p. 73). Page from Whitfield family album, snapshots on craft paper, ink captions. Source: Author's collection.

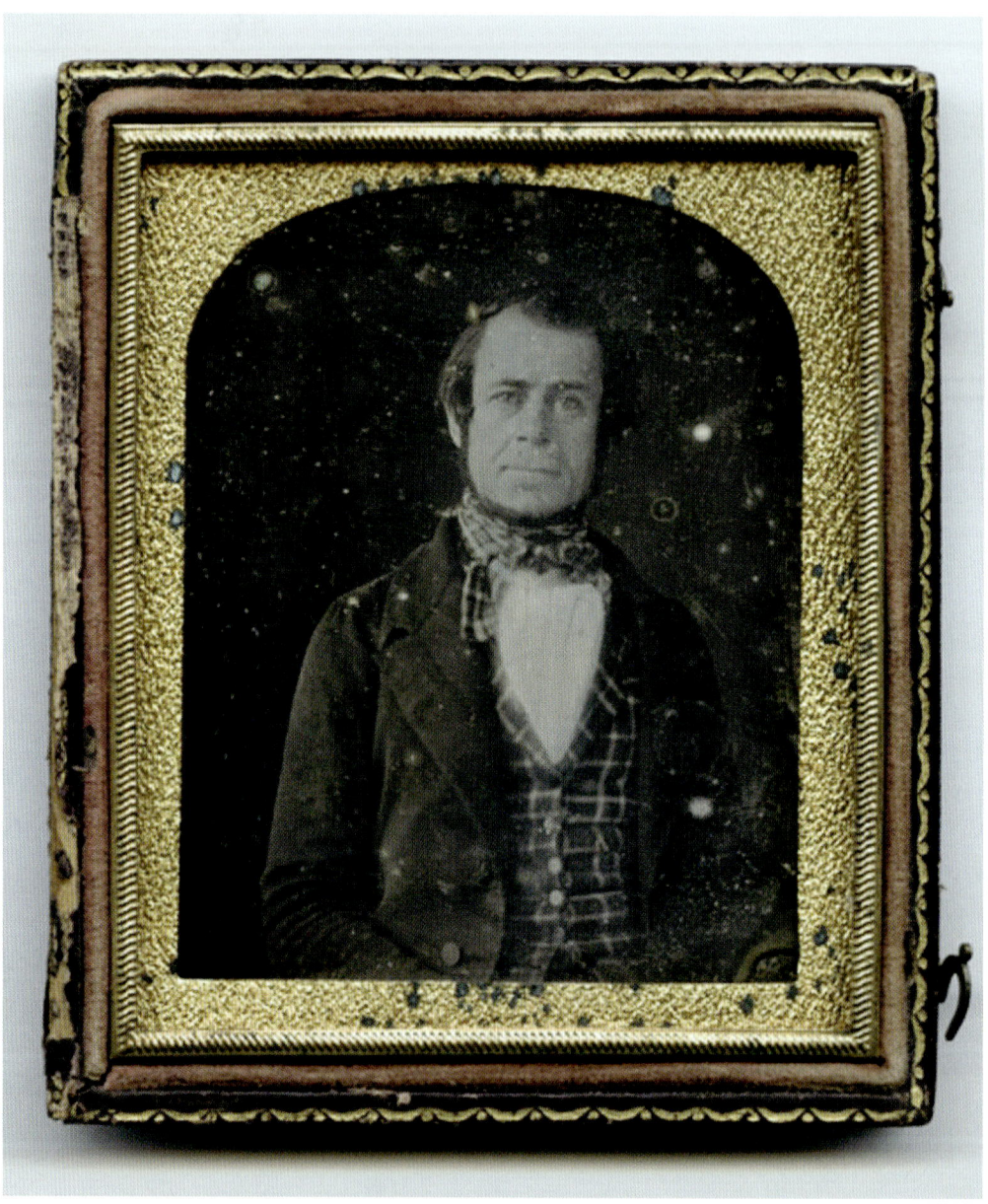

Plate 6: Anonymous, Irish American Daguerreotype, ca. 1850 (Fig. 3, p. 91). Author's collection.

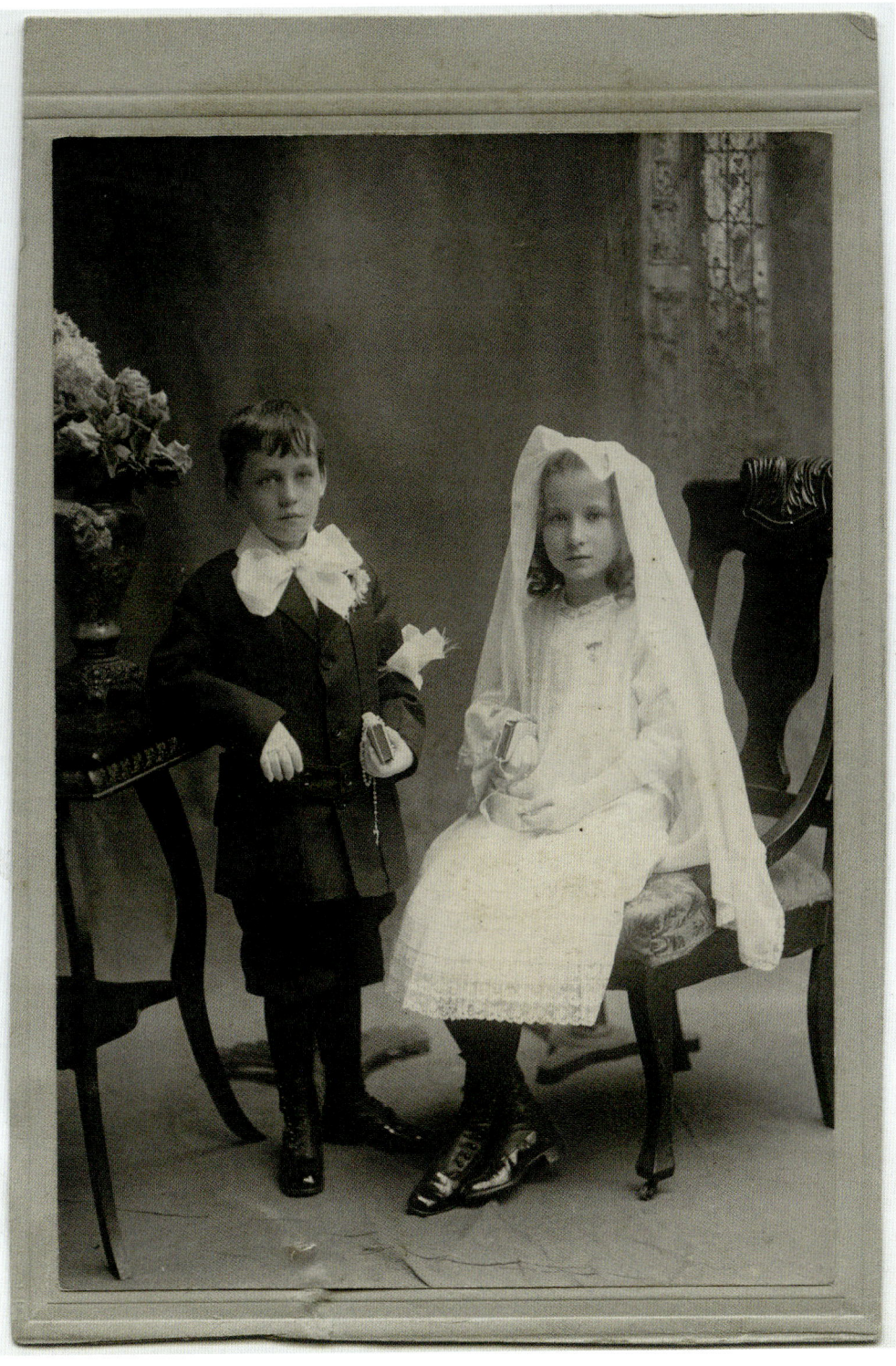

Plate 7: Anonymous, Francis Shackell Studios, n.d. (Fig. 7, p. 97). Edward Chandler Collection/
Author's collection.

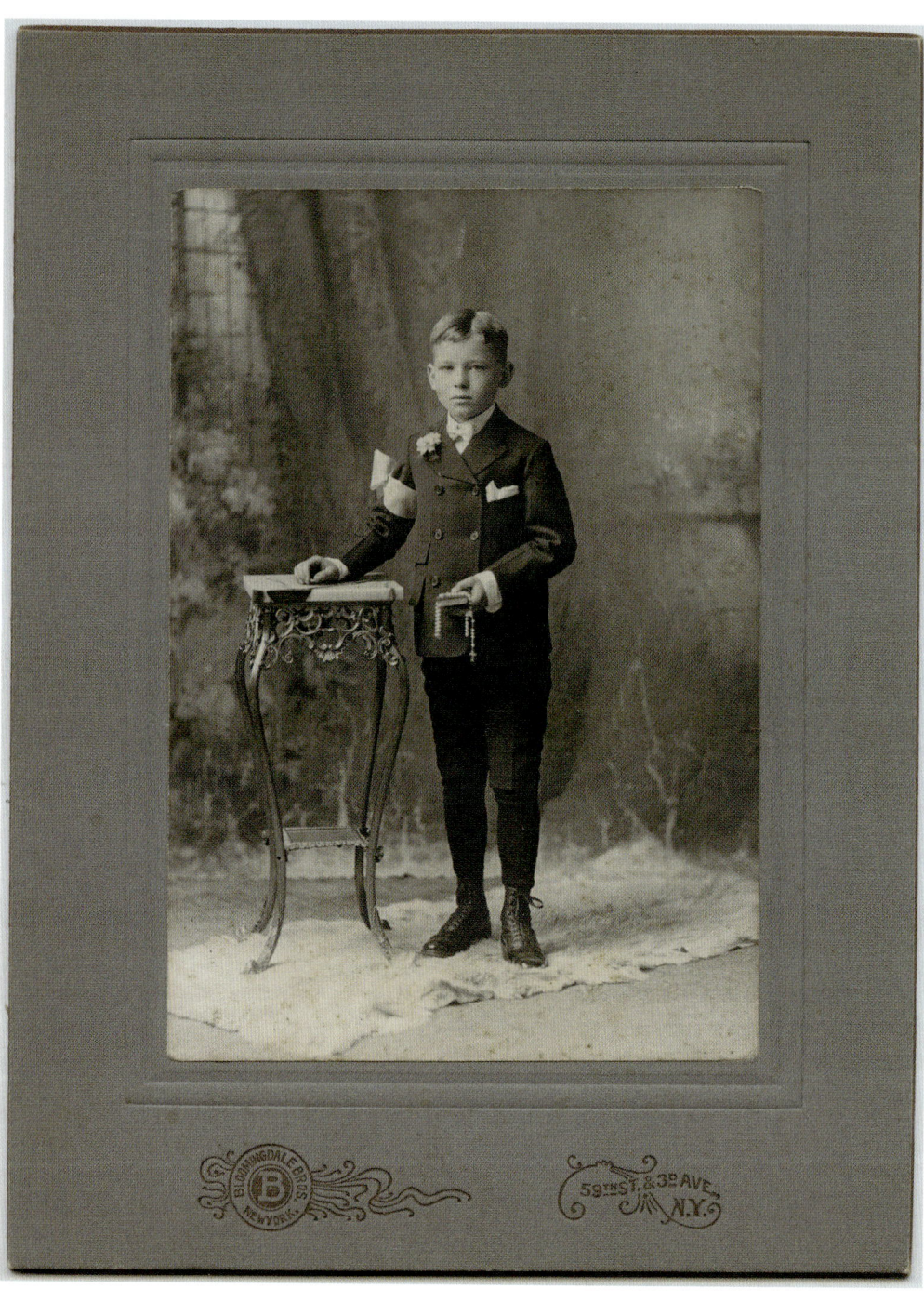

Plate 8: Anonymous, Bloomingdale Bros., New York, n.d. (Fig. 9, p. 100). Edward Chandler Collection/ Author's collection.

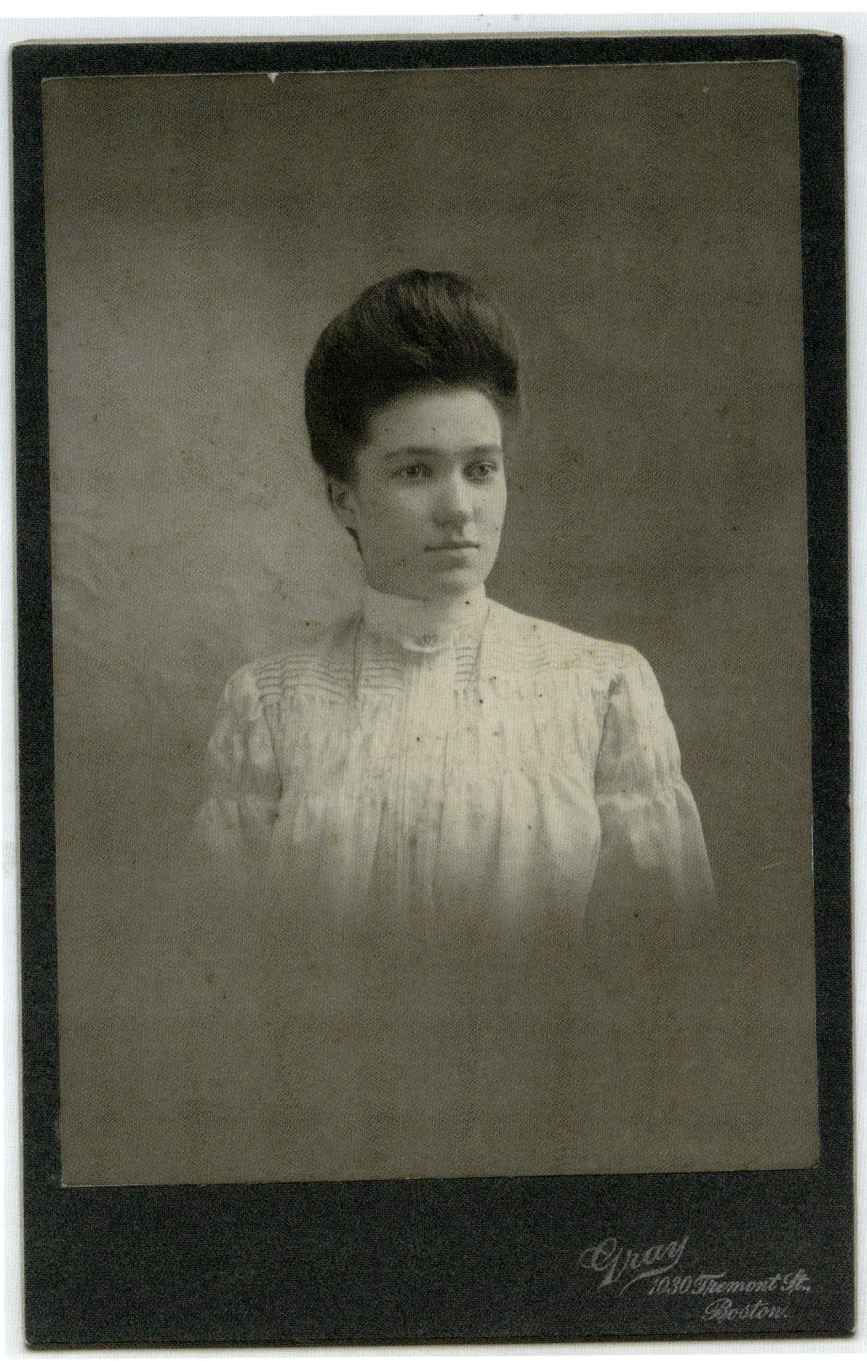

Plate 9: Anonymous, Gray Studio, Boston, n.d. (Fig. 11, p. 102). Edward Chandler Collection/
Author's collection.

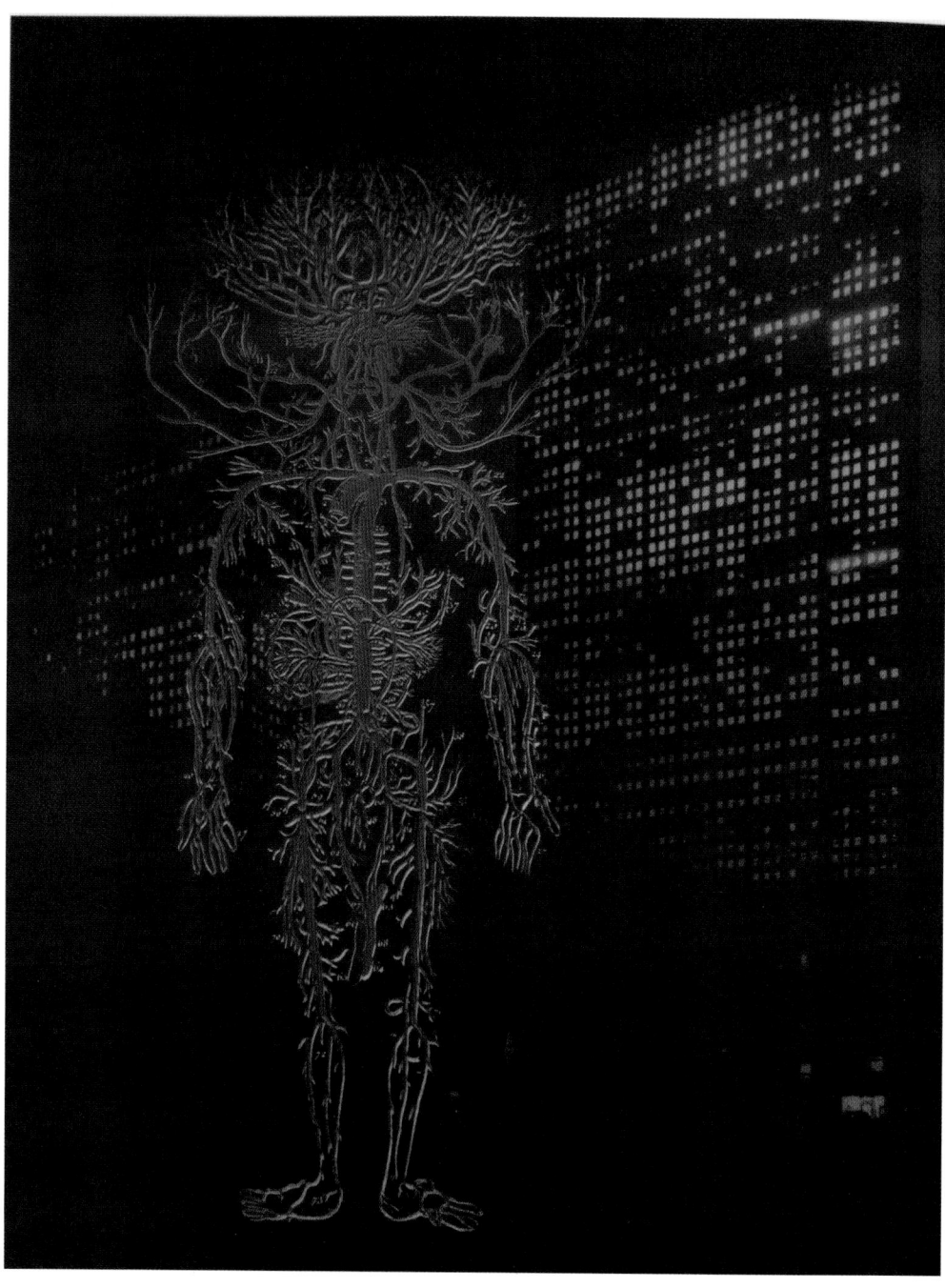

Plate 10: Josef Breitenbach, *We New Yorkers*, 1942, 38.4 x 30.5 cm (Fig. 2, p. 115). inv.-no. FM 96/3-33
© The Josef and Yaye Breitenbach Charitable Foundation, Courtesy of the Munich City Museum.

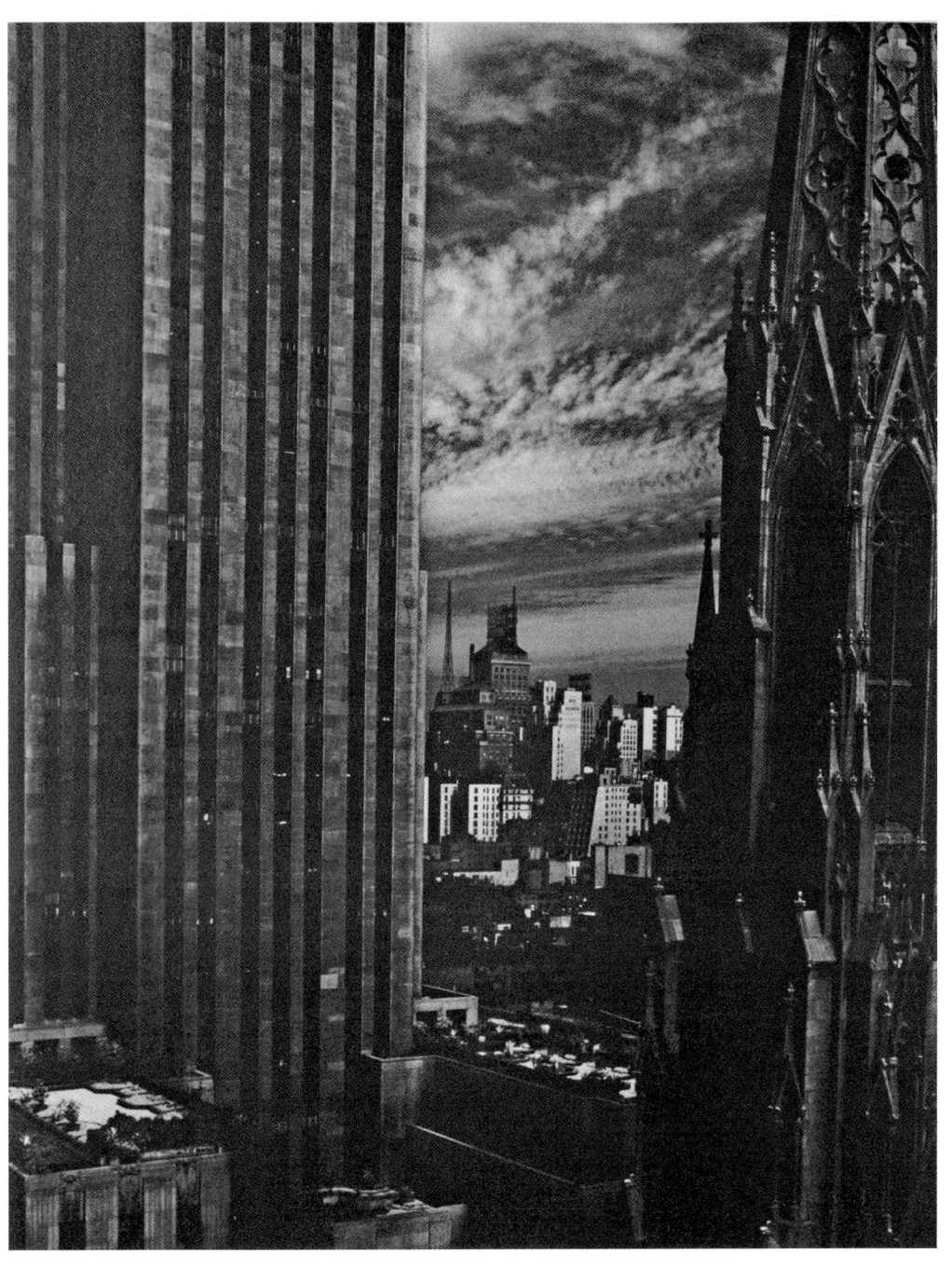

Plate 11: Hermann Landshoff, *New York*, 1941, 29.4 x 24.2 cm (Fig. 5, p. 121). inv.no. FM-2012/200.99
© bpk, Münchner Stadtmuseum, Sammlung Fotografie, Archiv Landshoff.

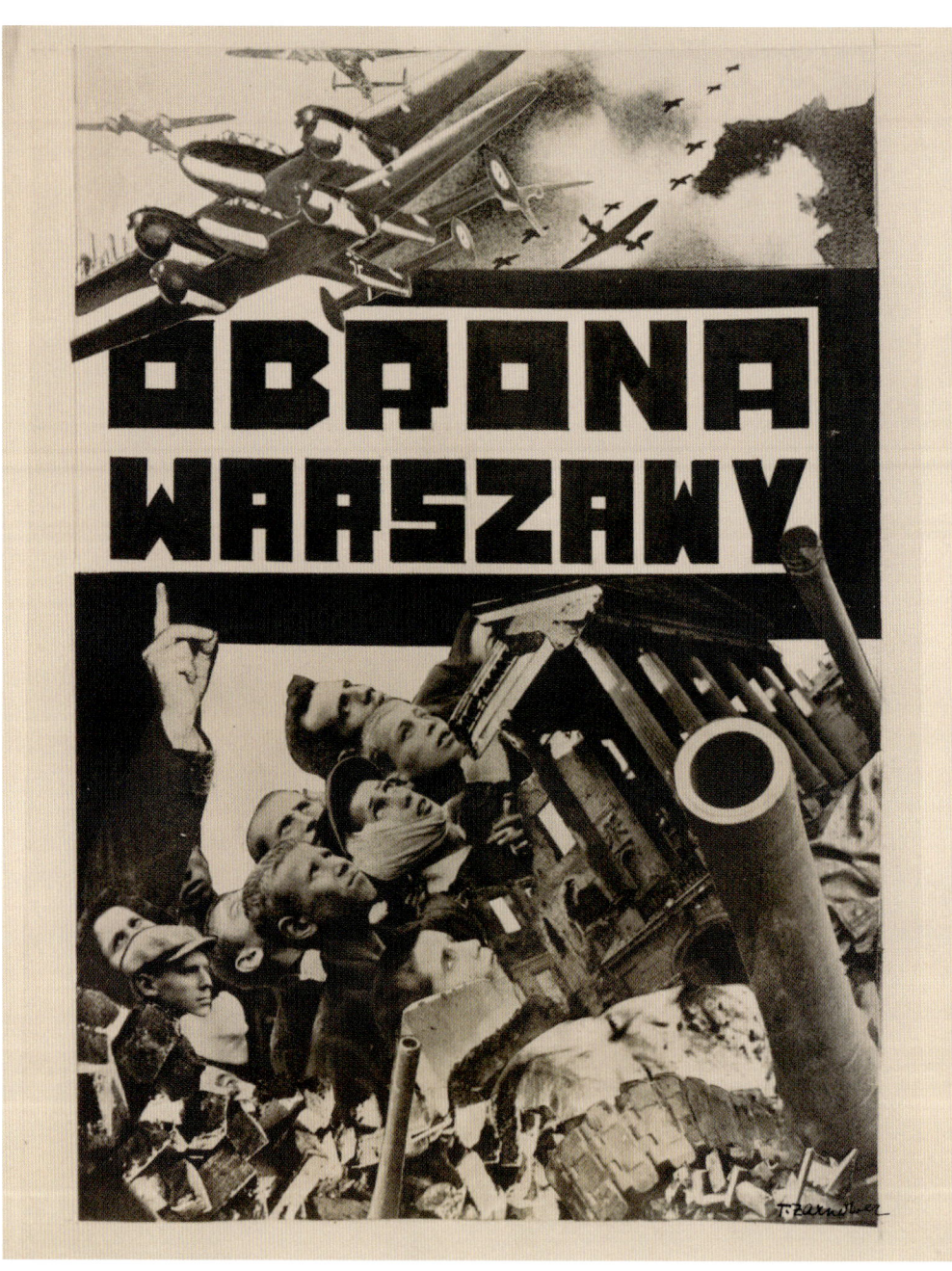

Plate 12: Teresa Żarnower, *Obrona Warszawy: Lud polski w obronie stolicy (wrzesień 1939)*
[The Defense of Warsaw: People of Poland in Defense of the Capital (September 1939)], 1942,
signed maquette for a front cover with title, photomontage (Fig. 1, p. 126). The New York Public
Library, New York

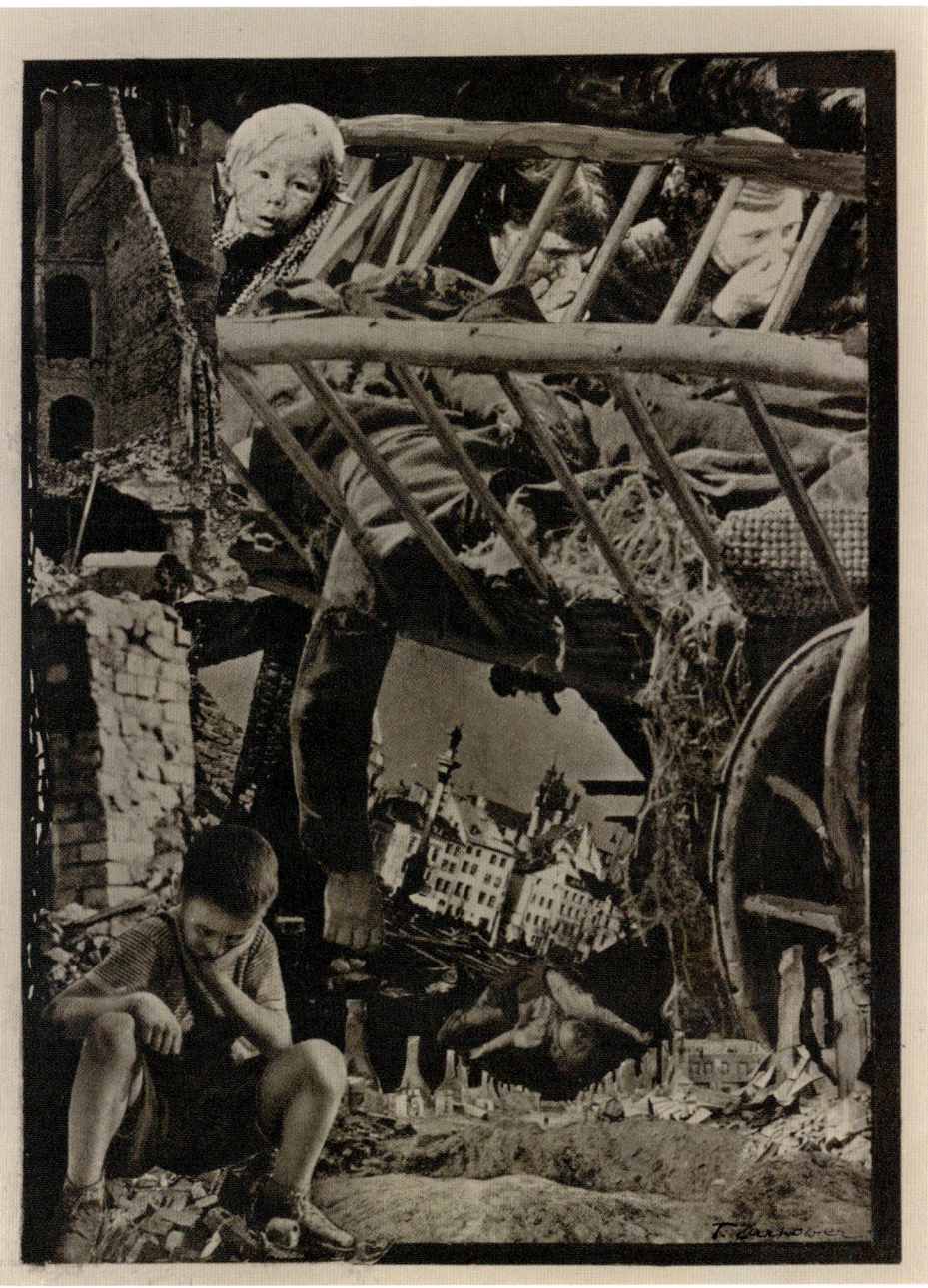

Plate 13: Teresa Żarnower, *Obrona Warszawy: Lud polski w obronie stolicy (wrzesień 1939)*
[The Defense of Warsaw: People of Poland in Defense of the Capital (September 1939)], 1942,
signed maquette for a back cover, photomontage (Fig. 9, p. 148). The New York Public Library,
New York

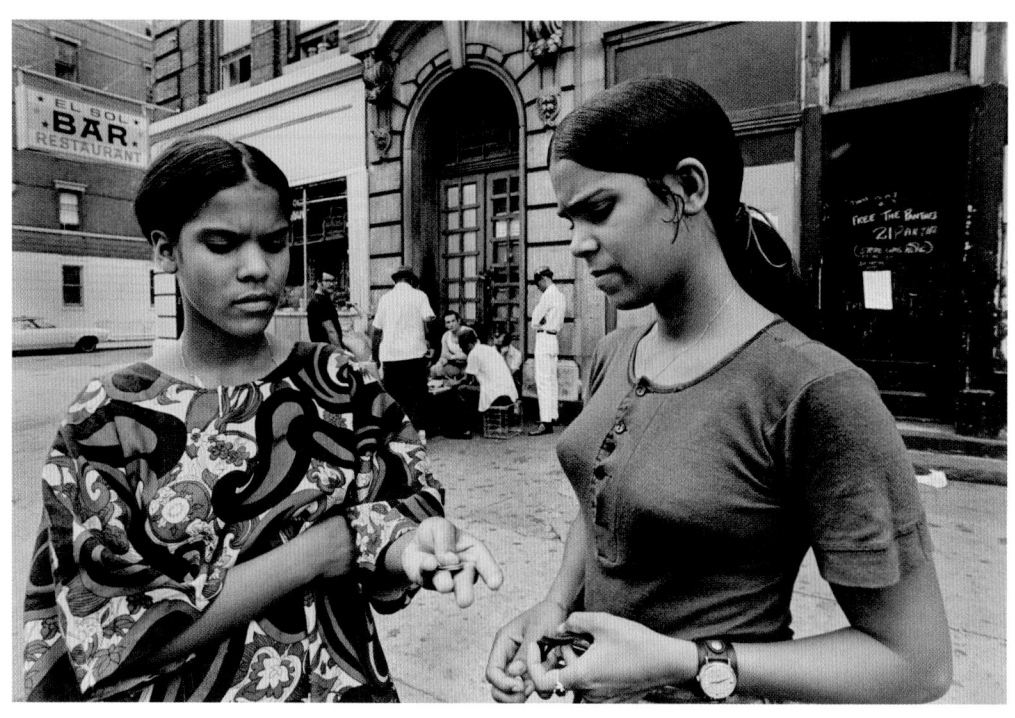

Plate 14: Winston Vargas, *Sisters, Washington Heights, New York*, 1970, printed 2016, gelatin silver print (Fig. 3, p. 167).

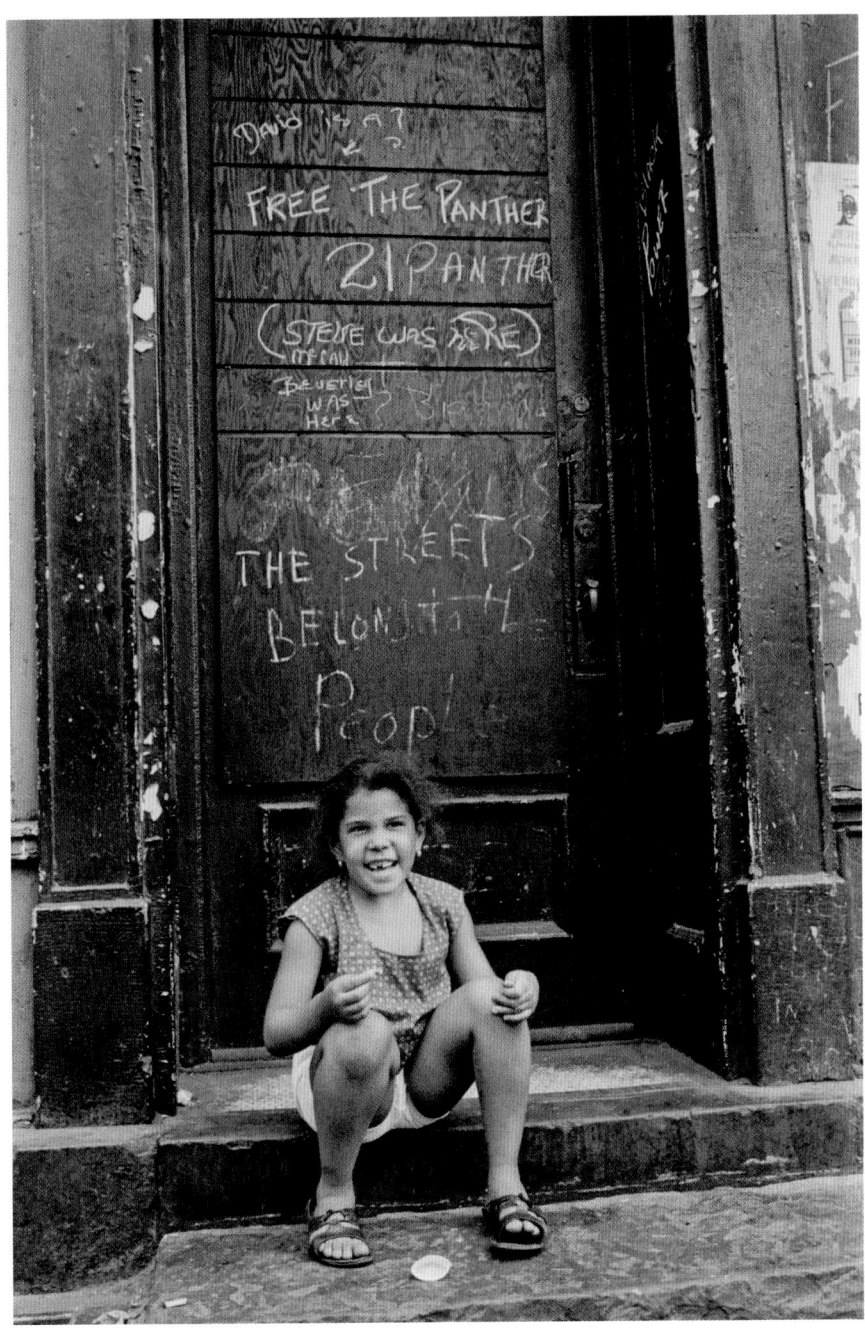

Plate 15: Winston Vargas, *Child Playing, Washington Heights, New York*, 1970, printed 2016, gelatin silver print (Fig. 4, p. 168).

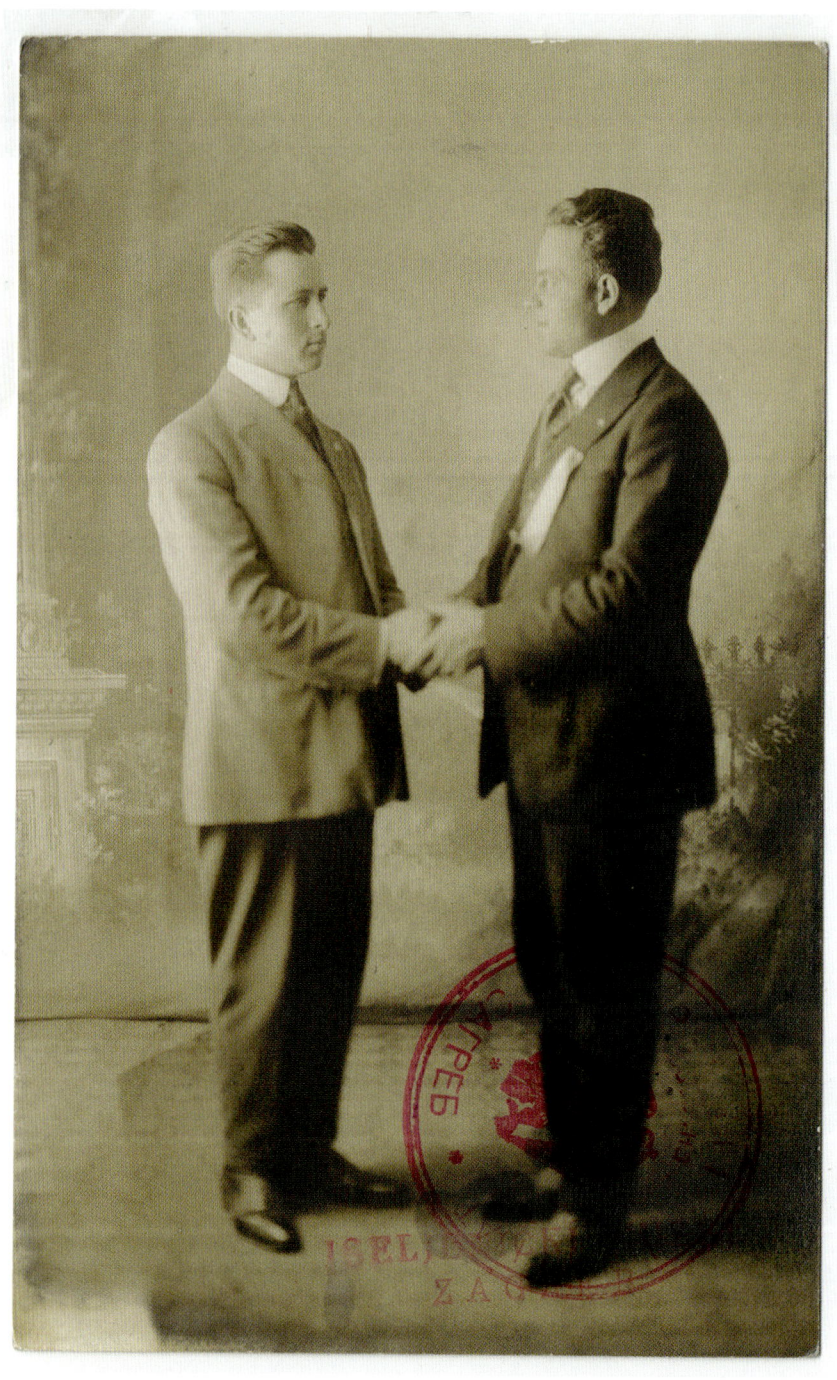

Plate 16: Unknown photographer, "Two volunteers from America" (Fig. 3, p. 190).
Croatian State Archives, Zagreb, Fond No. HR-HDA-1610-32-166.

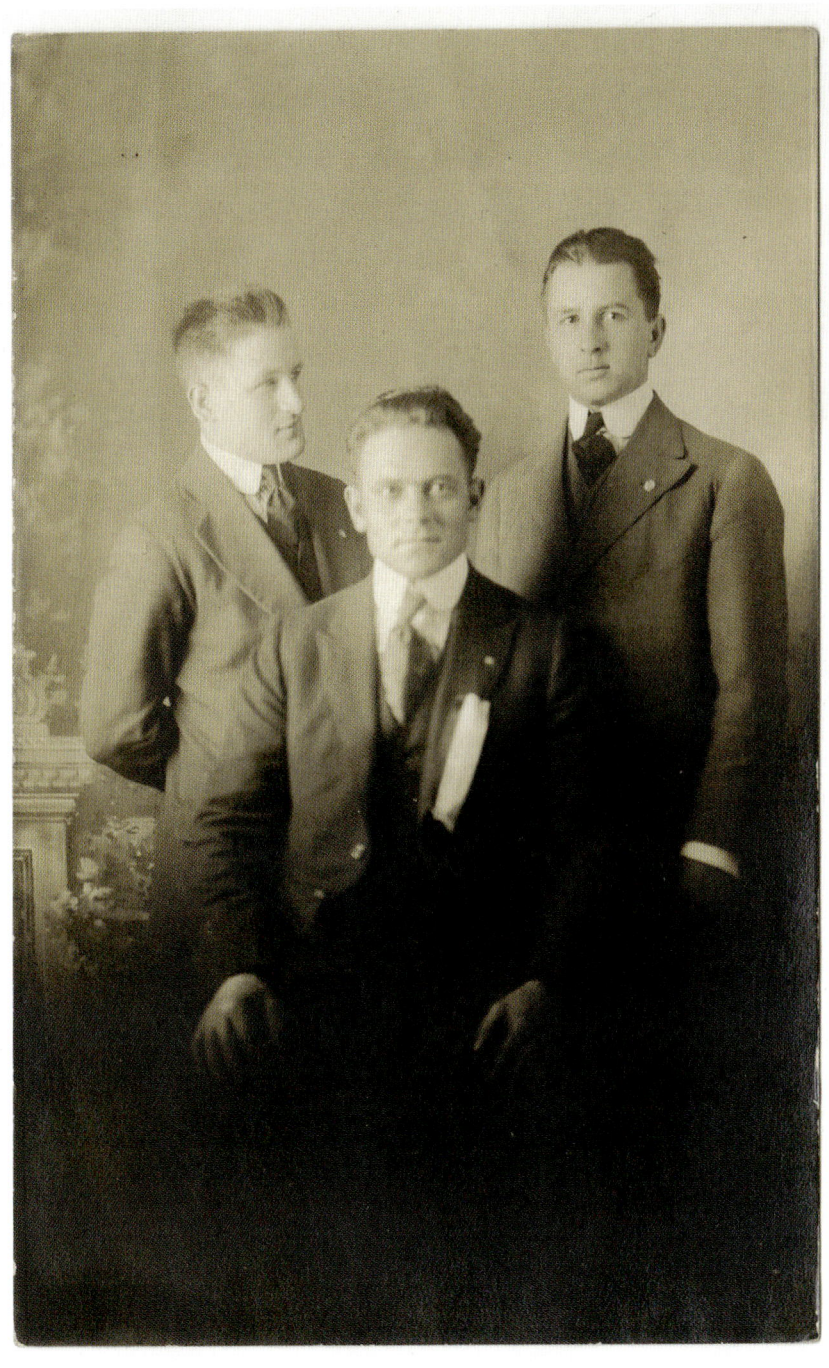

Plate 17: Unknown Photographer, "The group of volunteers, 1916" (Fig. 4, p. 190).
Croatian State Archives, Zagreb, Fond No. HR-HDA-1610-32-167.

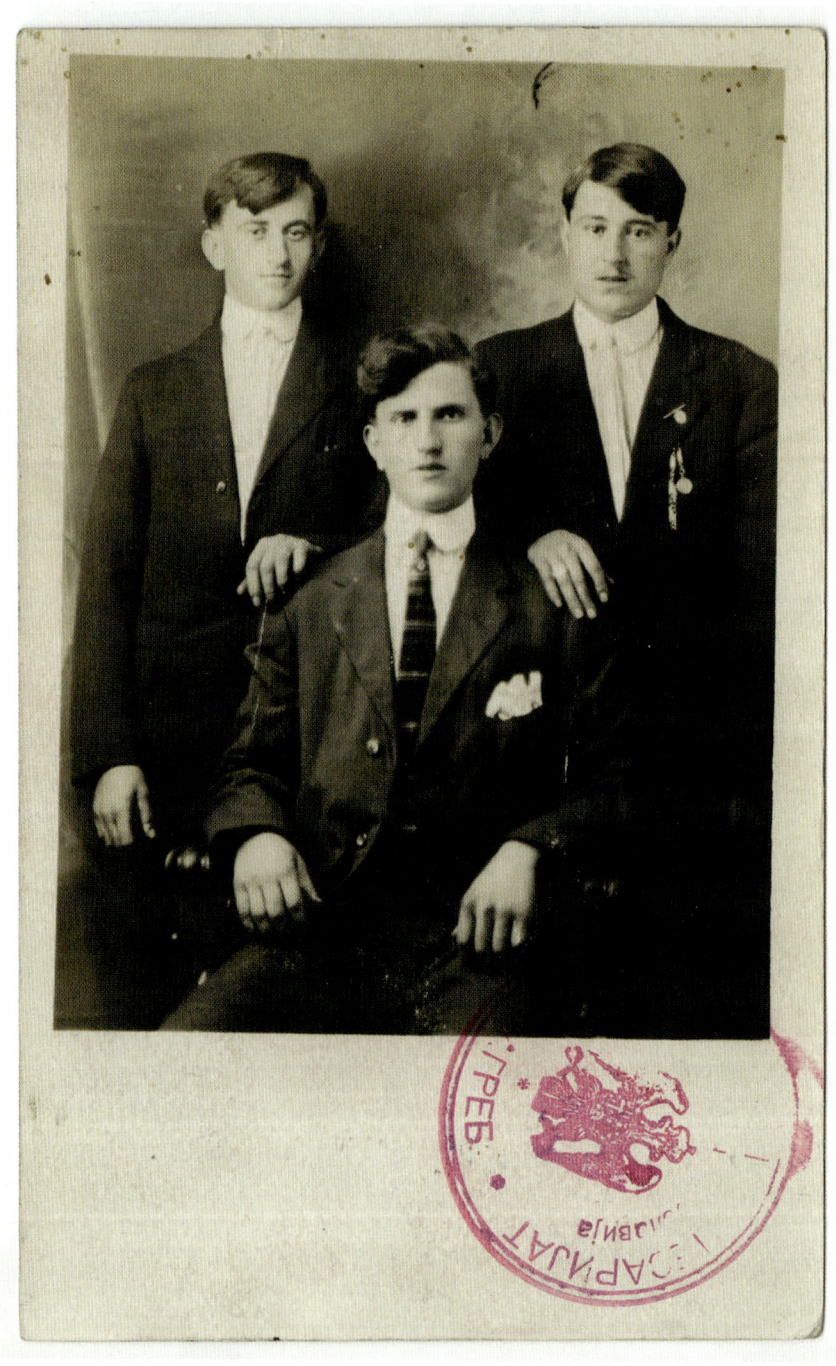

Plate 18: Unknown Photographer, "Volunteers 1916" (Fig. 5, p. 191). Croatian State Archives, Zagreb, Fond No. HR-HDA-1610-32-168.

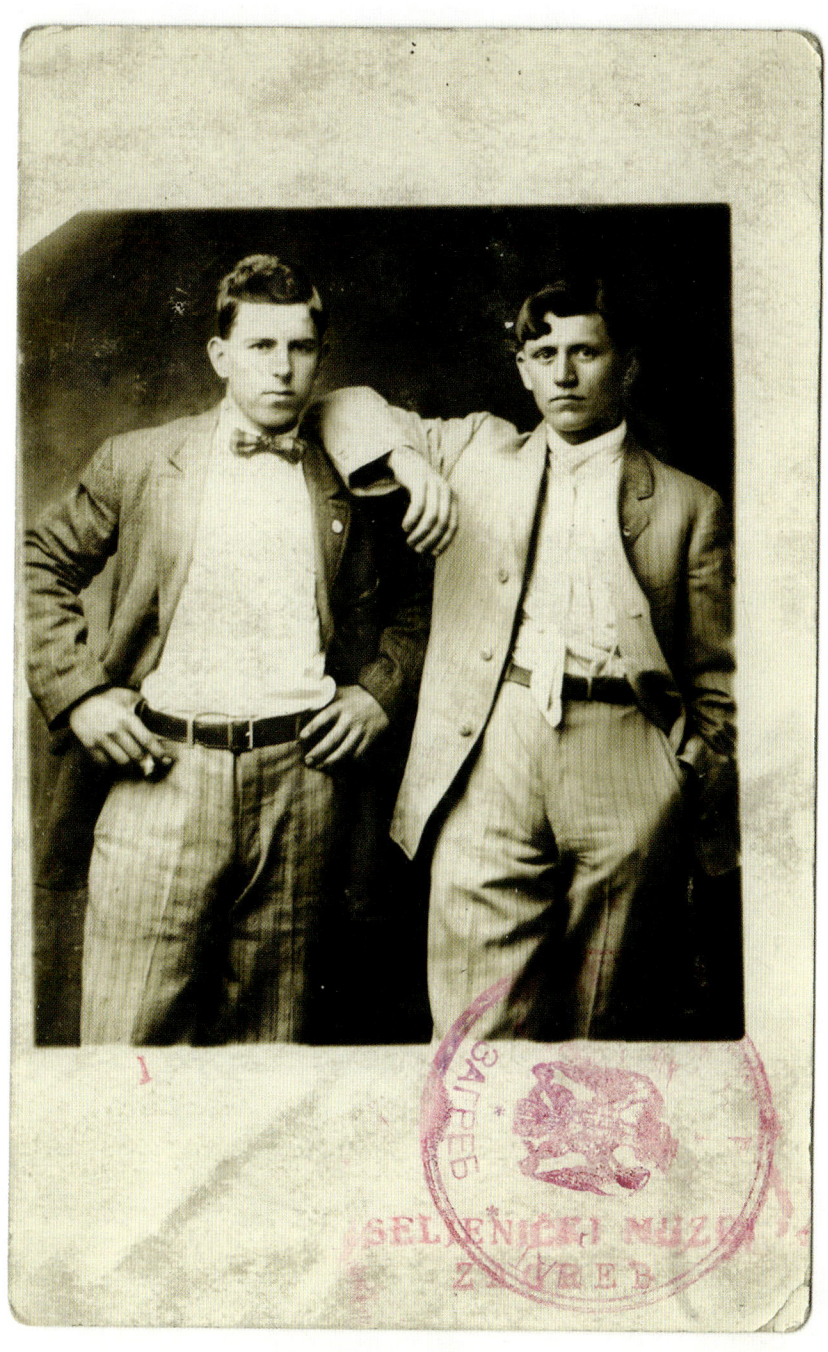

Plate 19: Unknown Photographer, "Two volunteers from America 1916" (Fig. 6, p. 191).
Croatian State Archives, Zagreb, Fond No. HR-HDA-1610-32-169.

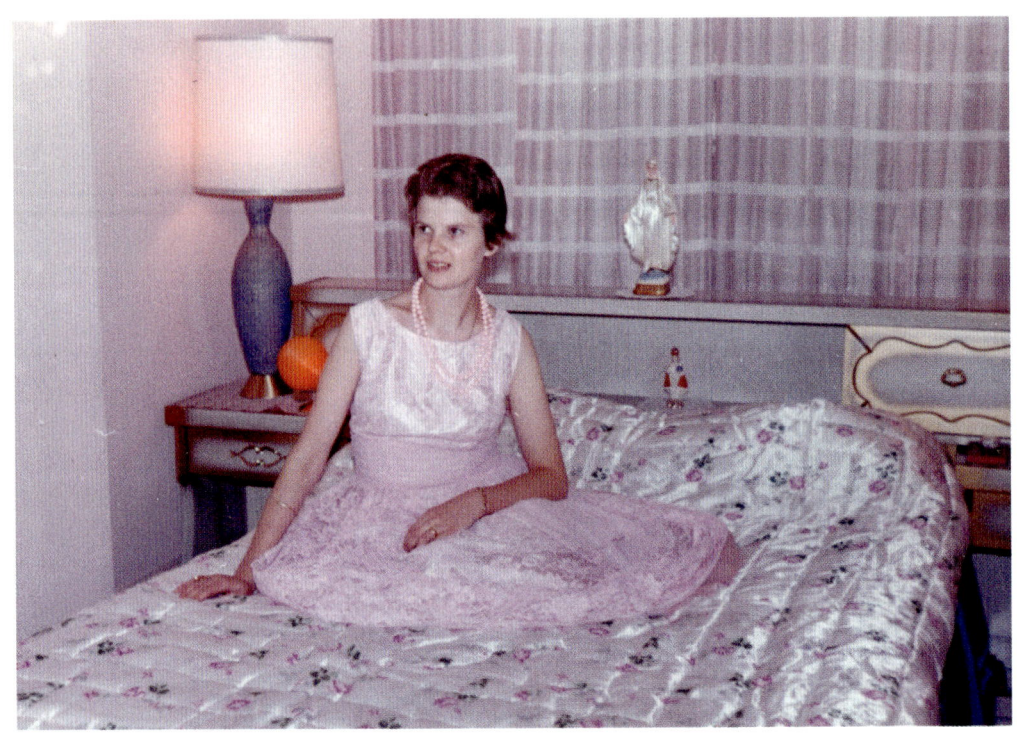

Plate 20: Image from the family album of Ljubica Zic, Astoria, Queens, New York, 1962 (Fig. 16, p. 201). Kristina Leko, *AMERIKA*, 2003–2005. In collaboration with Marcella Bonich, Nori Boni-Zorovich, Miriam Busanic, Margaret Zgombic, Ljubica Zic.

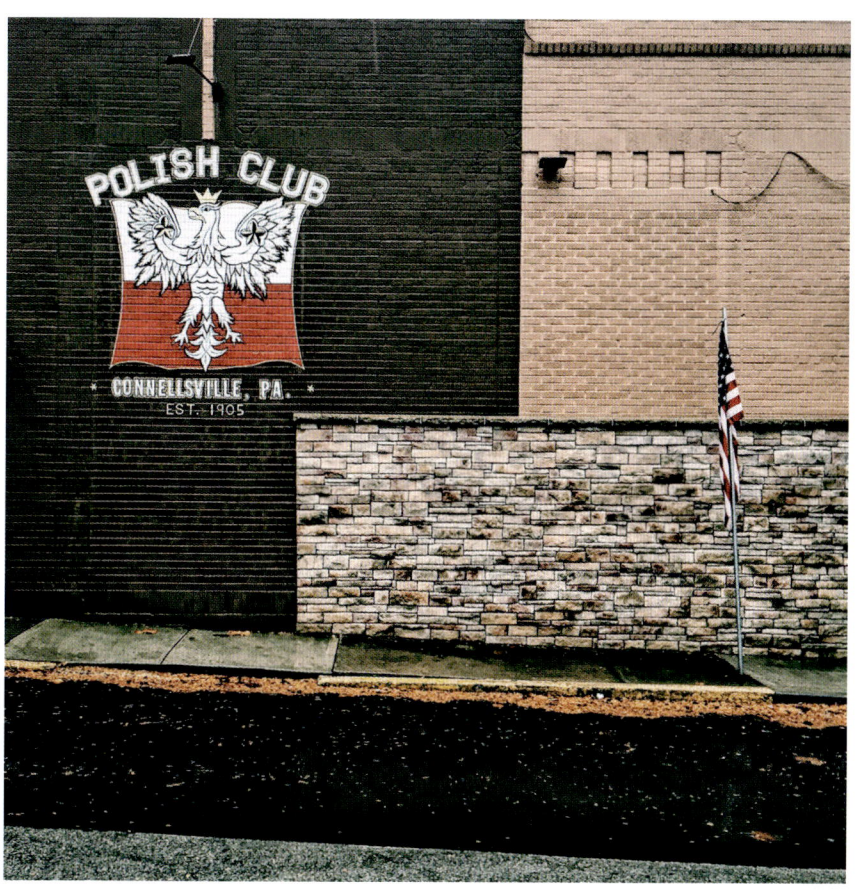

Plate 21: Brian Cohen, *Polish Club Connellsville*, 2017 (Fig. 2, p. 209). © Brian Cohen/The Documentary Works, 2017. Courtesy of the author.

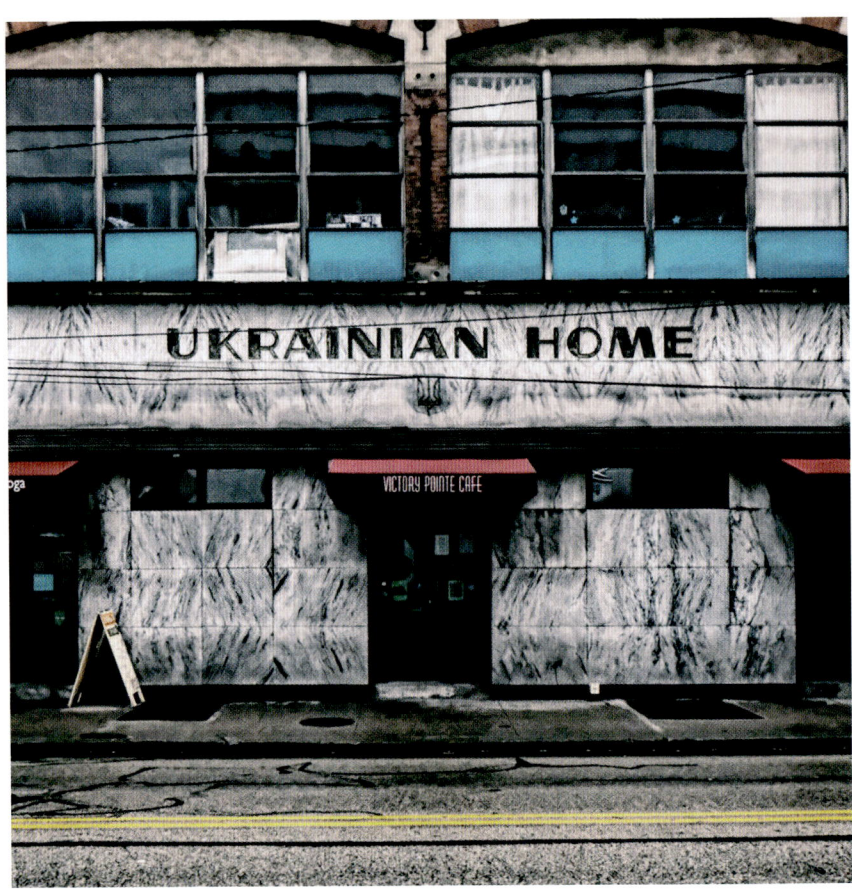

Plate 22: Brian Cohen, *Ukrainian Home*, Pittsburgh, 2017 (Fig. 6, p. 219). © Brian Cohen/The Documentary Works, 2017. Courtesy of the author.

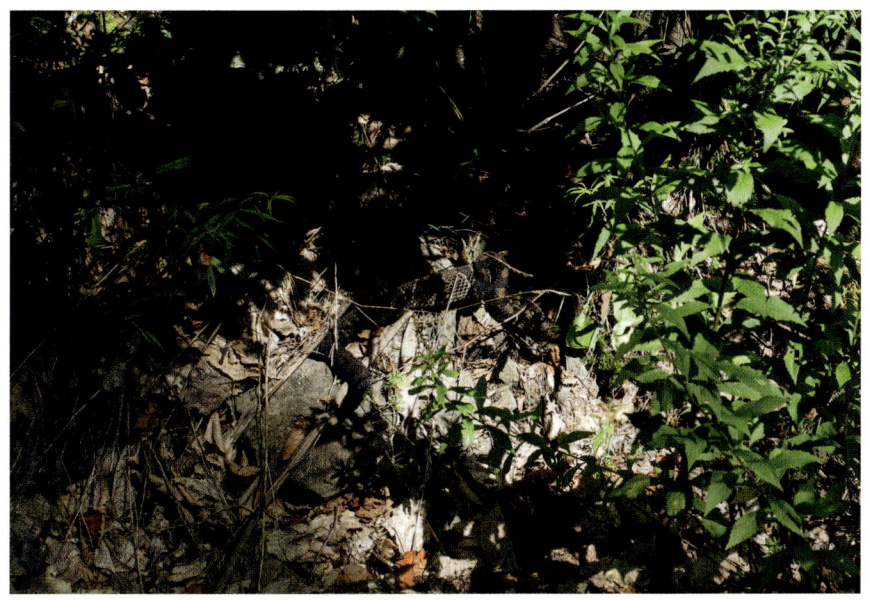

Plate 23: Giulia Mangione. Rattlesnake in the sunshine, Allegheny mountains, 2019 (Fig. 2, p. 232). Courtesy of Giulia Mangione.

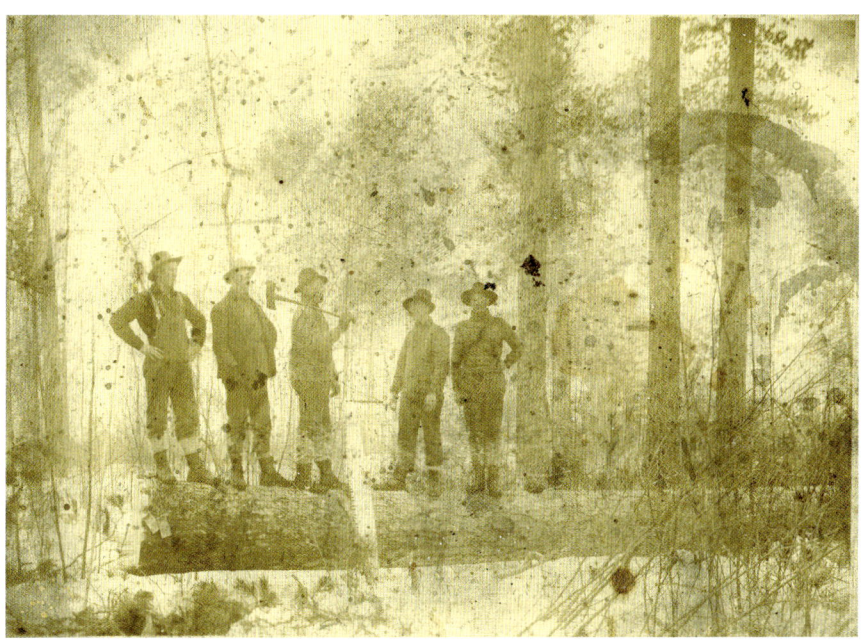

Plate 24: Unknown photographer. Immigrants from Setesdal, Norway, cutting trees, probably 1910–1920 (Fig. 4, p. 236).

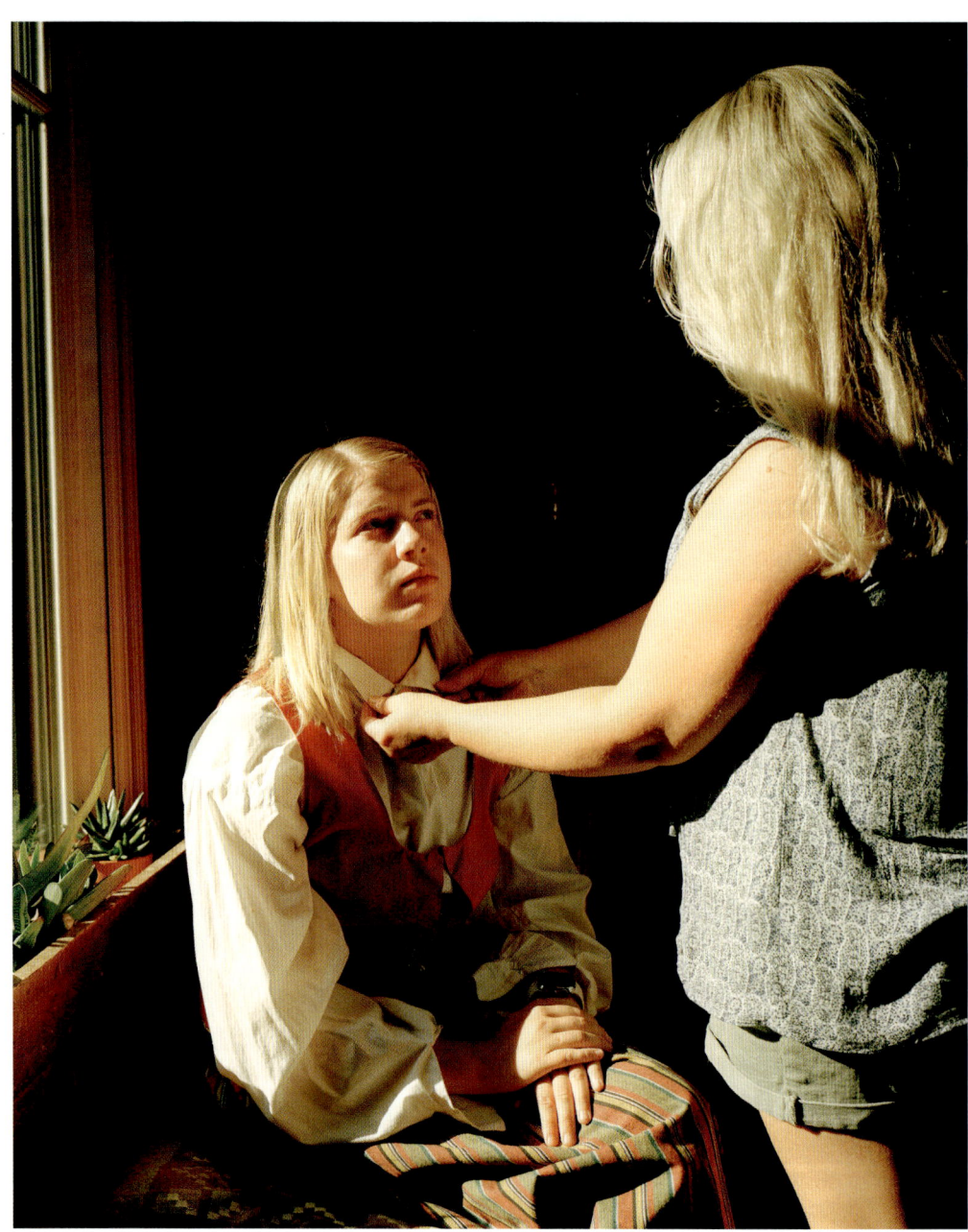

Plate 25: Giulia Mangione, 2019. Hilda Everson, daughter of Terry Everson, with her mother Charlotte, who is fixing the collar of the shirt of her *bunad* (national costume). The family is very interested in knowing and connecting with old Norwegian traditions. (27 on Giulia's list.) (Fig. 11, p. 240). Courtesy of Giulia Mangione.

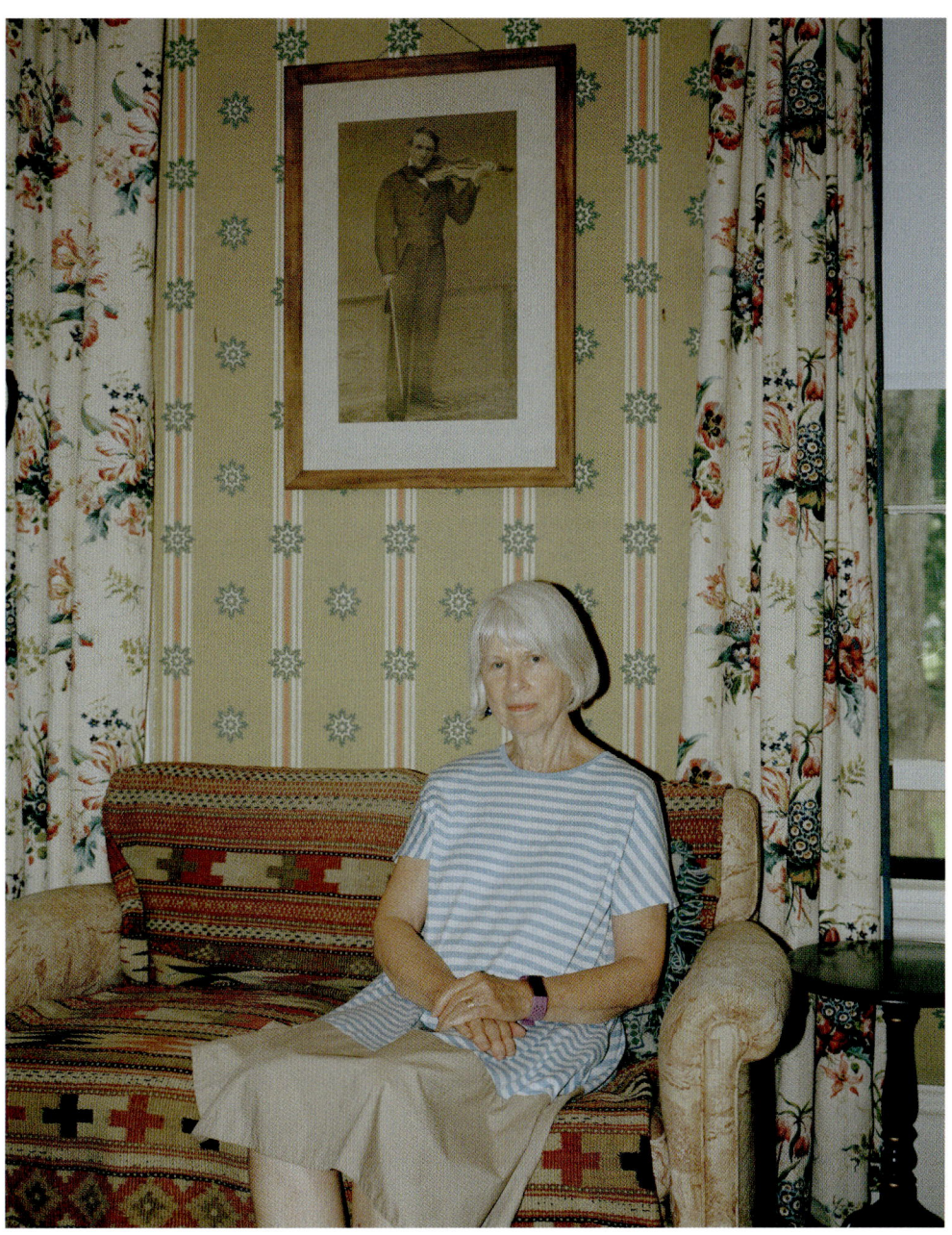

Plate 26: Giulia Mangione, 2019. Portrait of Olea Kaland Smith, great granddaughter of Ole Bull, from his second marriage. Olea is portrayed in the house where Ole and Sara Bull lived in Maine, United States, after the collapse of the colony (Fig. 12, p. 241). Courtesy of Giulia Mangione.

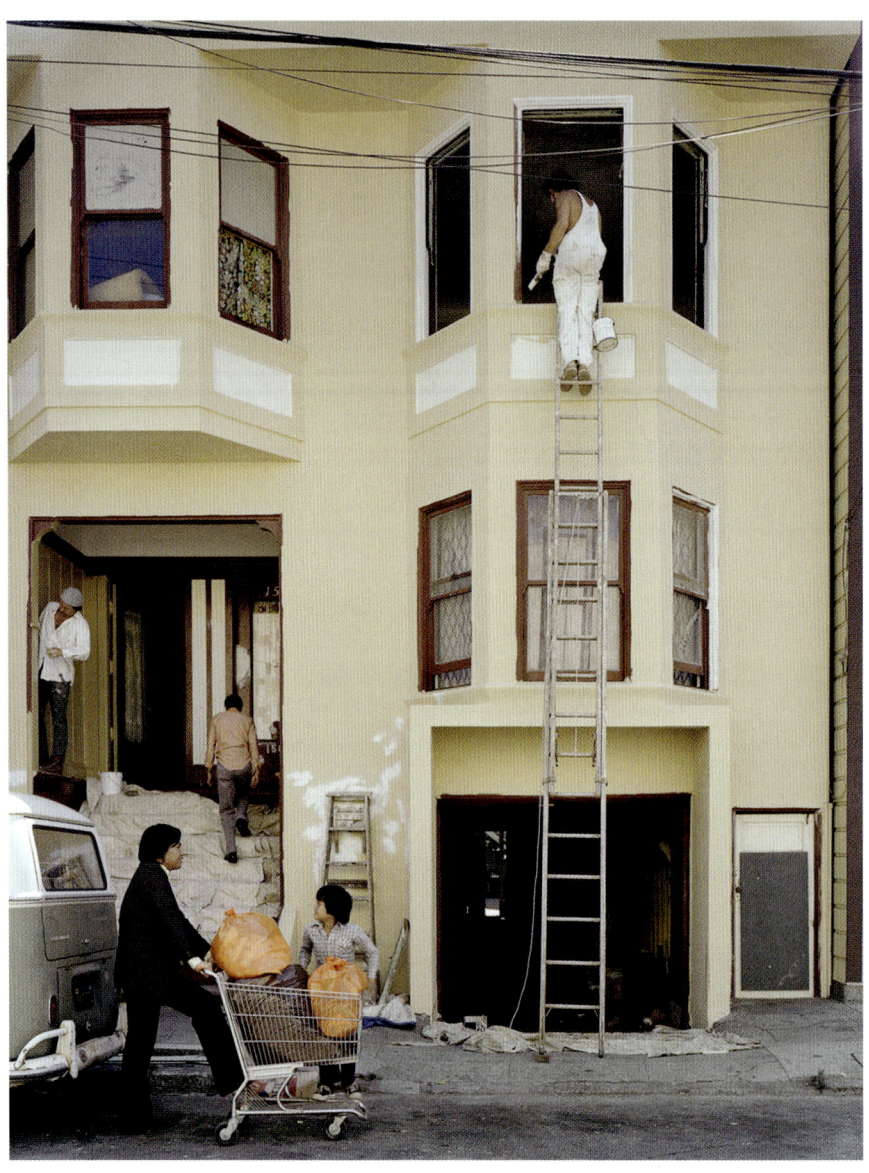

Plate 27: Janet Delaney, *Eviction, 158-160 Langton Street*, 1980. Chromogenic print. Dimensions variable (Fig. 1, p. 262). Courtesy of the artist.

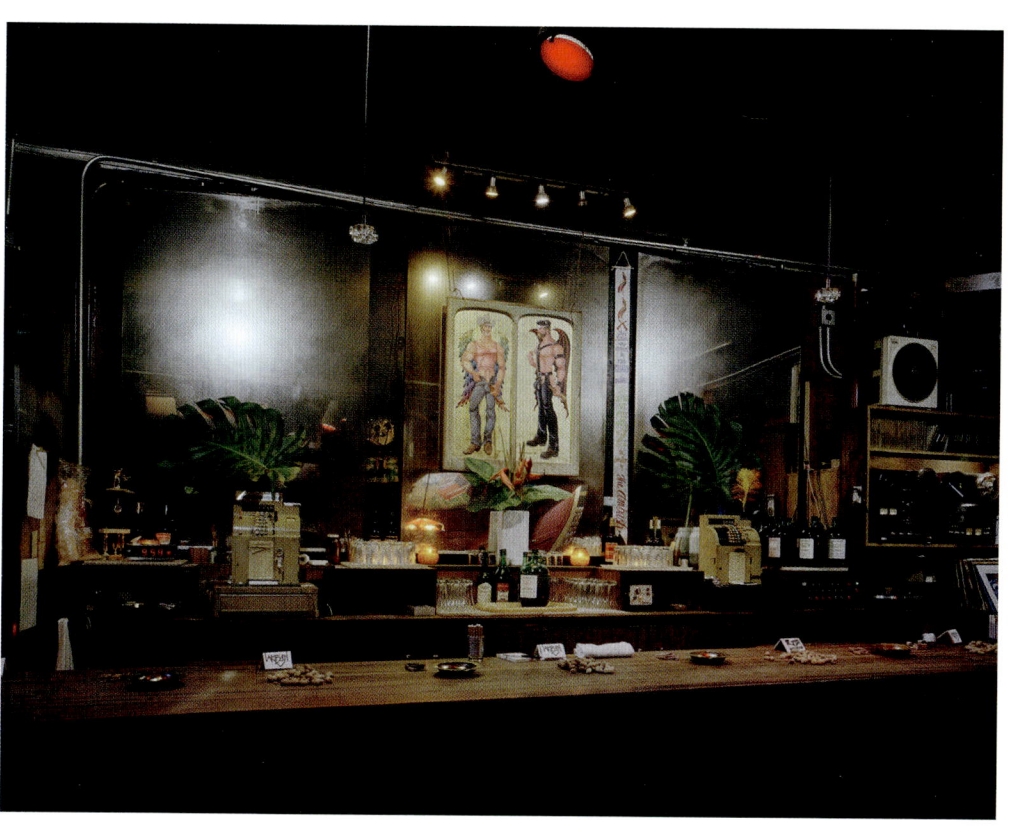

Plate 28: Janet Delaney, *Ambush Bar, 1051 Harrison Street*, 1981. Chromogenic print.
Dimensions variable (Fig. 3, p. 265). Courtesy of the artist.

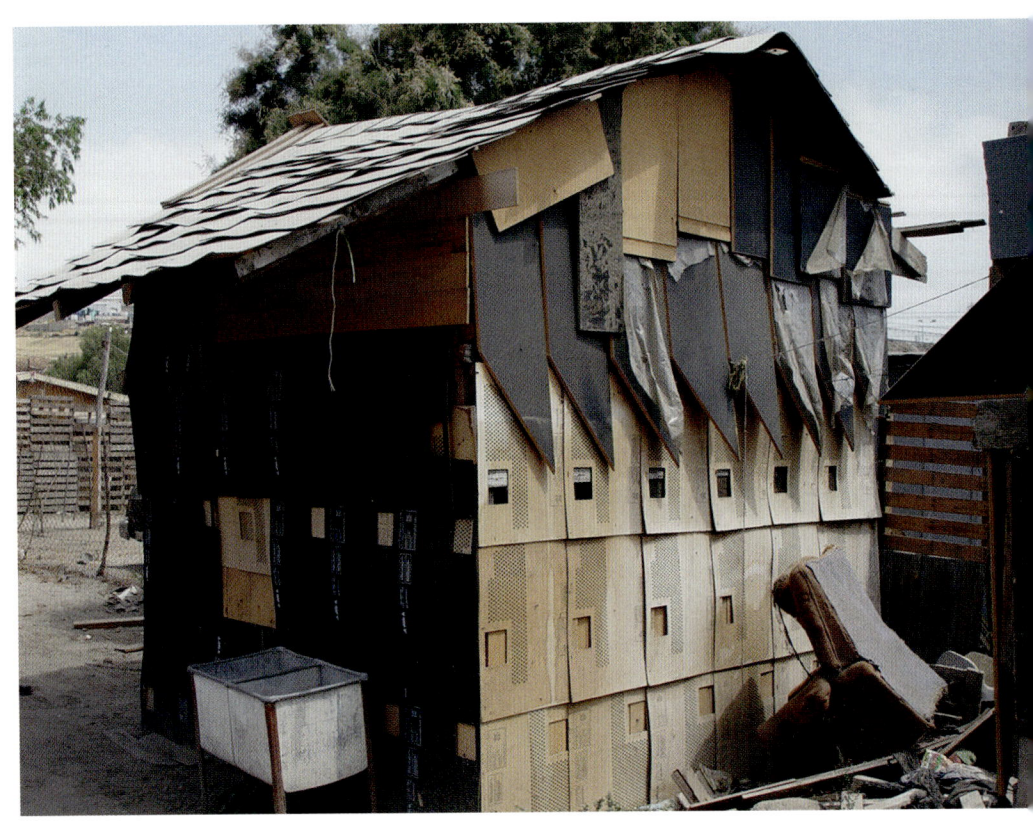

Plate 29: Ingrid Hernández, *Casa hecha con respaldos de televisión, Tijuana*
[House made of television backings, Tijuana], 2004. From the series *Tijuana Comprimida*
[Compressed Tijuana]. Digital print (Fig. 4, p. 268).

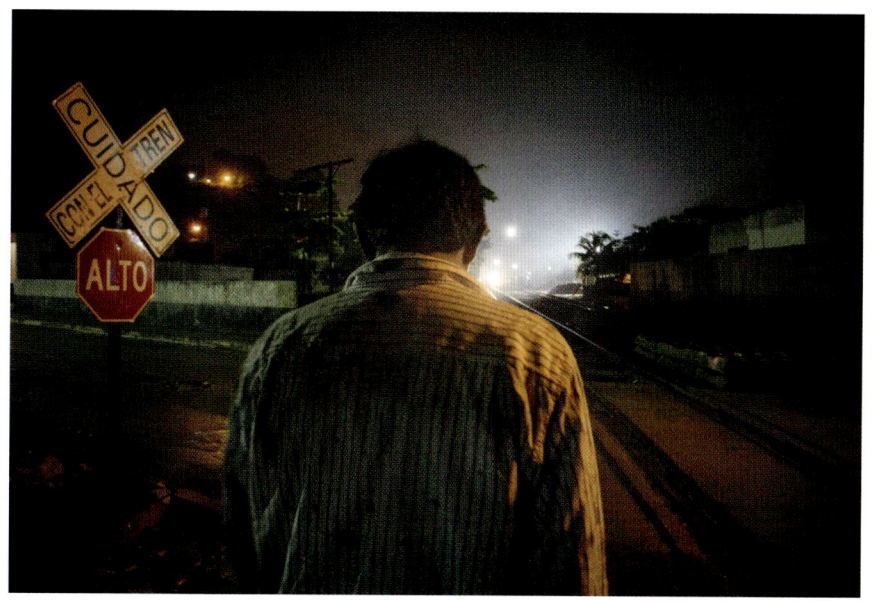

Plate 30: Moysés Zuñiga Santiago, *Manuel*, Coatzacoalcos, Veracruz, Mexico, October 29, 2012 (Fig. 3, p. 288). Photograph courtesy of Moysés Zuñiga Santiago.

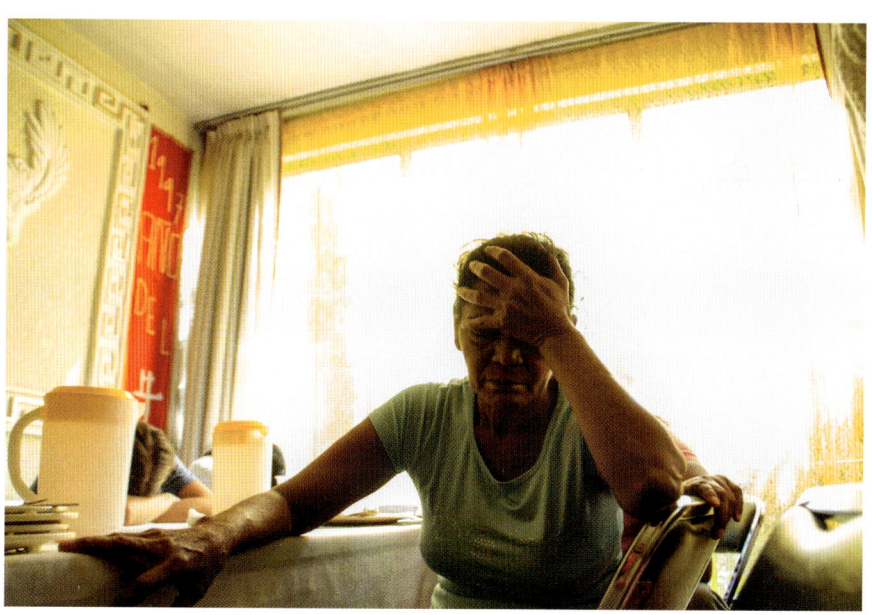

Plate 31: Moysés Zuñiga Santiago, *Narcisa González*, Tequisqulapan, Mexico, October 24, 2012 (Fig. 4, p. 355). Photograph courtesy of Moysés Zuñiga Santiago.

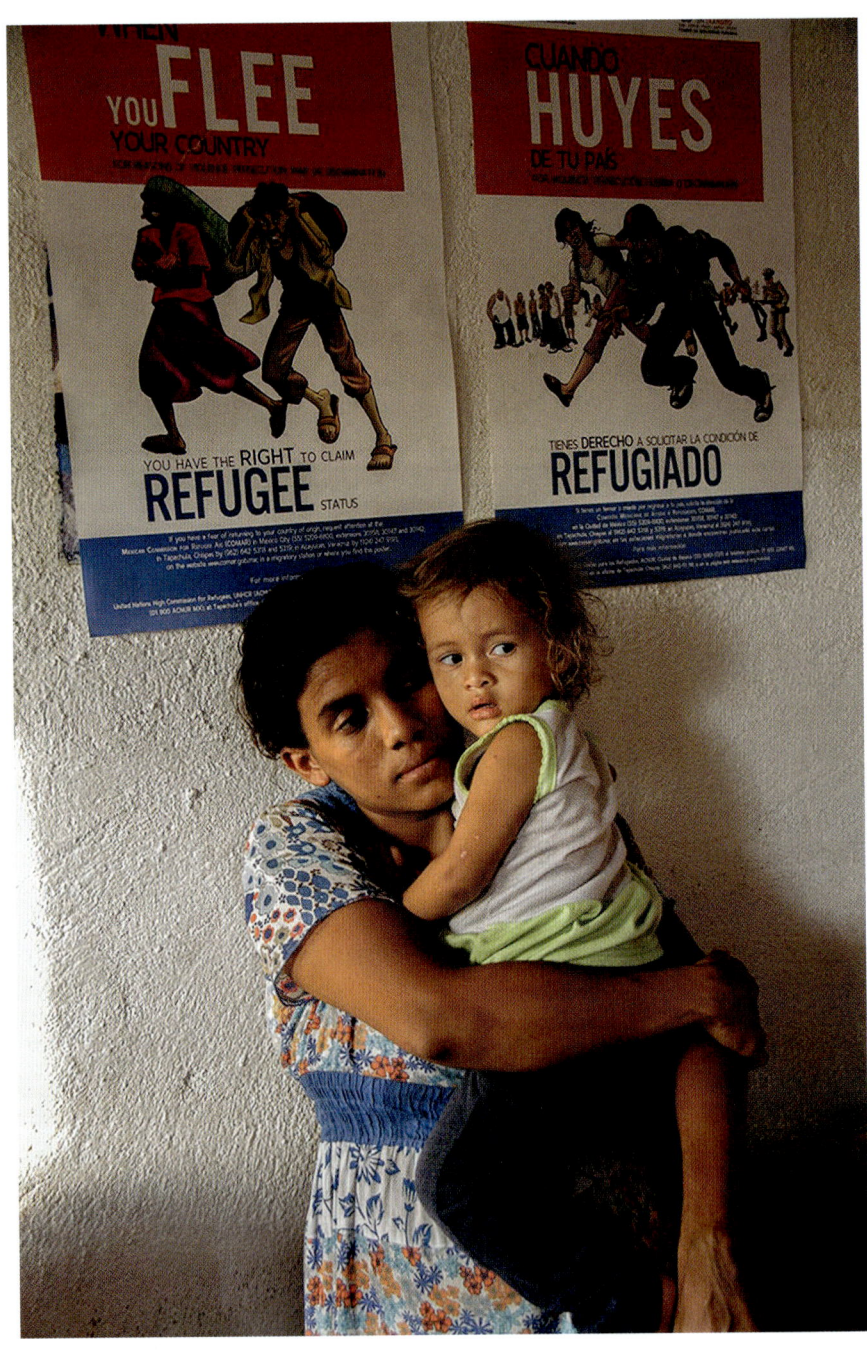

Plate 32: Moysés Zuniga Santiago, *Esther*, Arriaga, Chiapas, Mexico, May 6, 2014. (Fig. 5, p. 293)
Photograph courtesy of Moysés Zuniga Santiago.

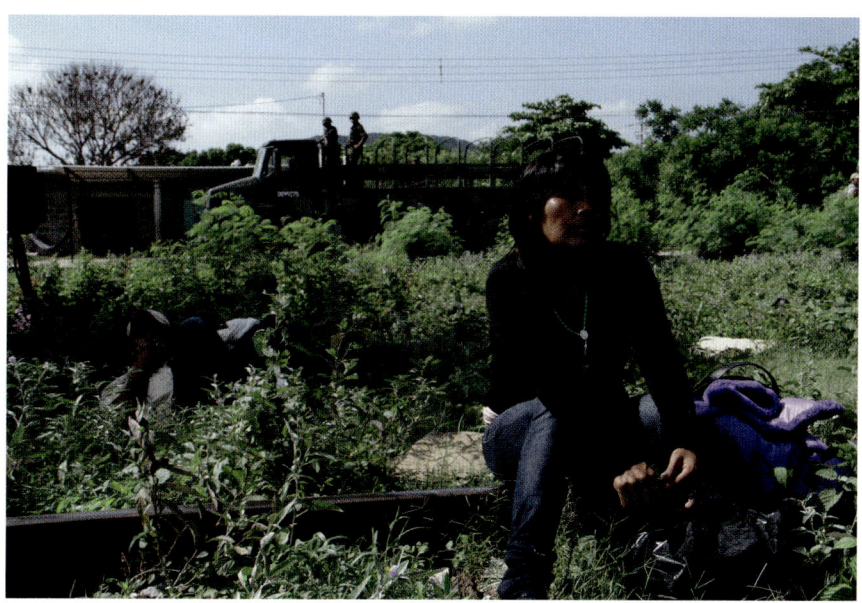

Plate 33: Moysés Zuniga Santiago, *Cristina*, Arriaga, Chiapas, Mexico, July 21, 2012. (Fig. 7, p. 295) Photograph courtesy of Moysés Zuniga Santiago.

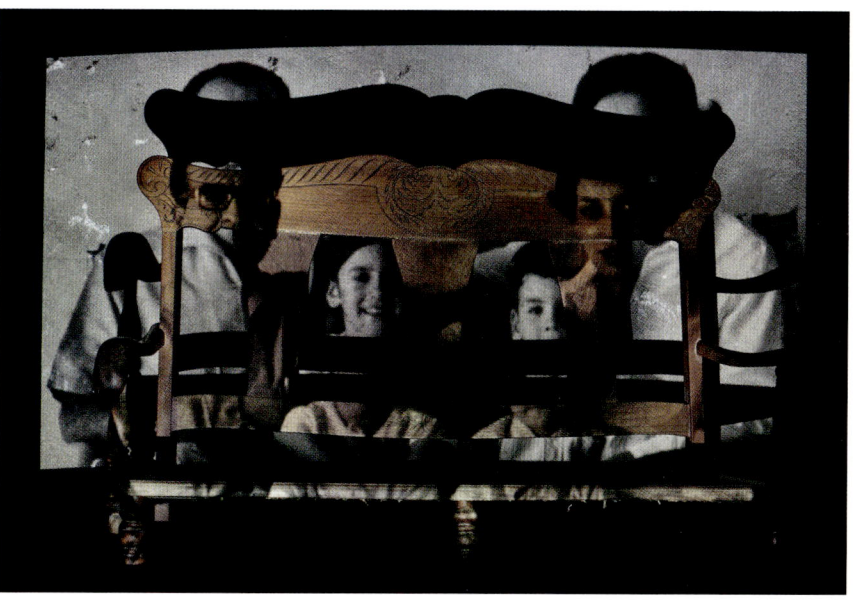

Plate 34: Muriel Hasbun, *Family Frames*, 2016.07.06, ca. 1960s, El Congo, archival pigment print, 2016 (Fig. 1, p. 304). Courtesy of the artist.

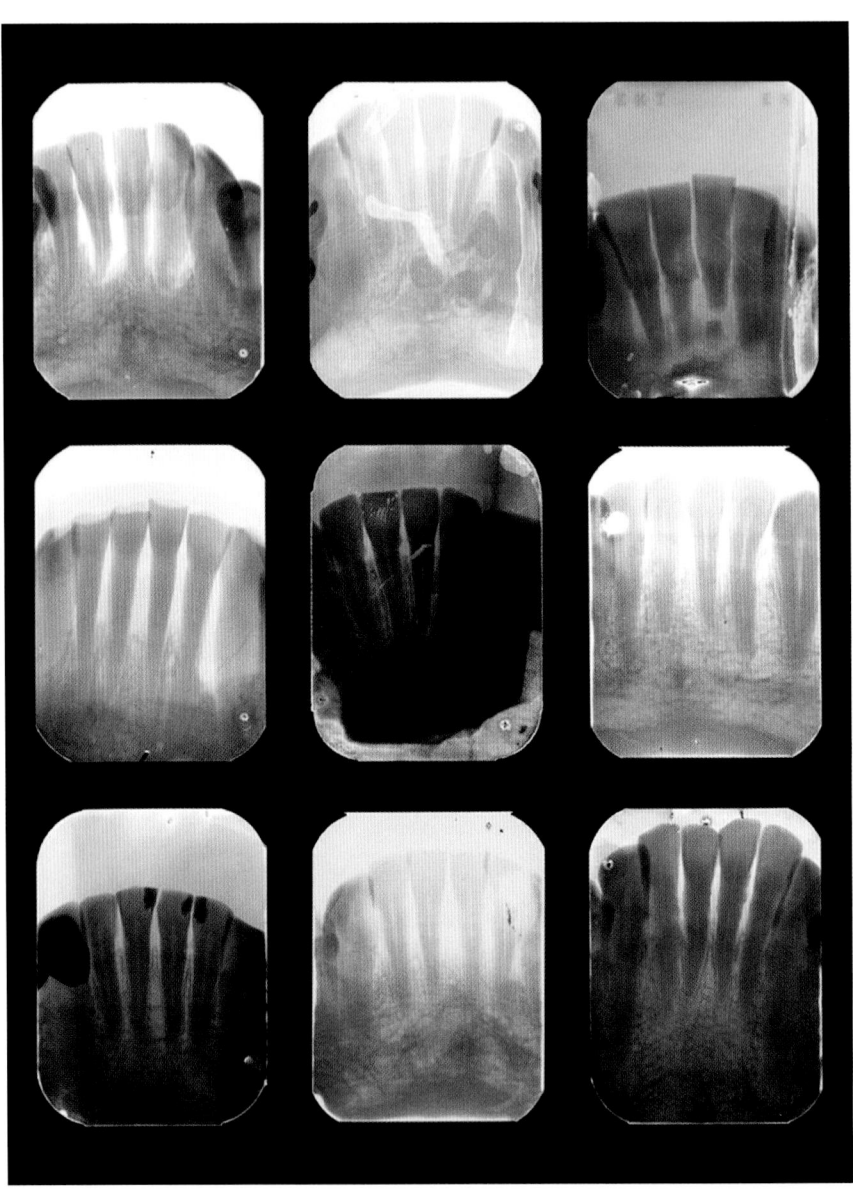

Plate 35: Muriel Hasbun, Study for *X post facto* (0.1-0.9), nine archival pigment prints, 2009
(Fig. 2, p. 304). Courtesy of the artist.

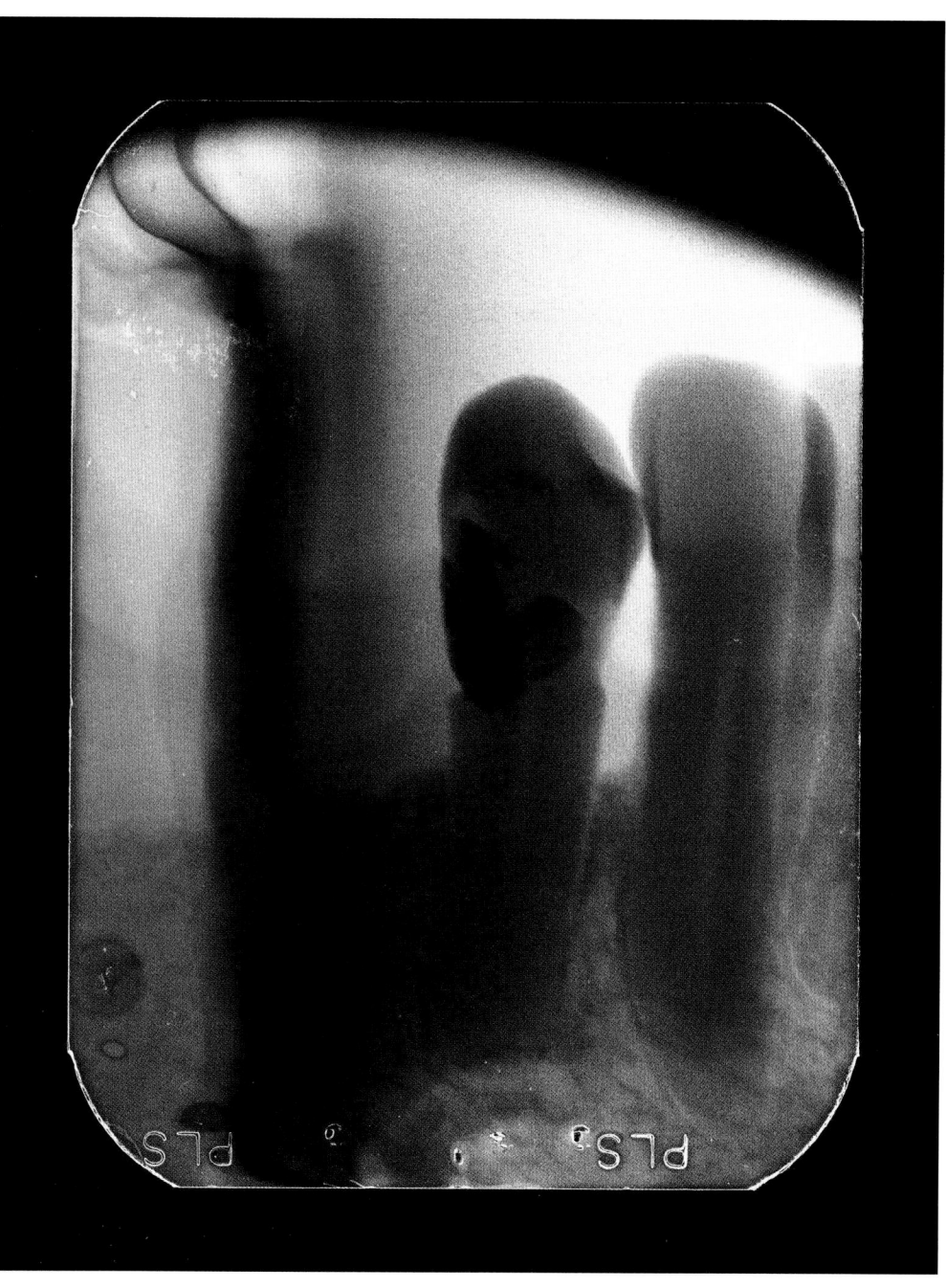

Plate 36: Muriel Hasbun, *X post facto* (12.3), archival pigment print, 2009/2013 (Fig. 7, p. 318).
Courtesy of the artist.

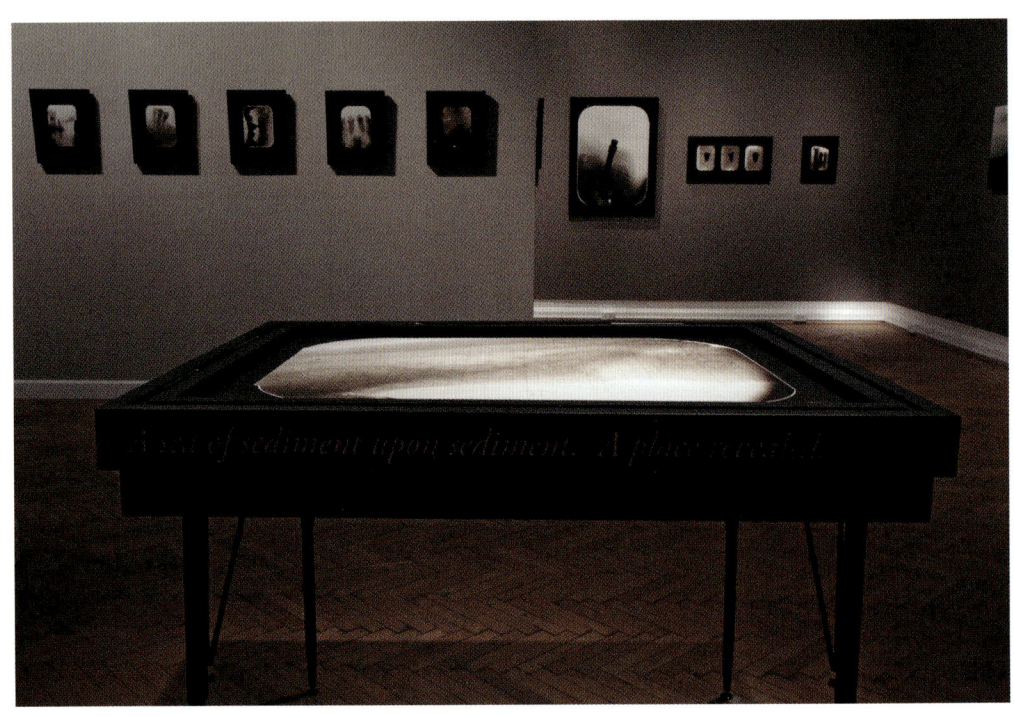

Plate 37: Installation view, *Inter Vivos: Margaret Adams, Gabriela Bulisova, Muriel Hasbun*, Corcoran Gallery of Art, Gallery 31, 2013 (Fig. 8, p. 319). Photo by Muriel Hasbun.